Health Policy

Health Policy

Understanding Our Choices from National Reform to Market Forces

EDITED BY

Marilynn M. Rosenthal and Max Heirich

Westview Press
A Member of the Perseus Books Group

RA
395
.A3
H42566
1998

ADF-6923

All rights reserved. Printed in the United States of America. No part of this publication may be reproduced or transmitted in any form or by any means, electronic or mechanical, including photocopy, recording, or any information storage and retrieval system, without permission in writing from the publisher.

Copyright © 1999 by Westview Press, A Member of the Perseus Books Group

Published in 1998 in the United States of America by Westview Press, 5500 Central Avenue, Boulder, Colorado 80301-2877, and in the United Kingdom by Westview Press, 12 Hid's Copse Road, Cumnor Hill, Oxford OX2 9JJ

A CIP catalog record for this book is available from the Library of Congress.
ISBN 0-8133-9023-0

The paper used in this publication meets the requirements of the American National Standard for Permanence of Paper for Printed Library Materials Z39.48-1984.

10   9   8   7   6   5   4   3   2

Contents

Introduction: Understanding Our Choices
Max Heirich 1

Section One:
How Can We Solve the Problem of Getting Affordable
Health Care to the Entire American Public?

Introduction
Max Heirich 13

Part One: The Alternate Positions and Their Critics

1. Next Steps Toward Health Policy Reform:
   A Conservative Approach
   William A. Niskanen 17

2. The Case for a Single-Payer Approach: A Liberal Voice
   Jim McDermott 23

3. Managed Competition as a Route to Markets That
   Serve Public Needs: A View from Near the White House
   Len M. Nichols 33

4. Health Reform: What Will It Take To Pass?
   A Moderate Conservative Stance
   Gail R. Wilensky 45

Part Two: Cost Containment: What's Working? What Isn't? Why?

5. Is Managed Care Working? The Payer Perspective
   Howard Bailit 59

6. Is the Health Care Cost Problem Solved?
   Karen Davis. 63

7. Managed Competition: Helping Hand for the Invisible Hand—How the Clinton Plan Would Use This Strategy
   Richard Kronick 69

8. Who's Afraid of Health Care Spending Growth?
   Mark V. Pauly 75

Part Three: Projecting Likely Economic Consequences of Planned Changes in Health Care: Strategies and Problems

9. Health Care Reform Projections and the Line Between Fact and Fiction
   Tami Mark 81

10. Paying for Health Care Reform: Alternative Financial Models Compared
    John F. Sheils 87

11. Financial Access to Health Care
    Katherine Swartz 99

Section Two:
Constraints on Choice: The Deepest Concerns of Interest Groups and the Public at Large

Introduction
Richard Lichtenstein 105

Part One: The Public and Health Reform Public Opinion Polls

12. Public Opinion on the Clinton Health Care Plan
    Karlyn H. Bowman 109

Contents

13. Health Care: The Limits of Polling
    Kathleen A. Frankovic 115

14. First Impressions and Second Thoughts: Public Perceptions of Health Care Reform
    John Immerwahr 121

Part Two: Interest Groups' Concerns with Health Care Reform

Professions

15. American Medical Association and Michigan State Medical Society
    Louis Zako 127

16. American Public Health Association
    Eugene Feingold 129

17. Health Care Reform: What Do We Do Now?
    Carol Franck 131

Business

18. Health Industry Manufacturers Association Position on Health Care Reform
    G. Gregory Raab 133

19. Health Care and the U.S. Auto Industry
    Charles T. Pryde 135

20. Small Business Association of Michigan Position on Health Care
    Gary Baker 139

Health Care Systems Providers

21. The Federation of Health Systems
    Michael D. Bromberg 143

22. Suggested Standards for Insurers
    Julie Goon 149

23. A Vision Renewed: Health Care Security
    Health Insurance Association of America 153

Insurers

24. Getting Inside Health Care Interest Groups
    Robert Asmussen 159

25. Blue Cross Blue Shield of Michigan Foundation
    Ira Strumwasser 161

Labor

26. Health Care in America: A Time for Change
    William Hoffman 163

Section Three:
Constraints on Choice: The Legislative Process—
Views from the Inside

Introduction
Marilynn M. Rosenthal 169

Part One: How the Executive Branch Positions Itself for Health Care Reform

27. President Clinton's Evolving Ideas on Health Care Reform: In His Own Words
    As compiled by Anand Parekh 171

28. The Politics of Health Policy Reform: An Inside View from the Clinton Administration
    Judith Feder 183

Contents

Part Two: How Congress Works

103rd and 104th Congresses

29. Political Strategies in the Long Run: Decades of Efforts at Health Care Reform
    An Interview with John Dingell 189

30. Inside the Senate Finance Committee
    An Interview with Katherine Hayes 197

31. The Politics of Health Care Reform
    Julie Kosterlitz 205

32. The Politics of Comprehensive Health Care Reform: Watching the 103rd and 104th Congresses at Work
    Sallyanne Payton 211

Section Four:
Change Without Legislation: The Managed Care Revolution

Introduction
John E. Billi 237

Part One: Managed Care: Its Permutations, Its Quality, Its Ethics, Its Costs, Its Politics

The Vision for the Future

33. Some Thoughts About Managed Care
    An Interview with Gail L. Warden 241

Issues

34. The Politics of Managed Care: The Regulatory Issues from the American Medical Association Perspective
    Thomas R. Reardon 247

35. Ford Motor Company's Perspective on Managed Care
    Charles T. Pryde 251

36. Will Managed Care End the Need for Managed Competition?
    Richard Kronick and Max Heirich 255

37. Managed Care: The Legal Viewpoint
    Sallyanne Payton 261

Research

38. Managed Care: Reform without Legislation
    Jon R. Gabel 267

39. How Well Does Managed Care Control Costs?
    Marsha Gold. 277

40. Managed Care: Stages of Development
    John E. Billi 283

How Does This Affect the Patient?

41. The Ethics of Incentives in Managed Care
    E. Haavi Morreim 289

42. Managed Care and Quality Assurance
    Tom Simmer 301

43. Provider Perspectives in Managed Care
    Macdonald Dick, Tom Carli, and Duane Kirking 305

Section Five:
The Realities of Health Care Reform:
Positions, Publics, Processes and,
Of Course, Power
Marilynn M. Rosenthal 315

About the Contributors

Robert Asmussen is executive vice president of Blue Cross Blue Shield of Michigan, Detroit, Michigan.

Howard Bailit is former senior vice president of Health Services Research, Aetna Health Plans, Hartford, Connecticut. He is a professor and head of the Health Policy and Primary Care Research Center, University of Connecticut.

Gary Baker is president of Online Technologies Corp. He was the president of the Small Business Association of Michigan, 1993-1994.

John E. Billi, M.D., is associate dean for Clinical Affairs at the University of Michigan Medical School.

Karlyn H. Bowman, is a resident fellow at the American Enterprise Institute in Washington, D.C., where she studies public opinion.

Michael D. Bromberg was the executive director of the Federation of American Health Systems in Washington, D.C. for 26 years.

Tom Carli, M.D., is a clinical assistant professor of psychiatry in the University of Michigan Medical School.

Karen Davis is president of The Commonwealth Fund.

Macdonald Dick, M.D., is the Ammon Rosenthal Collegiate Professor of Pediatric Cardiology and professor of pediatrics and communicable diseases in the University of Michigan Medical School.

John Dingell (D, Mich.) has served as a Congressman representing Michigan's 16th District since 1955. During the 103rd Congress, he was chair of the Energy and Commerce Committee, as well as chair of the Oversight and Investigation Subcommittee.

Judith Feder, Ph.D., was Principal Deputy Assistant Secretary for Planning and Education in the U.S. Department of Health and Human Services during the first Clinton Administration.

Eugene Feingold was, at the time this presentation was made (March of 1994), president of the American Public Health Association. He is professor emeritus at the University of Michigan School of Public Health.

Carol Franck is executive director of the Michigan Nurses Association.

Kathleen A. Frankovic, Ph.D., is director of surveys for CBS News.

Jon R. Gabel is director of survey research, KPMG Peat Marwick, in Arlington, Virginia.

Marsha Gold, Sc.D., is a senior fellow with Mathematica Policy Research, Inc.

Julie Goon is vice president of government affairs with the American Association of Health Plans.

Katherine Hayes is a legislative assistant to Senator John Chafee.

Max Heirich is an associate professor of sociology at the University of Michigan—Ann Arbor. In addition, he heads the Worker Health Program at the University's Institute of Labor and Industrial Relations and coordinates, with Marilynn M. Rosenthal, the University of Michigan Forum on Health Policy in Ann Arbor.

William Hoffman, Ph.D., was, at the time of this presentation, director of the Social Security Department, United Auto Workers, Detroit, Michigan. He is now president of Oster Enterprises.

John Immerwahr, Ph.D., is a Senior Research Fellow at the Public Agenda Foundation, and is also Assistant Vice President for Academic Affairs at Villanova University.

Duane Kirking, PharmD, PhD, is an associate professor of pharmacy administration in the University of Michigan College of Pharmacy.

Julie Kosterlitz is a contributing editor of *National Journal*.

Richard Kronick, Ph.D., is an associate professor, Department of Family and Preventive Medicine, University of California at San Diego. He served as a Senior Health Policy Advisor in the Clinton administration.

Richard Lichtenstein, M.P.H., Ph.D., is an associate professor of health management and policy in the University of Michigan School of Public Health.

Tami Mark, Ph.D., M.B.A., is a former Senior Analyst, Office of Technology Assessment, Washington, D.C.; she is a Senior Research Director, Project HOPE, Bethesda, Maryland.

Jim McDermott, M.D. (D. Wash.) is a member of the House of Representatives and a physician. He serves on the Committee on Ways and Means Subcommittee on Health.

E. Haavi Morreim, Ph.D., is a professor of medical ethics at the University of Tennessee's College of Medicine.

Len M. Nichols is a principal research associate with The Urban Institute in Washington, DC. He was the senior advisor for health policy at the Office of Management and Budget during 1993 and 1994.

William A. Niskanan is chairman of The Cato Institute.

Anand Parekh is an Inteflex medical student at the University of Michigan, Ann Arbor, Michigan.

Mark V. Pauly, Ph.D. is a professor in the Department of Health Care Systems at the Wharton School, University of Pennsylvania.

Sallyanne Payton, LL.B., is a professor of law at the University of Michigan Law School. She served as an advisor to the President's Task Force on National Health Care Reform in 1993 and subsequently as a Special Advisor on the White House Domestic Policy staff.

About the Contributors

Charles T. Pryde is the health policy and corporate issues manager for governmental affairs for the Ford Motor Company.

G. Gregory Raab, Ph.D., is vice president, government affairs for the Health Industry Manufacturers Assocation (HIMA).

Thomas R. Reardon, M.D., is a trustee of the American Medical Association.

Marilynn M. Rosenthal, Ph.D., is a professor of sociology in the University of Michigan—Dearborn College of Arts, Sciences and Letters. She is the director of the Program in Health Policy studies there and coordinates, with Max Heirich, the University of Michigan Forum on Health Policy in Ann Arbor.

John F. Sheils is vice-president of Lewin-VHI, Inc., Fairfax, Virginia.

Tom Simmer, M.D., is the senior associate medical director of quality management, Health Alliance Plan, Henry Ford Health System, Detroit, Michigan.

Ira Strumwasser, Ph.D., is executive director of Blue Cross Blue Shield of Michigan Foundation, Detroit, Michigan.

Katherine Swartz is associate professor in the Harvard School of Public Health's Department of Health Policy and Management.

Gail L. Warden is president and chief executive officer of Henry Ford Health System, Detroit, Michigan. In 1995, he served as the Chairman of the American Hospital Association.

Gail Wilensky is senior fellow at Project HOPE's Center for Health Affairs in Bethesda, Maryland. She served as administrator of the Health Care Financing Administration under the Bush administration and as deputy assistant to the president in the Bush White House.

Louis Zako, M.D., is past president of the Michigan State Medical Society.

Introduction
Understanding Our Choices

Max Heirich

What This Book Is About

During a critical period in health policy formation the University of Michigan Forum on Health Policy (sponsored by the Program in Society and Medicine of the University of Michigan Medical School) invited a series of key advisers, members of Congress, Congressional aides, business leaders, members of health provider interest groups, and others with a direct stake in the outcomes, as well as a few journalists and economists, to the campus to discuss what was happening. They engaged in frank discussions with one another and with the campus community about how choices for health care reform were changing through time. In addition, a student seminar traveled to Washington to observe the political process at work as various Congressional committees debated health care reform measures, and met with lobbyists, congressional staff, and others shaping the outcomes of those debates. The time period for these discussions, 1993 to 1996, included the period when the U.S. Congress was debating and rewriting the Health Security Act proposed by the task force appointed by President Bill Clinton. It extended through the congressional elections which became something of a political referendum on those proposals, and through the period following control of Congress by Conservative Republicans, when rapid changes were occurring in the organization and funding of health care, but were occurring independent of national legislation. The exchanges which took place on the University of Michigan campus between advisers to the White House and members of Congress, between economists and health policy experts of varying political outlooks, representatives of various interest groups affected by health care reform, and the academic community shed new light on the nature of the problem, the nature of the political process, and the realistic choices that now lie before us.

This book gathers together the heart of that dialogue, grouped and edited in a way to let it speak to the choices currently confronting Americans. It offers a rare glimpse into the frank exchanges that could sometimes occur between proponents of quite different solutions to the dilemma of health care reform. The book begins with papers presented shortly after the 1994 congressional elections, when it was clear that Congress would not endorse some variation of the Health Security Act proposed by the Clintons. Advisers to Newt Gingrich, conservative leader of the House, to former President Bush, and to President Clinton explained their different strategies for health care reform, discussed the heart of the differences between them, and what they saw as possible ways to proceed now. They were followed by experts who discussed different strategies for cost containment, and analysts who discussed what can and cannot be known about the most likely economic consequences of contending cost containment proposals. As had been true of the larger national debate, experts advocated three rather different roads to health care reform.

Many readers will be familiar with the broader strategies for health care reform that have been in contention during the 1990s. At one end of the spectrum have been advocates of a single-payer plan for cost control and for universal access to services. They urged Americans to imitate the Canadian model for health care, in which the government pays all health costs through a tax-based system, hospitals operate on annual budgets and serve all who come to them, and physicians' fees are set in consultation between the state or provincial government payer and medical associations.

At the other extreme have been advocates of free market solutions to health care dynamics, who argue that in the United States, government regulation of an industry, be it state or federal regulation, never works in practice. Instead, they argue, unfettered competition can bring down prices and produce innovation that will solve health care problems more creatively than monolithic national planning. Each problem in health care should be addressed individually, through a series of incremental reforms that leave the market place in tact. Make one reform at a time, they argued, and then see who is still left out. Interfere with normal market mechanisms as little as possible.

Clinton's advisers, in contrast, took a middle road between these two ideological positions, and their reform strategies borrowed evenly from each school's arsenal of proposals. Arguing that there was neither the political will nor the tax base necessary to reorganize American health care on the Canadian model, but that the market does not get services to everyone when left to its own devices, they urged the federal government to define the problems in health care that need solution and then enact laws that would create market incentives (positive and negative) for insurers and health care providers to provide services to all Americans, within a price range that could be afforded by those who pay for care. That middle position, as is well known, was attacked by advocates of each alternative.

Introduction: Understanding Our Choices

Single payer advocates found the Clinton version of managed competition unduly cumbersome and unnecessarily expensive because it continued a role for the American insurance industry, which they argued could be replaced more economically by a tax-based system. In contrast, free market advocates objected that the Clinton version of "managed competition" was more "managed" than "competition", and that government regulation lay at the heart of its reform strategies, a strategy they saw as long discredited in American political practice.

Readers who have followed the political debates about health care reform will be familiar with the arguments briefly described above. However contributors to this volume go far beyond the political arguments that surfaced in public debate. Because the discussions which took place at the University of Michigan involved key advisers in each camp who now were addressing each other and an academic audience already familiar with their general argument, advocates of each position cut to the heart of their own and opponents' assumptions, and provided both detail and analysis that often has been lacking in debates aimed at the general public. One does not have to be an expert to follow their remarks, but even those who know these arguments well will find much food for thought.

We hear, also, from experts who looked beneath the arguments and the economic projections made by proponents of each reform strategy, teasing out the current evidence about how serious the problems of access to health care actually are for various groups of Americans, and what can now be known and what remains unknowable about the most likely consequences of implementing each health care reform strategy. Then, with advisers' theoretical and technical proposals firmly in view, this book directs attention to the practical constraints that limit the freedom of the executive and legislative branches of government to choose and implement particular health care policies. Public opinion experts probe the deeper concerns of the public that limit choice, and representatives from a variety of interest groups who are active in the health care debate make clear their preferences and explain why this matters to them. Interest group representatives from associations of medical professionals, health care provider systems, insurers, business and labor explain their preferred solutions and occasionally explain why they are acting as a veto group blocking other reform proposals. Key participants in the executive wing, and in Congress, as well as keen observers from the press and academia, describe the practical political constraints that have shaped health care reform efforts in Washington. Although this helps explain how and why political gridlock stymied legislative health care reform efforts during this time period, we see these sections of the book as more than a retrospective look at what went wrong. Understanding how interest groups and congressional decision-making interact gives us a deeper understanding of the practical political realities that will affect what range of policy choices will be viable in the future.

This time period saw the failure of most legislative attempts, but the greater success of private efforts at health care reform. Within two years the health care delivery system had changed remarkably, and in some of the directions advocated by the Clinton health insurance reform task force. The majority of Americans now were enrolled in capitated payment, managed care plans, and hospital provider networks had consolidated, leaving far fewer competitors in health care delivery. This reform without legislation was accompanied by a drop in cost inflation. It was not clear, yet, whether this was true cost containment or simply a temporary drop in price increase, as had happened before during periods of high competition and rapid consolidation of the market, one that would reverse once competitors had been eliminated. The number of Americans lacking health insurance continued to climb, however, and the character of the health care system was changing fundamentally. We include papers given at a Health Forum devoted to the managed care revolution, in which advocates and critics of the changes now taking place discussed what is happening to costs, to access, and to doctor-patient relations.

The level of conversation that these Health Forums evoked between key advisers of different ideological convictions was unusually candid, and occasionally self-examining on their part. They paid their audience the compliment of assuming a fair degree of knowledge about the context of the current health care policy debate, the major positions that were in contention, and the nature of the political stalemate that now affects health care decision-making. A few of the economists assumed that their audience also understands the economic principles underlying the health insurance market. Readers who have such a background may want to go immediately on to the papers themselves, letting key players in health policy formation and analysis explain their understanding of the nature of the choices before us. Not all readers will be that familiar with the issues in question, however. For them, the rest of this chapter will provide a brief introduction to the debate by answering a series of questions.

What Is At Issue in the Debate About Health Insurance Reform?

The health safety net that Americans constructed during the first two decades following World War II has weakened. It offers no support to 40 million Americans currently, and until 1996 offered little support to another 25 million Americans whose most serious, ongoing health problems were not covered.[1] How much the 1996 legislation prohibiting exclusion of "pre-existing conditions" by health insurers will raise premium prices,

Introduction: Understanding Our Choices

and how this will affect the number of Americans without health insurance remains to be seen. How serious a problem all this creates is a matter of heated debate, but—given the cost of health care in America, lowered tax revenues and problems of state and federal deficits, as well as the problems the cost of health care now creates for the business community—there are no simple and obvious ways to mend that safety net. No wonder the debate about health care reform has drawn so much attention and concern: the stakes are high, both for the economic vitality of the nation and for the health of the population.

What is at issue in the health care policy debate, most Americans realize, is access to health care services for a constantly growing portion of the American public who can no longer afford to pay the cost of services, and for others who have had difficulty gaining access to care even when there is money to cover their costs. Equally at issue, of course, is the problem of cost containment: for over three decades, as most Americans are now aware, health care costs have risen at about twice the rate of general inflation, with only occasional and short-lived interruption to this trend. Under these circumstances answers to the questions, Who pays? How much? For what? And for whom? have major implications for all who are touched by the health care system. Those answers also affect who will have access to basic health care services and who will not. While problems of access and cost involve much more than the availability of health insurance, guaranteeing payment for services becomes critical for tackling the problems that remain.

Who Will Be Affected by the Outcome of This Debate, and Why?

The present American health care system seems to work fairly well for about three out of every four Americans. Thus the vast majority of Americans are well-served by the arrangements we have now, and most hope that others can be included without diminishing the quality or convenience of the care that they themselves now receive. For many workers, health benefits have been a hard-fought victory, an important part of their standard of living. Indeed, in recent years some of the largest labor unions have traded continued health benefits (which are not taxed) for what otherwise would have been higher wages. They are determined to make sure that health care reform does not decrease their income by lessening services they can have without increasing their wages in return. Many health care receivers, as well as providers of care and third party payers for care, look warily at proposals for reform, recognizing the need to do something but determined not to be a loser as health care reforms move forward.

Solving the twin problems of access and cost would be difficult enough, but even more is involved in this debate about health care insurance reform. The growth in health care costs has important implications for the economy as a whole. Health care employs more Americans than any other sector of the economy, and several parts of "the health care industry" have been consistent growth leaders in the economy for four decades. During the past quarter century health care has doubled its share of the gross national product.[2] Participants in the health care industry resist any changes that would weaken them financially; moreover for the sake of the economy as a whole the health care industry needs to remain strong. However, because of the formulas now used to reimburse health care expenses, other segments of American business, the federal and state governments, and private households often find themselves captive to increased price demands from health care providers. Since health care in the U.S. costs about twice as much per person as it does in most other industrialized countries, overhead costs for health benefits have affected American businesses' ability to compete in the international market (and with foreign products in the American market), contributing its part to the U.S. negative balance of trade. Increases in health care costs have also created serious problems for state and federal budgets. Solving problems of access and cost containment together, in ways that are equitable for business, government, and private households, consequently, is a high priority not only for those now left out but also for major institutional interests. The health care industry itself has too much at stake to remain passive in these discussions.

In addition to its impact on health benefits spending, businesses are affected by what the more rapid inflation in health care costs does to cost of living adjustments to wages. That also affects government obligations for social security and welfare payments. Not surprisingly, as medical costs have increased, public and private third party payers have refused to pay for some health expenses, passing those costs on to private households. Health care cost, thus, has become a two-edged sword. On the one hand, it cuts a bright swath: the increasing prosperity of American health care has helped keep the American economy vigorous in growth. But on the other hand, that growth creates serious problems for those who pay for it.

When Did the Health Care Cost Inflation Dynamic Begin, and How Does Insurance Affect It?

From 1920 to 1950 the cost of health care stayed steady relative to the growth of the economy, averaging between 3.5 and 4.5 percent of the gross national product. Then widespread introduction of health insurance began to change the cost of health care. Blue Cross Blue Shield hospitalization insurance had become available in the 1930s and some employers began to pay for it as a pre-tax "fringe benefit" during World War II. In the 1950s, labor-management contracts guaranteed this benefit for a large portion of the labor force.[3] During the 1950s health care costs increased a bit,

Introduction: Understanding Our Choices   7

with the cost of new hospital construction and widely available hospital insurance. By 1960, health care costs had increased to 5.5 percent of the gross national product, but few were hurting because of these higher costs.[4]

The cost of health care increased sharply after 1965, however, when Congress gave the federal and state governments responsibility for paying for the health care costs of the elderly and people on welfare, the first public health insurance legislation to survive the legislative process. The federal government provided Medicare insurance for persons over 65 who had retired, including both their hospital costs and part of their doctor fees. The federal government and the states split payment responsibility for persons on public welfare, and the states decided who among the poor could and could not be enrolled for welfare payments and consequently for Medicaid.[5]

Once public funding became available everything began to change quite rapidly. Within five years the overall cost of health care in the U.S. had doubled, and the cost of hospital care had quadrupled.[6] Hospitals, assured of a clientele that would need many services, began to expand their facilities and to invest in high tech equipment (such as intensive care units, dialysis machines, and expensive diagnostic equipment). They simply increased charges for their daily operating costs sufficiently to pay for these investments. When Congress responded by cutting off federal funds for hospital construction, the hospitals simply borrowed the money (at high interest rates) and continued their expansion plans. Indeed, hospitals that did not continue to upgrade risked losing their physicians (and the patient revenue each physician generated) to a more modern hospital. The cost of hospitalization increased still more rapidly, for now both the borrowed money and high interest costs had to be added onto the other expenses that were part of daily operating charges. Hospitals set a uniform daily rate, which meant that both private third party payers and the government were subsidizing the costs of upgrading and expansion. The pharmaceutical industry, hospital construction, hospital equipment, and hospitals themselves became growth leaders in the economy.[7] Gradually the entire area of health care delivery began to refer to itself as "the health care industry". Despite a variety of efforts to contain these costs, health care inflation has proceeded at twice the general inflation rate for most years since 1965.

Business and government, thus, became captive to cost inflation because of the obligations they had taken on and the ways that health insurance reimbursement arrangements worked. In 1960, health benefits cost business the equivalent of about 15 percent of their after-tax profits. In 1989, health benefits cost the equivalent of 98 percent of their after-tax profits.[8] (I.e., if they had not been paying for health care, business profits would have doubled.) For the federal government, health care spending commitments began to rival defense spending. The states found by the early 1990s that Medicaid's portion of the state budget had increased from about 3 percent to 15 percent, with the figure due to go higher still.[9] Health care costs were rising so sharply that few private households could pay for a major health crisis out-of-pocket. Many families without health insurance were forced into bankruptcy when a medical crisis occurred.

What Has Been Done Already to Try to Tame Health Care Cost-Inflation?

Neither the government nor business has stood by idly during the past 25 years that this accelerated cost inflation for medical care has been occurring. President Nixon tried imposing direct price controls and found they did not work: costs continued to rise because physicians and hospitals simply increased the number of services they billed at these fixed prices. Congress then passed legislation authorizing the establishment of Health Maintenance Organizations (HMOs) that would receive "capitated payments"— a fixed amount of money annually for each enrollee—in exchange for responsibility for the total care of that patient. It was hoped that HMOs would keep people out of hospitals (in order to preserve their income) and would emphasize preventive measures that would lower costs for care.[10]

Businesses responded to the cost increases by self-insuring for health benefits, and began to assume a more aggressive bargaining role for prices for services. Self-insurance began with passage of ERISA in 1974, which allowed businesses to self-fund retirement and health benefits programs. By the mid-1980s business health coalitions had formed in 93 metropolitan areas; they were monitoring health providers costs and designating some health care providers as Preferred Provider Organizations (PPOs). The larger companies bargained with their PPO for discounted rates, in return for a guaranteed volume of users. In addition, the business health coalitions often invited HMO chains to extend into their metropolitan area, as a way of increasing competition locally. After ERISA, the large health insurance companies that had developed during the 1950s and 1960s lost their large corporation accounts because these corporations self-insured. The insurance companies recouped in two ways: they got contracts to manage the health disbursements for large corporations; and they began to set up their own HMOs, so that they could compete for the business of actually providing health care to the employees of large corporations.[11]

With these changes, the corporatization of American health care began in earnest. Meanwhile government reforms of the 1980s intensified the dynamic for change that was occurring. The government still paid hospitals for each admission of Medicare patients. A new policy regrouped pay-

Introduction: Understanding Our Choices

ment into DRGs (diagnostically related groups of admissions), clustering diagnoses not by type of illness but by average cost for treating that illness. Medicare hereafter would reimburse hospitals a flat amount, depending upon the DRG category into which the initial admission diagnosis fit. Hospitals that could treat for less could keep the difference; if a patient's care cost more the hospital would have to absorb the loss.[12] Parallel Medicare funding policies for the reimbursement of physician's services (the Resource-based Relative Value Scale), introduced in 1992, provided government-set reimbursements for 85 percent of all procedures physicians use with Medicare patients.[13] In addition, government legislation encouraged the establishment of "for-profit" medical care whose income would be taxable and whose competitive business skills, it was hoped, would result in cheaper prices for care.[14]

What Interests Have Been Most Affected By Recent Health Care Reforms?

These changes in funding reimbursement have led to a fundamental restructuring of medical care and the relations between hospitals, HMOs, insurance companies, physicians, nurses, and patients. Hospital utilization has dropped sharply. HMOs now keep patients out of the hospital whenever possible and hospitals make more money if patients being paid for through DRG formulas are released quickly. More services are provided on an outpatient basis (because these were not subject to the DRG and R-BRVS payment rules). Consequently, some hospitals have closed, enough so that the community hospitals' bed count decreased by 100,000 beds between 1983 (when DRGs were introduced) and 1990.[15] Many public hospitals could not survive on their Medicaid and Medicare income and were sold to private for-profit companies. Many for-profit companies refused to accept Medicaid patients, thus aggravating the problems of getting access to care for the poor.

Hospitals themselves have regrouped, forming large hospital chains that can use economies of scale for purchasing and be in a better position to bargain for Preferred Provider status with large companies. For-profit and not-for-profit hospital chains now dominate the market. One out of every nine hospitals is now owned by a for-profit corporation.[16] HMOs use more primary care doctors and nurse practitioners, and less specialists than is true for indemnity-financed (fee for service) care, so that specialists are beginning to be in oversupply in many metropolitan areas. The relations between physicians and the business management of HMOs has varied, but the independence of physicians is very much an open question currently, affecting not only their incomes but standards of medical practice.

Have These Changes, Which Have Basically Restructured Health Care in America, Really Saved Money?

Until 1995 health care cost inflation continued at twice the rate of inflation. Capitated payment plans were about 5 percent cheaper than fee-for-service care, but their rate increases paralleled cost increases for health care in general. They were not changing the underlying dynamic but simply damping its effect a bit.[17]

In response to the health insurance reform debate of 1993 and 1994, many employers created incentives that moved their employees into capitated payment plans; by 1995 the majority of privately insured Americans were in HMOs or other programs that had a fixed cost annually. The HMOs expanded rapidly and entered a fierce competitive war. Hospitals and other health care providers consolidated into large provider networks as part of the restructuring of the health care market. For the first time in several years, health care cost increases for 1995 did not double the general inflation rate; it was not clear whether the dynamic of cost increase was changing or whether this reflected temporary price adjustments as competition led to greater consolidation of control over health care services.[18] It was clear, however, that everyone is being affected by the changes in health care delivery that the attempted insurance reforms have set in motion.

Because of the unique history of American health care, economic principles now affect much of its operation. However, the debate about health care reform cannot simply be reduced to a discussion of economics. When health problems arise, health care is not an optional commodity for private households to use or ignore, although many households now are forced to do so. Because health services often cannot be deferred, the lack of a universal insurance system to pay for health care now creates financial crisis or premature death for many Americans.

Because a wide range of earlier reform efforts failed to stop the inflation of health care costs or the erosion of access to health care services, the policy debates chronicled in this book become all the more important. How can we solve the problem of getting affordable health care to the entire American public? How do the deepest concerns of interest groups and the public at large constrain the choices that can be made? How have these affected the legislative process? In the absence of legislative overhaul of health care, how has private reform (the managed care revolution) affected access, cost, and quality of care?

Although this volume includes papers given at four different Health Forums, the argument remains remarkably coherent, as key advisers, technical experts, and decision makers discuss the choices before us and the practical constraints that affect how we proceed. We would like to have included the discussions that followed papers, as members of the audience and presenters interacted with one another. Space limitations preclude that choice. Nonetheless, the arguments presented here take account of one another, inviting the reader to probe more deeply the choices that now lie before us for health care reform.

Notes

1. Emily Friedman, "The uninsured: From dilemma to crisis." *Journal of the American Medical Association*, 265(19); 2491-2495, May 15, 1991.

2. Health Care Financing Administration, Office of the Actuary: Office of National Cost Estimates, "Trends in national health care costs, " 1991.

3. Paul Starr, *The Social Transformation of American Medicine: the Rise of a Sovereign Profession and the Making of a Vast Industry*. New York: Basic Books, Inc., 1984, 252-254, 311.

4. U.S. Government, Economic Report to the President, Annual Report of the Council of Economic Advisers, Appendix B: Statistical Tables, Table

5. Ted Marmor and Ann Marmor, *The Politics of Medicare*. Chicago: Aldine Publishing Co., 1970, 59-93, Starr, *op. cit.*, 368-370, Robert Stevens and Rosemary Stevens, *Welfare Medicine in America: A Case Study of Medicaid*. New York: Free Press, 1974.

6. Health Care Financing Administration, Office of the Actuary: Office of National Cost Estimates, "Trends in national health care costs, " 1991.

7. See, for example, *Standard and Poor's Industry Survey*, from 1959 onwards (beginning December 17, 1959, D20-22).

8. Katherine R. Levit, Mark S. Freeland, and Daniel R. Waldo, "Health spending and ability to pay: Business, individual and governments: Health care costs 1990. *Health Care Financing Review* 10, Spring, 1989, 3ff.

9. J. D. Rockefeller IV, "A call for action, " *Journal of the American Medical Association*, 265 (19) May 15, 1991, 2507-2510.

10. Joseph L. Falkson, *HMOs and the Politics of Health System Reform*. Chicago: American Hospital Association, 1986.

11. Katherine A. Lewis, *Private Sector Investment in HMOs*. Excelsior, MN: InterStudy, 1981; Leslie Scism, "Travelers Inc. and Met Life to form HMO; Met Life plans to purchase some Travelers assets to fund joint venture," *The Wall Street Journal*, June 14, 1994.

12. Commission on Professional and Hospital Activities, *Length of Stay by Diagnosis Related Groups, July 1984-July 1985, Discharges*. Ann Arbor, MI: CPHA Probe Series, 1986; Robert J. Fitzgibbon and Bernard E. Statland, *Survival Manual for the Clinical Lab*. Oradell, NJ: Medical Economics Books, 1985; Donald Lee Zimmerman, *DRGs and the Medicaid Program*. Washington, DC: Intergovernmental Health Project, George Washington University, 1984.

13. Resource-based relative value scales were discussed in detail in a series of articles appearing in the Journal of the American Medical Association (JAMA) 260, Oct. 28, 1988. See also Howard J. Anderson, "R-BRVS creates incentives for hospital-physician outpatient care," *Hospitals* 65:31, Feb. 20, 1991; Mary Jane Fisher, "New Medicare fee structure for doctors' services," *National Underwriter (Life and Health/*

Financial Service Edition) 95:3+, June 10, 1991; Joseph T. Donnelly, "R-BRVS as a financial assessment tool," *Health Care Financial Management* 47:44-46, Feb. 1993; William C. Hsiao, Daniel L. Dunn, Diane K. Verrill, "Assessing the implementation of physician-payment reform," *New England Journal of Medicine* 328:928-33, April 1993.

14. Eli Ginzberg, "For-profit medicine: A reassessment," *New England Journal of Medicine* 319: 457-61 September 22, 1988; David E. Lindorff, *Marketplace Medicine: The rise of the for-profit hospital chains.* New York: Bantam Books, 1992.

15. American Hospital Association, *Hospital Statistics:* Table 2-a, "Trends in utilization, personnel and finances in short term hospitals." Chicago: American Hospital Association, 1989-1990.

16. *Ibid.*

17. John Gable, "The changing world of group insurance," *Health Affairs* 7(2) Summer, 1988, 48-65; J. Gable, S. DiCarlo, C. Sullivan, C. and T. Rice, "Employer sponsored health insurance, 1989," *Health Affairs*, 8(2), Summer 1989, 116-128.

18. Milt Freudenheim, "Health costs for workers in U.S. rose last year, reversing 1994 drops," The New York *Times*, January 30, 1996.

SECTION ONE

How Can We Solve the Problem of Getting Affordable Health Care to the Entire American Public?

Section One

Introduction
How Can We Solve the Problem of Getting Affordable Health Care to the Entire American Public?

Max Heirich

How much reform of the health care system is necessary in order to get affordable health care to the entire American public? And what kinds of reform could make health more affordable—both to individuals who pay for it on their own, and to the public and private third party payers who now finance the bulk of health care spending? These questions underlie the arguments presented in Section One, and are supplemented by a related set of questions: What have we learned about strategies that actually work to contain cost increases? What's working? What isn't? and Why? And how reliable are the cost estimates being prepared to help us anticipate the most likely consequences of choosing one or another strategy for health care reform? These sets of inter-related questions engage the attention of the national experts whose differing views contend with one another in Section One. Most of the authorities are economists, as fits the focus on costs, possible enlargements of the market of health care consumers, and strategies for cost containment.

Part One is titled, "What is a Realistic Way to Make Health Care Reforms?" President Reagan's Council of Economic Advisers chairman, who went on to advise House Majority leader Newt Gingrich, President Bush's top health policy adviser and policy implementer, and one of President Clinton's most trusted health care economic advisers give strikingly different analyses of the problems that need to be addressed and the best route to finding affordable health care. William Niskanen, of the Cato Institute (a conservative policy institute) questions whether the "health care crisis" is of the proportions others claim, provides his own analysis of the size of various uninsured populations and the seriousness of access problems for different groups, and questions the conventional strategies for raising funds to cover their health care needs. He offers a radically different solution to the problem of access and cost containment than that of any of our other contributors to this debate. Len Nichols, of the Urban Institute (a liberal policy institute) and a major adviser to President Bill Clinton, offers an unusually frank discussion of the politics of economic planning, showing how key political decisions orient choice among economic options. He includes an equally frank discussion of the technicalities and limits of budget/spending projections, as seen from his earlier position at the Office for the Management of the Budget (OMB) and as an assessor of various projections done by health benefits management firms. Gail Wilensky, who was President Bush's top health adviser, lays out the alternate routes that can be taken in dealing with health benefits packages and their financing and the costs of doing each. She poses a trenchant challenge to the choices made by the Clinton Health Insurance Reform Task Force. To round out this discussion of routes to health care reform, we include a reprinted article by Jim McDermott, a physician and member of the U.S. House of Representatives. McDermott questions the market assumptions that underlie the debate among Presidential advisers. Instead he advocates reforming the U.S. health care system so that it more nearly resembles the Canadian health care plan, using government taxes to eliminate the need for insurance and making the government a single payer able to negotiate more reasonable rates for health care services.

In Part Two, titled, "Cost containment: What's Working? What Isn't? Why?" the debate continues, now focused more narrowly on ways to get *affordable* health care. Howard Bailit, a senior vice president for the Aetna Health Plans HMO, uses a variety of current economic data to argue that capitated payment plans with managed care have, in fact, begun to tame the cycles of constant cost inflation and may be making health care more affordable. Karen Davis, a former health policy economist in earlier Democratic administrations, and now executive vice-president of the Commonwealth Fund, musters her own economic analysis to challenge Bailit's conclusions, warning about the temporary nature of downward trends in health care spending and arguing that health care spending has *not* been brought under control. She closes with a discussion of the kind of challenge that Medicare and the growing number of elderly persons brings to cost control. Rick Kronick, of the University of California San Diego Medical School and a major policy adviser to the Clinton Task Force on Health Insurance Reform, re-examines the policy of managed competition which guided Clinton planning proposals for a Health Security Act. He explains why he believes the market needs to be "managed" if all Americans are to get access to health care, and explains the logic behind the cost containment strategies of the Health Security Act. Mark Pauly, an economist at the Wharton School, University of Pennsylvania, reexamines medical spending trends to ask "Who's afraid of health care costs?" and challenges a number of assumptions that have underlain most health policy debate. He sees quite different cost containment issues for public and private third party payers, insists that the problems are not being solved by managed care, and poses an ethical challenge to those who would limit discussion of health care needs to economic concerns.

In Part Three, titled "Projecting Likely Economic Consequences of Planned Changes in Health Care," three economists who are experts in health benefits analysis and cost projections sharpen our understanding of the limits of trying to forecast the costs of different health reform plans. Tami Mark, currently Senior Research Director with Project HOPE in Bethesda, Maryland, and formerly of the Office of Technology Assessment, describes the range of cost estimates that have been made, the five-step analysis OTA uses when projecting the most likely cost consequences of different health reform proposals, and concludes with observations of the relation between political will and slippage in cost outcomes. She recommends an incremental approach to health care reform, and cites the need for flexible reforms and ways to monitor their cost consequences. John Sheils, vice president of Lewin VHI, Inc., a benefits management company, explains how Lewin made cost estimates for providing universal insurance coverage for all Americans, with a uniform benefits package similar to the recommendations of the Clinton Task Force, and suggests how the additional costs would vary, depending on whether an employer mandate was used, an individual mandate, or a single payer plan. His conclusions may surprise you. Katherine Swartz of the Harvard School of Public Health discusses sources of error and slippage in making estimates of who is insured and uninsured, and of what the costs will be of implementing different proposals. Her discussion of who is uninsured, when—and what the *real* health implications of this are, clarifies a number of previously confusing arguments about health care reform. She also discusses the nature of data that are needed to let policy makers make more informed decisions, and challenges researchers to do better work in this regard. Section One of this book, in summary, lays out the economic assumptions that guide policy advisers of different ideological convictions, looks carefully at the evidence of what is happening to health care costs currently, and identifies both the potential and the limits of projecting costs for different policy choices.

In reading this section, it might be useful to consider some core questions as one ponders the strikingly different arguments being presented:

How important is it for all Americans to have guaranteed access to health care services?—a basic right for citizens in other industrialized countries, but an open question here.

How much cost would this add, to whom, and what strategies look most promising for controlling costs? What degree of risk is involved in trying them?

What limitations, if any, on current quality of services would be acceptable in order to extend coverage to all?

If there is a conflict of values between access to care for all and limits on public expenditure for budget balancing, how should they be resolved?

What do we, as Americans, take most seriously as underlying values and responsibilities to one another?

1

Next Steps Toward Health Policy Reform: A Conservative Approach

William A. Niskanen

President Clinton's Health Security Act is dead—the consequence of a misunderstanding of the popular concerns, a misdiagnosis of the major problems, the arrogance of the technocrats, and Clinton's own tendency to overreach his mandate. Unfortunately, many of its supporters have not learned the real lessons of the debacle, while many opponents of the Clinton plan still do not fully understand what is wrong with the U.S. health care system and what is needed to correct it.

Before Congress reconsiders health policy, all those concerned should reflect on the following questions:

- What are the major problems of our health care system?
- What are the major causes of these problems?
- What principles should guide the selection among the competing health policy reform proposals? And,
- What are the necessary and appropriate changes in health policy that only the *federal* government can make?

All of us—inside and outside Congress—should reflect on these questions *before* we jump back into the process of proposing or legislating specific health policy reforms.

The Problems

Most of the health reform plans considered to date focused on reducing the number of the uninsured with little attention to or with inappropri-

---

This presentation was made on November 18, 1994, at the University of Michigan Forum on Health Policy.

ate means to control costs. The number or percent of people who do not have health insurance, however, is *not*, by itself, a problem. We did not have a health care crisis in 1940 when few people had health insurance. We do not now have a crisis when few people have insurance against earthquakes, floods, and asteroids. Contrary to the Clintons' rhetoric, the employers that do not provide health insurance and their employees are *not* free riders; for the same labor skills, employers in a competitive labor market pay higher wages for the uninsured and employees pay higher taxes. Universal health insurance coverage is *not* necessary to control health care costs; broader insurance coverage, in contrast, would almost surely increase costs.

Those without health insurance present two quite different, rather small problems.

- Some of the uninsured do not receive some types of medical care that the rest of us, if necessary, would be willing to help finance. Those who are both uninsured and uninsurable, however, are only about one percent of the population under age 65 and could be folded into existing high-risk insurance pools for an annual subsidy of less than $1 billion. Most of the uninsured are a quite healthy lot and will be again within a few months.
- The uninsured, in fact, receive a substantial amount of medical care, for some of which the providers are not compensated. And the distribution of the costs of this uncompensated care is quite arbitrary. Again, this is a surprisingly small problem. As of 1991, the net amount of uncompensated care to the uninsured was around $20 billion, far less than the amount by which providers are undercompensated by Medicare and Medicaid. To the extent that these costs are shifted to private insured patients, most of the cost shifting is due to undercompensation by the public insurance plans, not the uncompensated care to the uninsured.

The primary problem of our health care system is the continuing rapid increase in the relative price and real expenditures for medical care. Over the years since 1965, the relative price of medical care has increased at a 2.5 percent annual rate, and real expenditures per capita have increased at a 5.2 percent annual rate. Payments for health insurance are now the most rapidly growing component of both private payrolls and government budgets. The rapid increase in health insurance premiums is the primary reason for the increase in the percent uninsured.

Some recent news stories have conveyed the perception that the relative inflation in medical prices and expenditures has eased. These stories are misleading. Despite substantial efforts by private firms and insurance companies to control costs, these trends have continued. The relative price of medical care increased 2.8 percent in 1993, and real expenditures per capita increased 5.4 percent in 1991—both *higher* than the average increase since 1965. And despite the increasing undercompensation of providers by Medicare and Medicaid, real federal expenditures for health programs increased 7 percent in fiscal 1993. The unsustainable increase in the relative price and expenditures for medical care has continued, but was progressively ignored as the debate on health reform developed. There are some who opposed any major reform on the basis that the major problems of our health care system are being resolved. They were correct to oppose the major reforms considered this year, but they were wrong in concluding that a major change in federal health policies can be long deferred.

The Causes

Most of the proposed health reforms seem based on a premise that broader health insurance would solve most of the problems of our health care system. Most of these problems, however, are a *consequence* of *too much* of the *wrong type* of health insurance. Too much because employer-provided health insurance is not included in taxable income. The wrong type because there is no similar exclusion for individual health insurance. The wrong type because the tax and regulatory preferences for the Blues displaced the older form of commercial indemnity policies with policies providing cost-based reimbursement. At present, patients pay about 5 cents on the dollar for insured hospital services and about 20 cents on the dollar for insured physicians services. The unusual form of health insurance has nearly eliminated any incentive for either the patient or the provider to control costs.

- One consequence of this condition is that insured patients spend too much on medical care; we have the highest quality medical care in the world but, at the margin, it costs more than it is worth.
- Another consequence is that the rate of inflation in medical care prices and expenditures, both over time and across types of treatment, is strongly related to the percent of costs covered by private or public insurance.
- The preference for employer-provided insurance, in turn, restricts the opportunity to choose your own coverage and risk pool or to maintain your policy when self employed, not employed, or changing jobs.

Most of the proposed health reforms, however, would broaden employer-provided health insurance and try to offset the problems of cost control, portability, etc., by price controls and other regulations. Again, the unusual form of American health insurance is the cause, not the solution, to most of the problems of the American system of health care.

The Principles

A valuable next step would be to reflect on the principles that should guide the choices among the proposed health reforms. Without claiming any unique ethical insight, let me suggest four principles to guide these choices and the major policy implications of each of these principles.

1. Government policy should not bias the choice of means by which health care is *financed*.

In other words, to the extent possible, government policy should be neutral with respect to whether any specific method of treatment is financed by employer-provided insurance, individual insurance, or by direct patient payment. The implications of this principle are clear: No monopoly purchasing cooperatives. No federal standard benefit package. No state mandates on insurance coverage. The tax exclusion for employer-provided insurance should be either eliminated or broadened to include both individual policies and medical savings accounts.

2. Government policy should not bias the choice of means by which health care is *provided*.

Again, to the extent possible, government policy should be neutral with respect to the choice of provider, method of treatment, and form of organization. And again, the implications are clear: No subsidies or restrictions by type of provider. No "any willing provider" restriction. No bias for or against home care, physician care, hospital care, HMOs, PPOs, fee-for-service, etc.

3. Any government subsidies for either health insurance or health care should be on the budget, transparent, and subject to periodic review and approval.

This principle, of course, rejects the three other major pieces of the Clinton plan: employer mandates, community rating, and price controls. Each of these measures is an effective tax on some group to pay for health insurance or health care to others and differs from explicit taxes only in that the coerced transfer does not go through the federal treasury.

We already make massive subsidies, of course, to provide health insurance to the aged, the poor, veterans, etc. Our political system may, and possibly should, subsidize insurance or care for some others. The point of this principle is that the government is likely to make a much better decision on this issue, both initially and over time, and the distribution of the burden of these subsidies will be much less arbitrary, if these subsidies are on the budget than if they are buried in mandates and regulations. The political test of whether broader subsidies for health insurance or health care is desirable is whether Congress is willing to reduce other spending or increase explicit taxes to pay for these subsidies. That may be the primary reason, of course, why most of the proposed new subsidies are not on the budget.

4. The focus of federal health reform should be on those policies that *only* the federal government can change.

This principle, of course, rules out any comprehensive reform plan that includes measures that could be changed by state and local governments or private organizations. Federal health reform should focus on changes in federal health programs, the federal tax code, on federal regulations, and, maybe, nothing else. There may be some health policies that the state governments could change for which a single national policy may be better, but I doubt it. I am especially unconvinced, for example, that the federal government should establish a single national policy on insurance regulation or medical malpractice. As with crime, the other major domestic policy issue of 1994, it is especially important to *decentralize* the policy choices on issues for which a uniform policy may not be best for all jurisdictions, because of regional differences in preferences or conditions, or when there is considerable uncertainty about what is the best policy. The guiding spirit of a wise federal health reform plan is humility, not hubris.

The Policies

At this stage, we should declare a 90-day moratorium on promoting specific health reform proposals, and I will follow my own advice. Let me conclude, however, with some suggestions about the types of federal policy changes that should be considered.

1. The most important broad reform would be to change the federal tax treatment of health insurance. Two quite different changes should be considered:
   a. Eliminate the exclusion of employer-provided health insurance from taxable income, *combined* with a revenue-neutral reduction in the payroll tax rate. This would be sufficient to eliminate the tax bias against both individual insurance and against direct patient payment. This policy would reduce health insurance coverage but increase wages and employment.

   OR

   b. *Replace* the exclusion of employer-provided health insurance with a revenue-neutral tax credit. Broaden the credit to individual policies (to eliminate the current bias against individual policies) and to medical savings accounts (to eliminate the bias against direct

payment). This policy may or may not reduce health insurance coverage and would require some other change in spending or taxes to offset the revenue loss of the broader tax credit.
2. Changes in the benefit structure of the major federal health insurance programs should also be considered. Three changes merit special attention:
   a) Income-test the deductible for both Medicare and Medicaid, maybe at 7.5 percent of adjusted gross income (the same rate as in the current federal tax code). This would gradually reduce the benefits of both programs as a function of the recipient's income.
   b) Eliminate the prohibition on balance billing on medical services reimbursed by Medicare. This would transform the Medicare reimbursement rates from price controls into lump sum payments, increasing the incentive of providers to serve Medicare patients and the incentive of patients to choose low price providers.
   c) Allow the state governments almost complete flexibility in designing the Medicaid benefit structure, eliminating most of the federal mandates as well as the restrictions on the use of federal funds from AFDC, food stamps, and other welfare programs. The case for decentralizing the decisions on these policies is powerful, primarily because of the uncertainty about the most effective combination of those measures in any jurisdiction.

3. Finally, most of the political demands for broader health insurance seem to be based on a concern about those who are both uninsured and uninsurable. We are a rich and generous nation, and we should help these people. In fact, state governments have already designed an effective if mis-designed policy to provide health insurance coverage to this group. At present, 28 states have created high risk insurance pools for those who have been denied coverage based on some severe preexisting condition. The premium on such high risk pool insurance is typically set up to 50 percent higher than for comparable coverage to the healthy people, and the states provide small subsidies to make these pools financially viable. The premium caps are set moderately high, and they have been quite effective both to encourage those affected to find other coverage and to limit the level of the subsidy. A hard liner would say that state governments can solve this problem without any federal policy, and they are correct. A political realist might conclude that we would be fortunate to limit the demands for new health insurance subsidies to provide coverage to this group.

I will leave you to surmise what may be my own personal preferences among the several types of federal health policies that should be considered.

2

The Case for a Single-Payer Approach: A Liberal Voice

Jim McDermott, MD

Throughout history, the medical profession has struggled in its conflict between belief and science. In the late 18th century, this struggle was exemplified by a religious adherence to Dr. Benjamin Rush's theory that bleeding patients would restore health. The result of this mistaken belief—as opposed to proven hypothesis—was that George Washington is historically thought to have been bled to death therapeutically.

Two hundred years later, American medicine is still locked in its ambivalence between science and belief. But in 1993, the issue is health care system reform. In the debate emerging from the presentation of President Clinton's plan, the challenge for our profession will be whether it can move beyond time-honored mantras to examine objectively and scientifically the options with which it is presented.

The Need for Change

Few would dispute the need for change. American physicians are the most dissatisfied and frustrated in the industrialized world.[1] Approximately 15% of our people have no health insurance at any one time, and at least 57 million nonelderly Americans lack health insurance for some part of the year.[2,3] This does not even include the underinsured and those on Medicaid whose coverage cannot begin to provide them with access that is consistent with good health care.[4] One hundred thousand additional people lose their health insurance every month.[5] Health care costs rise at 11% annually, further guaranteeing that more will become uninsured as employers become unable to bear the burden.[6] In a misguided attempt to control costs, insurance companies require physicians to spend extraordinary amounts of time defending their treatment decisions.

This paper appeared in the Journal of the American Medical Association (JAMA) 271(10), March 9, 1994. It is reprinted here with permission.

There is very little that individual physicians can do to remedy this situation. They have no power to affect systemic dynamics, they have little information on which to relate individual practice to that of others, and delivery decisions have largely been taken out of the physician's hands.

So the questions become how do we change general cost trends, how do we provide physicians the data they need to make prudent decisions, and how do we put control of the delivery system back in the hands of the caregivers? How do we bring about reform that provides universal access to care, controls costs, and recaptures the personalization of health care essential to illness prevention and healing?

Lessons Learned

Based on evidence from most of the industrialized world, the answer lies in providing health care through a single-payer system.[7] Single-payer health system reform severs the link between employment and health insurance. A single-payer system is essentially a financing mechanism that preserves the primary foundation of the American health care delivery system—the physician-patient relationship. The single payer—the government—provides the insurance for health care for all Americans, and the states negotiate the fees of health care providers. The health care delivery system remains primarily in private hands with free choice of provider. The government manages the rate of growth of price increases. This is the system that exists in varying forms in every society in the Western world, one that has brought health standards that are superior or equal to ours by most morbidity and mortality measurements, and one that has left its physicians and patients content.[8]

In single-payer systems throughout the world, patients choose their own practitioners, and physicians do not have to justify individual treatment decisions to insurance companies or their government or seek permission in advance to perform procedures. This is the system that has been proven to actually work to control costs, guarantee access, assure quality, and command loyalty by both patients and physicians.

Germans spend 57% of U.S. health care expenditures per capita on health care and on the first day of unification between East Germany and West Germany, every East German was included in the West German health care system without a moment's transition.[9] Canada spends 68% of U.S. health spending per capita.[9] Australia spends 51% of U.S. spending.[9] And all these systems have unrestricted free choice of provider. Interference in physician treatment decisions on a case-by-case basis in unheard of in these countries.

The single-payer system has been demonstrated to reduce administrative costs to less than 2%, instead of the 14% (range, 5% to 40%) we experi-

The Case for a Single-Payer Approach

ence in the United States at the hands of private insurance companies.[5,10] Overall, Americans spend at least 20% of their health care dollars on insurance company, physician, and hospital administrative costs.[11] Indeed, administrative cost is the fastest-growing sector of the American health care economy.[12] Medicare, on the other hand, our own single-payer system for elderly and disabled Americans, expends 2.1% on administrative costs.[4]

We have had virtually uncontrolled insurance free enterprise in the American health care delivery system since World War II, and it has brought us to our current dilemma. Health care cost inflation of 11% annually completely refutes the notion that competition between insurance companies will reduce costs.[5]

We can no longer ignore the implications of the fact that inability to pay medical bills is the leading cause of personal bankruptcy in the United States[8] or that out-of-pocket medical costs now consume more than 10% of average household income.[2] And most Americans know that the termination of their health insurance is but one pink slip away. On the other hand, our trading partners through single-payer systems have preserved freedom of choice of provider, enhanced quality, controlled costs, and provided unquestioned security of health insurance coverage.[12] To deny this reality is to argue for leeches in the face of penicillin.

That is why earlier this year I introduced the American Health Security Act, HR 1200, in the House of Representatives. It is based on proven systems. And because it is based on experience, it provides solutions that are based on the lessons learned from years of experiments in many other countries resulting in their current health systems.

American Single-Payer System

The American Health Security Act establishes a single-payer system that is federally financed, administered at the state and local level, and privately delivered. This means that physicians are not employees of the government or any insurance company—the private delivery system remains intact. Patients have unfettered free choice of provider. Access to providers (and providers to patients) is not limited by the insurance plan with which they are affiliated. This not only enables patients to choose the best provider for them, it also assures continuity of care, a critical element in quality enhancement, because patients are not required to lose their physician every time they need to change insurance plans because of changes in their economic situation. The financial imperatives to change insurance plans and therefore physicians with every variation in the patient's personal situation is a fundamental flaw in both the president's and the pure managed competition approaches. In a single-payer system, a patient is never impelled to leave his or her personal caregiver.

Key provisions of HR 1200 include universal coverage, cost containment through global budgets, a reformulation of quality review mechanisms to explicitly eliminate insurer interference in the physician-patient relationship, creation of a uniform database, promotion of primary care practice including general internal medicine and general pediatrics, and provision of the financing of insurance from the federal government. These key provisions operate to maintain stability in the delivery of care, to focus on the physician-patient relationship as the centerpiece of the health care system, and to provide total security to the patient in the form of uninterrupted insurance coverage that requires no changes in plans as circumstances change.

Under HR 1200, the premium for health insurance is collected by the government in a separate health security trust fund. Health care expenditures are based on a national budget based on the preceding year's national health care expenditures plus growth in gross domestic product and population. That money is then distributed to state health security funds according to population and health status. The states contribute approximately 14% of the budget.

The providers and the single payer negotiate the payment rate for services. The negotiation process itself anticipates that providers bring bargaining power to the table, as in Germany—bargaining power that is much greater than the negotiating posture physicians traditionally have had with insurance companies. Certainly, the bargaining position of providers will be much stronger with a government accountable for the public good than with the monopsony market power of insurance companies under any managed competition proposal. Competition is based on quality, not cost, which will lead inevitably to a minimalist approach to care.[11]

As long as they stay within the budget, providers and states are basically unconstrained in how they negotiate reimbursement, with one exception. We face a critical shortage of primary care in this country, where specialists outnumber our primary care providers 7:3.[1] If we do not address this issue forcefully by training more primary care physicians and then rewarding them, we will continue to confront both the health care problems created by insufficient primary care and the cost problems associated with excess specialty-oriented care.

To reverse this trend, HR 1200 requires states to weight reimbursement to favor primary care providers so that direct incentives are created to enter primary care and stay there. In addition, funding of graduate medical education is directly tied to the state's ability to produce primary care residencies in a 1:1 ratio with specialty residencies.

Quality

Compounding the failure to recognize the primary care crisis in this country is the inattention to quality-of-care issues. Yet the way we currently review quality and control utilization is as flawed as our existing financing system.

The HR 1200 bill scraps the existing system of case-by-case utilization review and substitutes a system of outlier identification. Based on practice profiles rather than individual cases, providers whose pattern of practice is consistently outside the norms of their peers are identified and their practice methods reviewed. This enables the profession to look at the practices of individuals who pose systematic quality problems and to reeducate them. It enables physicians to deviate from routine practices in individual cases without the concern that a particular case will trigger a review. It provides an opportunity to reach providers who are isolated from their peer community and might never be discovered in random case-by-case reviews.

Because HR 1200 strives to return the health care delivery system to the caregivers, precertification of procedures is explicitly prohibited. Rather, practice guidelines are developed based on outcomes data and research. The bill establishes a national clinical database to contain raw patient data based on patient charts rather than billing information. The database would be established by the year 2000 based on the use of uniform software. Patient identity would be shielded from nonproviders and access restricted. Other privacy protection mechanisms are included. With this database, valid outcomes research can be performed and systematized, and physicians will have much more information on which to base treatment decisions. Most evidence suggests, and HR 1200 assumes, that physicians respond to information.[13] The best way then to change practice patterns is not to regulate physicians, but to provide the data on what actually works.

In addition to enhancing our clinical research capacity, the database will enable broad-based epidemiological studies to be undertaken. Through it, we can track the course of the growing tuberculosis epidemic and evaluate the methods to contain it as well as monitor the incidence and origins of other diseases. It should become an important tool in the conduct of basic research.

Myths

The goals of health system reform outlined above will not be attainable unless we cast out the myths that make this struggle for reform unnecessarily difficult. The notion that government cannot do anything competently must be fairly examined. We must recognize that there are problems whose scope and impact are so large that solving them simply requires government coordination. Maintaining private financing to coordinate health care makes no more sense than privately financing our national defense, and defense is a smaller part of our economy than our health care expenditures.[14]

For example, the vigor of American biomedical research is largely a result of federal funding of research administered by the National Institutes of Health and conducted by private institutions. It provides a perfect illustration of the effectiveness of federal financing of privately conducted projects as seen in our major private research institutions. The funding of the National Aeronautics and Space Administration provides another excellent example of how federally coordinated programs have resulted in great private gain, such as the sharing of space technology to achieve the sophistication of the hospital intensive care unit.

From an operational standpoint, the potential for the government to bring real benefits is persuasive. The administrative cost of Medicare programs is just 2.1%[4] compared with the private rate of 14%.[5] Our publicly financed pension system, Social Security, has never missed a payment in its 60-year history. Its trust fund runs with a consistent surplus.

Nor are physician livelihoods threatened by a single-payer system. A Congressional Budget Office study demonstrated that if a single-payer system similar to Medicare had been in effect in 1991, we would have reimbursed health care providers $21 billion more than we did then and still reduced national health expenditures by $14 billion.[15] It is important to realize that the administrative savings achieved by eliminating insurance companies stays in the system and is converted to payment to providers for delivering more care.

What, in fact, happens to provider incomes in a single-payer system? Certainly the rate of growth is controlled—but the baseline does not change. Second, there will be changes in how the money flows to different specialty groups within medicine. It appears likely that the rate of increases in fees for internists and pediatricians, for example, is going to be greater than for cardiac surgeons. But that scenario will likely occur whether you have a single-payer system or not. Physicians in single-payer countries that retain the private delivery system prosper.[16]

In return for negotiated fee schedules, physicians are guaranteed that they will be paid 100% of the fee for every patient within 60 days of bill submission, paperwork is completely eliminated (Canadian physicians submit one diskette to their provincial governments monthly, which constitutes their entire non-chart related administrative burden), financial anxiety and discussion is eliminated from the physician-patient relationship, and insurance companies are not second-guessing individual treatment decisions.

The Case for a Single-Payer Approach

The Options

The alternative to single-payer health care reform is President Clinton's plan, a more regulated version of managed competition to attempt to achieve universal coverage and cost containment. Costs will be controlled by herding patients into plans dominated by health maintenance organizations that compete primarily on the basis of cost, not quality. Insurance companies are placed directly in charge of the delivery system, as evidenced by the fact that cost containment is based on unifying the delivery system and the insurance system through health maintenance organizations and enforced through capping insurance premiums and taxing higher cost plans, presumably fee-for-service plans.[17] Most physicians will become contractees of insurance companies.

While there is a great deal of rhetoric about patient choice being based on quality, all the incentives in the president's proposal are financial. To the extent that quality improves with plans above the average premium plan, consumers can select quality only to the extent that they can pay for it with out-of-pocket, after-tax resources beyond what their employer contributes to their health coverage. Quality enforcement is left to the insurance plans whose reporting to patients is based on average results. There are no mechanisms for identification of specific provider quality problems or for improving that provider's performance.

Enforcement of quality is essentially relegated to the patient who must evaluate quality report cards and choose plans accordingly to the extent the average premium permits. Since these sorts of quality assessments are extremely complicated for skilled professionals, it is difficult to imagine how the average patient is supposed to be able to distill this information. In effect, this aspect of the president's plan merely passes the buck to the people it is supposed to be protecting.

The only statement that can be made with certainty about the president's approach is that its applicability to the entire spectrum of any nation's health care delivery system has never been observed.[11] Its continuation of the patchwork of private-public insurance is destined to maintain large cracks that will leave many Americans still uninsured, assure high administrative expense,[12] and further establish the control of insurance companies over the delivery system.

Indeed, examined objectively, it is mystifying why the medical profession would prefer private financing. The expectation that physicians can have higher fees will certainly be defeated by the reality of fees set by insurance companies, which must be low enough to assure large insurance company profit margins. And there is at least as much reason to expect that needed care will be denied to subsidize executive skyboxes at the nation's stadiums as there is to believe that insurance companies will preside over better preventive care and improved health care delivery to rural areas. Insurance companies simply have no mandate to protect the public good.

Ultimately, a single-payer system and HR 1200 offer the solution that is most conducive to physician and patient satisfaction and to good medical practice. It is the only system that has actually worked to remove financial anxiety and coverage concerns from the physician-patient relationship. It is the only system that has in fact reduced administrative cost to its necessary minimum, thereby reducing physician overhead and freeing more resources for actual delivery of care. It is the only system that in fact operates without insurer interference in individual treatment decisions and restores the physician's role in the delivery system.

There are three major options controlling the health system reform debate. We can continue the current system, but the data show conclusively that it has failed by most major criteria and will only get worse. We can adopt managed competition in its regulatory form, which is completely untested but contains incentives that adversely affect quality and will institutionally remove physician control of the delivery system. Or we can adopt a plan that not only can be supported by objective data, but which has the potential for providing the best environment in which to practice medicine. For scientists, for clinicians, a single-payer system can prove to be the cure we have all been seeking.

References

1. Levinsky N. "Recruiting for primary care." *N Engl J Med*. 1993; 328:656-660.
2. *Half of Us, Families Priced Out of Health Protection*. Washington, DC: Families USA; April 1993.
3. Swartz K. "Dynamics of people without health insurance: Don't let the numbers fool you." *JAMA*. 1994;271:64-66.
4. Ford M. *Medicaid: Financing, Trends, and the President's FY 1993 Budget Proposals*. Washington, DC: Congressional Research Service; 1992. CRS report for Congress 92-168 EPW.
5. Iglehart J. "The American health care system: Private insurance." *N Engl J Med*. 1992; 326:1716.
6. *Managed Competition and Its Potential to Reduce Health Spending: A CBO Study*. Washington, DC: Congressional Budget Office, May 1993.
7. Glaser WA. "The United States needs a health system like other countries." *JAMA* 1993; 270:980-984.
8. Shikles J. *Canadian Health Insurance: Lessons for the United States*. Washington, DC: General Accounting Office; 1991. GAO report GAO/HRD 91-909.
9. Schieber J, Poullier J-P, Greenwald L. "U.S. health expenditure performance: An international comparison and data update." *Health Care Financing Rev*. 1992; 13:1-15.

10. Blendon RJ, Edwards JN, Hyams AL. Making the critical choices. *JAMA* 1992;267:2509-2520.
11. Angell M. How much will health care reform cost? *N Engl J Med*. 1993;328:1778-1779.
12. Himmelstein D, Woolhandler S. The deteriorating administrative efficiency of the U.S. health care system. *N Engl J Med*. 1991;324:1253-1258.
13. Merlis M. *Controlling Health Care Costs*. Washington, DC: Congressional Research Service; January 26, 1990. CRS report for Congress 90-64 EPW.
14. *Economic Indicators Report*. Washington, DC: Joint Economic Committee of Congress; June 2, 1993.
15. Rich S. Single payer health care savings seen: CBO reports system could cut $14 billion. *Washington Post*, May 9, 1993; section A:5.
16. Fuchs B, Sokolovsky J. *The Canadian Health Care System*. Washington, DC: Congressional Research Service; February 20, 1990. CRS report for Congress 90-95 EPW.
17. *The President's Draft Proposal for Health Care Reform*. Washington, DC: Office of the President; September 7, 1993.

3

Managed Competition as a Route to Markets That Serve Public Needs: A View from Near the White House

Len M. Nichols

My talk tonight has two parts. The first part is a brief review of the three broad steps necessary to construct a health reform package. The second part is a discussion of various cost estimation issues, given a package. This second part could be titled: What did we who worked on the Clinton HCR plan know and when did we know it, or alternatively, why did we do THAT?

Three Steps to Developing a Health Reform Package

Step 1: Define your goals.

Goals of Health Care Reform:

Middle Class Goals	Liberal Goal	Re-election Goal
Cost Containment Coverage Security	Universal Coverage	Deficit Reduction

The President's plan was designed to achieve all of these goals, an ambitious task by any standard. By the summer of 1994 most other bills aimed only for some variant of the middle class goals with some increased coverage and a bit of deficit reduction tacked on for good measure, mostly because the latter became a litmus test of "fiscally responsible" health care reform.

This presentation was made on November 18, 1994, at the University of Michigan Forum on Health Policy.

It seems to me that the necessary social consensus for universal coverage was never achieved, despite the fond hopes of the many and the repeated assurances of the few. I am afraid that the administration's inability to definitively establish the linkages among universal coverage, cost containment and coverage security served to seriously weaken the coalition that did support comprehensive reform at the outset.

Of course, data problems were serious here, since the evidence on the exact linkages between uncompensated care and private premiums is not definitive, and since the link from coverage security to universal coverage is probabilistic (most currently insured people simply don't believe they could become uninsurable until it happens).

Step 2: Identify your constraints.

For the president's plan, the constraints were very clearly laid out very early on:
- NO new broad-based taxes or broad-based tax increases
- DO NOT expand existing public programs
- Get every American insured before 2000

Note these constraints ruled out single payer plans, and also forced us to move rather quickly.

Step 3: Maximize the political appeal of the plan to achieve your goals subject to the constraints.

Step 3 can also be described, fundamentally, as deciding which groups you're going to redistribute economic welfare *from* and which groups you're going to redistribute economic welfare *to*.

Hard as it is to accept, there are only three ways to finance universal coverage:

- Broad-based explicit taxes
- Reduce insurers' and provider incomes, or at least reduce the rates of growth of insurer and provider incomes;
- Impose implicit taxes through mandates

Given the goals and the constraint of no serious tax increases, the president really had no choice but to:

- reduce public payments to providers through Medicare and Medicaid cuts;
- reduce insurer revenues from baseline by imposing restrictions on the growth of private sector premiums, i.e., premium caps; and to

- force as many people as politically feasible to pay for their coverage through mandates.

Once these broad contours were clear, and they were, very early on, the details of the exact managed competition framework finally proposed could be and were thought of as rather *technical details* designed merely to minimize the transitional pain, i.e., the rationing, that is implicit in the premium caps, by encouraging competitive forces underneath the caps.

Unfortunately for the administration, as wiser heads have concluded before, both God and the Devil really are in the details. For it was precisely in these relatively technical details regarding alliances and their rules about standard benefit packages, community rating, risk adjusting, etc., it was here that the absolutely *crucial* battle over the public characterization of the President's plan was lost.

Administration spokespersons still think of these details as indicative of their "moderate" view of government, merely setting reasonable rules for vigorous and effective private sector competition;

Opponents of the president's plan, however, painted these rules, and more generally, the explicit (and unavoidable) federal rulemaking AUTHORITY, as Orwellian BIG GOVERNMENT thrust unnecessarily and unwisely between "normal" Americans and their ever-solicitous Marcus Welbys.

As an analytical matter of political economy, I have to say I do believe the administration position is essentially correct, but, Sweet Lord have Mercy Upon Us, we did a spectacularly abysmal job of conveying that point to members of Congress, much less to the American public. The Administration never adequately explained why the insurance reforms were necessary and how exactly the reforms were going to make insurance markets function better.

Opponents of the President's plan surely overstated their case, as is normal in American political discourse, but I tend to think now that the fundamental objection was not over the merit of the rules, per se, but over the federal AUTHORITY to set the rules. This is why it came to be seen in that camp that the bill had to be killed outright, regardless of how it might be amended and seriously improved. The administration and its allies kept arguing about the detailed merits of the rules, but the larger debate which passed us all by and in the end rendered the prodigious efforts of Sens. Mitchell and Chafee sadly irrelevant, was always about the *locus* of authority.

As an aside, I submit to you that this larger debate about the locus of authority is precisely what the recent election results will sharpen into focus, and while we who lean toward the Democratic side of the aisle must yet endure some painful wailing and gnashing of teeth, I honestly believe the upcoming debate has the potential to be very good for the country, finally, after all these years of talking past each other, for the incentives for both sides to be closer to truthful have never been greater.

Cost Estimation Issues, or Why did we do THAT?

Well, you might ask, having decided to pursue extremely ambitious goals while imposing very tough constraints on ourselves and finally selecting a package of insurance market reforms that ARE difficult to explain to very smart people on good days, how did we spend the next 8 months of 1993?

Why, trying to figure out exactly how much this all would cost whom, of course, so that we could put forth a credible comprehensive health reform proposal with some non-trivial amount of deficit reduction. There are four classes of tasks in the quantitative analysis of a comprehensive health reform proposal:

1. premium estimation
2. subsidy estimation
3. overall budget effects (other federal programs and revenues)
4. effects on the national health spending and the national economy

I will consider each one briefly in turn.

1. Premium estimation

There are three major features of premium estimation:

- the benefit package, services covered and cost-sharing requirements;
- the populations that will have access to it
- the insurance rules that will govern that access

I've already indicated that a more or less separate team was given the autonomous task of working out the insurance market rules, so we in the quantitative estimation team spent most of our time on benefit packages and different populations.

It was also clear fairly early that the benefit package was going to be generous. It was finalized in May of 1993, and modified under cost pressures in September as the bill language was being finished.

Given the 1987 NMES, nationally representative, though old, expenditure distribution data for different sub-populations is available. However, data on the distribution of premiums and on the relation between premiums and actuarial values are virtually nonexistent, and what we really

Managed Competition as a Route to Markets that Serve Public Needs 37

needed was a way to predict the range of premium bids that would be forthcoming for a particular standard benefit package and how people would sort themselves in this range among HMOs, PPOs, and FFS plans. We gave up fairly early on, and concentrated on the predicted average bid, and basically assumed and hoped this was adequate. I believe it was the best we could do, and CBO agreed and did likewise. I also believe we would have had to be flexible in implementation if enrollment capacity at or below the average bid was insufficient in the early years, which very well could have been the case. Clearly, better data on insurance markets should be a very high priority, an even stronger priority as reform proposals become centered on voluntary coverage expansions instead of mandates.

In all our simulations up until the original benefit package was finalized, one major policy problem was the most difficult to resolve analytically: what to do with the under-65 Medicaid population.

- Some advocates wanted to abolish acute care Medicaid and put the beneficiaries into the community rated pool. Others argued for integrating Medicaid last, after all the other reforms had been phased in.
- Economists made clear that integration of Medicaid would cost everyone, especially the private sector. The literally $64 billion question was, how much?

There are two sources of these higher costs:

- legitimate per capita utilization and cost differences (particularly for the SSI and non-cash recipients)
- "induced" utilization increases, once in "mainstream" plans

The dispute over per capita costs was hard enough. We were shocked to learn that HCFA had two rather different opinions here (Office of National Health Statistics vs. Medicaid program actuary). Hard as this was, the absence of behavioral evidence was worse. How pessimistic should one be?

In the end, we implicitly adopted HCFA's more conservative estimate, 18-20%, and decided to:

- keep the Medicaid cash recipients, both AFDC and SSI beneficiaries, OUT of the community rate;
- pay plans a per capita amount for Medicaid cash-eligibles;
- put on tight premium caps in the first year to limit the "excess" Medicaid costs shifted; and to
- force all plans to spread these costs across all enrollees.

Beyond May of 1993, there was never any more serious discussion of going forward with a proposal without hard premium caps in the first year—the only question was how tight to make them.

Ergo, we had to propose rules about Medicaid and first-year bids that were arguably draconian, yet "merely" technical given our goals, belief set and the constraints. Private insurers predictably recoiled at the prospect of having to take former Medicaid recipients on demand and accept the government-set per capita payment for them, regardless of how "fair" we promised to make this per capita payment. The fundamental political problem was, we had no way of explaining the quantitative need for these rigid rules. We could hardly argue for the draconian rules on the basis of the HCFA actuary telling us the Medicaid tax on private premiums could be as high as 20%! The public relations battle was an uphill struggle, at best, from the beginning.

Let me make two more comments about premium estimation.

One, this is by far the most important estimate among the set of estimates required by comprehensive reform proposals. Eighty percent of the differences between CBO and the administration on the deficit impact of the HSA can be traced to their differing premium estimates (another 10% to differing assumptions about the number of large firms that would remain self-insuring outside the alliance/community rated sector, and a final 10% to the usual Medicare/Medicaid baseline technicalities). For what it is worth at the present moment, I believe truth was about halfway in between the administration and CBO estimates of premiums, though both estimates are within what one might call a "reasonable range." The upper bound of this reasonable range was in some ways defined by the final Lewin-VHI estimate, which CBO was more than happy to agree with. The other private sector estimates of the HSA premium, by Hewitt, Wyatt, and HIAA, by contrast, were irresponsible and alarmist, and only served to confirm administration fears that it could not obtain objective private sector analyses of the HSA and to confirm private sector fears that the administration was deliberately low-balling the estimates. This was truly not helpful.

Two, premium estimation is more difficult in voluntary as opposed to mandated markets, because adverse selection must be predicted as well as the usual demographic group heterogeneities in per capita costs. Because of the way the current health insurance market works (i.e., denial of coverage is preferred to raising prices to less favored enrollees), it is very difficult to get accurate data about the size of this effect. Estimating premiums in a voluntary community rated market is even trickier when Medical Savings Accounts are present to encourage the healthy to buy catastrophic policies. The CBO was rather generous to the Michel and the Bipartisan bills in giving them the benefit of the doubt about adverse selection in their numerical cost estimates while emphasizing the potential dangers of selection in the texts of their reports.

2. Subsidy Estimation

Before subsidies are designed, a fundamental decision is required: are they to encourage voluntary purchases of health insurance or to soften the consequences of mandates?

I've already said there was no doubt that universal coverage was a major goal, and an employer plus individual mandate combination was distinctly preferred to a purely individual mandate. The higher reaches of the Clinton administration became convinced that workers do not believe they are paying for their employers' health insurance payments with lower wages, and therefore the employer mandate had the appearance of more progressive taxation, when in fact of course, given the type of employer mandate chosen by the Clintons, precisely the opposite would have been true for many workers. Alas, it is the economist's fate to sing a lonely song sometimes.

No quantitative analysis of a purely individual mandate was done during 1993, and the idea was never seriously considered until Congress forced us to confront the issue in 1994. Ditto for a 50% employer mandate vs. the 80% preferred by the administration.

Given the decision to have an employer mandate, the first question is, a mandate to force employers to do what? Buy a premium, or pay a payroll tax? This was the first major presidential decision, in May of 1993, when the president recoiled at the explicit redistribution inherent in the pure payroll tax approach.

So, a premium requirement it would be, and this is of course more or less a head tax on labor which could have had serious job loss effects, were it not for the facts that:

- 60% of workers get coverage through their employer now;
- because of the method of accounting for the premium payments required of secondary employers, some firms would have paid substantially less than they are paying now, so job expansions in these sectors would partially counterbalance the losses elsewhere;
- wages are flexible downward in the long run, through incomplete inflation adjustments.

Three final points about subsidy estimation. An individual wage cap approach appears to have many advantages over the total firm payroll cap approach to employer subsidies written into the Health Security Act. We eventually talked Kennedy, Gephardt, and Mitchell into this, though

Gephardt abandoned it for a Ways and Means clone at the last minute in preparing his bill. The advantages of individual wage caps over total firm payroll caps are:

- better targeting of subsidies;
- better job effects; and
- less or zero incentive for outsourcing/sorting.

Outsourcing or sorting, to take advantage of the firm size/payroll subsidy schedule in the HSA and other bills, is potentially a very serious problem, though not insurmountable. It could be prevented, of course, but the subsidy design that would do so was not preferred among politicians inclined to do something "extra" for small businesses. There is, unfortunately, no good information on wage distributions within firms, and thus we had a difficult time analyzing the likely extent of the problem. CBO did the best work on it up until February of this year, and we got into this business pretty seriously during the discussions of small firm exemptions from the employer mandate in the first half of 1994.

Subsidy estimation is much easier when there is a full mandate than when participation in any subsidy program is voluntary. This is especially true with the Chafee-esque subsidies (in practically all the bills after Senate Finance) in conjunction with a new income tax deduction for individual payments for health insurance. Again, the lack of wage distribution data within firms made it difficult to predict how firms would respond to these new incentives. Clearly, this kind of data should be a high priority as well. We and CBO estimated the costs of these bills as if no claimable subsidy dollar would ever go unclaimed, and that may be overly pessimistic, at least in the short run.

3. Other Federal Programs and Revenues

- Medicare: OACT - OMB - HCFA/OLP (long standing proposals)
- Medicaid: OACT - OMB - HCFA/ASPE (differences over decomposition)
- LTC: ASPE/Lewin-VHI (Brookings/ICF) - OMB
  —everyone capped this program, because predictions are very soft.
- AHC/GME/PHS: PHS and OMB (with some help from Mr. Moynihan's staff and friends)
- VA/DOD/FEHB: OMB - departments
- Revenues: Treasury

Interactions between the mandate and subsidy programs and the existing federal programs were always delicate and done at the end of a set

Managed Competition as a Route to Markets that Serve Public Needs

of iterations that defined a discrete stage in the process. The main reason the cost estimates moved so much between September and November of 1993 was that we finally had time to take into account all the various interactions. Ira understood the numbers in September were not ready for prime time, but I really think he felt he had no choice but to release them when he gave the plan to the Hill on Labor Day weekend.

Tobacco taxes are fairly straightforward to estimate. There were, however, three difficult parts of the revenue estimates:

- 1% of payroll "corporate assessment," which depended upon behavioral assumptions about large, self-insuring firms. During 1993, the Treasury believed inertia was a much stronger force than CBO came to believe. Straight financial calculus supports CBO. But it always seemed odd to me to assume that most large firms would quickly join something voluntarily they were trying mightily to kill.
- the effect of restricting health insurance premium payments from cafeteria plans required a behavioral assumption and the data on which to base this judgment are relatively weak.
- the indirect tax effects of the mandate, revenue gains resulting largely from the premium caps reducing total employer spending for health insurance below currently projected baseline levels, even with the mandate, and thereby leading to wage increases and subsequently to tax revenue increases. Our lower premium estimates contributed to the discrepancy with CBO here.

These indirect revenue gains were unexpected when we began the cost estimation process, for a priori we thought employer mandates would depress wages in the long run. We came to see that the revenue gains that came out of the models, given all the other pieces of the HSA puzzle, were directly dependent on the tightness of the premium caps.

Therefore, guess what: the tightness of the premium caps became a prime lever for jacking up or down the amount of estimated deficit reduction. The administration's rhetorical zeal for deficit reduction through health reform probably contributed to premium caps that were perceived to be "too tight" even by many administration allies, at least in the early years. In retrospect, it seems particularly unfortunate that deficit reduction got mixed up with health reform. Deficit neutrality, yes, deficit reduction and universal coverage, NOT a smart combination.

4. National Health Expenditures

I would suspect you're going to hear a lot more about this tomorrow from Tami Mark, but the simple fact is there is no fully integrated data set that permits intellectually satisfying overall health care system estimates. All NHE numbers are fictions: useful fictions, but fictions nonetheless.

One can do a reasonable job with aggregate premium spending and subsidy costs (based on per capita expenditure estimates and estimates of the number of newly insured), and then complete the picture with the aggregate federal program costs and state and local levels of effort under reform.

But accurate predictions of the demand for specific health care services in response to the multiplicitous reforms being considered, much less the supply side response of providers to the same huge set of often contradictory changes are very difficult, and I wouldn't want to watch anyone try.

An unexamined question in our deliberations was: what share of GDP is appropriate for America to devote to health care? The president and Ira wanted this to fall. Why??? What level is right? There is no intellectual basis for a particular share at the present time.

Summary

A large number of talented, knowledgeable, and dedicated people worked extremely hard to produce accurate cost estimates for the tremendously large number of health reform proposals that floated and sank over the last two years.

The uncertainties are large, and we clearly need much better data on insurance and labor markets. But the major uncertainties center around behavioral responses that are largely unknowable a priori. It makes me think we should discontinue most of the current surveys run by HHS and set up a panel study, like the Michigan Study of Income Dynamics, and follow households and employers through time. We need to know what kinds of products and prices were offered to employers by insurers, what choices the firm made, and then what choices households made, given the choices the firms had already made. Learning about the reasons for these choices is crucial to being able to predict how voluntary coverage expansions could work.

At the same time, the uncertainties can be bounded by sensitivity tests and the literature and natural experiments we can observe, so I do not believe any of the published official estimates of the administration or CBO were irresponsible or dangerously inaccurate.

I spent just enough time at OMB, however, to take increasing comfort with the fail-safe mechanisms that began with Chafee's original Mainstream Coalition group, and were incorporated into every serious bill after Senate Finance finished their markup. These "pay as you go" constraints differed from bill to bill, but they typically postponed expanding the subsidy eligibility or required some other compensating reduction in benefits if the dedicated financing streams proved inadequate to meet the next year's updated projected spending levels. More money than originally projected could be spent typically only with an additional act of Congress. This would seem to allow for adequate flexibility for changing circumstances and attitudes while at the same time protecting the federal purse from overly optimistic cost estimators who have been known to find employment in the executive branch from time to time.

Thank you again for the opportunity to be here. I'll stop now and respond to any questions you may have.

4
Health Reform: What Will It Take To Pass? A Moderate Conservative Stance

Gail R. Wilensky

Despite all of the recent activity on health care reform, we are only at the start of what will be a difficult and contentious process. The Clinton administration's clear hope is that the result will be health care legislation in 1994. As of this writing that outcome is very uncertain. If it is the "big bang" of health care reform (that is, reform that requires large spending increases or substantial pain) or nothing, I believe that it will be nothing. If it is possible to fashion a more modest package of reforms that does not involve mandates, spending limits, or big entitlement cuts, legislation is possible. Were 1994 not an election year, legislation would be unlikely because of major divisions over fundamental issues and vision. It is an election year, however, and fear of returning to their constituents empty-handed may bring members of Congress to the table. Whether there ultimately will be a willingness to pass whatever the majority can agree to, even if it includes less than what are now the president's minimum requirements, will determine whether any legislation is passed.

The principal forces driving reform are ballooning costs, increasing numbers of uninsured Americans, and increasingly insecure Americans who are insured. Yet enormous changes are proposed in the Clinton plan that have little directly to do with providing insurance to 36 million uninsured Americans, or with providing health security to the remaining 215 million Americans. Rather, the top-down restructuring of the health care system reflects the Clinton administration's predilection toward an interventionist government, which will reconfigure the way health care is financed, organized, and delivered in the United States.

The Clinton administration has promised a benefit package comparable to the health benefits of Fortune 500 firms to all Americans, whether

---

This paper appeared in the Spring 1994 issue of Health Affairs and is reprinted here with that publication's permission.

or not employed. It also has promised a major new prescription drug benefit and a home care benefit for the elderly, as well as an early retiree benefit that is 80 percent government-financed for persons ages 55 to 64. The health plan is to be funded by a tobacco tax; a community-rating system that shifts large amounts of money from younger, healthier workers in lower-cost areas to older, sicker workers and retirees in higher-cost areas; highly optimistic spending reductions in Medicare and Medicaid; and limits on premium increases in the private sector. The latter, among other effects, is assumed to lead to increased (taxable) wages and thus to increased personal income tax collections.

Strengths of the Clinton Proposal

The major strength of the Clinton proposal is a clear commitment to the concept of universal coverage, with a set of policy mechanisms for achieving that coverage. In addition, the plan contains a set of subsidiary reforms that are both highly desirable and common to most other health care proposals. These include elimination of preexisting condition clauses in insurance coverage, strategies for reducing paperwork and administrative tasks associated with inconsistent forms and billing, the provision of needed information on outcomes and quality for specific plans and providers, limited tort reform, and the beginnings of a risk adjustment process. An additional strength is the clear commitment of the Clinton administration to regard health care reform as a high-priority domestic policy goal. This is reflected in the frequent direct references to health care reform, the appointment of First Lady Hillary Rodham Clinton as the administration's point person on health care, President Clinton's address to a joint session of Congress in September 1993, and the Clinton's personal delivery of legislative language in October 1993.

Concerns about the Clinton Proposal

Reforming health care is not an easy task. Most Americans mistrust central government, like the quality and easy availability associated with the current health care system, would like to see everyone with good health care, and are reluctant to pay any higher taxes. The Clinton administration has made the difficult task of health care reform even more difficult by promising major new benefits—to the elderly, early retirees, the uninsured, the unemployed, and the poorly insured—at a time when the American public is cynical about its politicians and, especially after the economic plan, is in no mood for broad-based tax increases. The president has promised too much, too quickly, to too many, without credible financing.

I have at least four areas of concern with the administration's proposal: (1) spending limits and premium caps to control spending; (2) employer mandates; (3) the use of a regulated, complex structure to control the health care sector, including a regulated National Health Board and mandatory, monopoly health alliances; and (4) funding by questionable financing. These policy issues must be resolved before a political resolution can be achieved.

Spending limits and premium caps. The most serious issue to resolve involves the use of spending limits and premium caps. The Clinton administration says that its plan uses market forces and relies on market-based incentives, but in fact it uses direct regulatory mechanisms to control spending. The administration's actions reflect its fundamental distrust of markets and its greater level of comfort with regulated systems.

Although other countries have attempted to control spending by using spending limits and price controls in addition to limiting the use and availability of expensive technologies, the history of the United States with price controls is that they are short-lived and unsuccessful. The use of price controls, which is the less polite name for premium controls, will set prices rather than serving as a so-called safety net. The use of Medicare diagnosis-related groups (DRGs) and other forms of price controls has shown that government-set prices become the prevailing prices even though providers could always compete beneath these established prices.

The use of spending limits and price controls also is an area in which conservative Democrats tend to align themselves more with mainstream Republicans than with their own Democratic leadership. While it would be possible to remove this aspect of the health care plan, doing so would put at risk several other key elements of the plan. For instance, Democratic support of the sharp reductions in Medicare spending requires the use of spending limits in the private sector. Removing the spending limits in the private sector would make the administration vulnerable to charges of massive cost shifting to the private sector, an issue of particular concern to its congressional supporters; it also would remove the administration's estimated increase in personal income tax receipts. Thus, removing private-sector spending limits would severely jeopardize funding.

In addition to the practical problems of jettisoning these provisions of the plan, philosophic issues are at stake as well. There are only two ways to get spending right: rely on spending limits and price controls (in this case, premium caps) or rely on market forces. The administration's dilemma in part reflects the split in the Democratic Party, which is particularly pronounced on health care matters. A sizable minority distrusts major government intrusions in price setting and spending decisions, but the majority is uncomfortable with market forces, believing that they have been ineffective at controlling spending in the past and will continue to be ineffective in the future. This had led the administration to attempt to keep a foot in both camps. However, the political right recognizes premium caps and spending limits as the regulatory mechanisms they are.

Employer mandates. The second most serious issue involves the use of employer mandates. The way that the administration has proposed to guarantee universal coverage is to require employers to finance 80 percent of the average price of the health care plan in their region and to require employees to purchase a plan and pay the difference. Others are assured coverage by being required to choose a plan from the alliance and receiving varying levels of subsidies, depending on their income.

This is a funny kind of employer mandate, however. The employer is not actually required to provide health insurance coverage, but rather to serve as a mandatory financial conduit to the health alliance. Many businesses are objecting that employers are being removed from any involvement in negotiating health care networks and prices, at a time when they have become most active in this area, and are being replaced by institutional entities that do not yet exist. Use of the employer mandate also has raised concerns about the future viability of small businesses and the potential impact of the mandate on low-wage employees, which has led to the proposed use of subsidies to low-wage small businesses to limit the adverse effects of this mandate. This had led in turn to concerns about the resulting economic distortions as firms attempt to maximize their subsidies.

Many people, but especially Republicans and conservative economists, have questioned whether employer mandates will result in substantial job loss for low-income workers and/or economic failure for new small businesses. Most economists agree that there will be some job loss. However, they disagree on the magnitude of the effect. Job loss from mandates has been estimated to be as small as 200,000 and as large as three million. The latter estimates, however, reflected a mandate that did not provide subsidies to small, low-wage firms and therefore cannot be directly attributable to a proposal such as the administration's. Most economists believe that as long as money wages can adjust demand to reflect the effect of the employer mandate, the amount of job loss will be relatively small. Estimated job losses in the range of 500,000 to around a million would seem most probable. However, substantial economic distortions could be introduced as small firms attempt to reconfigure themselves to take maximum advantage of the subsidies being paid to firms that have both fewer than 75 employees and an average annual wage of less than $24,000. Alan Kruger has estimated that these distortions could cost about $10 billion, which is the equivalent of about one million jobs lost.[1]

The various concerns about employer mandates have led to some proposals that rely on individual mandates rather than employer mandates and to other proposals that do not require employers to finance the purchase of insurance but only to make group purchase of insurance available to employees. Many believe that an individual mandate has certain advantages: reducing the economic distortions that we see under the Clinton proposal, allowing government to target subsidies more efficiently to individuals who are believed to need subsidization, and removing the political concerns about mandates on employers. But countering that attraction is the fear that reliance on individual mandates would appear harsh and would represent too much change from the current system, while the lack of a mandate on either the employer or the individual would allow some number of persons to be uninsured, thus violating the administration's number-one requirement for health care reform: universal coverage.

While employer mandates are not quite as basic an issue to resolve as the one involving spending limits and price controls, its resolution will be contentious nonetheless. The business community itself remains split on this issue, with large employers not objecting to employer mandates and smaller employers very concerned unless they are to be heavily subsidized. Finally, it is one of many areas about which the public has shown mixed views. For the past several years polling data have shown that the public supports the concept of an employer mandate, with approval rates that have varied between 54 percent and 67 percent.[2] But polling data also have shown that the public withdraws that support if the mandate is assumed to cost jobs (which it will, although the magnitude of job loss is subject to dispute). An October 1993 poll showed a large number of people supporting the notion of "businesses encouraging the provision of health insurance," although it is unclear what the public thinks this phrase means.[3]

Other effects on economic growth. The rate of change in spending in sectors of the economy related to health care will also have an effect on the economy. Many reform proposals seek to reduce spending by improving incentives for purchasers to be more cost-conscious and by pushing for more efficient provision of services. However, if we are successful in reducing paperwork, or in pushing out of business small insurance companies that have excluded medium- to high-risk persons, or in downsizing the hospital sector, we also will reduce employment in each of these areas. The economic dislocation from such changes will depend in large part on the speed with which such changes occur and the size of the reduction. If we were to accomplish the spending goals of the administration, there would be sharp reductions in hospital spending and in the existing administrative structure associated with health care (although potentially large increases in other administrative costs). Substantial numbers of relatively low-wage, low-skill workers are employed in the health care sector, and absorption of these workers into the economy will take some time. This is not an argument for maintaining the status quo in health care, but rather a recognition that sudden changes in spending can produce local distortions, and dislocations that are difficult to accommodate. They also are changes that are not easily compensated for by increased spending elsewhere, even in different sectors of the health care industry.

Furthermore, the economic effects of the president's health care reform proposal need to be considered in the context of other recently adopted or proposed policies of the Clinton administration. For example, Labor Secretary Robert Reich recently proposed and subsequently withdrew a 50¢-per-hour increase in the minimum wage. Any increase in the minimum wage, on top of the increase implied by an employer mandate, would exacerbate concerns about potential effects on low-wage workers. Furthermore, the increase in marginal tax rates passed in August 1993 will affect some successful small businesses. Approximately 40 percent of all U.S. businesses file as subchapter S—that is, they file as individuals. Those that have been financially successful are at risk of having an increase in their marginal tax rate; this, combined with changes resulting from an employer mandate, could have cumulative effects on the economy.

National health board and regional alliances. The Clinton plan proposes powerful new bureaucracies and gives new regulatory powers to existing bureaucracies such as the Department of Health and Human Services (HHS). The new entities include a National Health Board, with powers to set per capita spending, allocate the per capita spending to the states, review and provide oversight for prices of breakthrough therapeutics, and take over the functions of health alliances that are not performing in a satisfactory manner. The proposal also establishes mandatory monopoly purchasing groups: the regional health alliances.

Purchasing groups, which are an important part of almost all health care reform proposals and are used to provide market power to small firms and individuals, are used in the Clinton plan for purposes that extend far beyond those that are necessarily associated with purchasing groups. The administration's purchasing groups have strong oversight powers to implement the directives of the National Health Board, including decisions of where people will enroll if their health plans are oversubscribed, setting provider fee schedules for fee-for-service providers, establishing information requirements for plans that will be allowed to market in their areas, negotiation and enforcement of premium caps, enforcement of mandatory participation, and so forth.

The problems with use of these highly regulatory entities, however, are not nearly as difficult to resolve as are the problems mentioned above. Most health care reform proposals use the concepts of national health care boards and purchasing groups, even if they do not have the regulatory power that is assumed in the Clinton proposal. If employers or individuals must offer or obtain health insurance, some entity must decide what that health insurance package needs to include, which means that there is a need for a health care board of some sort. In addition, many proposals recognize the value of purchasing groups as a way to give small firms and individuals better market leverage for their health care dollar.

Thus, while the precise functions of a national health care board and health alliances will be subject to negotiation and change, their fundamental concepts are not the subject of controversy as is the case for spending limits, price controls, or employer mandates. Most policy analysts believe that ultimately there will be a national health board of some sort, although one with far less regulatory power than has been envisioned, and that there will be health alliances or purchasing groups, although it is unclear whether these will be voluntary or mandatory and what the size of firms that are required or encouraged to participate will be.

Questionable financing strategies. My final set of concerns has to do with the proposed financing and with the accuracy of the spending and savings estimates. By promising major new benefits to the uninsured and the already insured, the administration has put itself under enormous fiscal pressure. Its response has been to propose reductions in Medicare and Medicaid that far exceed any experience in the United States, and to couple these reductions in public programs (amounting to almost one-sixth of baseline spending) with a very tight premium cap for the private sector. Ultimately, savings can only come from paying providers less, providing less in the way of quantity or quality of services, or finding ways to increase the efficiency with which health care is provided. The administration nominally invokes the third, although most of the savings would come from paying various providers less.

Medicare and Medicaid. The largest source of funds to finance the Clinton health care proposal comes from reductions in Medicare and Medicaid spending. The administration proposes a reduction of $124.4 billion in spending in the Medicare program over five years. This amount is in addition to the $56 billion in reductions that was included in the economic plan passed by Congress in August 1993. This means that the administration is proposing more than $180 billion of reduction in Medicare's projected spending in the 1990s, mainly through reducing payments to providers.

The Medicare reductions involve some 28 specific payment changes that range from reductions in the hospital update factor and reductions in payments for capital, which together provide over $28 billion in savings, to changes in hospital outpatient department payments and in physician reimbursement, which account for an additional $25 billion in savings. While a few changes could be viewed as attempts to produce savings by affecting use, such as changing the coinsurance rate for home health agencies or establishing coinsurance for laboratory services, the vast majority of savings occur because of reductions in provider payments. Although this has gone largely undiscussed to date, these reductions will affect the availability of services to the elderly as providers respond to reductions in funding and reorganize or restructure how they provide services. In addition, these reductions will further stress the schism between a price-controlled Medicare system, in which providers can attempt to compensate for low payments by volume increases, and a managed care-oriented system for the non-elderly, in which providers respond by limiting less necessary use of services.

The almost exclusive reliance on reductions in provider payments—both in the financing of the Clinton health care reform package and in the changes included in the economic plan—makes these Medicare reductions both politically unlikely and of questionable wisdom substantively. The administration had a difficult time convincing a majority in Congress to agree to the $56 billion reduction in August 1993. The likelihood of persuading an uneasy Congress to add $124 billion of Medicare reductions in an election year seems remote.

There is certainly potential for reducing Medicare spending. However, promising the same service level to the same population in a program having the same basic incentives, yet removing $180 billion of projected spending over a five-year period, would be a serious mistake unless the elderly understand that it will affect the level and availability of their health care. And financing new benefits for the elderly by these proposed reductions will only exacerbate Medicare's current fiscal fragility. To me it represents a political cynicism that bodes ill for the future.

The administration also proposes several changes to the Medicaid program. The disproportionate-share payment program, which has been a major source of Medicaid spending growth, would be eliminated. In its place the Clinton plan would put a small reserve of funding for hospitals treating large numbers of low-income persons. This is a reasonable proposal since the justification for the disproportionate-share program was to finance the costs of treating large numbers of low-income uninsured persons, which will no longer be an issue under the Clinton proposal. Eliminating disproportionate-share payments or making this amount of money available to the states under flexible guidelines is included in many other health care reform proposals as well.

The remaining Medicaid reductions are more problematic. The administration assumes that health alliances will be able to provide Medicaid services at 95 percent of what would have been paid if the cash-eligible beneficiaries were still on Medicaid. In addition, those who have been on Medicaid will be subject to a stringent cap placed on their spending growth, since these persons will be part of the health alliance and thus subject to the Consumer Price index (CPI) cap on payments. It is also assumed that $85 billion in federal savings will occur as many who had been on Medicaid get coverage under the employer mandate, with the states being required to continue their current financial efforts on behalf of the noncash Medicaid population. While these savings seem unreasonably high, until more information is known as to how precisely these calculations were made, I am reluctant to criticize these estimates.

Accuracy of estimates. Whether the administration's financing estimates are accurate and whether the financing is adequate to support the benefits promised will be resolved by the Congressional Budget Office (CBO). Under existing budget rules new benefits can be enacted only if new funding sources are identified or existing spending levels reduced, and these spending and financing estimates must be agreed to by the CBO. But if history is any guide, these estimates—no matter how conservative—will be wrong, and they will be wrong in only one direction: Government spending will be underestimated, and government savings will be overestimated. A few examples of our inability to accurately forecast expenditures associated with new benefits will make the point.

The glaring mis-estimation has to do with Medicare itself. Passed in 1965, the Hospital Insurance component was estimated to cost $9 billion by 1990; actual costs were $67 billion (no longer-run estimates were made for the Supplemental Medical Insurance component).[4] More recent mis-estimates are shown by experiences with the Medicare catastrophic legislation, or the savings attributed to the 1990 budget act. Most of the catastrophic program was never in place long enough to assess the accuracy of the projections, but one part that was had to do with the removal of a three-day hospital stay requirement before Medicare would pay for nursing home care. The cost of this change was independently estimated by the Health Care Financing Administration (HCFA) and the CBO at $150 million per year.[5] In the one year that the change was in effect, the provision was estimated to have cost $1.4 billion.[6] This means that both HCFA and the CBO were off by a factor of nine in a program change for which it was believed there was adequate information for an accurate prediction. The 1990 budget deal was expected to reduce Medicare and Medicaid spending by about $40 billion. Within months of the agreement, however, it was clear that rather than a reduction, there were be a net increase in spending of at least $60 billion within the relevant time frame of the budget deal. In fact, technical revisions to the 1990 budget act have now added about $190 billion worth of spending to that agreement.[7] This history, combined with specific concerns about the Medicare and Medicaid reductions, has led to overwhelming skepticism about the claims of conservative estimates of funding health care reform.

As a result of the concern over the financing estimates, a number of proposals involve a "spend-as-you-save or pay-as-you-save" provision, such as the Health Equity and Access Reform Today Act (S. 1770), sponsored by Sen. John H. Chafee (R-RI). This is an attempt to recognize that despite the best efforts at projecting expenditures or savings in policy changes, only after we have implemented change will be know how much we will spend or save. Given the size of the health care sector, this has been suggested as a way to limit the damage that major changes otherwise could impose on the federal deficit. If not a "pay-as-you-save" provision, some attempt to limit future government financial exposure may be needed if the legislation is to be supported by the more conservative members of Congress.

The Politics of Health Care Reform

In assessing the politics of health care reform, the usual response is to outline areas with the greatest differences between the Democrats and the Republicans. While this remains important, the most significant split is within the Democratic Party. Conservative Democrats and mainstream Republicans tend to agree on some of the fundamental issues: opposing spending limits, price controls, and employer mandates and sharing a distrust of the Democratic leadership. Of course, significant splits exist within the Republican ranks as well.

Democratic divisions. To understand how significant the divisions within the Democratic Party have been, it is instructive to think back to the summer of 1992. This was a time when partisan Democrats would have dearly loved to have embarrassed a weakened Republican president by passing health care reform legislation that they knew he would be forced to veto. Senate majority Leader George J. Mitchell (D-ME) was advocating Health America, a bill that incorporated spending limits, price controls, and employer mandates; it was cosponsored in the Senate by Edward M. Kennedy (D-MA), Jay Rockefeller (D-WV), and Donald W. Riegle, Jr. (D-MI). But Health America never went to the floor of the Senate because it was clear that it did not have the 51 votes required for passage. In the House the Health Cost Containment and Reform Act of 1992 (H.R. 5502), cosponsored by Fortney (Pete) Stark (D-CA) and Richard A. Gephardt (D-MO), also contained spending limits, price controls, and employer mandates. It too was not brought to the House floor, for while substantial efforts were made to garner the 218 votes needed for passage, it was clear that it would not pass. This was a time when there were 10 more Democrats in the House and one more Democrat in the Senate than there are now. Thus, even when the legislation would have been "for show," in that it would have been vetoed by the president, there was enough division within the Democratic Party, primarily from the conservative Democrats, to prevent passage of the legislation containing the most critical elements of the Clinton administration's health care plan.

This division between conservative Democrats and party leadership is complicated by the existence of a third group—the single-payer group. This group is lead by Rep. Jim McDermott (D-WA) and has almost 90 members in the House but only two or three supporters in the Senate. The leadership group, which wants universal coverage through an employer mandate and spending limits with price controls, includes about 110 supporters in the House and around 40 in the Senate. The conservative Democratic forum in the House is more easily identified and has 60 to 70 members. The conservative Democrats in the Senate are a less identifiable group made up of eight to 10 senators. These conservative Democrats do not want employer mandates, may or may not support individual mandates, want reliance on market forces, and are against total private sector spending limits.

Republican divisions. Within the Republican Party there are three identifiable groups. One group, including the House leadership and a majority of House Republicans, favors incremental changes, for example, insurance reform, administrative simplification, tort reform, more flexibility for the states regarding Medicaid, full tax-deductibility of premiums for the self-employed, the option of a medical savings account instead of the tax exclusion of employer-provided insurance, and small additional investment in community health centers and rural health centers. A second group, including 25 House Republicans and 20 to 25 Senate Republicans, wants a less regulatory type of managed competition, involving individual mandates or no mandates rather than employer mandates, no overall spending limits and price controls, and purchasing groups that are either voluntary or, if required, limited to small firms. A third set of Republicans wants individual vouchers or tax deductions with medical spending accounts, some with the incremental reform that the first group of Republicans favors and possibly with an individual mandate or otherwise strong encouragement to have some type of insurance. There is a substantial amount of diversity within this third group, but they number 25 to 30 in the Senate (some of whom also sponsored the less regulatory managed care legislation) and at least 25 in the House.

Forging alliances. The big unknown is what it would take to bring these camps together and whether it will occur in time for passage of some legislation in the 103d Congress. At the moment the dynamic appears to be moving toward the more moderate group of Democrats and Republicans. This group's preference is embodied by the Cooper/Grandy bill, which has neither a mandate on employers or employees nor spending limits but is otherwise a managed competition structure, and the Chafee bill, which has an individual mandate and steep Medicare cuts (similar to those included in the Clinton plan), voluntary purchasing groups, and no spending limits. But both bills include a tax cap, which will be a significant impediment to their passage. Unions hate such caps, and since President

Clinton has already alienated labor with the North American Free Trade Agreement (NAFTA), he may be loath to do it again. Most economists believe that a tax cap or the substitution of a refundable tax credit for the current tax exclusion of employer-provided insurance makes eminent policy sense as a way to make purchasers more cost conscious and is therefore an important element in market-oriented reform. But a tax cap also translates into a middle-class tax increase, which causes politicians political heartburn. Since a tax cap produces tax revenue, there also would be a severe shortfall if the cap was excluded from legislation. Thus, including a tax cap brings a political and financial problem, but so does not including it.

In addition, guaranteed universal coverage—a prerequisite for presidential support of any health care reform plan—requires either an individual mandate, an employer mandate, or universal provision by the government. But employer mandates raise concerns, which have already been discussed, about economic growth and the employment of low-wage workers. Individual mandates are also of concern because they depart from current practice and because they sound harsh to individuals.

Ultimately, it is possible that the conservatives will cave in on the employer mandate issue, but I do not believe that this will occur in 1994. Alternatively, the administration may yield on its universality requirement and support the Cooper/Grandy bill, which provides universal access, although not necessarily universal coverage. This also seems unlikely.

Were 1994 not an off-year election, I believe that there would be little chance of passing health care reform. But many members of Congress have promised health care reform, and 435 members of the House and one-third of the Senate need to return to their constituents for support and re-election. This provides a powerful incentive to forge alliances and pass some legislation.

If it is all or nothing, then I believe that "nothing" is more likely, given the problems of the tax cap and the fact that leadership Democrats may not support legislation that does not ensure universal coverage. And while bipartisan support exists for many of the component policies contained in incremental reform, there has been a reluctance to vote on such a package. Right now it appears unlikely that the congressional leadership or the Democratic health care leadership of John D. Dingell (D-MI), Stark, Henry A. Waxman (D-CA), Gephardt, or Thomas S. Foley (D-WA) in the House, and Mitchell, Kennedy, or Rockefeller in the Senate would allow a vote in either house on an incremental package. A vote on this type of "downpayment" strategy will occur only with the support or concurrence of the President; at present, that does not appear likely.

To pass a health reform bill this session, there will need to be movement toward a consensus by the spring of 1994. The absence of this consensus will reinforce the belief that we are heading toward a stalemate.

Health Reform: What Will It Take To Pass?

There are also the beginnings of a sense among some in Congress that the bill introduced by the president is so flawed that there is a need to begin again, perhaps with a bipartisan commission composed of members of the legislative and executive branches. If by late spring no legislation appears to have the momentum for passage, either this strategy or an incremental bill may represent the best hope for the near term.

The interest in health reform is strong, but the near-term passage of legislation is not inevitable.

Notes

1. Alan Kruger, Princeton University, personal communication, November 1993.

2. Kaiser/Commonwealth/Harris poll, 1992; and *New York Times*/CBS News poll, 16-19 September 1993.

3. *USA Today*/CNN/Gallup poll, 28-30 October 1993.

4. Estimated amount is from Committee on Ways and Means, *Actuarial Cost Estimates and Summary of Provision of the Old-Age, Survivors, and Disability Insurance System as Modified by the Social Security Amendments of 1965 and Actuarial Cost Estimates and Summary of Provisions of the Hospital Insurance and Supplementary Medical Insurance Systems as Established by Such Act, P.L. 89-97* (Washington: U.S. Government Printing Office, 1965). Actual amount is from *1993 Annual Report of the Board of Trustees of the Federal Hospital Insurance Trust Fund*.

5. Original estimates contained in 1989 Mid-Session Review budget documentation. Actual outlays contained in unpublished budget documentation for fiscal year 1994 President's Budget.

6. *Ibid.*

7. Tim Muris, former associate director, Office of Management and Budget, personal communication, September 1993.

5

Is Managed Care Working?
The Payer Perspective

Howard Bailit

Introduction

The health care system is undergoing a historic restructuring, and there is great concern about the impact of these changes. Specifically, are health maintenance organizations (HMOs) reducing the rate of health care cost increases and providing adequate care to patients? What impact is managed care having on physicians?

To examine these issues, I first consider the organizational changes that are taking place in the delivery system. Then, I briefly review recent data on the growth of medical premiums, HMO quality, and changes in medical student selection of residency programs.

Delivery System

About 75% of the commercially insured population is now enrolled (1996) in some form of managed care program. Most states are involuntarily enrolling certain segments of their Medicaid populations into HMOs, and Medicaid HMO enrollment is now approaching 40%. Finally, the Medicare population is also joining managed care plans at a rapid rate, enticed by reductions in out-of-pocket costs and additional benefits such as drugs and dental. The bottom line is that managed care is now the dominant system for organizing medical care and traditional indemnity insurance will soon cover only a small percentage of the population, probably less than 20 percent by the turn of the century.

With managed care has come a major restructuring of the delivery system. These changes are best described as a consolidation of payers,

---

This presentation was made on November 18, 1994, at the University of Michigan Forum on Health Policy. It was updated in December 1996 by the author.

providers, and buyers. For managed care organizations (MCOs), once HMO market penetration reaches 20 to 30 percent, economic forces cause HMOs to consolidate. In many cities such as Portland, Minneapolis, Boston, San Francisco, and Phoenix, three to five MCOs have 80% or greater market share. With consolidation comes significant market power to drive down prices paid to providers and to bring about changes in delivery methods to reduce unnecessary utilization.

In response to these forces, many hospitals have formed alliances with other hospitals and are also moving to integrate vertically with physicians through various kinds of organizational arrangements such as physician-hospital organizations, management service organizations and ownership of practices. These large hospital and physicians systems are sometimes called integrated delivery systems, a loosely used term that covers a multitude of different organizational structures.

The ultimate goal of these integrated systems is to capture market share and position themselves to negotiate with MCOs on a more level playing field. This has been a difficult process because of the great excess supply of hospital beds and physicians, conflicts between hospitals and physicians, and the difficulty of integrating and managing these complex delivery systems. So far, MCOs have the clear advantage and are forcing providers to downsize and operate more efficiently.

The final consolidation that is at an early stage of development is voluntary and state sponsored health plan purchaser coalitions. There are some 175 of these coalitions nationally, and some are very well-developed and effective in forcing MCOs to keep premium increases to a minimum. Some of the better known business purchaser coalitions are in Minneapolis, Memphis, and Cleveland. Two states, California and Florida, have buying cooperatives for small businesses. In addition, states such as Kentucky and Connecticut are combining their Medicaid members with state and municipal employees to purchase health benefits, giving them significant market power. Finally, many large pension funds and employers also have considerable market clout. There is good reason to believe that these purchasing coalitions will continue to increase in number and mature operationally to force MCOs and providers to accept lower profits and operate more efficiently.

Impact of Managed Care

The key question is, what impact are these delivery system changes having on the cost and quality of care? There is no definitive answer to this question, because we are in a very dynamic period and the data are inadequate. However, it is possible to gain some important insights on the impact of managed care up to this point.

Medical Care Expenditures. The data are very clear: commercial health insurance premiums have declined dramatically for the past three years and for 1996 average about a 2.2% increase. Indeed, HMO premiums have actually declined by 5-10% in many areas of the country. These numbers have to be compared to 10 to 20% increases in premiums in the late 1980s and early 1990s. Managed care has, in all likelihood, played an important role in the decline of medical premiums.

However, it is premature to conclude that managed care has brought commercial insurance premiums under "permanent control." Some argue that these are one-time savings that result from going from indemnity plans to HMOs or that the insurance cycle is about to swing upward again forcing HMOs to go back to 10% plus premium increases. Others suggest that the aging of the population and the introduction of new technology into the system will force premiums to again rise at unacceptable rates.

While we cannot come to any firm conclusions, it is reasonable to conclude that managed care has had a positive impact on controlling health care costs. Whether or not the impact is long lasting, or even adequate to the size of the problem, remains to be seen.

Quality of Care. Many studies have examined the differences between indemnity plans and HMOs in the process and outcome dimensions of quality. Overall, the evidence indicates that there are either no differences or a slight advantage to HMOs. Some recent evidence suggests that the sick poor and the elderly with chronic diseases fared worse in HMOs. It is not surprising to find these conflicts in study results, and it is very likely that there never will be a definitive answer to the quality issue. HMOs are rapidly evolving and improving, and indemnity plans are rapidly disappearing. As such, the argument between indemnity insurance and managed care plans is probably moot.

The more important issue is, how well are managed care plans performing against the expectations of purchasers? Here, the evidence suggests that purchasers, especially the large ones, are demanding documented evidence on performance. These demands have led to HMO and PPO voluntary accrediting agencies such as the National Committee for Quality Assurance and the Joint Commission for the Accreditation of Health Organizations, and the establishment of many private sector firms that evaluate HMOs for buyers such as MEDSTAT, Value Health Sciences and many consulting companies.

Largely because of managed care and the market forces of competition, plans have to publicly make available standard data on key performance measures (e.g., the Health Plan Employer Data and Information Set). Although it is not clear how this information is used in purchasing decisions, there is at least anecdotal evidence that large purchaser groups do consider performance quality. As price variation decreases in more mature managed care markets, many experts believe that plans will have to differentiate themselves on process and outcome measures of quality and that this will result in major improvements in the care patients and populations receive.

Physician Career Choice. A very difficult problem that both federal and state governments have been unable to resolve is the large percentage of medical graduates who seek careers in subspecialty practice. Compared to other countries, the United States has many more subspecialists (65%) than primary care physicians (35%).

Managed care appears to be having a dramatic impact on physician career choice. Simply put, the number of medical graduates going into primary care—family practice, general internal medicine and pediatrics—is increasing. In contrast, some subspecialties such as anesthesiology and radiology are no longer able to fill available residency positions. The reasons for this reversal in career choice is that the market is demanding more primary care physicians who play a key role in HMOs as care managers and coordinators and fewer subspecialists. Thus, it is the market place rather than government that is finally bringing about long-needed changes in physician specialty mix.

Conclusion

I have presented evidence that managed care is having a positive impact on the cost and quality of care and physicians' career choices. The evidence is not definitive, but it is reasonably convincing for most people, and in part this is the reason for the dramatic growth of managed care over the past five years.

Certainly, managed care has many problems that need to be addressed, and it is foolish to believe that there will ever be a perfect system for delivering health care. Further, the managed care system that we know today is rapidly evolving and will probably look much different several years from now.

In the larger picture, this country has decided to use the market place rather than government to deal with the very difficult problem of controlling the demand for medical care and health care costs. The market place has responded and the rapid changes that are now taking place are sometimes painful and difficult to accept. This has resulted in significant opposition to managed care from many provider organizations and some consumer groups. This is not surprising, and the issue is whether the American people can accept this rapid change in the health care system.

6

Is the Health Care Cost Problem Solved?

Karen Davis

Opponents of health care reform argue that market forces are adequate to control rising costs, and that federal legislation is unnecessary. The argument that the health care cost problem is solved has a familiar ring to it. It was used by supporters of the Voluntary Effort, a coalition of hospital and physician organizations in 1977 to 1980, to argue that federal legislation to control hospital costs was unnecessary.[1] With the defeat of the Carter administration legislative proposal to contain hospital costs in the fall of 1979, health care costs again began to soar.

This paper reviews evidence on recent trends in health care costs, examines the reasons why these trends may or may not continue, and discusses long-term policy options. A historical look at trends in health care costs is especially insightful, because while there have been temporary periods of health care cost slowdown, there has been a strong underlying upward trend that has reasserted itself after periods of moderation.

Trends in National Health Expenditures

In 1993, the U.S. spent 13.9 percent of its Gross Domestic Product on health care, up from 5.3 percent in 1960.[2] The Congressional Budget Office has estimated that health care expenditures will increase from $884 billion in 1993 to $1.6 trillion by the year 2000.[3] Health care spending will increase to 18.9 percent of Gross Domestic Product by the year 2000 if we fail to take effective steps to alter this course.

Why are rising costs a problem? After all, some sectors of the economy must rise faster than the economy as a whole. In fact, we greet with considerable relief quarterly reports that the real Gross Domestic Product is in-

---

This presentation was made on November 18, 1994, at the University of Michigan Forum on Health Policy.

creasing at a healthy rate. The concern with rising health care costs reflects an underlying belief that we are failing to receive value for the resources invested in health care, and that inefficiency and unnecessary services are consuming resources that could be better used, for example to provide health care to the uninsured or to be used in other sectors of the economy such as education.

Workers increasingly recognize that employer health benefit costs cut into wage increases. Employee health care benefits now average 12% of employee wages and are a cause of labor-management disputes. A recent study by the Service Employees International Union found that real worker wages declined from $11.01 in 1980 to $10.55 in 1992,[4] measured in 1992 dollars. If health costs had risen no faster than Gross National Product over this period, real wages would have been constant rather than falling.

Rising health care costs also impose burdens on taxpayers. Medicare and Medicaid are the most rapidly increasing components of the federal budget. Medicare real spending per Medicare beneficiary was $974 in 1968 (measured in constant 1990 dollars).[5] By the year 2000 the Congressional Budget Office projects that it will increase to $5,729 per beneficiary.

Out-of-pocket health care expenses impose direct burdens on families. The average non-elderly household spends 3.7 percent of its income on health care in 1992, and even with Medicare, the average elderly household spends 11.9 percent of its income on health care, up from 10.6 percent in 1984.[6]

High health care costs are a major reason why 40 million Americans are uninsured. A survey by the Henry J. Kaiser Family Foundation and the Commonwealth Fund in 1993 found that 59% of the uninsured said they were uninsured because they couldn't afford health insurance, and another 22% were uninsured for job reasons such as they had lost their job or their job didn't provide health insurance coverage.[7] Three percent were uninsurable and couldn't obtain coverage because of health reasons. Only seven percent were uninsured because they didn't want coverage.

Businesses argue that high health care costs undermine their ability to compete in international markets. The validity of this argument depends in part on whether health benefits substitute dollar-for-dollar for wages. But nonetheless, it is certainly the case that the U.S. spends far more on health care than other industrialized countries, and that our health spending is increasing at a faster rate than other countries. Over the period from 1980 to 1992, real per capita health spending in the U.S. increased at an annual rate of 4.6 percent, compared with 2.0 percent in Germany, 3.3 percent in France, 3.9 percent in Canada, and 4.2 percent in Japan.[8]

Historical Evidence on What Works

There have been periods in U.S. history where health care cost increases have moderated. For example, real annual increases in hospital expenses per adjusted admission slowed below historical rates in 1973-1974, 1979-1980, 1984, and 1993.[9] Interestingly, these were all periods of major policy change or consideration of major policy change. The Nixon Economic Stabilization Program of wage and price controls from 1972 to 1974 is largely credited with the slowdown in the 1973-1974 period. The Carter administration's hospital cost containment proposed legislation and the health industry's Voluntary Effort are largely responsible for the slowdown in the late 1970s. The Medicare system of setting flat hospital payment rates based on patient diagnostic case-mix account for the 1984 slowdown. Consideration of the Clinton health care reform plan in 1993 may be a factor in the more recent slowdown, as well as other forces in the market.

What occurred after each of these periods, however, is that health care costs continued their upward rise. The 1993 national health expenditure increase of 7.8 percent, after adjustment for economy-wide inflation, is in fact on a par with the historical average, not a market slowdown. What many are viewing as a slowdown is in fact simply a reflection of economy-wide price stability. The gap between inflation in the medical care Consumer Price Index versus the all-item Consumer Price Index continues at about three percentage points.[10]

Policy Options

There are those who believe that market forces have solved the health care cost problem. The empirical evidence finds scant evidence to date for that belief. The best assessment is that what moderation has occurred has only succeeded in bringing the rate of increase down to historical long-range rates of increase, which are largely viewed as unacceptable.

It is possible that as market forces continue to expand, more moderation and savings will occur. But the opposite is more likely to be the case. The historical evidence certainly gives little comfort that slowdowns will be permanent. The driving engines of cost increases, particularly technological advances, the training of more physicians to provide specialized care, and to some extent aging of the population, continue unabated.

Further, there is no solid evidence that managed care achieves consistent savings over time. The Congressional Budget Office analyzed the managed care literature in 1992, and reported mixed results. It found that savings varied significantly depending upon the type of managed care plan.

Staff model HMOs, which employ their own physicians and operate clinical facilities seem to generate 10 percent savings compared with traditional fee-for-service health care. These savings are achieved largely through reduced hospitalization rates. In recent years, however, even the fee-for-service system has experienced a sharp contraction in days of hospital care—narrowing the difference between HMOs and fee-for-service plans. IPA models (Independent Practice Association) which contract with physicians in private practice, show little or no savings.

It is particularly troubling that studies to date have found no difference in the rate of increase in health care costs over time between staff model HMOs and indemnity insurance plans. A long range strategy must be capable of altering the upward trend in health care spending as a percent of Gross Domestic Product.

Another element of uncertainty is the future of consolidation in the health care and managed care industry. As health systems and managed care plans merge or fail, the concentration of market power on both the purchaser and the supplier side will increase. The outcome of this concentration of economic power for the ultimate payers—whether businesses, workers, taxpayers, or families directly—is uncertain.

The truth is we do not know enough about the impact of managed care on costs or on quality to embrace it as a national system. This issue is too crucial to turn to a system that has not been fully tested.

Another alternative is to build on the Medicare experience. For those hospitals and physicians providing care on a fee-for-service basis, Medicare-like fee schedules could serve as the basis of payment. Hospitals would be paid a prospective payment rate per patient based on patient diagnostic case-mix. Physicians would be paid according to a resource-based relative value schedule. Overall expenditure targets similar to those used by the Medicare physician payment system could be established to control the rate of increase in total health expenditures. If spending rose in excess of targets, any overage would be subtracted form future fee increases.

Such a system could be combined with offering everyone a choice of capitated managed care plans. Administratively, this could be accomplished either by having employers offer employees a choice of plans or opening up existing or new purchasing alliances, such as the Federal Employees Health Plan, Medicare, or state public employee health plans, to smaller firms and individuals.

Choice between capitated managed care plans and regulated fee-for-service plans has a strong advantage over a "pure" managed competition approach. It guarantees budgetary savings and restraint in growth in health care outlays over time.

Most importantly, it would continue to offer patients a wide array of choices. They could continue to be cared for by their own physician without incurring severe financial penalties. The option of enrolling in either a capitated HMO or a fee-for-service plan should help assure better care in both systems. If HMOs were not responsive to patient concerns, had long waiting times, and substandard providers, patients could disenroll and be cared for in the fee-for-service system. If expenditure limits and price limits made fee-for-service unattractive to physicians, they could join HMOs. The best competition should come from having attractive alternatives, rather than forcing all Americans into capitated plans.

Notes

1. Karen Davis, Gerard F. Anderson, Diane Rowland, and Earl P. Steinberg, *Health Care Cost Containment*, Baltimore, MD: The Johns Hopkins Press, 1990.
2. Health Care Financing Administration, Office of National Health Statistics.
3. Katherine R. Levit, Cathy A. Cowan, Helen C. Lazenby, Patricia A. McDonnell, Arthur L. Sensenig, Jean M. Stiller, and Darleen K. Won. "National Health Spending Trends, 1960-1993." *Health Affairs*, 13(5):14-31, Winter 1994.
4. Service Employees International Union, 1992.
5. Health Care Financing Administration, Office of National Health Statistics.
6. Congressional Budget Office calculations based on data from the Consumer Expenditure Surveys of the Bureau of Labor Studies, 1984-1992.
7. Louis Harris and Associates, Inc., Kaiser/Commonwealth Fund Health Insurance Survey, 1993.
8. G.J. Schieber, et al., *Health Affairs*, Fall 1994.
9. ProPAC analysis of AHA National Hospital Panel Survey data.
10. Data from the Bureau of Labor Statistics, in "Health, United States 1993."

7
Managed Competition: Helping Hand for the Invisible Hand— How the Clinton Plan Would Use This Strategy

Richard Kronick, Ph.D.

When the Clinton Task Force on Health Insurance Reform was formed in 1993, it seemed obvious that the free market, left to its own devices, was not solving the growing problems our health care system faced. Each year payers found themselves captive to steeply rising costs and each year fewer Americans had private insurance to pay for their health needs. Nor was public subsidy for health care equitably distributed. It seemed clear, at the time, that some form of public intervention was needed to make sure that the health care market got services to all who needed them, and at prices we could afford.

One of Alain Enthoven's many contributions to our understanding of health care economics is the insight that a perfectly "free" market in health care will not produce desirable results. The theory of managed competition, which Enthoven and others developed, starts with the assumption that an "unmanaged" market for health plans, in which individual consumers make choices among health plans without having the benefit of a sponsor, will not reward physicians, hospitals, or health plans for high-quality, economical care. When the market is unmanaged, health plans prosper most easily through risk selection, market segmentation, and the provision of biased information to consumers who are making choices. These are much easier routes to a profitable market share than the hard work of organizing the delivery system for quality and economy. Moreover, risk selection as a strategy for profit-making guarantees that services

---

This presentation was made on November 18, 1994, at the University of Michigan Forum on Health Policy. It was edited by the author in June 1997.

to persons who seem likely to cost more to care for than the income they bring in will be avoided. As a consequence, totally "free" market competition creates undesirable results: it encourages pursuit of profit through practices that have nothing to do with the quality of services provided or their economy.

The theory of managed competition argues that these inadequacies of the invisible hand can be overcome if a third party manages the basis for competition among health plans. The third party can overcome market tendencies that fail to serve the public interest, by introducing a variety of strategies that (1) share costs fairly among the public; (2) make risk selection and market segmentation difficult; so that services get offered to everyone; and (3) give the public sufficient information to make informed choices among competing health plans. In addition, the third party should administer a system of risk-adjusted payments that ensure that plans which do a particularly good job of caring for people with more expensive health needs do not put themselves out of business because their overall costs for care are higher than competitors.

The Health Security Act proposed by the Clinton Health Insurance Reform Task Force in 1993 would have created a third party, the health alliance, that had sufficient control over access to customers to motivate health plans and insurance companies to stop current practices of risk selection, market segmentation and biased information that now work to the public's disadvantage. More specifically the health alliances would have (1) insisted that competitors charge everyone in a community the same rate for health insurance premiums, and that they accept all applicants without waiting periods or preexisting condition exclusions. (2) The alliances also would have required every health plan to offer the same package of benefits, so that providers could not offer unique benefits—such as those which appeal to younger and healthier segments of the public—to capture particularly profitable market segments that require few services, while discouraging the less healthy from enrolling, nor could they engage in other forms of risk selection that place an unfair burden for the cost of care on their competitors. (3) The alliances also would have collected and made public comparative information on the cost and quality of services offered by competing health plans.

As would be true of any form of managed competition, the Health Security Act attempted to balance two inherently competing tensions. On the one hand managed competition is meant to save markets in health care from failing, doing so without substituting government allocation and political control for market-based allocation mechanisms. On the other hand, any third party that performs a variety of functions in the public interest must be held publicly accountable. To make a health provider market work better, we need a public sponsor with a substantial presence in that market. This, however, raises concerns that actions of the sponsor will be influenced by political pressure from providers and health plans. Consequently the Health Security Act proposed a variety of protections to insulate alliances from such pressures—such as requiring their board membership to be composed of employers and consumers of care, and circumscribing their power in a variety of ways. Skeptics, however, were not convinced that these protections would be sufficient to allow alliances to be "market forces" rather than regulatory agencies.

During the Congressional debates on the Health Security Act in 1994, I defended its proposals against attacks by advocates of managed competition who nonetheless opposed this bill. Among its strongest critics were Alain Enthoven and Sara Singer, who criticized the Health Security Act, asserting that it would create "weak market incentives and no real opportunity for market forces to work." As corrections they proposed four reforms of its provisions: (1) limiting mandatory participation in the health alliances to individuals and employer groups with less than 100 employees; (2) limiting tax-free employer contributions to employee health benefits to the level of the lowest-price qualified plan in the region; (3) not guaranteeing a limit on employer or individual premium contributions; and (4) eliminating caps (upper limits) on the price of health insurance premiums.

While some of these proposed changes would indeed increase the strength of market incentives, at the time I argued against these changes because they would have created other problems. Only the largest employers (those with more than 5,000 employees) have shown an ability to be innovative as purchasers. Limiting participation in the alliances to small companies and the self-employed—to those who now have least success in bargaining for reasonable rates—is not likely to change that dynamic. Moreover, these alliances would serve people with low incomes, rather than the general population. Many of their subscribers would be within 200 percent of poverty. Thus alliances would become sponsors of programs for the poor, which in the U.S. health care market have been inferior in quality to those available to the more wealthy. It is not good policy to create an institution that perfects the market primarily for the poor. Second, many of the Medicaid recipients, uninsured, and other low-income employees of very small businesses have greater health care needs than upper-income people. To group them together with the employers of 50 to 75 employees, thus, would place an unfair premium rate on small employers. Third, while larger employers would be welcome in the alliances, problems of adverse selection would be much more serious. The only feasible options would be either to prohibit firms with more than 100 employees from joining an alliance, or burdening firms and individuals who are required to be in the alliance with a higher liability than they would have otherwise. Firms with more than 100 employees who join an alliance are likely to be those with employees with expensive health problems, i.e., the firms that could not do as well bargaining for insurance rates on their own. Other objections to small purchasing alliances as an alternative to the Health Security Act alliances could be raised as well, but these are the most important concerns that would affect cost.

The Health Security Act would have changed the demand side of the market by creating powerful monetary incentives for individuals to choose less expensive health plans. Enthoven and Singer argued, correctly, that the incentives would be even stronger if there were a cap on the amount of an employer's voluntary contributions to pay for employee health benefits that would be tax-free. The administrative burden on the Internal Revenue Service would be much greater, however, and would add expense of its own. If purchasing alliances are small in size this would make it even more difficult to monitor, because many would be paying higher prices for insurance than groups with larger or more evenly distributed risk pools. Moreover, the cost of care varies by metropolitan area, which further complicates the task of monitoring tax limits.

Enthoven and Singer also strongly objected to the fall-back proposal in the Health Security Act of a cap on the rate of increase in premiums, arguing that this proposal would undermine competition, create wrong incentives, and put quality at risk. Premium caps were included in the Health Security Act because they were the only mechanism that would convince the Congressional Budget Office to 'score' the proposal as being somewhere close to budget neutral. Much of the financing for new subsidies for low income uninsured workers came from converting federal Medicaid expenditures for acute care, growing at approximately 10% per year, into subsidies to be paid through health alliances, growing at approximately half that rate. Although many of us who were involved in drafting the Health Security Act thought that the growth of expenditures would be reduced even without premium caps, some wanted a 'guarantee' of these lower growth rates; the premium caps were a response to the desire for a guarantee. Certainly they would have been extremely messy to implement, at best; whether they would have led to the many dire consequences feared by Enthoven and Singer is a counterfactual to which we are unlikely to be able to observe an answer.

When the managed competition legislative proposals got to Congress, additional debate emerged around proposals for community-rating of premium charges, a requirement that a health insurer charge the same price to everyone in a community, grouping all members of the community into a common risk pool and using the health care utilization experience of the community as a whole as basis for premium price. Opponents argued that this would destroy the insurance market as it now operates. Some argued that it would destroy incentives to offer worksite prevention services, to economize in use of services, or to bargain for discounted rates, since everyone in the community would pay the same price, regardless of personal actions. Advocates insisted that community rating was necessary in order to share fairly the burden of paying for pre-existing conditions that now get excluded from insurance coverage. I would add that while community rating might reduce employer incentives to act in ways that would bring down costs, it would increase an alliance's interest in sponsoring those activities. If you can get individuals in the market making choices that lower cost you can bring the prices down. That, however, requires choices among roughly comparable products, rather than among very different products aimed at special market segments that let providers engage in risk-selection.

There was also some debate about requiring all health plans to offer similar products. Some suggested this would discourage innovation that could lead to lower costs. Others suggested that it would drive prices up toward the top of the premium cap: large networks of providers would form, in order to guarantee profits as providers were required to absorb all who needed health care. (Each health care provider would gather a pool of customers large enough to balance out the higher costs of providing health services to poor Americans.) Once large provider networks formed, there would be less competition and providers could fix prices by common agreement, as happens in other markets where a few large producers dominate the field. One could expect costs to head toward the top prices allowed. These skeptics doubted that a combination of community-rated pricing and standardized products would lead to real cost containment, under these market conditions.

The small industry devoted to analyzing the causes of the demise of the Health Security Act has advanced a plethora of explanations for the political debacle. One explanation is simply that is was a bad policy proposal; health alliances- overreaching government institutions- that would have destroyed the market for health care services rather than facilitating the creation of an environment to reward quality and economy. We will have a chance to observe during the coming decade the extent to which a market without a public sponsor will provide quality and efficiency in health care delivery for those Americans with health insurance; sadly, we already know the answer for those 40 million uninsured Americans.

8
Who's Afraid of Health Care Spending Growth?

Mark V. Pauly, PhD

Introduction

I have been asked to talk about "cost containment" for medical services, and to describe what is working (or works), what isn't (or wouldn't), and what the future may bring. I will tell you what I know about those questions as part of this talk, but I will also address what is in some sense a more fundamental question about medical care "cost containment": Who cares? In my view (and from the perspective of welfare economics), understanding or determining what level or rate of growth in "cost" we should incur is much more important than ticking off the effectiveness of various nostrums for spending limits. From a public policy perspective, doing something about the uninsured is also more important than limiting cost growth and, as well, economics will say that there need be relatively little connection between policies directed at either problem.

Why Contain Costs?

From the most simple view of an economy, the objective of limiting the growth of one item of total spending is difficult to understand. Given some overall rate of growth in national output, high growth in one component of total spending must be offset by lower growth in another component. Our health care spending grows faster than that of Japan, but their spending on seafood grows faster than ours. (Their total GNP also grows faster than ours, which is a much more serious problem.) Why is spending on doctor visits or drugs for migraine headaches somehow less valuable than spending on fish? The answer obviously is that there is nothing intrinsically less valuable or less beneficial in medical services than food, flowers, refrigerators, or locomotives. The real question is not the level of spending,

---

This presentation was made on November 18, 1994, at the University of Michigan Forum on Health Policy. It was edited in June 1997 by the author.

or the change in the share of GDP. After all, the share of services in general, as well as medical care, has been increasing in the U.S. as far back as we have data; to a considerable extent this appears to happen because our agriculture and manufacturing are more productive than in many other developing countries. Instead, the real question is whether the inputs we use to produce medical services would produce outputs of greater value if used elsewhere. The real question is a benefit-cost question—are the benefits all citizens get from medical care services larger or smaller than the cost of those services in terms of other goods and services foregone.

This is all rather abstract. To be more specific: do we know that the large number of well (and not-so-well) educated young workers who got jobs in the medical care industry over the past decade could have provided services of greater value if they had taken jobs doing something else? I do not think anyone really knows the answer to this question, although there are currently some distorted incentives in our system that point in the direction of an affirmative answer. The important questions, however, are not whether "costs" can be contained or limited to a lower rate of growth than would otherwise occur. The questions are (1) how much lower than present is the ideal rate of growth and (2) what mechanisms can we devise to pick the ideal rate (or convince us that the rate we experience is close to ideal)?

I think the answer to the first question is unknown. Health policy analysts should therefore stop talking as if they know they answer, and politicians who pretend they do should be ignored. There are some ways of answering the second, which I will turn to at the end of my talk. Before I do that, however, I want to clear up some misconceptions about our levels of medical "cost," review recent experience on cost growth, and talk about methods that may slow its rate.

Cleaning Out the Underbrush

I have tried to put "cost" in (verbal) quotation marks in what I have said so far, because we really do not know what the economic costs of medical services are. Instead, what we can measure is medical care *spending*, but, especially in this industry, spending is probably not a good index for cost. Economics teaches us (as they say) that in competitive industries, price will come to be equal to marginal cost, so that spending can be thought of as the product of quantities times marginal cost. This is still not the same thing, for any product, as total (opportunity) cost, if marginal cost is rising as we often assume. It can provide a good measure of how much of other goods could become available for small reductions in spending, but it probably overstates what we could have if we abolished or took a big cut out of some particular good or service. But there is an even more serious problem in going from medical care spending changes to what we could have of other goods—prices in this industry may well exceed marginal costs. The presence of patents, the effects of state-enforced exclusive licensure, and buyer ignorance may cause prices to contain elements of profit or rent. Indeed, much of the difference in health care spending as a share of GDP between the U.S. and most European countries is explained by the higher earnings of U.S. physicians and, especially, by the higher wages of nurses and other health professionals in the U.S. Likewise, about a quarter to a half of the growth in real health care spending in the U.S. during the 80s was represented by increases in health worker wages and incomes at rates higher than wages in general.

These observations suggest that much (though by no means all) of "cost containment" would simply represent a redistribution of income from health professionals and owners of firms producing drugs and medical products to consumers and taxpayers. Since nurses, doctors, and technicians are Americans too, it is not obvious why public policy should favor this redistribution.

The other point that is important to make is that there is one cause of excessive medical spending and possible (though not certain) cause of excessively high rates of spending growth: the tax subsidy offered to insured medical spending through the exclusion of employer-paid insurance premiums from income and payroll taxes—even though they undoubtedly represent part of the compensation employees receive. The impact of these tax breaks is that nearly half of increases in health insurance premiums may be offset by lower taxes, leading to an obvious bias in choosing types of coverage that are not worth what they really cost. Paradoxically, the most economically uncontroversial cause of higher spending growth in the health care sector is put there by government policy itself.

What Is Happening to Medical Spending Now?

Perhaps surprisingly, government statistics to answer this question have recently been subject to major revisions, resulting in substantial changes in estimates of spending growth in recent years. For example, the growth of national health care spending in 1991, initially set at over 11%, was subsequently revised downward by two percentage points. The most recent figures, for 1992 and 1993, show nominal growth rates of less than ten percent. But after adjustment for the lower economy-wide rate of inflation in those years, compared to previous years, the real rate of growth in medical spending is still at about 5%, at or only slightly below the historical trend. (The private sector growth rate has fallen somewhat more, but the public rate is up, fueled both by Medicaid and Medicare.) That is, the real growth rate has fallen a percentage point or two since reaching a high level of almost 7% in the late 1980s, but is still, as of this writing, comfortably in the range of historical experience. If we can put together a number of years of real growth below 5%, and if further revision of the statistics do not cause additional changes, we may be able to declare a modest slowdown.

However, since the growth trend in real Gross National Product is still, as of this writing, substantially below the growth in medical spending, the share of GNP going into medical care is bound to continue to increase over the long term. As noted above, however, it is impossible to tell whether this trend is desirable or undesirable without knowing what the additional spending is buying.

Whether or not total medical spending is falling or not, there are some changes in private sector organizational arrangements which may bear on how we interpret those figures. The most important change is doubtless the sudden rapid spread of a wide variety of managed care insurance arrangements. While we as yet have no definitive empirical conclusion, there is circumstantial evidence to suggest that the spread and/or high levels of managed care are associated with lower spending growth rates. Studies in California show that, in parts of the state with both high managed care penetration and large numbers of competing hospitals, hospital spending grows more slowly.

Table 1 provides some informal evidence bearing on the generalizeability of this phenomenon. This table shows hospital spending growth rates and managed care market shares for the states with the ten highest and the ten lowest growth rates. The average managed care share is nearly twice as great for the slow-growing states as for the fast growing states. However, there is one state with a high managed care share among the fastest growing states, and there are several states with very low spending growth that nevertheless have a negligible managed care share. The messages are obvious: managed care has something to do with low rates of health spending growth, but spending growth depends on much more than the managed care share.

The other change in private sector arrangement that might affect spending growth is one that has yet to happen. Health economists generally cite the exclusion of employer-paid health insurance from employee taxable income—a tax subsidy—as a probable cause of high health spending (as well as horizontal inequity). It is less clear whether the tax subsidy leads to higher growth, but it probably does not help. The fundamental message, however, is that, if the tax subsidy were removed, private sector spending growth rates, whatever they turned out to be, would have a much stronger claim to being undistorted reflections of citizen preferences to buy medical care rather than other goods and services.

The other problem with the U.S. medical care system is the presence of a sizable minority of persons without insurance. High rates of spending growth probably have relatively little to do with this phenomenon, and elimination or reduction in the uninsured would have little effect on cost growth.

Let us take the last proposition first. The rough numbers are as follows: the uninsured are about 16% of the population, but the uninsured currently obtain about 75% as much care as do the insured. It therefore follows that if this minority were covered and their spending increased 25% to 100% of the currently insured, *total* medical care spending would rise by (.25 x 16%), or approximately 4%, a negligible difference.

Table 8.1 Rate of Growth in Hospital Spending, by State

State	Hospital Spending 1989-92	HMO Share 1991 (%)	Average
High Spending			
South Carolina	14.1	2.5	
Kentucky	12.6	6.2	
New Jersey	12.3	12.0	
Alabama	12.2	6.6	
Nebraska	11.9	5.8	
Kansas	11.8	8.2	7.62
Souh Dakota	11.6	3.1	
Louisiana	11.4	6.9	
Hawaii	11.3	22.9	
Arkansas	11.3	2.0	
Low Spending			
Nevada	4.2	9.8	
Arizona	5.9	25.0	
Maryland	6.8	22.2	
California	6.8	33.4	
Oregon	7.0	26.4	
West Virginia	7.3	0.0	15.9
Michigan	7.4	16.1	
Maine	7.4	2.9	
New Hampshire	7.7	10.3	
Florida	7.8	12.4	

What have high private medical costs got to do with the uninsured? Some journalists have incorrectly asserted that the possible presence of cost shifting from the uninsured is a major reason why those who are insured are experiencing increases in premiums. This hypothesis is inconsistent with facts and theory: the number of uninsured has increased only very slowly over the last decade. Even if all costs were shifted to consumers, the addition to spending growth is negligible, relative to the other influences. Moreover, there is strong skepticism about whether providers do cost shift, both because cost shifting is limited by the willingness of private insurers to pay yet higher prices, and because costs can only be shifted if providers were initially failing to charge the profit maximizing price, an implausible assumption for doctors, drug companies, and some hospitals.

My overall conclusion, partly dependent on my own preferences about social policy but also tied to the information I have just presented, is that "cost containment" is not really a serious problem for the private sector. It is a problem for Medicare and Medicaid, but those government-run insurances should take care of their own spending problems by using the same managed care devices that private sector buyers have found to be effective. They may also have to face up to the fact that, if taxpayers are not willing to pay for higher costs, they may be forced to deliver fewer and lower quality services to their beneficiaries, just as private sector insurers have done. Again, I hasten to add that this is not my personal preference but it is the inevitable outcome in a world, such as the world of medical care, where you get at most what you pay for.

9

Health Care Reform Projections and the Line Between Fact and Fiction

Tami Mark

In today's political environment the enactment of significant public policies hinge on what "the numbers" (i.e., budget estimates) indicate the impact of those policies will be. One can point to a number of factors to explain this demand for numbers: the professionalization of politics and policy making, the Federal budget deficit, discretionary spending limits, and Americans' resistance to higher taxes to name a few. The preeminence of numbers was no where more evident than in the health reform debate.

When President Clinton addressed Congress on September 22, 1993, and unveiled the Clinton health reform proposal, he made a point of saying that the Administration's estimates had been reviewed by an outside group of actuaries and economists from major accounting firms and Fortune 500 companies. The numbers—the Administration stated—were good and achievable.

However, following President Clinton's health reform speech, the following headlines appeared:

In the Washington *Post*, the headline read, "Clinton challenged on Health Plan's Cost Impact." The first paragraph said that "Martin Feldstein, chairman of President Reagan's Council of Economic Advisors, had asserted that the plan would cost the government $120 billion more in its first year than the Clinton Administration had estimated."

The New York *Times* ran a story with the headline "Health Insurance Data Called Faulty," that stated that the White House estimates of insurance costs were sophisticated guesses based on incomplete and largely outdated information."

Who was right? Were the numbers "fact" as the Administration had claimed? or fantasy as Senator Moynihan (Chairman of the Senate Finance

---

This presentation was made on November 18, 1994, at the University of Michigan Forum on Health Policy. It was edited in June 1997 by the author.

Committee) had maintained? Where do these numbers come from anyway and what are they based on?

A Congressional board asked OTA a similar question in the summer of 1993. OTA, formally known as the Office of Technology Assessment, was a congressional agency that serves as a nonpartisan analytic arm of Congress. It was one of four congressional agencies, the other three being the Congressional Budget Office, the General Accounting Office, and the Congressional Research Service.

In June of 1993, OTA was asked by Senator Stevens to indicate the cost of different approaches to health care reform. Although Clinton had not yet been elected, health care reform was an important issue during the campaign and was likely to be high on the domestic agenda after the election. Since OTA did not typically "cost out" legislation, it decided to approach this task, not by producing new numbers, but rather by reviewing the estimates that had already been done of the costs of different reform approaches. This preliminary study found that when one puts the estimates of health reform costs done by different groups side-by-side, for example, what one group estimates a single payer system would cost versus another group (Table 9.1), one finds that there is a substantial amount of variation in the estimates.

Table 9.1 Estimates of Single Payer Approaches' Effect on National Health Spending (1991) (in billions)

Group	Single Payer Costs 1991 $ (in billions)
Lewin-VHI	+$21.2
GAO	- $3.0
PNHP	- $18.0
CBO	- $69.0 TO + $.90
Meyer, et al.	- $241.0 TO + $20.0

Source: U.S. Congress, Office of Technology Assessment, 1993.

There are a number of possible explanations for this variation. One explanation is that analysts had different interpretations of how various health reform policies would be implemented, and in particular, differed in their interpretations of policies not yet written into legislation.

When this information was presented to OTA's Congressional board, the board asked OTA to go back and to try to narrow the differences between analysts, or at least try to explain in greater detail why those differences existed.

The first task undertaken upon beginning this subsequent study was to speak with organizations involved in costing out health care legislation, including Lewin-VHI, CBO, the Urban Institute, the Administration, and others. These groups were asked to describe the "model" or "models" that they used to estimate health care reform impacts. The first response of these organizations was that most aspects of their estimation process were not written down, or at least not in one, easy-to-access document.

The second point some of them made was that they do not have one model, per se, but a bunch of analytic tools and that they use them depending on the type of legislation being costed out.

What we eventually came to understand was that at the heart of most analyses are not super-computers and complex algorithms, but rather a few simple steps. Let me give you an example of how national health expenditures were estimated under managed competition, at least to the best of our understanding. The estimates typically involved five steps:

1) Analysts first estimate what premiums typically are in traditional indemnity insurance plans or non-HMO plans;
2) They then assume that HMOs save some percentage over traditional indemnity plans;
3) Analysts then estimate how many people would leave their non-HMO plan and join an HMO given the incentives in the bill;
4) They calculate the total savings by multiplying the cost savings per HMO switcher by the number of switchers;
5) Finally, some analysts make assumptions about additional future savings due to plan competition.

Data are used to derive these estimates—for example, information on premium costs and the number of people in HMOs. The estimates also hinge on some key assumptions—how many people will join HMOS and how much will HMOs save?

The OTA report not only tried to describe what the models looked like but also examined how much evidence there was in support of key assumptions.

The good news is that health service researchers have been busy gathering information and doing studies on these key issues and in many instances there is an extensive literature on the key issues or assumptions. For example, there have been scores of studies of HMO savings. Most of these studies indicate that HMOs are less expensive than traditional indemnity insurance plans. If one also considers that employers, searching for cost savings, are moving to managed care plans, and the common sense idea that capitation offers providers a disincentive for utilization, one might conclude, with some degree of confidence, that HMOs can reduce health care costs relative to status quo.

The bad news is that we often do not have a good idea of the magnitude of the impact of specific policy changes, particularly if it is a complex and major policy change. For example, although most studies have found HMOs save money over FFS plans, the savings reported span a wide range (Table 2). Moreover, one might question whether these savings estimates would apply under a vastly changed health care system. What happens if the bill includes an "any willing provider" clause or requires plans to offer an out-of-network option? Will new technologies create efficiencies and reduce health care expenditures or contribute to the growth of health care costs?

Table 9.2 Assumed and Estimated Savings from Health Maintenance Organizations

Author	Savings from "average" HMOs
Lewin-VHI Health Security Act, 1992	3.3%
CBO, Managed Competition Proposal, 1993	4%
CBO, Managed Competition Proposal, 1992	7.5%
Economic and Social Research Institute, Managed Competition Proposal, 1992	10%, 15%
Mathematica, Medicare Risk Program for HMOs	10%
Rand Health Insurance Experiment	25%
Health Care Strategies Associates	27%

The bottom line of the OTA report was that the numbers were not fact, nor were they fantasy, but something in between.

Having said that, it is important to recognize where the "facts" are in the numbers and where the "fantasy" is. No matter how much data we have and how sophisticated we make the models, unless we have some experience to generalize from, costing out any major health reform proposal is likely to involve value judgments.

A good part of the art to the estimates of the Health Security Act was in predicting what the government would do. The Health Security Act financed its expansion of health insurance and other programs through savings, for example, in the form of reduced Medicare and Medicaid expenditures.

If you look at the history of government cost controls, in this country and abroad, in many situations they have worked. Medicare and Medicaid have been operating for a long time, and there is evidence that the controls in these programs have reduced the growth rate of expenditures. Therefore, we can have some confidence in the technical feasibility of reducing the growth of expenditures by using government cost controls. A more difficult question is whether the premium caps in the Clinton proposal would have been politically feasible. If the premiums caps did "not work," the subsidies needed to finance insurance coverage expansions would have been substantially higher than estimated and the revenue estimates lower.

To a large extent, whether or not the government cost controls proposed in the administration's health reform proposal would have worked as intended boils down to a political and subjective question—do you believe a particular government has the will and ability to enforce those cost controls, given pressure from special interests?

If analysts are going to play the role of objective scientists, then these types of distinctions between data, evidence, guesses, and political judgment need to be highlighted.

The final point I would like to make is that while I am suggesting that there were inherent uncertainties in the health care cost estimates, I do not believe that, in general, these types of uncertainties need be a barrier to moving ahead with the expansion of health insurance coverage.

One option is to implement reforms incrementally. Many states, such as Minnesota, that are implementing reforms are taking an incremental approach. The Medicaid experience is also exemplative. As Victor Fuchs recently put it, we should expect modest attempts to increase coverage and contain costs, accompanied by an immodest amount of sound and fury.

A second option is to build flexibility into reform policies. If you look at the cost controls in Medicare, for example, you find that the payment system is constantly being modified. Similarly, if you look at Germany's cost containment structure you see lots of innovation and change as public opinion and provider sentiment evolve and as the health care system changes.

Finally, to be able to have a reactive and flexible system, we need to develop a way to monitor its impact on costs, access, and quality. It is well known among policy makers that the NMES data—the basis for most of the 1992 health reform estimates—were collected in 1987. Moreover, until recently there was very little reliable data on employers' health care expenditures.

To conclude, research and data did inform policy makers about the cost impacts of various approaches to health reform, but there is often a point where the data stops being informative and politics and opinion take over. Finding that line and highlighting it for policy makers is a critical but extremely difficult task for health policy analysts.

References

U.S. Congress, Office of Technology Assessment, An Inconsistent Picture: A Compilation of Analyses of Economic Impacts of Competing Approaches to Health Care Reform by Experts and Stakeholders, OTA-H-540 (Washington, DC: U.S. Government Printing Office, June 1993).

U.S. Congress, Office of Technology Assessment, Understanding Estimates of National Health Expenditures Under Health Reform, OTA-H-594 (Washington, DC: U.S. Government Printing Office, May 1994).

U.S. Congress, Office of Technology Assessment, Understanding Estimates of the Impact of Health Reform on the Federal Budget, BP-H-132 (Washington, DC: U.S. Government Printing Office, July 1994).

10

Paying for Health Care Reform: Alternative Financial Models Compared

John F. Sheils

Health expenditures in the United States grew from about 9 percent of Gross Domestic Product (GDP) in 1980 to about 15 percent of GDP by 1994. Yet, despite this massive infusion of national wealth into our health care sector, the number of persons without health insurance actually grew from 25 million in 1980 to about 39 million by 1994. The relationship between cost and access is simple; as health care costs rise faster than incomes, fewer and fewer individuals and employers can afford insurance. Consequently, most of the major health reform bills introduced in recent years emphasize both expansions in insurance coverage and cost containment.

The health reform debate of 1994 revealed three simple truths. First, universal coverage cannot be achieved without mandates. Second, universal coverage requires a large transfer of income to pay for covering lower income families. Third, the real cost of subsidizing lower income families will grow year after year unless we control the growth in health care costs. Consequently, early reform bills included mandates, significant income transfers, and cost controls.

As 1994 wore on, health reform efforts in Congress stumbled over these three issues. Each new bill offered throughout the year progressively delayed and ultimately eliminated mandates for universal coverage. Controls on the growth in health spending were eventually dropped as were tax penalties designed to create incentives to enroll in managed care plans. Ultimately, health reform stalled all together over an inability to agree on how to finance universal coverage.

In this paper, we describe the financial impact of alternative methods for financing universal coverage. We present estimates of the financial

---

This presentation was made on November 18, 1994, at the University of Michigan Forum on Health Policy. It was edited in May 1997 by the author.

impact of an employer mandate, an individual mandate and a tax financed single payer plan. In addition, we also illustrate the financial impact of an employer mandate with and without delivery system reforms based on the principles of managed competition.

Health Care Financing Options

Universal coverage could be achieved through an employer mandate, an individual mandate or a single payer plan. Under an employer mandate, such as that proposed by President Clinton, all employers are required to cover their workers and dependents while non-workers are required to obtain their own private insurance. In an individual mandate, all individuals who are not otherwise covered under an employer plan must obtain private insurance on their own. Under the single payer model, all individuals are covered under a single government program financed through the tax system. We assume that these financing models would apply only to the non-Medicare population and that Medicaid acute care coverage is abolished for the non-Medicare beneficiaries, leaving the Medicaid population to qualify for subsidies under the same rules that apply to the general population. These options include:

- **Employer Mandate:** Under this option, employers are required to provide coverage for their workers (employed 17.5 hours or more per week) and their dependents with the employer paying 80 percent of the premium. Also non-working individuals who are not otherwise covered under Medicare would be required to purchase coverage on their own, subject to premium subsidies for low-income persons.
- **Individual Mandate:** Under the individual mandate, all individuals who are not otherwise insured by Medicare or an employer would be required to purchase insurance. Employer plans would, however, be required to provide at least the standard benefits package and premium subsidies would be provided to assist low-income families.
- **Single Payer Plan:** Under the tax financed plan, all working and non-working individuals not otherwise covered by Medicare would be covered under a single government program financed by a payroll tax sufficient to cover the cost of coverage for workers and their dependents (9.8 percent). Employers would be required to pay 80 percent of the payroll tax with workers paying the remainder. Some employers may continue premium financed supplemental coverage for services that are not covered under the uniform benefits package (e.g., eyeglasses, adult dental, etc.).

In all three of these scenarios, we assumed that the benefits package would cover hospital care, physicians services, prescription drugs and mental health up to certain limits. We also assumed that the package would have a $200 deductible per person ($400 per family) and a 20 percent copayment requirement up to a maximum out-of-pocket payment of $1,500 per individual ($3,000 per family).

Subsidies would be provided to low-income families under all three of these models. We assumed that families with incomes below the federal poverty line are excused from patient cost sharing requirements. We also assume that premium subsidies are provided to workers and non-workers with incomes below 200 percent of poverty on a sliding scale with income. These subsidies are not required under the tax-financed single payer model because family payroll tax payments are varied automatically with income. In addition, under the employer mandate we assume that subsidies would be provided to employers so that each employer's spending for health care will not exceed 7.9 percent of payroll.

The Health Benefits Simulation Model (HBSM)

We developed these estimates using the Lewin Group Health Benefits Simulation Model (HBSM). HBSM is a "microsimulation" model of health spending. The core of the model is a representative sample of households in the United States. For each household in the sample these data provide information on health insurance coverage, health spending, income, employment and basic demographic characteristics. The model uses these data to show how expenditures for households and employers will change as they become covered under a new health insurance system. These estimates reflect changes in both health benefits costs and administration.

HBSM estimates the impact of health reform for each individual household in the sample. The model simulates these changes in coverage, utilization and reimbursement for each household in the HBSM database under the health reform initiative. Because the model is based upon a representative sample of the population, it produces aggregate estimates of the impact of policy proposals on the total number of persons affected, aggregate health spending, and program costs. Cost estimates are provided for employers, governments and households. However, because the model develops estimates based upon analyses performed on an individual-by-individual basis, the model also provides estimates of the impact of these policies on various socioeconomic groups.

The basic data source used in this analysis is the March 1993 Current Population Survey (CPS) conducted by the Bureau of the Census. These data provide detailed information on individuals by demographic characteristics, income, and employment by firm size and industry. Because the

CPS does not include health spending data, we merged the CPS with the 1987 National Medical Expenditures Survey (NMES) data which includes health care utilization and expenditures information for households with various population, income and employment status groups. Health expenditures data in the model were then controlled to replicate aggregate health expenditures estimates for 1994 by type of service and source of payment provided by the Health Care Financing Administration (HCFA).[1]

The Financial Impact of Alternative Financing Options

Using HBSM, we estimated the financial impact of the employer mandate, the individual mandate and the single payer plan assuming they are first implemented in 1998. Under all three scenarios utilization of health services would increase by about $50.7 billion in 1998 as coverage is extended to the uninsured (Table 10.1). This estimate reflects our assumption that utilization of health services among previously uninsured persons would increase to levels reported by insured persons with similar age, sex, income, and health status characteristics.[2]

Table 10.1 Summary of Changes in Health Spending, by Source of Payment Under Alternative Universal Coverage Options in 1998: National Estimates

	Individual Mandate	Employer Mandate		Single Payer
		Without Managed Competition	With Managed Competition	
Source of Payment				
Household Spending	$25.2	$0.2	($2.8)	($27.5)
Employers	$1.5	$16.6	($6.2)	$22.4
Insuring Firms	$1.5	($17.8)	($37.0)	($7.3)
Non-Insuring Firms	--	$34.4	$30.8	$29.7
Net Fed. Program Cost	$53.4	$59.5	$56.6	$46.4
State and Local Governments*	($25.2)	($29.2)	($29.2)	($28.5)
Net Change in National Health Spending				
Net Change in Spending	$55.0	$47.1	$18.3	$12.8
Utilization	$50.7	$50.7	$50.7	$50.7
Managed Care Savings	--	--	($36.4)	--
Admin. Costs	$4.3	($3.6)	$4.0	($37.9)

*Assumes state maintenance of effort in funding for Medicaid program.
Source: Lewin Group estimates using the Health Benefit Simulation Model (HBSM).

The impact of reform on administrative costs, however, would vary across the three reform models. We estimate that under universal coverage, national health spending would increase by $12.8 billion under the single payer plan, $47.1 billion under the employer mandate and $55.0 billion under the individual mandate.

Administrative costs include the transactions costs involved in transferring the resources required to provide health services. These include the insurer's cost of marketing, claims processing, utilization review and insurer profits. Provider administration includes the cost of confirming coverage, submitting claims, and forming managed care networks. We estimate that administrative costs would be reduced by $37.9 billion under the single payer plan due to consolidating coverage for all Americans under a single program with uniform coverage and reimbursement rules. Administrative costs also would be reduced by about $3.6 billion under the employer mandate due to the use of a standard benefits package, and the elimination of medial underwriting. However, administrative costs would increase by about $4.3 billion under the individual mandate reflecting the fact that individual non-group policies are over twice as costly to administer as employer group plans.

Our analysis indicates that employer health spending would increase under all three health reform plans including the individual mandate. Employer costs would increase by $16.6 billion net of subsidies and cost shift savings (i.e., reduced provider overhead charges for uncompensated care) under the employer mandate. Health spending for firms that do not now offer insurance would be $34.4 billion under the employer mandate. However, spending would decline by about $17.8 billion for insuring firms as working spouses who are now covered as dependents on their spouses' employer plan are required to take coverage on their own job. Under the single payer plan, employer spending would increase by $22.4 billion as all employers are required to contribute the cost of covering their workers through the payroll tax. Employer costs in insuring firms would increase by about $1.5 billion under the individual mandate due to the cost of upgrading existing health plans to the minimum standard benefits package.

All of these programs would require additional federal funding to pay for subsidies and coverage for persons who are not associated with employment. The single payer plan would require $46.4 billion in federal funds over and above what is collected in payroll tax revenues under the plan. Federal spending would increase by $53.4 billion under the individual mandate and $59.5 billion under the employer mandate. State and local governments would save up to $29 billion under all three options as insurance is extended to individuals now receiving care through public hospitals and other indigent care programs.

Targeting of Federal Subsidy Dollars

Our analysis shows that the employer mandate results in higher costs to the federal government ($59.5 billion) than under the individual mandate ($53.4 billion). This is because under the employer mandate, premium subsidies would be provided to employers with low-wage workers even though many lower-wage workers are in dual-earner families with relatively high combined family incomes. Consequently, a large portion of these employer premium subsidies would be used to subsidize coverage for many dual-worker families in upper income groups.

This does not occur under the individual mandate because subsidies are provided directly to families based upon their total family income. For example, in our analysis, we found that 32 percent of all subsidies under the President's plan (i.e., employer and family subsidies) would go to dual-earner families with incomes in excess of 300 percent of the federal poverty line, while nearly all of the subsidies provided under an individual mandate would go families in the lowest income groups. Thus the individual mandate does a better job of "targeting" subsidy dollars to low-income families.

Distributional Impact on Households

The three health reform models examined in this analysis would have a significant impact on household health spending. We define household spending to include family premium payments, direct payments for health services and taxes dedicated to finance health programs. For example, the individual mandate would result in a net reduction in household health spending of $437 per family for those with incomes below $10,000; largely because of the premium subsidies provided under the program (Table 10.2). However, health spending would increase among middle income groups as currently uninsured persons purchase insurance under the individual mandate.

The employer mandate would tend to be less costly to middle income households than the individual mandate because it requires employers to contribute to employee premiums. However, the employer mandate generally would result in a loss of wages to persons affected by the mandate as employers adjust to these new employee compensation costs, which largely offsets savings in out-of-pocket spending. Once these wage effects are included, the net impact of the employer mandate on households would be roughly the same as under the individual mandate.

Table 10.2 Net Change in Household Health Spending for Households Headed by Persons Under Age 65 Under Alternative Health Reform Plans in 1998: National Estimates

Family Income	Individual Mandate	Employer Mandate		Single Payer	
		Before Wage Effects	After Wage Effects	Before Wage Effects	After Wage Effects
Under $10,000	($437)	($730)	($761)	($772)	($940)
$10,000-$14,999	$330	($265)	($408)	($438)	($610)
$15,000-$19,999	$669	($104)	$561	($466)	($689)
$20,000-$29,999	$907	$318	$649	($298)	($539)
$30,000-$39,999	$556	$108	$355	($437)	($682)
$40,000-$49,999	$413	$96	$279	($432)	($649)
$50,000-$74,999	$71	$114	$78	($179)	($120)
$75,000-$100,000	($41)	$110	$78	($179)	($120)
$100,000 and Over	$125	$351	$43	$675	$2,993
Total	$278	$8	$168	($266)	($126)

Source: Lewin Group estimates using the Health Benefits Simulation Model (HBSM)

Our wage effect estimates are based upon empirical evidence indicating that employers are likely to pass on much of the increase in employer costs to employees in the form of reduced wages and lost jobs.[3] Studies indicate that 88 percent of the change in employer costs under reform would result in changes in wages to employees.[4,5] Conversely, in firms that see net savings under reform, most of these savings are assumed to be passed on in wage increases as labor markets force adjustments to overall employee compensation.

The single payer plan would tend to reduce heath spending for middle and lower income groups while increasing health care costs for higher income groups. This is true even after accounting for wage effects resulting from the employer payroll tax. This reflects the impact of shifting from premium based financing to a more progressive tax-based system.

The impact on individual households will vary depending upon their health status and their current level of coverage. For example, under the President's health reform plan, about 48 percent of all families would have seen an increase in family health spending of $20 or more per year. About 50 percent would see a spending decrease of $20 or more per year while only two percent would see a change of less than $20 per year. About 28 percent would see a spending decrease of $1,000 or more while 26 percent would see an increase of $1,000 or more. These wide variations in impacts across families are the inevitable consequence of imposing uniform benefits and standard premium contribution rules in a system with diverse sources of financing and coverage.

Managed Competition

The underlying principle of managed competition is that health care costs can be controlled by encouraging competition among health plans on the basis of price and quality. Under a managed competition model, all individuals in a given region would select from among several health plans providing a uniform standard benefits package. Insurers would be required to accept all applicants and would be prohibited from varying premiums with the health status of the individual. Information on premiums and consumer satisfaction for these plans would be provided to facilitate consumer choice of health plans. Price competition among plans would be encouraged by limiting tax and premium subsidies to the premium amount for the lowest cost plan in the area so that individuals face the full incremental cost of enrolling in higher cost plans. These financial incentives would encourage increased efficiency in health plans through expanded use of managed care.

We estimate that this managed competition model would result in managed care savings of about $36.4 billion in 1998 (see Table 10.1). However, administrative costs would increase by $4.0 billion due to the added cost of utilization review and network formation in these managed care plans. Overall, national health spending would increase by $18.3 billion under an employer mandate with managed competition compared with a net increase of $47.1 billion under an employer mandate without managed competition. The net cost of the employer mandate to employers, governments, and households also would be lower under managed competition. Managed competition also could be implemented under an individual mandate or a single payer system.

In estimating managed care savings, we assumed that managed competition would effectively shift the population into managed care plans with a cost performance comparable to that observed in existing health maintenance organizations (HMOs). Our estimates of managed care savings are based upon Lewin Group studies of managed care savings.[6,7]

Voluntary Coverage Options

At the close of the 1994 legislative season, Congress was considering several health reform bills which would encourage people to take coverage voluntarily rather than mandating coverage. For example, Senator Mitchell introduced a bill that included insurance market reforms, tax deductions for premium payments, and direct premium subsidies for low-income persons as inducements to obtain coverage. Our analysis indicates that insurance market reforms alone will do little to expand coverage. We also found that providing additional tax deductions for insurance purchases would have little impact on coverage because the families benefiting most from these deductions would be in upper income groups where most individuals are already insured. However, we found that direct premium subsidies for low-income persons would induce a significant portion of the nation's 39 million uninsured persons to obtain coverage.

We estimate that under the Mitchell Bill, about 22.3 million of the uninsured would become covered. The percentage of the population without coverage would drop from 14.9 percent to about 5.9 percent. Only about five percent of newly insured persons would be individuals who are excluded from coverage under today's system due to health status.[8] Of those who take coverage, 39 percent (8.6 million) would be persons below poverty who qualify for full premium subsidies. About 25 percent (5.7 million) of those who become insured would be persons between the poverty line and 200 percent of poverty where partial subsidies are provided.

Program enrollment rates would vary with income. For example, under the Mitchell Bill, there would be no premium for persons below poverty with premiums phased in between the poverty line and 200 percent of poverty. Based upon Medicaid program experience, we estimate that among persons below poverty, where no premium contribution is required, about 73 percent of individuals would enroll. A family at 125 percent of the poverty level would receive a 75 percent premium subsidy leaving the family to pay 25 percent of the premium ($1,739), which would equal about 11 percent of income for families at this income level. Based upon an analysis of the private insurance coverage data, we estimate that the percentage of persons electing coverage at this contribution level would drop to about 33 percent. The percentage of persons taking coverage drops to 21 percent for families at 175 percent of poverty where families must pay 75 percent of the premium.

The Importance of Community Rating in Reform Plans

To a large degree, the cost impacts of health reform are driven by the health service utilization characteristics of individuals who would find themselves in the various community rated pools created under these reforms. For example, several health reform proposals would pool families in small firms with families where there is no worker (excluding Medicare recipients). This is important because as compared with workers, the non-working population uses about twice as much hospital care and is about three times as likely to report themselves to be in poor health.[9] Consequently, pooling small employers with non-workers can result in an increase in small employer premiums of up to 30 percent while reducing premiums for non-workers by as much as 50 percent.[10]

For example, under President Clinton's health reform proposal, all persons in a given health plan would pay the same premium for their type of family regardless of their age or health status. This means that younger, healthier populations would cross-subsidize the cost of care for older and sicker groups. In particular, it implies that employers and workers would cross-subsidize non-workers. We estimate that in 1998 the average monthly per capita cost of the uniform benefit package under the bill would be roughly $158 for workers and dependents, while the monthly per capita cost for non-workers would be about $319 (Table 10.3).[11] The resulting community-rated per capita premium would be about $182 per month. This community rate is about half the actual cost for non-workers but about 15 percent more than the actual cost for workers and dependents.[12]

Table 10.3 Average Monthly Premium Cost Per Person Under the Regional Alliance Under the President's Health Reform Plan in 1988[a,b]

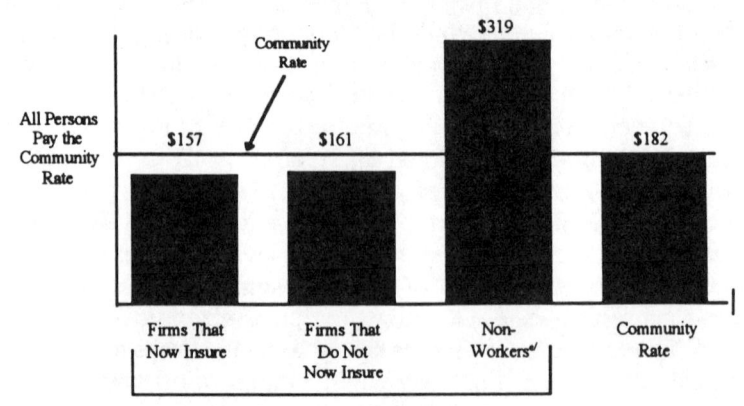

Average Cost Under Regional Alliance

[a]Includes premium surcharge and cost constraints. Excludes the Medicaid cash population which is not included in the community rate.
[b]The actual cost is an overall average that may differ significantly from what individual groups may be paying in premiums.
[c]Non-workers include early retirees, some disabled individuals and many pregnant women and other higher cost groups who would be covered in the community rated pool (i.e., alliance) created under the bill.
Source: Lewin Group estimates using the Health Benefit Simulation Model (HBSM).

This employer cross-subsidy of non-workers substantially reduces the Federal cost of assuring universal coverage. This is because most of the non-worker population is in the lower income groups that would qualify for premium subsidies under the Act. Thus, the Federal government would subsidize premium purchases for non-workers at the community rate of $182 per month rather than their actual cost of $319 per month.[13,14] Several of the bills introduced subsequent to the President's proposal would have had similar impacts due to the way that community rated pools were formed in these bills.

Caveats

Enacting any of these reform plans would involve implementing a program that has never before been attempted on a broad scale in the United States. Consequently, there are few data on the likely outcomes of such programs that can be used to estimate program impacts. In particular, a dramatic restructuring of the health care financing system could substantially alter consumer, employer, and provider incentives which could have a significant impact on program costs.

Although our analyses are based on the best data and research now available, the data available to us are quite limited. Thus, these estimates should be treated as illustrative of potential impacts rather than point estimates of actual outcomes. In fact, our analyses have shown that the ultimate impact of health reform on government health spending, employer health costs, and wages is very sensitive to assumptions on employer and consumer behavioral responses under the new incentives created under reform.

Furthermore, these estimates are based on projections of the growth in health spending over time which are especially sensitive to a number of factors including general economic growth and underlying health care cost trends. Moreover, our cost analysis is sensitive to trends in medical technology and other factors that drive health care. Consequently, policy makers should recognize that any major health reform initiative will require continued refinements in program design and financing over time.

Notes

1. See: Lewin-VHI, "The Health Benefits Simulation Model," (Report to the Office of Research, Health Care Financing Administration, Washington, D.C., April 13, 1990.)
2. See: John F. Sheils et al., "Potential Public Expenditures Under Managed Competition," *Health Affairs*, Supplement, 1993

3. See, for example, Jonathan Gruber and Alan B. Kreuger, "The Incidence of Mandated Employer-Provided Insurance: Lessons from Workers Compensation Insurance." in *Tax Policy and the Economy* (1991); Jonathan Gruber, "The Incidence of Mandated Maternity Benefits," *American Economic Review*, (forthcoming); and Lawrence H. Summers, "Some Simple Economics of Mandated Benefits," *American Economic Review* (May 1989).

4. See, for example, James Heckman, "What Has Been Learned About Labor Supply in the Past Twenty years?" *American Economic Review*, (May 1993).

5. This estimate is consistent with estimates presented in the literature. For example, Gruber and Kreuger, *op. cit.*, find that about 85 percent of the costs of mandated worker's compensation benefits are shifted to employees in the form of reduced wages, while Gruber, *op. cit.*, found that virtually all of the employer's cost of mandated maternity benefits are shifted to the employee.

6. Lewin-ICF, "Effects of Managed Care, Uninsurance and AIDS on Health Care Use," (report to the Health Resources and Services Administration, Washington, D.C., 16 July 1992).

7. David Stapleton, "New Evidence on Savings From Network Models of Managed Care," (report to the Healthcare Leadership Council), Lewin-VHI, May 5, 1994).

8. John Sheils, et al., "Health Insurance Coverage Under Alternative Health Reform Proposals," (Report to the Henry J. Kaiser Family Foundation, Lewin-VHI, Inc. November 4, 1994).

9. Lewin-VHI analysis of: the 1987 National Medical Expenditures Survey Data and the 1989 National Health Interview Survey Data. Data available from author.

10. Lewin-VHI, "Permitting Voluntary Enrollment in Regional Alliances Under the Health Security Act: The Impact on Spending for Employers and the Federal Government," (report to the Henry J Kaiser Foundation, April 21, 1994).

11. Non-workers include early retirees, some disabled individuals and many pregnant women and other higher cost groups who would be covered in the community rated pool (i.e., alliance) created under the bill.

12. Lewin-VHI, Inc., "The Financial Impact of the Health Security Act," December 9, 1993.

13. The higher premium costs under this program are partly offset by federal premium subsidies to employers.

14. There would also be a net increase in household premium payments under this scenario.

11

Financial Access to Health Care

Katherine Swartz

Three years ago, no one would have predicted the changes we've been seeing in the numbers of people insured by managed care organizations — currently about one in five Americans. Similarly, I doubt that anyone would have predicted the rapid increase in numbers of physicians participating with managed care organizations and sharing the risk that actual costs of care may exceed expected costs. Nonetheless, I have been asked to make some predictions so I will address what we can — and what we cannot — predict will happen to the numbers of people with (or without) financial access to medical care. In particular, I will discuss financial access in the context of likely scenarios for health care reform in the next few years: (1) no major changes initiated by the federal or state governments — only market based or market driven changes will occur; (2) state initiatives for insurance market reforms will occur in some states. Finally, I will discuss why it is often difficult for researchers to get the same answers from the same data when estimating individuals' financial access to health care.

Numbers of Uninsured People

Currently we have about 40 million people without any form of health insurance on any given day. But because people are uninsured for different lengths of time, more than 40 million people are uninsured at some time during a year. In 1992, for example, there were 60 million people who lacked insurance for at least a month. These two different numbers — 40 million and 60 million — provide a good example of how easy it is to confuse the public with data. I and two colleagues estimated the distribution of lengths of time that uninsured spells last (Swartz and McBride, 1991; Swartz, Marcotte, and McBride, 1993a, 1993b). That research showed that half of

---

This presentation was made on November 18, 1994, at the University of Michigan Forum on Health Policy.

all uninsured spells end within six months and 18 percent of all spells last more than two years. But in spite of our careful explanations of the difference between using point-in-time data and longitudinal data, various people have incorrectly applied the distribution of the lengths of uninsured spells to the point-in-time data. They applied the 18 percent to the 37 million people who were uninsured at a point-in-time in 1992, and argued that there were fewer than 7 million people who were hard-core uninsured and in need of public assistance. For me, this was a sobering illustration of how easy it is for people to deliberately misuse data.

Consequences If There Are No Reforms

Let me suggest what I think will happen if we do nothing or if state reforms of the insurance market occur. My predictions are based on what we know about the incentives in each of these scenarios.

If there are no major reforms initiated by the federal or state governments, experience rating of individuals and small groups will become more sophisticated.

More firms will choose to self-insure and to the extent they can avoid law suits charging discrimination in hiring, they will seek to avoid hiring people whom they suspect will cost more in terms of health care costs.

More employers will require employees to pay a higher share of the total premium. When health insurance was first offered as a fringe benefit by employers, it was the norm for employees to pay more than half of the premium. But with the tight labor markets of the last half of the 1960s and then the wage and price control period of the Nixon Administration in the early 1970s, employers began to pay close to 100 percent of the premium for employees and often a majority share of the premium for family policies. If anyone had told me three years ago that employers would be able to make employees suddenly pay 25 to 40 percent of the total premium — without increasing wages — I would not have believed it. And yet that is what we are seeing now. It says a lot about people's uncertainty about job security that they are for the most part not arguing. I should add one note to this development, however. Note that if employers are in effect switching to a defined contribution to premiums, it decreases the employer's incentives to avoid hiring older people or people who are likely to be sicker.

These three changes imply three outcomes for the numbers of people without financial access to medical care. First, we will definitely have more people without health insurance. Second, we will see a continuation of the decline in employer provided health insurance for workers. Employer provided health insurance creates incentives for employers to be inefficient in decisions about production processes and in decisions about whom to hire or to lay off. For example, if an employer has to provide health insurance to employees, an employer would rather increase the number of workers working over-time than expand to another shift with all new employees — over-time does not involve more health insurance costs. Similarly, employers would prefer to hire part-time workers or temporary workers rather than full-time, permanent workers if part-time workers or temporary positions do not have to have health insurance provided as part of compensation. Third, we will see an increase in the number of people who choose to forego health insurance coverage through their employers because they cannot afford their share of the total premium.

In short, we will have an increase in the number of people without health insurance. The people who will be uninsured will likely have chronic health conditions, have lower incomes, be younger (because they will view the costs of insurance as greater than their expected medical care costs), and older (because they would be more costly to an employer). We do not, however, know the magnitude of the increase in the number of those people. One reason we cannot estimate the magnitude is that the recent rapid shift of employers requiring employees to pay greater shares of the total premium is something we have not experienced before. We cannot assume we know how people will react to this sudden change. A second reason we have a difficult time estimating the magnitude of the increase in the number of uninsured if there are no major reforms is that if Medicaid funding is reduced, the number of uninsured will increase dramatically. Medicaid has been the safety net of health insurance for perhaps as many as 10 million people who lost employer-provided health insurance during the economic recession of the early 1990s.

Now suppose we assume that some states initiate reforms of the health insurance markets in their states. The principal initiatives will consist of programs to create a limited number of uniform benefits packages for the individual and small group markets so that insurance companies have to compete on price, or subsidized programs of health insurance for special groups of people (e.g., children, early retirees, people with incomes below two times the poverty level), or reductions in state mandated benefits that must be contained in any insurance policy.

These types of state initiatives are all directed at sections of the insurance market that don't appear to work. For example, forcing companies to sell insurance policies or managed care plans that meet any of five or six descriptions, forces the plans to compete on price. Individuals have a much easier time comparing policy types and insurance companies' prices for the different types of policies. In essence, this type of reform tries to ease information problems for consumers.

The state initiated reforms that include plans for subsidies are the most problematic. Most of the proposals for subsidies have subsidies that vanish once a person's income is above 200 to 250 percent of the poverty level.

For a family of four, this is about $30,000. If health insurance for a family costs about $5,000 per year, the premium as a fraction of family income is between a fifth and a sixth — and most people would not say that's affordable. Unless the subsidies are also linked to insurance policies that cost less — which means that the policies provide less extensive benefits or are more catastrophic in nature with high annual deductibles — I do not think these programs will achieve their objective of encouraging more people to buy health insurance. I particularly do not think that people with incomes between 100 and 250 percent of the poverty level can afford —even with subsidies — to pay more than 10 percent of their income for health insurance. Thus, I am convinced that state initiatives to reform the health insurance market and to encourage more people to purchase health insurance will need to consider ways to lower the costs of the health insurance package. We need to think a great deal more about what is in a minimum package of health insurance benefits.

Alternatively, states may choose to bypass reforms of the insurance market and simply expand funding of public health clinics or community health centers. There is a growing sentiment that it may be cheaper for states to simply expand the ability of the public sector to provide health care for people without health insurance than it is to expand eligibility criteria for Medicaid. For example, language and cultural problems, or certain types of illnesses such as tuberculosis, seem to need specialized "response teams". If that's the case, then public resources might be more efficiently spent on community health centers or clinics than on subsidized enrollment in a managed care plan or a fee-for-service insurance plan. Clearly, we need to estimate the relative costs and benefits of alternative mechanisms for providing access to health care for disadvantaged groups within our society.

Why Is It So Difficult to Predict Consequences?

Probably the most important reason for the difficulty in obtaining agreement on predictions of social policies' consequences is our fuzziness with data. What can researchers and policy analysts do? First, researchers need to maintain objectivity. We should not go looking for something and discard all evidence that does not fit with prior hunches. Additionally, we should always be looking for robustness in a finding. That is, if we estimate that a particular characteristic or factor is statistically significant in predicting some behavioral response, we should be sure that finding is not sensitive to the data set used for the estimation or to the functional form used for modeling the behavioral response. If a finding is sensitive to the data or the functional form, we should be quite suspicious of it. Further, some types of numbers fluctuate a lot from year to year — for example, state aggregate expenditures for hospital care. It is particularly important in these situations to examine several years worth of data and to investigate what is underneath the numbers and what might explain the volatility. For example, are there incentives or situations in some years which would explain why hospitals or states might be late in their cost reporting? I have seen a table on premium changes over the last few years that shows a marked slow down in the rate of increase in premiums in the past year. Bailit thinks this is due to increased competition in the health insurance market place. However, the packages of benefits have by and large not remained the same — substance abuse and mental health benefits in particular have been scaled back — and employees are paying more of the total costs of care when they seek care. Both of these changes would be expected to sharply slow the rate of increase in health insurance premiums, even without increased competition in the health insurance market.

Complex survey design is the second reason why it is difficult to predict consequences. During the past decade, the complexity of survey framework designs has increased tremendously. As a consequence, researchers need to be aware that sample weights ought to be used not just for estimating population numbers for tabular analyses but also for multivariate analyses. Because researchers are not always aware of the complex weighting of a survey, the demand for software for estimating multivariate models with weights has been slow in coming. The problem of researchers misunderstanding when weights are needed has led recently to a number of different interpretations of the same data. Researchers need to take the time to understand how a survey was conducted: what the sample framework design was, how the survey questions were worded, what skip patterns were employed (because not everyone is asked every question), what the sequencing of questions was (because it is well known in the polling literature that people's responses to certain types of questions can change simply because another question may have been asked before or after the questions). It is important to realize that complex survey framework designs are needed if we are to obtain large enough numbers of people with a particular characteristic in population-based surveys.

A third factor that researchers have to bear in mind when predicting the consequences of social policies is how we might be able to predict what we do not really know. For example, would people — especially low income people — really buy health insurance if it were available at premiums lower than the current premiums? There is great debate over this point. One way to find out would be to run a demonstration or large experiment (which could even be a natural experiment in terms of gathering information about a market induced lower premium) and gather data. We would then be able to estimate marginal changes in people's behavior in response to lower premiums. However, what might we expect to be people's response if we change everything about how health insurance can be purchased — e.g., with large purchasing cooperatives for people not employed by large firms? The truth is we do not know. Another example of something we don't know much about is how managed care organizations/health maintenance organizations control the growth of new technology that raises health care costs. We assume that financial incentives to slow cost growth work but we need more data on who controls what within managed care organizations before we can predict behavioral responses to changes in reimbursement methods.

Finally, we all need to realize that it is difficult to predict the consequences of changes in policies or changes in the marketplace because there are time delays between when we can gather data and when we would like to predict what might happen. For example, I mentioned at the outset that no one would have predicted three years ago how many people would now be insured by managed care organizations/health maintenance organizations. But of course, right at this moment we would like to know more about who these people are and why they have switched so that we can predict what will happen in the next three years. But to do that requires time just to interview people and then to analyze the survey data. By the time we find out why people have switched during the past three years, another two years will have passed and the people who may switch during the next two years may be different than the people who have already switched to managed care organizations. In this age of televised live war action, we also cannot have instant analyses of social behavior.

Summary

If we are going to convince the public (and politicians) that there is a problem of access to health care, we need to be more careful about explaining results of analyses of data. This also means we need people in the media (journalists as well as their editors) who are willing to spend the effort to explain the results of research analyses. We also need to challenge interest groups and others who misuse data analyses, and avoid the current "balanced reporting" that seems to require a contrary view for every point made.

Similarly, we need researchers who are willing to spend time digging for data and trying to understand institutions. Unfortunately, the incentives for academic researchers are almost all for researchers to publish quickly, which usually means using government collected data sets or small polls that may not be designed for the use to which the researcher puts them.

SECTION TWO

Constraints on Choice: The Deepest Concerns of Interest Groups and the Public at Large

Section Two
Introduction
Constraints on Choice: The Deepest Concerns of Interest Groups and the Public at Large

Richard Lichtenstein

The health care industry is large, extremely complex and of critical importance to the United States. The industry employs over 10 million people, includes some 5,200 hospitals, 15,000 nursing homes and thousands of other facilities and businesses. It accounts for over $1 trillion per year in expenditures and, perhaps most importantly, it provides Americans with the security and peace of mind that result from the lifesaving capabilities of modern medicine. Radically transforming such an enterprise could never be an easy task, and trying to do this with one piece of legislation just might be impossible. Change is always threatening, to some degree, but the possibility the Clinton health plan raised of the wholesale reconstruction of the health care system was sure to raise anxiety levels enormously. Not only would such a prospect cause some Americans to fear the loss of the protection that the system provides against illness and death, but it also would threaten the careers, livelihoods and fortunes of others who work in and invest in that system.

Once President Clinton outlined his plan for health care reform in September 1993, it did not take long for the political process to swing furiously into action. No matter whether one assessed the overall impact of the plan to be positive or negative, there was one thing clear about it—it was going to involve painful sacrifices and there would be plenty of pain to go around. Although the public was generally receptive to the plan when it was first introduced, public enthusiasm for the plan diminished over time. This seemed to be associated with people's growing awareness of the sacrifices the plan would exact from them and it also paralleled the plan's declining chances of passage. Perhaps more important to the political process, and to the eventual demise of the plan, was the work of the interest groups. The interest groups and their lobbyists spent millions of dollars to affect the course that health reform would take. Although a few interest groups, such as Public Citizen and the American Public Health Association, thought the plan did not go far enough, most set out very quickly to either squelch the plan entirely, or to ensure that if pain was to be suffered, it would be suffered by someone else, not by them.

The first part of Section Two summarizes the attitudes of the American public toward the plan, as measured by the ubiquitous public opinion polls conducted throughout the period. The chapters on public opinion polls by Bowman, Frankovic and Immerwahr provide an excellent discussion of both the value and the limitations of such polls. As summarized by Immerwahr, the polls revealed certain enduring values held by the American people: a desire for a personal relationship with health care professionals; a commitment to universal coverage; a preference for "painless solutions"; and an ambivalence toward governmental intervention in the health care system. All by themselves, these four core values illustrate the difficulty inherent in fashioning an acceptable approach to health care reform — since achieving universal coverage was likely to involve some governmental intervention, some form of increased taxes or other costs and, very likely, some diminution of professional time and caring available to each patient. But the polls also revealed something else: they proved meaningless for use in assessing people's attitudes toward the details of the Clinton health plan. The plan was too detailed and too complex, and the public was simply not sufficiently well-informed about these details to guide any political action.

Section Two also provides a sample of the widely varying positions taken by selected interest groups. Not surprisingly, each group criticizes the Clinton plan and articulates its own health reform proposal based upon its own assessment of what would help and what would harm its particular interests. All the groups ostensibly advocate cost containment and universal coverage, but most want these goals to be attained in a way that is least disruptive to their usual way of doing business. Most take the position stated explicitly by Charlie Pryde of the auto industry: "We are not the problem," and they urge that the solutions hold them harmless. What is interesting, and perhaps surprising, is the extent to which groups that, politically and ideologically, are on the same side of most other issues take conflicting positions on health reform. Thus, a business coalition (the South Central Michigan Health Alliance) calls for governmental regulation of the diffusion of medical technology in order to contain costs, while the Health Industry Manufacturer's Association (HIMA) rails against such regulation. The Small Business Association of Michigan urges that universal coverage be attained through individual rather than employer mandates, while the investor-owned hospital industry strongly advocates employer mandates, etc.

Section Two: Introduction

When reading this section, it may be useful to keep in mind the following value-laden questions, the answers to which are reflected in the positions taken by the public and by the interest groups: What is the responsibility of the individual with regard to obtaining health insurance and health care? What is society's responsibility to individuals who, for various reasons, do not have access to health insurance or health care? To what extent should government mandates or regulations, in contrast to free market solutions, be used to achieve the nation's health care goals? And, finally: To what extent should the freedom to operate without external constraints enjoyed by some people or interest groups be restricted in order to achieve equality and fairness within the health system for the entire population?

12

Public Opinion on the Clinton Health Care Plan

Karlyn H. Bowman

Hundreds of polling questions were asked during the course of the 1993-1994 health care debate. The polls were generally informative and responsible, particularly the early ones on the issue. The polling proceeded in four waves. The first wave of polls explored attitudes about the current system. The second wave began after President Clinton announced his health care reform plan in September 1993, and the pollsters probed attitudes toward his approach. This group of polls provided much useful information about the concerns people had about reform.

The third wave of questions attempted to discover how much support existed for reform proposals and approaches different from the President's. No matter how carefully these questions were worded —and many were impressive attempts to convey enormously complex material to the public —the questions were virtually meaningless as a guide to action. Polls suggesting that Americans were opting for an employer mandate over a single-payer system, for example, were attempts to provide certainty where none existed. The pollsters asked these questions in the face of substantial evidence that the public was not well informed about the plans under discussion. These questions did not illuminate public thinking. They were asked because polls that mined familiar ground no longer made headlines. In the highly competitive business that polling has become, pollsters were going beyond areas where opinion was firm and meaningful. The fourth wave of polling attempted to measure the political consequences for the November 1994 elections of a politician's vote for or against health care reform. These kinds of questions are a familiar fixture of polling, but they yield very little.

This presentation was directly adapted from Karlyn Bowman's monograph "The 1993-1994 Debate on Health Care Reform: Did the Polls Mislead the Policy Makers?" (Washington, DC: AEI Press, 1994).

Early Opinion

Early polling on health care reform showed that people had fundamental concerns about the system. In 1982, Louis Harris found that only 19 percent said the health care system worked pretty well and needed only minor changes to make it better. Forty-seven percent opted for the response "there are some good things in our health care system, but fundamental changes are needed to make it better," and 28 percent said that the system had so much wrong with it that it needed to be completely rebuilt. Over the next decade, opinion on this question did not change significantly. In April 1994, the comparable figures were 14, 54, and 31 percent, respectively. Though many questions were asked about whether the system was in crisis, the responses were not consistent, probably indicating that that "crisis" formulation didn't capture the way most people were thinking about their health care system.

Survey data clearly indicated that most Americans were satisfied with the quality of care they and their families received (73 percent in a Roper Starch Worldwide survey in 1993) and with the availability of medical care when they needed it (74 percent). There were, however, clear concerns about cost. In the same Roper Starch Worldwide survey, 56 percent said the costs of the medical care they received were unreasonable; 40 percent said they were reasonable.

The public's generally positive assessment of the care they received contributed to the demise of the Clinton health care bill, as many people perceived that their own care could be jeopardized by the administration's approach.

Predispositions

Knowing how people evaluated their own health care was essential to understanding how the debate over the Clinton bill developed. So, too, was understanding fundamental predispositions people brought to their thinking about health care. Two important convictions shaped public thinking on the issue.

In 1938, 81 percent of those surveyed told Gallup that the government should be responsible for providing health care for people who were unable to pay for it. When that question was repeated over 50 years later, in 1991, a virtually identical 80 percent gave that response. Americans thus believe that the federal government has an important role to play in this area. This important conviction about basic governmental responsibility in the area does not translate into support for universal coverage. In assessing public opinion, the administration confused a strong commitment to the *goal* of universal coverage with support for its approach. Admittedly, some poll questions provided false leads.

Poll after poll showed that strong majorities supported a health care package that guaranteed every American private health insurance that couldn't be taken away—79 percent in a January 1994 Gallup poll. Seventy-two percent indicated that they would still favor universal coverage if their taxes went up (although an amount was not specified). Seventy-three percent indicated in the same poll that President Clinton should not sign a bill that did not guarantee such coverage. These kinds of responses no doubt convinced the administration of the correctness of its position on universal coverage. But Gallup posed a final question: Suppose the effect of guaranteed coverage was to limit the availability of health services. Would you still favor guaranteed coverage? The support for guaranteed coverage seen in the other questions turned to substantial opposition. Sixty-nine percent opposed universal coverage if the availability of care would be limited. The fact that availability of care might be affected became a centerpiece of the arguments of those who opposed the Clinton plan.

The public's commitment to universal coverage was never open-ended. Universal coverage is a goal. But support for it is tempered by other considerations, most notably concerns about limitations on care and costs.

Also important to understanding how the health care debate developed was the public's deep skepticism of the federal government. Although Americans are ambivalent about the role the federal government should play in our society, the weight of polling evidence for the past 15 years has been on the federal government as a problem causer and not a problem solver. Skepticism about a large and expanding governmental role in health care contributed to the Clinton bill's demise. The response of one man from Denver in a focus group conducted by the Public Agenda Foundation illustrates this: "Any time government is in it, it is going to get worse." A plurality of people consistently told the pollsters that the Clinton plan created too much government involvement in the nation's health care system, and many believed that there would be less access to medical care, lower quality care, and more delays under a government-run national health insurance program than under the present system.

The public also felt that the choices they currently had might be limited under the Clinton plan. Given the importance of choice in our democracy, public concerns in this area also became important in raising doubts about the plan. Three times in the 1990s, ABC News and the *Washington Post* asked people whether they would choose an inexpensive health care program that "does not allow you to choose your own doctor" or "an expensive health care program that allows you to choose your own doctor." Between 25 and 32 percent opted for the less expensive program and around six in ten opted for the expensive program where they could make their own choices. People want to be able to make choices on their own, and they react negatively when government appears to be limiting those choices.

The Clinton Plan

When the Clinton plan was announced, many polls showed approval of the plan. At the same time, the polls showed that Americans didn't know much about it. "Support," then, was basically an endorsement of the President's attempt to address health care problems, not a vote of confidence in his specific plan.

As the debate went on, polls showed increased public concerns about what would happen to the cost and the quality of care if the Clinton plan became law. People were even divided about the fairness of the Clinton approach. In November 1993, ABC News and the *Washington Post* found that the more people heard about the Clinton plan, the less they liked it (53 percent), whereas 41 percent said the more they heard, the more they liked it.

The polls told us a great deal about the reservations people had about the Clinton plan; what they couldn't reveal was how people perceived competing plans. Yet that is what the third cluster of polls during the health care debate tried to do.

The Third Wave

The polls designed to assess competing plans and approaches were good-faith efforts. But people didn't know enough about other approaches for opinions to be useful to policy makers. When Americans were asked in March of 1993, for example, whether they had heard the term "managed competition," 60 percent had not. About the same number had never heard of "pay-or-play" or single payer. These numbers did not change during the course of the debate. Pollsters and politicians who suggested that the polls provided unambiguous conclusions about specific programs were seriously misreading the opinion data. Democratic pollster Peter Hart was quoted during the debate as saying that the public "knows things that it hates, it knows a couple of things that it definitely believes—and everything else, color it confusion." Hart was right of course.

The final wave of polling attempted to measure the impact of voting for or against health care reform on election outcomes. This kind of polling is very common but it rarely provides much insight, because the questions are usually asked in isolation with no points of comparison to other things that could affect a vote decision. These include the extent of concern about other issues, perceptions about the nation's economy, and views about a candidates character. These can be important in candidate choice. The voting decision is just not as simple as some of the questions the pollsters used about health care. A more realistic approach comes from a question asked by CBS News and the *New York Times* in November 1993. In it, 9 percent said that the health care issue was going to be the single most important issue to them in their congressional election. Sixty-seven percent said it would be important but that other issues would be important, too. And finally, 20 percent said that a candidate's position on health care reform would not influence their vote.

Conclusion

Many actors in the health care debate misread the public mood in part because they did not understand how to interpret public opinion data. While the public wanted (and still wants) government policy makers to pay attention to their concerns about our health care system, this desire does constitute an endorsement of a greatly expanded federal effort in the area. Although universal coverage was and is a goal the public supports, it is not the only thing people care about in this area. While many were and are dissatisfied with aspects of the health care system (particularly its costs), most people were and are generally satisfied with the care they receive and did not want their own care to be compromised in any way. Many mistook the "support" the Clinton plan received early on, when it was simply an endorsement for the President's interest in a policy area people care deeply about. These are the lessons from the polls in the 1993-1994 health care debate.

13

Health Care: The Limits of Polling

Kathleen A. Frankovic

Pollsters were able to measure some very important aspects of public opinion as they affected and were affected by the 1994 health care debate. They could report on Americans' feelings about their own health coverage, on public worries about the future of the American health care system, and on the overall trust (or lack of it) in what the Clinton administration proposed and what Congress was going to do about it.

But what polling couldn't do was evaluate the minutiae of the health care debate. The ability to track opinion put a premium on finding change in opinion, even when much of the difference between polls could be attributed to different questions or sampling error. The apparent changes that some saw were frequently artifacts of the polling process itself. Worse, even the measurements that were well-conceived were too often over-interpreted. Meaning was attributed when there was none.

In most cases, media polls (and media coverage) follow the election model. There is conflict, there are winners and losers, and the plebiscitary nature of American politics overwhelms the policy issues. James Fallows, in the January 1995 issue of *The Atlantic*, writes: "Health care became a battle in which some would win and others would lose — and Clinton lost." (p. 36)

Examining the continuous ballot box that polling provided for the health care reform debate demonstrates the limits of public opinion polling to give us adequate information about public opinion.

In the health care debate, the "election" —the battle Fallows spoke of — was between President Bill Clinton and the opponents of health care reform — all of them. The media poll instinct, to track changes in opinion and cast the change in terms of the conflict — who's winning and who's losing — highlighted this "battle." Being able to indicate that the Presi-

---

This presentation was made in October 1994, at the University of Michigan Forum on Health Policy.

116   Kathleen A. Frankovic

dent is losing, of course, is far more interesting than reporting that he is winning. In the course of 1993 and 1994, the health care issue became part of the general political environment, generating its own edition of The American Political HOTLINE — a daily compendium of political news and polls from the major national and many state and local news outlets. Polls were an important part of this daily scorecard, often summarized without comment, amplifying the volume of poll reports without necessarily enhancing the signal.

Deciding Who's Winning

During the health care debate, polling organizations were able to rate the importance of health care reform and evaluate the way the President was managing reform. In examining how important health care reform was to the public, the polls suggest the importance of national leaders in elevating an issue in the public's mind. In this case, the President himself was one of the leaders.

The Issue

In mid-1992, when asked to name in their own words the most important problem facing the country, only 2% of the public named health care. Even after the presidential election, only 9% cited it (health care was overwhelmed by concerns about the economy — both real and stimulated by the campaign itself). In September 1993 — at the time of President Clinton's health care address to Congress — 19% named health care, more than named anything else. For the next full year, health care and crime dominated the public's concerns. Only in October, when it was clear that Congress would NOT enact any reform, did health care slip. In recent polling, however, it continues to be one of the top three problems.

Table 13.1 Responses to "Most Important Problem Facing the Country"

Problem Cited	Date Polled						
	7/92	1/93	9/93	12/93	8/94	10/94	1/95
Health Care	2%	9%	19%	13%	21%	5%	10%
Crime	-	3	10	22	28	23	17
Economy	34	28	15	11	4	7	10
Unemployment	20	14	16	11	6	10	9
Deficit	5	11	9	5	3	2	10

Concern about health care persists and is real, but public opinion on policy specifics remains unclear. When asked specifically about health care reform, Americans consistently believed that something was wrong with the system. For many, fixing the system was a critical problem for the country. Between mid-1991 and early 1994, fewer than one in 10 Americans believed the health care system worked well and needed only minor changes. Nine out of ten wanted fundamental change or a complete overhaul. And even after a year's campaign AGAINST the President's health care reform package, only 19% felt the health care system needed only minor changes. Seventy-nine percent believed that the system needed fundamental changes or to be completely rebuilt. Throughout the entire period of debate, three-quarters of Americans believed the health care system was in crisis.

One key to the problem with this polling: The public's view of the system overall was at odds with their own private assessment of health care for their family. About three-quarters consistently reported they were satisfied with the quality of their family's health care. It was the COST of their family's health care that many Americans were dissatisfied about. And there was underlying concern about the portability of their health care coverage. In September 1993, 40% of the public reported that they or someone else in their household had decided to remain in a job they wanted to leave MAINLY because they didn't want to lose health coverage. While this is likely an overreporting of health care as the SINGLE reason for remaining in a job, it still suggests how potent concern about health care was to many Americans.

The President

Throughout the one year of Congressional debate over health care, support for the way the President was handling health care reform rose above 50% only once — and that happened ONLY after the September health care address. For most of the year, only two in five Americans approved of the way Clinton was handling health care reform, while half or more disapproved. Opinions about his management of health care reform tracked very well with attitudes about the overall performance of Clinton himself as President.

The underlying POLICY attitude Americans expressed in polls about health care reform was simple — did they TRUST Bill Clinton to do the right thing about health care. This attitude seemed inextricably linked to opinions of the President, with very little change during the year. As the President's overall approval rating hovered around 40%, so did trust in his ability to handle health care reform.

Only two-fifths of the public had some faith in Clinton's ability to handle health care reform, but even fewer had faith in Congress, and expectations for action shrunk as time went on. Only at the end of 1993, in the two months following the program's announcement, did even a third of the public believe Congress would produce health care reform in the following year. By mid-1994, that figure dropped even lower, with only 18% believing some reform would pass.

As expectations for passage dropped, so did faith in Clinton's proposal. Those believing it would be fair to them dropped from 51% to 38% in six months; those who believed it would improve health care in the United States dropped from 53% to 35% in the same period. In the debate, the cost issue was used effectively against Clinton. The equation that bigger government meant higher costs and lower quality was reflected in rising fear and distrust about the President's plan.

Limitations of Polls

The difference in pollsters' questions between the overall assessments of government and the need for reform, and the specifics of health care reform plans illustrates the limitations of polling on this issue (as well as underscoring the failures of the "election" poll model on policy questions). Polls about health care reform (CBS News polls included) presented respondents with a bewildering array of health care choices — at a time when many Americans barely understood what "HMO" and "PPO" meant.

Specific questions — whether about the Clinton plan or other plans — weren't really measuring public *opinion*, not at a time when only about a quarter of the adult population ever felt that they had a good understanding of what was in the Clinton health care plan. Pollsters were measuring American reaction to the words and constructs the *pollsters* presented to them.

Despite the limited public knowledge, pollsters still asked questions that attempted to learn what Americans thought should be part of a basic health care package — only to discover that what Americans thought should be part of a *basic* package (including psychiatric treatment and long-term care) went far beyond what most of them had. Other polls tried to explain the differences among single-payer plans, the Clinton plan and the Cooper-Breaux plan (usually requiring paragraphs to do so) and then asked respondents to choose among them.

The instinct to use the election model of polling on questions about specifics never really paid off. Opinion rarely changed as opinion was never real.

Conclusion

The pollsters' dilemma, as well as the plebiscitary nature of the discussion, may have served only to exacerbate the already-existing skepticism about government reform. By the end of the Congressional debate, although Democrats still held an edge on the health care issue, Americans were prepared to blame everyone concerned — Republicans, Democrats, and the President — for the failure of health care reform.

In the long run, that doesn't mean health care reform is dead. Even after the Republican election victory, 62% of the public said they thought the new Congress should try to pass health care reform legislation. So after all of this polling, what is clear is that Americans still want change in the nation's health care system. What is not clear is what exactly that change should be.

14

First Impressions and Second Thoughts: Public Perceptions of Health Care Reform

John Immerwahr

There are many complex policy issues where the public is content to let leaders hammer out a solution outside the spotlight of public attention. Health care policy is not one of them. Many Americans are deeply concerned about health care and they have strong feelings about it. While people may not know very much about the details of health care reform proposals, they do have strongly held values which they bring to bear on health policy debates. For better or for worse, these values provide the road map for those who are in the health care policy arena. Proponents of any given proposal know that they must appeal to those values which are constant with their proposal, and attempt to persuade the public in the areas where the public's principles are violated. Opponents of any given policy will invariably exploit the areas of conflict in order to whip up public opposition. The situation is even more complex because public opinion is a moving target, and the parameters set by public opinion tend to change as the debate matures and develops.

The essential public opinion questions, then, are these:

- What are the public's current values concerning health care?
- Which of those values are most likely to change as the debate matures?

Traditional public opinion polls can answer the first question, but are ineffective at giving us guidance toward answering the second.

In order to forecast how public attitudes may change, Public Agenda, a New York based non-profit research and education organization, con-

---

This presentation was made in October 1994, at the University of Michigan Forum on Health Policy.

ducted a study of public opinions using an innovative methodology.[1] Public Agenda interviewed 564 respondents in 13 cities around the country. Respondents were recruited according to demographically balanced quotas reflecting current census data. On arrival at a focus group facility in their area, the respondents were given a "pretest," which, in effect, was a traditional public opinion survey. (Indeed the results of the pretest matched results of random sample surveys taken at about the same time). The respondents then participated in a two-hour intervention, which included a video and slide presentation and also group discussions moderated by trained focus group leaders. The intervention exposed the respondents to a series of health policy reform options and allowed them to discuss pros and cons of each option. The materials were carefully reviewed by independent experts for balance and fairness. Following the presentation, respondents completed a second questionnaire. Our hypothesis is that the post-test results give some indication of how public thinking changes as people spend more time discussing and thinking about the options. The study was conducted in Fall 1993, and our own interpretation is that projections were in some ways validated by the shape of the health care debate as it developed through 1994.

The Public's Starting Place

There are several main themes that have dominated the public's thinking about health care for a number of years. The results given here, unless otherwise indicated, are from the Public Agenda pretest, but other surveys have documented similar findings.

1. A desire for a personal relationship with health care professionals.

Americans place tremendous emphasis on a personal relationship with health care professionals who listen to them and take them seriously. Presented with a list of nine health care goals, the respondents in the pretest gave the highest priority to "medical professionals who take their time with patients." Eighty-nine percent gave this a six or seven on a seven point scale and 81 percent gave the highest priority to having "medical professionals who are concerned with patient well-being, not the cost of care." These two items received the highest ratings of any items in the inventory.

2. A desire for universal coverage.

Americans are upset by the fact that many people currently do not have adequate health care coverage. They are even more disturbed by the fear that one day they themselves may lose their health care coverage. The years of downsizing, restructuring and the shift to temporary and part-time work for many Americans have made a deep impression on people and have raised their anxiety about health care coverage. Seventy-percent of our respondents gave "medical care that is good and available to all regardless of income" a top priority. Public Agenda also asked people to compare how important each factor was to how well the country is doing in providing that element of health care. Personal care and universal coverage top the list of both importance and dissatisfaction. Comparing these two results gives us a dissatisfaction index that highlights those areas which are both most important and where the country is perceived to be doing the worst job.

3. *A belief in painless solutions.*

As in any other area, health care policy offers both painless and painful solutions. By "painless" solutions, we mean those that appear to impose no unwanted changes or sacrifices on health care consumers themselves. Cutting excess profits is typical of what we mean by a painless solution. As most people initially think about it, the suffering will be born by the rich and greedy, while the benefits are perceived as accruing to average Americans. Painful solutions, by contrast, are seen as imposing direct sacrifices on average Americans. Examples of painful solutions include options such as rationing, higher taxes, diminished choice of provider, and less personal attention from physicians.

Through the 1980s and early 1990s, a number of research findings suggest that large majorities of the public were convinced that health care reform problems could be solve by painless solutions such as cutting waste and fraud, or capping malpractice payments. In 1991, for example, the Public Agenda found that 83 percent of the public thought that universal coverage could be funded entirely by cutting excess profits, malpractice and waste. The public was convinced, in other words, that it could achieve an important goal (universal coverage) without having to do anything that would impact on the health care of individual consumers.

4. *An ambivalence about government.*

Hundreds of surveys (as well as recent elections results) have also confirmed a deep ambivalence about government-based solutions. On the one hand, people see government as the ultimate provider for essential services that people cannot provide for themselves. In survey after survey, large majorities say that government should take a role in providing health care, helping with higher education bills, and dealing with poverty. At the same time, Americans have little trust and confidence in their own government, especially when it comes to saving money. The most direct evidence for this is the current interest (played out in the 1994 elections) in term limits, spending and tax cuts.

Constancy and Change

The principles we have noted above have been documented in hundreds of surveys. What the existing surveys do not tell us, however, is how these principles are liable to change as the debate develops. The Public Agenda post-test was designed to predict whether these attitudes would change or remain constant as people took the time to debate and discuss the issues. The results of the study are particularly interesting in light of the subsequent health policy debate which occurred in the months after the study was completed.

In some areas we saw little change between the pretest and the posttest. Even after a two-hour discussion, people's views did not seem to budge at all. On other areas we saw much more mobility, suggesting that people may be more flexible on these issues.

1. Constancy:

We saw virtually no change in the public's commitment to personal care, or in the public's commitment to universal coverage. This is not to say that people support these values under all conditions. Indeed, the public clearly is not willing to obtain universal coverage at any price. But what is clear is that people do not back off of either of these elements as goals, even after they spend time thinking about it and discussing it.

In effect, what people are saying is that they want a health care system that covers everyone without destroying their personal relationships with their health care providers. They want the safety net of universal coverage without having to adopt some kind of "cattle car" medicine. They also appear to be telling us that they are unwilling, without a great deal of persuasion, to be flexible on either of these values.

2. Change:

We saw much more evidence of potential change on the other two main areas. There is, for example, a clear change in the public's belief that the problems can be solved by painless solutions. In one of the most interesting questions in the survey, we gave people a choice between two methods for adequately controlling health care costs. One approach stressed controlling costs by cutting waste from the health care system (a characteristically painless approach), the other proposed controlling costs by relying on managed care, reduced choice and rationing. The posttest showed a small but noticeable shift away from the belief that we can have it all.

The same result was preserved when we looked at the public's response to specific policy suggestions. Painless solutions tended to lose support between the pretest and the posttest. For example, in the pretest one of the most popular approaches to controlling costs was to regulate insurance premiums. While this approach remained popular in the posttest, the intensity of its support dropped significantly.

By contrast, several of the painful approaches picked up support between pretest and posttest. Despite the high level of public discomfort with rationing, there was a noticeable increase in support for rationing expensive procedures with a low chance of success — from 43 percent in the pretest to 53 percent in the posttest — and for rationing expensive life-extending procedures (as opposed to care to ease pain and suffering) for people over 85. Support for this kind of rationing rose from 38 percent to 44 percent. Indeed, some rationing proposals (such as limiting coverage for heroic measures) edged into majority support in the posttest.

Attitudes toward government involvement in health care also changed as the respondents spent more time thinking about and discussing the issues. As the discussions developed, we heard more and more anti-government attitudes. In thinking more about health care, the balance between desire for government assistance and suspicion of government tends to tip against government. Consistent with what other surveys have found, the Public Agenda pretest noted modest support both for national health insurance and for local agencies to offer plans and negotiate lower insurance rates.

As the discussion evolved, however, people became increasingly skeptical of the ability of government to play a positive role. The focus group discussions were particularly revealing here. The main stumbling block for many people was the idea that government could actually play a useful role in saving money. People frequently raised the issue of defense spending as their point of comparison:

> You've seen the good job the government has done in paying $60 per hammer and all of the stories you've heard about that kind of stuff. I am sure they'd do a wonderful job negotiating with the doctors and hospitals. *St. Louis man*
>
> The same ones who buy $2,500 toilet seats are going to be the ones who are going to negotiate healthcare prices down? I doubt it. *Chicago man*

Support for both universal coverage and local agencies dropped over the course of the discussion.

These findings suggest, then, that some elements of the public's position are subject to change. As people spend time with health care issues, people do tend to become more realistic. People begin to see, for example, that health care is expensive and that costs are likely to go up, and they come to realize that it may not be possible to achieve health care goals at no real cost. But the discussion also tends to move people even further away from the notion that government can play a useful role.

Note

1. John Immerwahr and Jean Johnson, *Second Opinions: Americans' Changing Views on Healthcare Reform* (New York: Public Agenda Foundation, 1994). Available from Public Agenda Foundation, 6 E. 39th St., New York, NY 10016, (212) 686-6610.

15
American Medical Association and Michigan State Medical Society

Louis Zako, M.D.

Prior to President Clinton's proposed health system reforms, the American Medical Association (AMA) and the Michigan State Medical Society (MSMS) advocated several reforms to improve access to health care coverage, assure continued excellence in our health care system and address the underlying issues affecting health care costs. Every citizen should have access to coverage for a defined level of benefits, through programs that empower patients to make choices about coverage and providers.

MSMS joined the AMA in applauding several of President Clinton's proposals: insurance reforms to ban exclusions based on preexisting conditions and to implement community rating; the basic level of benefits; measures to reduce administrative complexity and cost; reforms to ERISA, which governs self-funded benefit plans; and the emphasis on preventive services. We supported the President's efforts toward antitrust relief for physicians, but did not believe his proposal went far enough to assure a level playing field for physicians.

We disagreed with proposals that would develop and enforce a national budget by a national health board, restrict the availability of fee-for-service programs, or create quotas and other measures that would have federalized our medical education system. We felt attention to medical liability reform was inadequate.

Changes in the market today are being fueled less by government initiatives than by purchaser demands for accountability relating to costs, quality and access. Competition among insurers is based less on price than on other measures, as insurers are called upon to demonstrate success in outcomes, access, and patient satisfaction.

This presentation was made on March 26, 1994, at the University of Michigan Forum on Health Policy.

In Michigan, and throughout the country, physician-directed networks are demonstrating their value in meeting quality and service goals, and are becoming increasingly sophisticated in their ability to assume risk for providing services to a defined population.

To empower *consumers* to make more informed choices about health care, MSMS would like to secure passage of a Michigan Patient Bill of Rights, which among other things, would require disclosure of benefit and coverage information and restrictions to patients, and would prohibit excluding coverage to individuals with preexisting health conditions.

We advocate continued refinement and elimination of regulatory barriers that inhibit development of physician sponsored networks.

Streamlining administration of health care is another goal. We advocate implementation of a single set of standards for claims reporting and physician credentialing.

16

American Public Health Association

Eugene Feingold

The health care reform debate of the past few years was concerned almost entirely with making insurance for the care of illness more widely available at an affordable cost. Although that's very important, it's not enough to protect and improve the health of the American people.

And that should be our goal — protecting and improving the public's health, and reducing disparities in the health of different population groups. The public health system focuses on that goal by preventive services and interventions which protect entire populations from disease and injury. The major health problems we face today — tobacco-induced illnesses, drug abuse, HIV, poor nutrition, sedentary life styles, and violent injuries — call for public health interventions, rather than simply reforming the way we pay for medical care.

Unfortunately, a very small and decreasing proportion of national health expenditures — less than 1% — is devoted to public health services. We need to change our spending priorities to enhance and strengthen the public health system, so that public health workers can carry out their mission, as the community's agent for prevention and education, to protect and promote the public's health.

We also need to superintend the rapid changes that are taking place in the medical care system, to make sure that they operate in the public interest. The medical care system is being increasingly integrated vertically and horizontally. Health care financing is being rapidly restructured by employers and insurers in their own interests, while broader public interests are ignored.

We need a way of overseeing these changes, reviewing their effects, and modifying them in the light of their results. Public health agencies, which have a legal and constitutional responsibility for the public's health,

---

This presentation was made on March 26, 1994, at the University of Michigan Forum on Health Policy.

are the logical entities to enforce the public interest in this arena. This is a role which public health agencies have played to only a limited extent in the past, and do not now have the capability to carry out. But if not the public health agencies, who will do it?

We also have to broaden our outlook and understand that health problems stem not only from diseases of the body, but also — even especially — from diseases of society. The basic determinants of health are living conditions, education, nutrition, and protection from environmental hazards. These in turn are heavily dependent on jobs and income. Yet, among full-time workers today, almost 20% earn less than the poverty level, and that proportion has dramatically increased in the last 20 years. Most striking has been the suggestion of an international study that mortality rates for different income groups seem to be not so much a matter of absolute income levels as of relative inequality of income within each country. And the gap between rich and poor is at record levels in the United States.

Both state and national governments have failed to adequately address these broader economic and social problems. Congressional efforts to transfer programs to the states and balance the budget while protecting national defense and social security are likely to make the situation worse. The states, under pressure to be competitive by keeping taxes down, and under pressure to take care of social needs no longer funded by Washington, are also unlikely to spend what's needed to maintain essential services.

Until we do something to improve this situation, poor health will continue.

17

Health Care Reform: What Do We Do Now?

Carol Franck

Is health care reform dead? Certainly not. But we will probably see a more incremental or evolutionary approach to health care reform rather than the revolutionary approach that many of us envisioned. Congress and the American public were afraid to rearrange one sixth of the American economy with a single bill. Much of the way we deliver health care would have been affected by this type of massive legislative approach.

American nurses fought hard for the concept of universal coverage because we believe that it is the key component necessary for achieving comprehensive reform in an incredibly flawed system. The reason we were unable to achieve universal coverage was primarily the lack of consensus about how and who would finance this benefit.

President Clinton and the health care reform task force deserve much credit for proposing an extremely worthwhile initiative and for putting it at the top of the nation's agenda. Their inexperience and lack of sophistication in working with the United States Congress, however, became a significant liability when dealing with such a complex proposal.

The partisan politics and fear-mongering special interest groups cannot go unrecognized. The campaign mounted by the insurance industry, for example, was an abomination, embarrassing to us all. To a lesser extent, but equally worth noting, were some of the provider groups who lent their high status to misinform and misdirect the public. They must bear some responsibility for the bill's failure.

We must continue to work on the issues this bill addressed, but in a less complex fashion and from the standpoint of the consumer. By the year 2000, 20 percent of the American economy will go into health care, and each American will pay $7,200 out of pocket for coverage. Medicare and Medicaid will consume 40 percent of all tax revenues.

This presentation was made on March 26, 1994, at the University of Michigan Forum on Health Policy.

The uninsured population will increase to more than 55 million and will not be limited to the young, the poor and those who do not care. In addition, the percentage of Americans over age 65 has tripled to 12 percent of the population since 1990.

Many of the major reform issues will be reintroduced in Congress in the next year on an issue basis rather than as part of a global reform. Such issues from the nursing arena include Medicare and Medicaid reimbursement, graduate nurse education, the removal of barriers and discriminatory practices against nurses, and work force and quality protections.

Much of the action on health care reform is likely to shift largely to individual states. Some states are clearly way ahead of the rest. The State of Hawaii, for example, has had near universal coverage for more than 20 years. Minnesota passed legislation about three years ago addressing issues of health care at the state level. Other big players will be managed care corporations, and insurance companies that are hospitals, health systems, pharmaceutical companies, provider groups, and other suppliers of health care services. As we see the development of these very complex health care delivery systems, we are going to see reform legislation that will deal with health care systems in new ways.

Nurses have concerns about incremental health care reform. There is a potential that incremental reforms could hurt the nursing profession and seriously diminish the quality of patient care. The American Nurses Association (ANA) is concerned that in the absence of comprehensive health care reform, current restructuring practices, such as replacement and layoffs of nurses, cross-training and poor staff, will continue unchecked, leaving patients and the nurses who care for them inadequately protected. Additionally, alternative delivery systems proposed in the Health Security Act that would provide new job opportunities for nurses may not be there. Other aspects of incremental reform, such as greater Medicare cuts or an emphasis on deficit reduction, done without the benefit of comprehensive system reform, could aggravate the current restructuring situation.

At the federal level, Nursing's Agenda for Health Care Reform will remain our guiding document. It's likely ANA will begin to shift some of its efforts to support increased activity at the state level. How we achieve the principles of Nursing's Agenda for Health Care Reform may differ dramatically from state to state, however, because of differences in how the organizational elements are put into place in each state.

ANA has also begun a broad multi-year campaign addressing quality of patient care that will include components such as policy analysis, job protection measures for nurses, public relations campaigns, lobbying, and re-training of the nursing work force. The final things we will address are the serious threat to quality of care and patient safety, as well as job security for registered nurses.

18
Health Industry Manufacturers Association Position on Health Care Reform

G. Gregory Raab, Ph.D.

Background

Health care reform is essential to secure proper medical care for tens of millions of Americans and to provide incentives to control costs. Health care reform must also preserve the ability of the U.S. medical technology industry to innovate, so that patients have access to high-quality care.

To assure patient access to state-of-the-art medical technology, the Health Industries Manufacturing Association (HIMA) supports government health care policies that provide an environment which encourages innovation. HIMA opposes price controls on medical devices and global budgets, since either action would choke off innovation. HIMA supports the concept of technology assessment, but opposes establishing a centralized bureaucracy to conduct such assessments.

Health Care Reform

HIMA supports reform of the health care system that would (1) expand access to state-of-the-art health care for all Americans; (2) control costs through market-based incentives, so that we spend scarce health resources wisely, secure value, and eliminate excessive utilization; and (3) preserve the quality we now enjoy without dampening innovation.

HIMA believes that any health care reform legislation must:

- specify that decisions about the use of medical technology are made locally;
- extend effective malpractice reform to medical technology manufacturers; and

---

This presentation was made on March 26, 1994, at the University of Michigan Forum on Health Policy.

- achieve cost-containment through market-based incentives, not price controls or global budgets.

Technology Introduction. Local health plans (not a national board) should be empowered to review, adopt, and use medical devices once they have been cleared by the FDA. Health plans should be given the discretion to pay for any investigational technology, as well as the routine costs associated with making these technologies available to patients.

- In the House, support inclusion of the Richardson amendment (currently contained in the Energy and Commerce Committee mark) in any bill that receives serious legislative consideration.
- In the Senate, support inclusion of the approach to technology introduction currently contained in the Chafee bill (S. 1770) or the Breaux bill (S. 1579) in any measure that receives serious legislative consideration.

Medical Malpractice. Any health care reform legislation that takes up the question of malpractice reform must extend a cap on non-economic damages not only to health care professionals and health care institutions but also device manufacturers.

- The Administration's bill covers only health care professionals and health care institutions; the Cooper bill in the House (H.R. 3222) and the Chafee bill in the Senate (S. 1770) cover all three elements — professionals, institutions, and manufacturers — and include a unified cap that limits non-economic damages.
- HIMA supports a unified cap of $250,000 for non-economic damages, as well as other reforms that make the medical liability system more rational, including, among others, alternative dispute resolution mechanisms, limits on attorney fees, and periodic payment of damages.

Cost-Containment. Health care reform legislation should achieve cost-containment through market-based incentives, not price controls or global budgets.

- It is imperative that health care reform legislation provide proper levels of funding to assure patients access to a fair and reasonable benefits package.
- Adequate funding for this benefits package can be achieved by reforming the existing policies and incentives in today's system that lead to excessive use of health care resources.

19
Health Care and the U.S. Auto Industry

Charles T. Pryde

Industry Health Costs

Controlling health costs is of the highest priority to America's auto companies. In 1995, Chrysler, Ford, and General Motors spent $6 billion on health care —more than they spent on steel. They provided health benefits to over 2.7 million people —one out of every 94 Americans. Due to the highly competitive nature of the global automobile marketplace, and the significantly lower health costs in other auto-producing countries, controlling health costs is critical to competitive success.

Long-Term Objectives

The nation must develop a health system that provides coverage to every American, with an equitable means of financing, and effective cost control. While the effort to achieve these objectives through federal legislation was unsuccessful in 1994, it must eventually be achieved.

Current Legislative Environment

Multi-state employers who provide health benefits to their employees, retirees, and families currently face a threatening legislative environment. At present, there is no public consensus for comprehensive national health reform. Absent such legislation, states are becoming more aggressive in their reform efforts. As they consider broader reforms, they will increasingly seek to regulate and tax employer health plans. In addition, if savings from Medicare and Medicaid are attempted by significantly reducing reimbursement rates to providers, greater cost-shifting to the private sec-

---

This presentation was made on March 26, 1994, at the University of Michigan Forum on Health Policy. It was subsequently edited by the author.

tor will result. And enactment of anti-managed care legislation is an ever-present threat. These trends will mean higher health costs for employers, and less autonomy over health benefit design.

The auto companies oppose enactment of legislation at both the state and federal levels that would significantly increase health benefit costs or reduce autonomy. Our argument is based on this proposition: "We are not the problem. We provide good benefits to our people at costs already inflated by cost-shifting from a number of sources. Therefore, do not impose additional costs upon us, and do not hinder our ability to control our existing costs." This general proposition is translated into the following issue-specific positions.

Priority Issues

ERISA Preemption: Uniform national rules governing employer benefit plans are provided under ERISA and must be preserved. If waivers are granted to individual states, multi-state employers will be subject to a multiplicity of state rules regarding mandated benefits, plan administration, reporting requirements, etc. The result would be increased complexity, increased costs, and loss of the ability to offer uniform health plan choices to all employees of a firm.

Health Benefit Taxes: The manufacturing sector already pays a hidden tax in the form of cost-shifting. This "tax" has been estimated at 28 percent of health costs. If new revenue is needed by federal or state governments to finance health system changes, it should be obtained by broad-based taxes, rather than by tax increases on those employers currently shouldering the burden of costly benefits. Increasing the tax burden on benefits will cause some employers to drop coverage, further exacerbating the downward trend in employment-based health coverage.

Managed Care: Use of managed care is one of the most important means of controlling costs and assuring quality. Anti-managed care provisions, such as "any willing provider" laws, are highly detrimental. Employers and managed care entities must retain the ability to selectively contract with health providers of their choice. This freedom to contract is essential in any aspect of business in order to secure quality services at cost discounts based on volume.

Medicare and Medicaid Spending Cuts: The growth rates of these health entitlement programs must be reduced, but the means of doing so are critically important. Savings achieved through program changes such as greater use of managed care and increased detection of fraud are desirable. Drastic cuts in reimbursement rates to providers, however, will result in greater cost-shifting to private payers. While this lowers costs to government, it raises costs for those in the private sector who purchase health services, and does nothing to moderate overall health spending. Reimbursement rates under Medicare set by the federal government, and rates under Medicaid set by the states must fairly compensate providers.

Insurance Reforms: Whether enacted by the federal government or the states, reforms that allow individuals and small groups to purchase coverage at reasonable rates, regardless of pre-existing medical conditions and job changes, are desirable. These incremental reforms, however, will not significantly reduce the number of uninsured, and will not substitute for more profound system reform. Similarly, medical spending accounts, which may be beneficial if individuals who use them are more cost-conscious regarding discretionary health spending, will not have a significant impact on overall health spending levels.

20

Small Business Association of Michigan Position on Health Care

Gary Baker

The Picture in Michigan

Cost, access and quality define the interest of the small business community and these concerns must drive the debate about health care reform. Small business continues to be the largest creator of new jobs in America today. If small business is going to continue to replace the jobs being lost to large manufacturers, small business must be free from the damaging impact of mandated health care costs.

Our nation has the best health care system in the world, and Michigan is among the leaders in providing that care.

Admittedly, some people are without insurance in Michigan: about 10 percent of our residents voluntarily elect to go without insurance or are without insurance due to economic hardship. Nationwide, a greater percentage of the population—some 37 million people or about 15 percent—are uninsured, but most are only temporarily without coverage as a result of moving from job to job or are dependents leaving their parents' coverage after high school or college but prior to employment.

Michigan employers know all too well that the cost of health care is rapidly rising. Some of the cause has been the result of generous benefit packages negotiated by labor unions, which raised the expectations of employees in all businesses.

The Small Business Association of Michigan (SBAM) believes we do not need to redesign the entire health care system to cover those without insurance and to control costs. Simply providing insurance to those without it would, in part, control costs because these individuals are now receiving health care at the most expensive point in the entire health care

---

This paper was presented at the University of Michigan Forum on Health Policy on March 26, 1994.

delivery system—the emergency room, which cannot deny medical services.

Those who have insurance coverage end up paying that bill, just as the insured pay a portion of the cost of Medicaid and Medicare. Why? Because government reimbursements to doctors and hospitals rarely cover the actual cost of the medical services covered by government programs. This accounts for roughly 30 percent of the cost of insurance premiums.

Small business agrees with the President's basic goal, which is to offer basic health care coverage to all Americans. What we disagree with is the proposed mandate being placed on employers to pay for it. Any mandate for coverage should be placed on the individual. Making individuals responsible for their own health care cost will make them consumers of health care and force them to make economic choices.

What Should Be Done

Michigan should be moving in a direction that will create a Michigan health reform plan. The plan should fix the problems with health care without throwing out the many things that are good about our current health care system. We believe that the states will have a great deal of discretion to implement a health care plan following a skeleton of federal guidelines.

We believe that small businesses should be allowed to pool their resources to form their own health alliances rather than simply writing checks to a quasi-governmental pool over which they have no control. Multiple, competing health alliances would encourage market-based cost containment and innovation.

A Michigan plan should contain the following provisions:
  a) Guarantees access to health care coverage by requiring every individual enroll in either an employer sponsored plan or an individual coverage pool unless covered through Medicare or Medicaid. The pools would provide for a guaranteed-issue coverage by insurance carriers and no limitations on pre-existing conditions.
  b) Individuals would be able to carry coverage with them when changing employers, or coverage pools.
  c) Require NO NEW TAXES to implement. Continue Medicaid to assist in paying for coverage for persons who earn up to 150% of the poverty level.
  d) Development of a electronic information and claims processing and payment system.
  e) 100% tax deduction for non incorporated employers and employees who make premium payments for basic health care coverage.

f) Encourage the use and full implementation of tax-free medical spending and savings accounts made available by authorizing legislation at the state and federal level.
g) Costs would be contained and brought down through wellness/prevention screening, medical malpractice reform, extensive utilization review, case management, alternative health care arrangements, and by limiting state mandated benefits that frequently exceed those desired by individuals or their employees.

21

The Federation of Health Systems

Michael D. Bromberg

Principles of Reform

The Federation of American Health Systems believes that access to health care coverage should be universal and should be financed on ability to pay. Any health reform proposal should reform Medicare and Medicaid by purchasing coverage in health plans instead of services. The Federation has long favored health reform which eliminates the perverse incentives in our tax code. Congress needs to replace the current rewards for volume with rewards for cost effectiveness.

A competitive bidding system will contain health care costs without destroying the quality of health care Americans expect and deserve. This can be achieved by limiting the amount of health insurance premiums tax employers and employees may deduct or exclude from taxable income. This one change would foster cost containment better than any other regulatory or market-based reform. It would change the behavior of all stakeholders by offering positive economic incentives for organizing and purchasing cost effective health plans.

Health insurance is the only fringe benefit which is not capped, and a small fraction of the approximately $60 billion in lost revenue from the tax exclusion could subsidize care for the neediest segment of the population. Lower income employees could be granted exemption from such a change in the tax code to assure a fair and equitable redistribution of the tax subsidy for private insurance.

A more efficient health system can also be achieved by: eliminating the current state-level regulatory barriers that impede the development of

---

This statement was originally prepared for the Committee on Energy and Commerce, Subcommittee on Health and the Environment and the Subcommittee on Commerce, Consumer Protection and Competitiveness, October 14, 1993. It was extensively edited for this publication in June 1997, by the author.

managed care plans; eliminating state-mandated benefits above the basic benefit package; privatizing Medicare and Medicaid by converting them to programs that buy health coverage instead of health services; accelerating the development and use of "best practice" treatment standards; and eliminating the high cost of defensive medicine by capping malpractice awards for non-economic damages and establishing an arbitration system.

Clearly, the Federation had much in common with the proposal put forward in the 103rd Congress by President Clinton. The Clinton HSA established a minimum benefit package that affords Medicaid recipients the same access to health providers as any other privately insured individual. The plan offered Medicare beneficiaries the opportunity to continue their private coverage when they reach eligibility for Medicare. It called for insurance reforms to assure all Americans access to coverage, regardless of health status. The plan also overrode state barriers to the growth of managed care. Although what most consider a critical component of malpractice reform, capping non-economic rewards, was absent, the President's health reform proposal did address some malpractice issue, such as contingency fees, alternative dispute resolution and periodic payments. The President's proposal also created purchasing alliances to receive competitive bids from integrated health plans.

Much of the Clinton plan was bold and innovative. However, the obsession with deficit reduction threatens to override the opportunity for structural reforms, which would prove that a market-oriented approach is a feasible method of cost containment. The President's plan called for unprecedented and unrealistic reductions in spending for the Medicare and Medicaid programs. Congress, after much debate, recently passed a budget reducing Medicare spending by the largest amount in the history of the program: $56 billion over the next five years. The Administration's plan calls for more than twice that amount, $124 billion, in additional reductions. Medicaid funding would be reduced by $114 billion.

Access to universal coverage should be financed through a broad-based mechanism, not by deep cuts to providers of health care to the poor, elderly and disabled. Hospitals are labor intensive institutions which will not be able to absorb such massive underfunding of the Federal programs without a) reducing services, and b) eliminating jobs or cost of living wage increases for their employees.

Global Budgets

The President's plan included a global budget enforced through limits on annual increases in insurance premiums. We strongly oppose a global budget or price controls. When price controls "work" they do so by rationing access to care and further limiting access to expensive new technology. A

The Federation of Health Systems

global budget would mean reducing care for all Americans to the lowest common denominator as shown by the impact of expenditure caps tried in Canada and several European nations.

A global budget would also have a detrimental effect on many states, because expenditure caps reward high-cost states. For example, the current per capita health spending in South Carolina is 56 percent as high as Massachusetts; a Federal cap based on historical spending would allow South Carolina 44 percent fewer dollars per resident annually than Massachusetts. Over the first five years of a seven percent global cap, Massachusetts could spend $8,258 more per person than South Carolina.

As you can see, global budgets freeze the current system's inefficiencies in place, they make no pretense about reform and they do not address any of the underlying reasons for rising costs, such as the unrestrained demand for unlimited health care services. Global budgets further undermine any effort to stimulate competition among health plans.

Premium Caps

The task force and the President rejected across-the-board price controls, but included price controls on insurance premiums. Such premium caps would drastically undermine efforts to organize delivery networks envisioned by the President. Unless modified by Congress, price controls on premiums will become an obstacle to reducing costs; price ceilings will become the floors. Insurers would not be likely to set lower premiums when their future pricing options are limited by government caps.

Premium caps would also inhibit the growth of new and innovative health plans, ones that would require large amounts of risk capital to develop health services delivery networks, whether they be formed by insurers, employers or providers.

Managed Competition

The Federation of American Health Systems endorsed the managed competition concepts contained in the "Managed Competition Act," introduced by Representative Jim Cooper (D-TN) and by Senator John Breaux (D-LA) and others in the Senate and House. These bipartisan measures rely on the creation of large purchasing pools for small employers and also on the purchasing of coverage at reduced costs by individuals from accountable health plans which submit competitive bids to purchasing cooperatives.

The Managed Competition Act shared many features of the President's plan. Several of these features provided for universal access to health insurance through: establishing a standardized benefits package to be offered by health plans; subsidies for individuals' purchase of coverage based on their income; requiring health plans to offer coverage to everyone; and prohibiting insurers from denying coverage for pre-existing medical conditions.

Both plans include features that make health insurance more affordable, and enhance the quality and efficiency of care. These include: establishing regional purchasing groups through which individuals and small businesses purchase coverage; preempting state anti-managed care laws; requiring health plans and providers to report on the quality of their health care and outcomes and enrollee satisfaction; and promoting administrative simplification.

Security and Choice

The President listed six criteria essential for meaningful health reform. The first is security. We applaud the Administration's proposal to assure Americans that health coverage will always be there. But a point of concern lies in this guarantee: losing the quality of care received.

Choice is another criteria mentioned by the President. Parts of his plan would have resulted in increased choice. An example is the provision of employee choice from a variety of plans, instead of accepting the single choice of their employers. However, others parts of the plan restricted choice. An example is the regulatory authority granted to alliances to freeze enrollment in plans where global budgets are exceeded. Choice can be restricted when the growth in the weighted average premium in an alliance rises faster than inflation. For example, if all plan premiums in an alliance grow at the same rate of inflation, but some individuals elect to switch to a higher cost plan, the growth in the weighted average premium in that alliance would exceed inflation. In this case, consumers who want to switch to higher cost plans can be penalized by having their choice denied by the alliances, even when the desired plan did not increase its premiums from the previous year.

This raises serious constitutional and policy questions about whether government can cap private spending decisions by consumers, especially those which involve no government funds and for which there exists no national emergency nor shortage of supply.

Basis for Consensus

The concept of managed competition already enjoys the endorsement of an unprecedented number of diverse groups in the private sector. Managed competition also has strong bipartisan support in the Congress, a necessary element for avoiding gridlock on the important issue of health care reform. With the exception of global budgeting and price controls, the government and the private sector have never been closer to a compromise on health care reform.

The managed care revolution has been underway for a decade. Indemnity insurance is giving way to a new system which restrains excessive treatment. There has been little talk about rationing during this debate, but rationing of health care is a central issue.

Managed care does not withhold needed care; it manages care to restrain unneeded services. Price controls and global budgets limit care without regard to medical necessity. The Clinton HSA attempted to try both at the same time. But that would be detrimental to managed care by putting controls ahead of case management, budgets ahead of needed care and regulators ahead of patients.

Our industry stands ready to help President Clinton use his leadership and consensus-building skills to implement a national health care reform policy that builds on the best features of the current American health care system.

22

Suggested Standards for Insurers

Julie Goon

Since the 1992 presidential campaign, when health care reform emerged as a high profile issue, our national leaders have been searching for legislative solutions to address the public's concerns about health care. Republicans and Democrats alike, despite their disagreements over the government's proper role in the health care system, have pursued the twin objectives of controlling costs and expanding access to care. At the same time, significant progress has occurred in both of these areas as a direct result of the growth and evolution of managed care in the marketplace. Competition and private sector innovations have succeeded while lawmakers and policy makers have foundered in their quest for practical solutions.

President Clinton's "Health Security Act," which was a response to growing public concern about the issues of cost and access, failed in the 103rd Congress for a variety of reasons. Despite its good intentions, the proposal was too complicated, too costly and too ambitious for its own good. Even its supporters struggled at times to explain and defend its complex provisions to a suspicious and wary public. The task force that developed the plan was considered by many to be overly secretive and out-of-touch with the concerns of ordinary Americans. Most members of Congress, including key Democrats whose all-out support was crucial to the plan's ultimate success, were excluded from the process by which it was initially developed. The Clinton administration underestimated the importance of cultivating political support and it vastly overestimated the public's willingness to trust government.

Repeated delays in the plan's release made it difficult for supporters to sustain momentum on the public relations front. When the plan was finally

---

This presentation was made on April 1, 1995, at the University of Michigan Forum on Health Policy.

unveiled, committee chairpersons spent much of their time squabbling over jurisdictional matters instead of working together to move the bill through Congress. In January of 1994, President Clinton defiantly told Congress in his State of the Union address, with the entire nation watching, that he would veto any bill that did not provide "universal coverage." This statement later made it impossible for him to negotiate a less sweeping compromise when it became evident that far-reaching reforms could not be achieved. In the end, Democrat leaders in Congress found that their majorities were too slim. Sensing the public's anxiety, many rank and file Democrats were unwilling to line up and vote for a plan that they did not have a hand in crafting. A wide range of interest groups presented yet another obstacle as they coalesced against the bill, sending Congress a unified message that the marketplace should be allowed to work. As a result of the combination of all of these factors, the proposal died an unceremonious death without ever coming to a vote in either the Senate or the House.

The failure of the Clinton health care plan was an enlightening experience for our national leaders. Congress learned a great deal about what it could and could not do in its pursuit of health care reform. First and foremost, it became clear that a "big government" solution was not acceptable. Congress recognized that wholesale reforms should be shelved in favor of more modest, incremental reforms. A number of lawmakers came to realize that the marketplace, if left to its own competitive devices, could achieve much of what was attempted by the President's task force.

When the Republicans became the majority party in the 104th Congress, they were presented with an opportunity to demonstrate that incremental reforms improving the health care system could be enacted with bipartisan support. Medicare reform was the Republicans' first big challenge. They over-reached in their effort to overhaul the system, and their sweeping Medicare reforms were vetoed by the President and later used as campaign fodder to suggest that Republicans wanted to balance the budget on the backs of seniors. This experience, coupled with the lessons learned from President Clinton's efforts in 1993-94, led to the movement of the Kassebaum-Kennedy health insurance reform bill. Although this measure moved slowly in the early and late stages of the legislative process and generated partisan quarrels all along the way, it was ultimately approved by overwhelming margins in both the Senate and House and signed into law by President Clinton. It is the most significant new health law in years. In the 1996 campaign season, incumbents from both parties — especially those in tight races — eagerly claimed credit for the passage of this popular legislation.

At the same time the 103rd and 104th Congresses were grappling with legislative reforms, the health care marketplace was experiencing fundamental changes as the growth of managed care generated more competition, based on both cost and quality. A "dynamic transition" began to take place as more consumers enrolled in managed care plans, the "big players" shifted towards managed care, the industry consolidated, economic fat was squeezed from the health care system, and physicians and hospitals tried to establish integrated systems. As the health care system transformed itself, true cost control was achieved — to the delight of purchasers and to the dismay of many "players" in the shrinking fee-for-service sector whose interests were well-served by the chaos of the old system.

Regrettably, critics of managed care have tried to use the uncertainty inevitable in this period of transition to link managed care to assorted "horror stories" — widely circulated by the media — involving patients who have had bad experiences with the health care system. While isolated instances of substandard care or patient dissatisfaction in the fee-for-service sector are recognized as unfortunate, but inevitable, in a health care system that involves millions of tests and procedures each day, any such instance in a managed care plan is exploited as critics try to portray managed care plans in the worst possible light.

Ultimately, these "horror stories" resulted in proposed legislation on the so-called "gag" issue and laws passed on maternity length of stay and mental health parity. These measures were considered in the closing weeks of the 104th Congress with little serious debate and little understanding of the far-reaching consequences of what was being proposed. While such proposals may be politically popular in the short-term, Congress may also find that it is hazardous in the long-term to establish regulations in a competitive marketplace without knowing what the end result will be.

Another unintended consequence of the passage of such legislation is the shift, suggested by the recent pattern of legislative activity, in the traditional roles of the federal government and state governments with respect to health care issues. Historically, state governments have regulated the insurance markets, while the federal government has had oversight over public health programs. However, as state mandates have proliferated in recent years, more and more employers have moved to self-insure in order to become exempt from state regulation. This, in turn, has prompted special interest groups to pressure Washington to regulate self-insured employers at the federal level.

It is a virtual certainty that these pressures will continue to be felt in the coming session. The extent to which lawmakers are willing to resist these pressures and trust the marketplace will determine whether competition is stifled or allowed to flourish. Recent history has shown that cost containment and quality improvement are best achieved, not through legislative mandates, but through private sector innovations that empower consumers and expand health care options. Constructive health care reform will continue in the marketplace only if the 105th Congress recognizes this important reality.

The American Association of Health Plans and its 1,000 member plans have worked diligently to try to unleash the full potential of managed care to deliver quality health care at an affordable price. Our "Philosophy of Care," which we formally adopted in 1995, affirms our commitment to high standards of quality and professional ethics, and to the principle that patients come first. It states in the clearest possible terms that we believe patients should receive "the right care, at the right time, in the right setting." If our plans are allowed to carry out this philosophy, unencumbered by mountains of regulations and mandates, consumers can look forward to a future of better coverage and more options for quality health care services.

23

A Vision Renewed: Health Care Security

Health Insurance Association of America

The Health Insurance Association of America (HIAA) remains committed to the Vision for Health Care Reform we first adopted in December 1992, which was and is as follows:

> Our vision is a society of healthy individuals and communities. Our Nation, through systemic change, will build upon our employer-based system to create a consumer-responsive, prevention-focused, affordable and cost-effective health care system which fosters individual responsibility, human dignity, improved human status, and enhanced quality of life for all.

The goals we first articulated four years ago remain as relevant today as they were then. We seek a health care system that will:

- Promote a healthy and productive existence for all Americans, maximizing the dignity and quality of life for each individual.
- Encourage Americans to take personal responsibility for maintaining good health regarding lifestyle factors within their ability to control.
- Recognize, as a society, that heroic efforts to extend life are not always appropriate or desirable. Dignity, quality of life, and the potential of returning to a healthy existence must be considered in treatment decisions and in the allocation of resources.
- Provide compassionate care to all people, especially to those who are chronically or terminally ill and cannot recover from their illnesses.

This presentation was made on November 18, 1994, at the University of Michigan Forum on Health Policy.

- Stabilize health care costs as a percentage of individual financial capacity—earned income and other sources.
- Harmonize health care spending with other essential national requirements—the environment, education, the economy and security.

In particular, HIAA is dedicated to assuring that every American has access to high-quality and affordable preventive and medical care; and is adequately protected from the financial consequences of illness, crippling disease, sudden disability or the need for long-term care.

While we continue to believe a few of its provisions are ill-advised, in general we applaud Congress' recent enactment of the Health Insurance Portability and Accountability Act of 1996, the "Kassebaum-Kennedy bill." The Act establishes the framework necessary to assure responsible portability throughout our employment-based health insurance system. By clarifying the tax treatment of long-term care insurance and services, it also helps millions of Americans to protect themselves and their families against the financially devastating consequences of long-term, debilitating illness.

Clearly, more needs to be done to achieve the health security goals we all share, and we have learned that they will not be achieved overnight. We will have to proceed incrementally, step by step.

In this Vision Renewed, HIAA offers a set of principles to guide us in this quest for health security. HIAA believes that reform of our health insurance system must be guided by the following principles:

Principle 1: "Personal Responsibility." Public policy should encourage all Americans to take personal responsibility for maintaining coverage for their own (and their family's) medical care, long-term care, and income-replacement needs, if not through a plan arranged by their employer, then individually. Consumers who responsibly protect themselves and their families by purchasing and maintaining medical, long-term care or income-replacement coverage should not be required to bear the costs of those who have chosen not to protect themselves (except to the extent all taxpayers are asked to bear such costs for the truly needy).

Principle 2: "Build on the Employer-Based System." The best and most expeditious way to expand health coverage to more Americans is to build on the employment-based system that serves us well. Employment-based coverage encourages virtually all employees to participate—the young and the old, the more healthy and the less healthy—because the employer pays a large part of the cost. Employers' active participation in financing, selecting, and administering coverage has been and will remain critical to maintaining open, flexible, and innovative health care and ben-

A Vision Renewed: Health Care Security

efit systems. Therefore, public policy should seek ways to encourage more employers to arrange and contribute toward coverage for their workers.

Principle 3: "Tax Equity." Because not all employers are financially able to contribute toward medical and other benefits for their workers, the tax advantages available for employer-sponsored coverage should be available to individuals who purchase medical or long-term care coverage directly.

Principle 4: "Affordability is Key." Affordability is driven by underlying costs, and cost is the enemy of broader coverage. Managing costs, both of services provided to their enrollees and of administrative functions, is a primary responsibility of private health plans. Some sources of cost pressure, however, are rooted in societal structures, such as the legal system and government-established health programs, that only government can address directly. Therefore:

- Government should not interfere with innovative private efforts to control health care costs through managed care or other means.
- Government should not interfere with customers' ability to choose a benefit design that meets their needs and that they can afford.
- Government programs should be fully financed through explicit funding mechanisms. The true cost of government programs should not be shifted in a hidden or indirect way to private entities. Allowing government to shift costs to private health insurance plans, for example, raises the price of those plans and makes them less affordable.
- Whenever government establishes rules for private markets, such as the health insurance market, the costs and benefits of those new rules should be carefully weighed. New requirements should not be imposed unless the benefits clearly outweigh the additional costs to insurance purchasers.
- Existing societal structures, such as the tort system, should be re-examined periodically to determine whether the benefits they provide to the public at large outweigh the costs they impose. If not, changes should be made to bring the costs in line with the benefits provided.
- The nation needs a new approach for dealing with newly developed or experimental medical and surgical treatments that have not been proven to be safe and effective. In order to keep premiums as affordable as possible for employers and individuals, private health plans should not be required (whether by regulation or threat of litigation) to cover new treatments whose effectiveness has not been proven through appropriate clinical trials.

- Government and private insurers should work in partnership in identifying and prosecuting fraudulent activity of any kind against public or private insurance plans and in recovering losses due to fraud.

Principle 5: "Customer-Driven Private Markets." In health insurance as in virtually all areas of economic life, customers' needs are best met by a competitive, pluralistic private marketplace. Private marketplaces quickly respond to changing customer demands, abandon failed approaches and embrace promising new ideas. Therefore, government's primary role should be to foster a dynamic private marketplace driven by customer demand rather than by government mandate. Moreover, to assure effective competition, it is critically important that all players — public and private alike — abide by the same rules. (Such rules include, for example, licensing requirements, taxes or assessments, consumer protection rules, etc.)

Principle 6: "Quality and Value." The discipline of the private marketplace is much more effective in bringing about real quality improvement than government-imposed procedural requirements. A prime example of this reality is the systematic approach health plans have taken to assessing and improving quality as managed care has developed and grown over the past two decades.

Private health plans of all types compete to provide the best value-for-dollar to their customers. This customer-responsiveness is the best guarantee that plans will continue to make quality improvements that customers believe add value. Therefore, government requirements, which tend to be rigid and not responsive to changes in the marketplace, should be kept to a minimum and should focus on basic consumer protections, such as fair and effective grievance procedures for resolving disputes. Private, marketplace-driven initiatives to assess quality and customer satisfaction should be encouraged.

Principle 7: "Groups, Individuals and Risk." A basic principle of insurance is that premium charged must be matched to the risk assumed for those insured. If the premium is too low, revenue will be insufficient to pay all the claims expected. If the premium is too high, potential customers will decide to take their chances and forego purchasing insurance. The application of this principle differs considerably, however, depending on whether the decision to buy insurance is being made by an individual or a group. It also differs by the size of the group.

When all (or most) members of a group participate in an insurance plan, and the group is large enough, the risk being assumed can be estimated from the characteristics of the group as a whole; it is not necessary to evaluate each individual member of the group. This is why employer-sponsored insurance works so well — the employer's contribution assures that virtually all members of the group will participate in the plan.

When the decision to buy insurance is made on an individual-by-individual basis, however, the only way to evaluate the risk being assumed is to evaluate each individual applicant thoroughly. Because people who know they will use insurance coverage are highly motivated to buy it, almost regardless of cost, and because people who believe they are unlikely to use insurance coverage are very sensitive to price, a failure to properly evaluate the risk of each applicant will virtually guarantee either that premiums will be insufficient to pay claims or that they will be too high for many people to afford.

Therefore, when the decision to buy insurance is made by individuals, insurers must remain free to fully evaluate the risk presented by each applicant, to accept or deny coverage, and to charge a premium appropriate to the risk assumed.

Principle 8: "Protecting vulnerable populations." Society as a whole has an obligation to care for vulnerable populations who cannot otherwise afford health care. The financial burden of the subsidies necessary to fulfill this obligation must be spread broadly and equitably across the entire population.

24

Getting Inside Health Care Interest Groups

Robert Asmussen

In the early 1990s, health care reform, presented as a sweeping governmental overhaul of our health care system, was stymied by partisan politics and the conflicting positions of various health care interest groups. The debate nonetheless shifted the consciousness of all health care providers, insurers, payers, and consumers to a higher level of understanding of the complexities of the health care industry. Three important issues in this debate revolve around availability, affordability, and quality.

1. *Availability*: The debate drew attention to the vast numbers of individuals who are uninsured nationwide, as well as those who are locked into low-paying jobs because of the health benefits provided. Many issues related to the uninsured are linked to the practice of insurance carriers in the small group market. In today's market, competition is based on risk selection rather than focusing on managing care. Blue Cross Blue Shield of Michigan is the only carrier in Michigan that accepts all applicants regardless of age, gender, or past claims experience. BCBSM uses a community rate that makes coverage more affordable to the population at large, rather than just targeting the young, healthy and profitable components of the market.

While many states have implemented insurance market reform, Michigan has not. Due to adverse risk selection, our products are becoming increasingly unaffordable to the population BCBSM is intended to serve. BCBSM would favor individual and small group insurance regulation because it would promote competition based on efficiency, customer service, and cost management rather than competition based on risk selection.

2. *Affordability*: Comprehensive legislative changes to reduce health care costs through increased use of managed care were unsuccessful, but the debate has accelerated the shift to managed care in the private market. A

This presentation was made on March 26, 1994, at the University of Michigan Forum on Health Policy. It was edited in June 1997, by the author.

survey, conducted in 1993 of businesses nationwide, projected that by 1996 62 percent of all employees would enroll in managed care products. In Michigan, a state with a relatively low managed care penetration rate, the managed care market has increased from 36 percent in 1988 to 55.3 percent in 1995. BCBSM's membership reflects these market trends. Our traditional business is declining and our managed care products are accounting for an increasing share of membership.

The debate on how to control costs raised the concept of personal responsibility, a concept that the private market embraced. This is evidenced by new "demand management" products in the market intended to assist health consumers in managing the personal choices that they make. Demand management focuses on early identification and treatment of illness or disease indicators, and then provides the individual with information on managing health for future disease prevention, working with individuals prior to the onset of illness and arming them with information necessary to lead healthier lives. The net outcome is a better quality of life for the individual and lower costs in the health care system.

3. *Quality*: Quality has always been an important concept in health care. However, the health care reform debate also helped to emphasize the issue of quality in our health care system. Quality continues to be an amorphous concept that is difficult to quantify, but there are significant efforts underway in both the public and private sector to measure quality of care in various ways. Many markets use the Healthcare Employer Data and Information Set (HEDIS) and other report cards to assess health care insurers. The Michigan State Legislature has introduced a bill to establish a statewide database to provide consumers with comparative health care data. Practice guidelines and provider reporting mechanisms are frequently utilized to ensure that a baseline level of quality is achieved in our increasingly complex health care system.

Conclusion

In the end, it is unclear whether the private sector initiatives will resolve the dilemmas of the current health care system. It is likely that the number of uninsured will continue to grow; health care costs, although mitigated, will continue to outpace the growth in the Gross Domestic Product; and employer health care costs and the deficit will force the health care debate back to the forefront of the American agenda.

25

Blue Cross Blue Shield of Michigan Foundation

Ira Strumwasser

As the executive director of the Blue Cross Blue Shield of Michigan Foundation, which is affiliated with a health insurance company that has both managed care plans and managed fee-for-service indemnity, I don't have a particular perspective or delivery system to defend. I would like to move our consideration of the issues in a slightly different direction. I would like to talk about the impact of managed care and cost containment on the uninsured. We haven't heard much about that today, and quite honestly it hasn't been as prominent in the dialogue as many of us would like.

I am a proponent of managed care and as well of cost controls. There are implications, however, of these delivery mechanisms for the uninsured in our society to which we must pay attention. We all know the numbers. There are about 40 million people in America, give or take a few million, who are uninsured. Recent data suggest that this number is growing. We could reach 50 or 60 million uninsured people within the next 10 to 15 years. We know through the work of Dr. Bashshur of The University of Michigan School of Public Health that there are about one million people in Michigan who are uninsured. This number doesn't count the underinsured, people who have inadequate, limited or inappropriate and unnecessary coverage. This represents about one tenth of Michigan's population. About half of these people are working mothers in low-paying service jobs who have no company-provided health coverage.

Stu Altman of Brandeis University, in a presentation to Grantmakers in Health, argued, and I agree, that despite all of the problems with our health-care delivery system, we've developed a pretty good health-care delivery system. People may not get enough care, they may not get the right care, or may not get the care they need on time or in the most appropriate setting, but in America we've developed a pretty good health care

This presentation was made on April 1, 1995, at the University of Michigan Forum on Health Policy. It was edited in June 1997 by the author.

safety net. This safety net is represented by our hospital systems. Hospitals make a lot of money. Hospitals call them margins because they are, for the most part, non-profits. There is a lot of "margin" in the hospital systems. According to data presented by Altman, there is about $30 billion in profits available to the U.S. hospital system. Thirty billion dollars can pay for a lot of uncompensated care. Why am I talking about the uninsured, about uncompensated care and $30 billion in profits? Altman's data show that hospitals work at a loss on Medicaid and Medicare while they make huge profits, in the vicinity of $35 or $36 billion, on private insurance.

The managed care revolution is here to stay. So is cost containment. What are we going to see as we move into managed care? Hospital profitability is going to be reduced. The calculation is simple and straightforward. Hardly a day goes by in which we don't see numbers like $450 million cut out of the Medicare budget being discussed. We're going to reduce hospital profits, and put Medicaid into block grants, then reduce the cost shift from private payers—guess who is going to suffer. Doctors and hospital administrators are wonderful people, but they run a business—an increasingly competitive business. When they have extra money they are able to provide care for the uninsured, so-called charity or uncompensated care. If their businesses are less profitable, they will be forced to provide less uncompensated care.

If our health care safety net falls apart, we may have 50 or 60 million people without any access to care. The working poor and their children will probably be the first to suffer, followed by those on public assistance (Medicaid). We need to think about the implications of managed care, and cost containment and budget cutting for these citizens. We need to think about what we're going to do about it and, more importantly, what kind of society we choose to be.

26
Health Care in America: A Time for Change

William Hoffman

Over the past 15 years, wage and salary incomes of blue collar workers in the private sector rose nearly 83 percent. But in "real" terms—after adjusting for inflation — wages fell by 4.1 percent, i.e., prices rose faster than wages by 4.1 percent. Health care cost increases during that period ran at **nearly two and a half times** the rate of increase in general inflation. In fact, increased health care costs accounted for a full four-fifths of the decline in real earnings during the past 15 years. Put another way, if the health care cost component of inflation were excluded the decline in real wages since 1979 would have been only about .8 percent rather than 4.1 percent.

Rising health care costs have reduced workers' standard of living in two ways: first, directly, by eating away at wages through higher health care premium payments, copays, deductibles, etc.; and secondly, indirectly, by reducing the amount and frequency of wage increases in order to offset the higher cost of health care borne by employers. Without immediate and effective controls, health care costs will continue to soar, the possibility of increases in wages and improvements in other benefits will be further diminished, and the standard of living of workers will continue to erode.

Access to health care for millions of Americans continues to decline despite the steady rise in the cost of health care. We have a strong stake in improving access to health care in this country. During the past 10 years, many UAW members have lost health insurance coverage after they were laid off. All too often, this has happened in the context of plant closings and bankruptcies.

At the same time, UAW members have been faced with continuous demands from private and public sector employers to cut back on benefits such as prescription drugs, dental, vision, or mental health benefits; or to

---

This presentation was made on March 26, 1994, at the University of Michigan Forum on Health Policy.

increase employee cost sharing by adding or increasing deductibles and/or copayments. Employers have also attacked health care coverage by introducing periodic worker contributions for spouses and dependent children; and reducing or discontinuing retiree and dependent health care benefits before age 65 and Medicare complementary coverage after age 65.

The skyrocketing costs of health care pose a fundamental threat to the job security of millions of Americans employed in the private sector. In Canada, employer health care costs are approximately one-half those in the United States; in Japan, about one-third. Multinational corporations feed on this kind of disparity by transferring more production and plant investments outside this country. Since older companies have a higher ratio of retired to active workers than their newer competitors, and older active workforces than newer companies, and since health care costs tend to rise with age, older companies experience higher health care costs for their active workers, putting them even more at risk to increasing international competition.

The UAW believes that all employers should share equally in the costs of providing a basic level of health care protection to all Americans. All employers currently pay the same contribution (i.e., the same percentage of wages) to Social Security in order to provide a basic level of retirement and disability income to workers. The same principle should be applied to the financing of health insurance coverage for workers and their families. That is why the UAW has supported, and continues to support, reform legislation which would result in a single-payer system.

Medicare and Medicaid

The elderly continue to suffer from the relentless increases in health care costs, which directly affect the Medicare system and its recipients. While Medicare premiums and deductibles have risen to the point where they are three times what they were 20 years ago, the average retirees' Social Security benefits have risen by only 63 percent. Despite these huge increases, Medicare still does not cover many essential services, including long-term care, important portions of mental health care, dental care, and critically important, prescription drugs. The recent election of "anti-entitlement" forces in Washington will bring an escalation in the already heated debate over Medicare entitlements, and will do little to encourage improvements either in the cost of the program or its benefits.

Despite the increasing health care needs of the poor, cutbacks in Medicaid—the federal-state program developed for insuring the poor—continue at a relentless pace. Presently, even members of this nation's neediest families—those with family incomes below the federal poverty standard—may not qualify for Medicaid benefits if they are not in families with dependent children, disabled, or otherwise categorically eligible for Medicaid.

Widely different eligibility standards and benefit levels between states undermine the program. Beneficiaries, particularly the working poor, suffer from uneven quality and access to care, constantly having to face the question of whether they are "in" or "out" of the system. Because of inadequate reimbursement levels, many physicians refuse to accept Medicaid beneficiaries, who are then forced to go to overburdened public health clinics or hospitals. Ironically, because of the low levels of Medicaid reimbursement, many of these institutions are in dire financial straits or have already closed their doors, further reducing access to care. Comprehensive, universal coverage, regardless of income, is the preferred solution to the problems in the Medicaid system.

The financial burdens of the Medicare and Medicaid programs add to the problems faced by private payers. Public health programs, such as Medicare and Medicaid, have cut back on reimbursements in all areas, and the costs that are not covered have been shifted increasingly to private employers. This has led to a situation where, whenever possible, hospitals increase their charges to private payers in order to offset the inadequacy of public payments. The net result is that private employers are paying higher rates to subsidize the public programs.

Long-Term Care

Long-term care is a national health care policy issue that has been the subject of much debate, but remains unresolved. The growing number of elderly in our country, resulting from advances in preventive care and greater availability of new technology, signals the need for a comprehensive long-term care policy. Medicaid provides some long term care benefits, but does not go far enough in providing access to needed services.

A successful system would provide a comprehensive range of home, community, and institutional services available according to individual need for care and capacity for functioning. In addition, relief for informal caregivers, and limited out-of-pocket costs should be a part of any program.

The UAW has negotiated pilot programs with major employers which begin to address the problem. These programs have been expanded, and have been very successful. But a national public program policy is necessary to pick up where Medicaid, the private sector, and collective bargaining leave off.

Laid-off Workers and Retirees

The problems in the health care system have put extra pressure on laid off and retired workers. The UAW continues to fight to maintain health care coverage for all members, whether they are active, laid off, or retired. In fact, some of our collective bargaining agreements provide for continuation of health insurance coverage for a significant period of time after workers are laid off. But due to the lengthy nature of layoffs for some in these industries, our members often lose their health insurance coverage. Furthermore, many UAW contracts, particularly in independent and smaller workplaces, provide much more limited health insurance coverage continuation than do the major private-sector UAW-employers. Thousands of UAW members working for these employers lost their health insurance benefits shortly after being laid off.

These workers are faced with an impossible situation: they cannot afford the exorbitant costs associated with maintaining individual health insurance policies, yet they usually cannot qualify for Medicaid. The federally mandated COBRA health insurance continuation requirements provide little relief, because most laid off workers cannot even afford to pay the group rates available under COBRA.

Rising health care costs, increasing sizes of retiree groups, plant closings, bankruptcies, and changes in accounting rules for post-retirement health insurance benefits put forth by the Financial Accounting Standards Board (FASB), are all reasons retiree health care protections have been cut. But whatever the cause, the underlying fact remains: employers are increasingly walking away from their responsibility to provide health benefit protection for America's retirees.

The only fair and equitable answer to the problem of lost and unaffordable health insurance for laid off and retired workers is a comprehensive national health insurance program that insures health care for all citizens.

National Health Insurance

The crisis in America's health care system continues to worsen, and a comprehensive solution is needed soon. Reform that includes universal coverage, cost containment, and more equitable financing is essential. We need a system that ensures universal access to care, comprehensive benefits, a single-payer system, elimination of waste and inefficiency in the system, effective cost containment, and control over and improvement in quality. If we do not act soon, health care costs will continue to rise faster than inflation, over a million Americans will lost their coverage each year, and the cost of health care will explode the federal deficit. Any reform of the health care system should include:

- Universal Coverage with Comprehensive Benefits
- Cost Containment
- Fair Financing

There are several ways that fair financing could be achieved for comprehensive reform. One way would be through a progressive tax, such as would take place under a single-payer system. A second would be to build upon the current system by requiring all employers to provide health care coverage to all workers.

A system that would require all companies to contribute to the cost of health care for their employees would lead to the establishment of a "level playing field" between employers. This level playing field would provide several important benefits.

First, it would eliminate the cost shifting that currently takes place in our health care system. Employers that currently provide health insurance coverage to their workers would not longer have to subsidize employers that fail to provide such coverage. Instead, all employers would be required to pay their share.

Second, if all employers were contributing to the costs of the system and their contributions were "leveled" through the use of community rating, employers would no longer be penalized if one of their workers happened to develop a serious condition that required expensive treatment. Also, they would no longer be penalized because they had an older workforce.

We must continue to fight to bring the United States in line with other industrialized countries in the world by instituting a reformed national, comprehensive, and fair health care system. Even as we reemphasize the need for national reform, we will also continue our efforts to reform the health care system within the communities where we live and work. Recent efforts to encourage community-wide initiatives to improve access and quality of care while reducing overall costs hold great promise. National legislative efforts for comprehensive national health insurance will be aided by local community action.

SECTION THREE

Constraints on Choice: The Legislative Process — Views from the Inside

Section Three

Introduction
Constraints on Choice: The Legislative Process— Views from the Inside

Marilynn M. Rosenthal

There has been a great deal written about how the federal government works, particularly the gradual changes in power relations between the White House and Congress, the breakdown in party discipline in Congress and the growing influence of the interest groups. This section is a case study in the results of these changes.

The section begins with a roundup of President Clinton's statements on health care reform during his first term. These reflect what he hoped to accomplish with the Health Security Act and health care system reform in general. These statements are at the heart of his vision for a better, more efficient and effective health care system. While not including the overwhelming details of the 1,300 pages constituting the Act itself, these statements capture the main thrust of what the Clinton administration sought to do. These also reflect the language of presidential politics.

Judith Feder, who was then U.S. Deputy Assistant Secretary of Health, presents the views and language of a bureaucratic insider. Both these pieces reflect two things: the administration's goals for health care reform and Washington political public relations—how the executive branch wanted the public to understand the President's goals.

This is followed by four powerful articles, two by insiders intimate with what went on in selected corners of Congress and two by particularly well-informed observers. All four of these people were "there" in various ways. Congressman John Dingell, who was Chair of one of the five committees of the House of Representatives debating the Health Security Act, presents a unique view of what happened in his own committee. He also talks from a long, historic view of efforts at health care reform over four decades, going back to when his father, also a Congressman, supported significant health reform. Many observers felt that Dingell's Committee was a bellwether because so many diverse congressional views were represented on it. If the HSA couldn't get through this Committee, then it couldn't get through Congress. Furthermore, Dingell is seen as the consummate congressional politician. His frustration is clear in this chapter.

Katherine Hayes, a staffer for Senator John Chafee on the Senate Finance Committee, provides an unusually candid picture of how that committee carried out its work. She captures the shifting views and coalitions that formed and dissolved as the Finance Committee tried to reach acceptable compromise. She also describes the important work and influence of staffers and the special role played by the most respected lobbyists. This piece is a rare picture of internal committee dynamics.

The two analytical pieces by Kosterlitz and Payton provide overviews of why health reform failed. First there is a general discussion from a national journalist's (Kosterlitz) point of view. This is followed by Payton's close analysis of all the dynamics from the initial work of the White House task force, to the intricate work of all the committees in Congress. This second piece is presented through the eyes of a law professor with extensive experience in Washington, including a stint in the White House. Professor Payton also brings expertise in administrative law to her analysis. She provides a detailed and informed picture of the 103rd Congress as well as the 104th from a close and astute observer of congressional politics.

While thinking about the rich material in this section on the dynamics and convolutions of the legislative process, several questions present themselves. Why did the Clintons so badly misread the legislative process in the President's first term? Have the ways in which Congress works become too arcane to serve the national needs in effective ways? What kinds of Congressional reform are needed and are possible? Has interest group politics usurped the democratic process? How can incrementalism be used to resolve the most important and chronic problems in the American health care system: access, quality and cost control?

27

President Clinton's Evolving Ideas on Health Care Reform: In His Own Words

As compiled by Anand Parekh

"Americans are blessed with the world's finest doctors and nurses, the best hospitals, the most advanced medical technology, and the most promising research on the face of the earth. We cherish—and we will never surrender—our right to choose who treats us and how we get our care. But today our health care system is badly broken.

Next year we will spend more than one trillion dollars on health care—and still leave 37 million Americans without health insurance, and 25 million more with inadequate coverage. Skyrocketing health care costs have forced workers to trade wage increases to maintain health benefits and crippled our nation's manufacturers in global competition. And every month that passes without health care reform adds billions to our national deficit" *(October 27, 1993, letter in The President's Health Security Plan).*[1]

"All of our efforts to strengthen the economy will fail unless we take bold steps to reform our health care system. America's businesses will never be strong; America's families will never be secure; and America's government will never be solvent until we tackle our health care crisis" *(January 1993, State of the Union Address).*[2]

"Instead of putting people first, Washington favors the insurance companies, the drug companies, and the health-care bureaucracies. The most advanced health-care system in the world is being strangled.

This chapter is a compilation of portions of President Clinton's statements on health policy, taken from a variety of sources and put together in relatively chronological fashion. Taken as a whole, it presents the important elements of the President's thinking on health policy issues.

And working Americans are paying the price. Since 1980, the average cost of individual health insurance rose from $1000 to $3000 a year. Today health-care costs are the number one cause of labor disputes, bankruptcies, and growth in the federal deficit. People can't change jobs because insurance companies will deny them coverage claiming pre-existing conditions. Small businesses are caught between going broke and doing right by their employees. Drug companies raise prices three times faster than inflation. Working men and women are forced to pay more while their employers cover less" (1992, *Putting People First*).[3]

"Seventy-six percent of insured Americans have policies with lifetime limits, which means they can find themselves without any coverage at all just when they need it the most" (*January 1994, State of the Union Address*).[4]

"When I launched our nation on the journey to reform the health care system I knew we needed a talented navigator, someone with a rigorous mind, a steady compass, a caring heart. Luckily for me and for our nation, I didn't have to look very far. For eight months, Hillary and those working with her talked to literally thousands of Americans to understand the strengths and the frailties of this system of ours. They met with over 1,100 health care organizations. They talked with doctors and nurses, pharmacists and drug company representatives, hospital administrators, insurance company executives and small and large businesses. They spoke with self-employed people. They talked with people who had insurance and people who didn't. They talked with union members and older Americans and advocates for our children. The First Lady also consulted, as all of you know, extensively with governmental leaders in both parties in the states of our nation, and especially here on Capitol Hill. Hillary and the Task Force received and read over 700,000 letters from ordinary citizens. From them we have learned a powerful truth. We have to preserve and strengthen what is right with the health care system, but we have got to fix what is wrong with it" (*September 22, 1993, Address to the Joint Session of Congress*).[5]

"Health care should be a right, not a privilege" (1992, *Putting People First*).[6]

"Every American must have the security of comprehensive health benefits that can never be taken away. That is what the Health Security Act is all about. The Act is grounded in six basic principles: security, simplicity, savings, quality, choice and responsibility" (1993, *The President's Health Security Plan*).[7]

"Security means that those who do not now have health care coverage will have it; and for those who have it, it will never be taken away. Under our plan, every American would receive a health care security card that will guarantee a package of benefits roughly comparable to the benefit package offered by most Fortune 500 companies. Equally important, for both health care and economic reasons, this program for the first time would provide a broad range of preventive services including regular checkups and well baby visits.

The second principle is simplicity. Today we have more than 1,500 insurers, with hundreds and hundreds of different forms. These forms are time consuming for health care providers, they're expensive for health care consumers, they're exasperating for anyone who's ever tried to sit down around a table and wade through them and figure them out. Under our proposal there would be one standard insurance form, not hundreds of them. We will simplify also—and we must—the government's rules and regulations, because they are a big part of this problem.

The third principle is savings. Rampant medical inflation is eating away at our wages, our savings, our investment capital, our ability to create new jobs in the private sector and this public Treasury. In addition, health care premiums for small businesses are 35 percent higher than those of large corporations today. We want to give groups of consumers and small businesses the same market bargaining power that large corporations and large groups of public employees now have. We also want to save money by simplifying the system and cracking down on fraud and abuse in the system.

The fourth principle is choice. We propose to give every American a choice among high-quality plans. You can stay with your current doctor, join a network of doctors and hospitals, or join a health maintenance organization. If you don't like your plan, every year you'll have the chance to choose a new one. We also believe that doctors should have a choice as to what plans they practice in. Choice is important for doctors, and it is absolutely critical for our consumers. We've got to have it in whatever plan we pass.

The fifth principle is quality. Quality is something that we simply can't leave to chance. Our proposal will create report cards on health plans, so that consumers can choose the highest quality health care providers and reward them with their business. At the same time, our plan will track quality indicators, so that doctors can make better and smarter choices of the kind of care they provide. We have evidence that more efficient delivery of health care doesn't decrease quality. In fact, it may enhance it.

The sixth and final principle is responsibility. Responsibility means insurance companies should no longer be allowed to cast people aside when they get sick. It should apply to laboratories that submit fraudulent bills, to lawyers who abuse malpractice claims, to doctors who order unnecessary procedures. It means drug companies should no longer charge three times more for prescription drugs made in America here in the U.S. that they charge for the same drugs overseas. We need to restore a sense that we're all in this together and that we all have a responsibility to be a part of the solution" (1993, *The President's Health Security Plan*).[8]

"Right now I'll say again: There is no guarantee for anyone that health care will be there tomorrow. I want to be clear on this. We'll debate many points of this plan. But this point must remain nonnegotiable: The health care plan must guarantee every American a comprehensive package of benefits that can never be taken away. And I will only sign a bill into law that meets that fundamental commitment to the American people" (*October 30, 1993, Radio address by the President*).[9]

****

Editorial comment by Anand Parekh:

The health reform debate shaped by the 1993 Health Security Act accelerated several trends that already were in motion at the time. Health care providers began to regroup, forming new partnerships that could survive and thrive under the proposed new market conditions. HMOs increasingly took over private physicians' practices and gained greater control over the day-to-day practice of medicine. Employers, meanwhile, responding to the idea of an "employer mandate," increasingly restructured their employee benefits packages to push their employees to obtain health care from HMOs and other "managed care" preferred providers who offered less expensive care. Thus, the impact of the Clinton administration proposals for health reform was profound, independent of its eventual fate in Congress.

Strong attack of health care reform came from small employers who resisted mandatory health benefits. They claimed that the requirement even with proposed government subsidies would raise the cost of doing business enough to eliminate a million jobs. Economists challenged the ability of the National Health Board to control industry, noting that regulators frequently become controlled by those whom they try to regulate. The American Medical Association and the American Hospital Association united in attacking the idea of global budgets as impractical and inappropriate ways to control health care spending.

Republicans, on the whole, challenged the core concept of regulation as the way to reform health care, arguing that the Clinton plan was more "managed" than "competition" and calling for a return to "market forces" as the way to deal with costs. Eventually four bills came out of congressional committees; however, all the bills were grossly watered down from the key proposals in our plan. Sensing widespread uneasiness about health care reform in general and a chance to gain control of Congress, Republicans stalled action on the legislation until after the November elections.[10]

****

"In 1994, we almost came to blows over health care, but we didn't do anything. And the cold, hard fact is that each year, another 1.1 million Americans in working families lose their health care. And the cold, hard fact is that many million more—most of them farmers and small business people and self-employed people—have seen their premiums skyrocket, their co-pays and deductibles go up. Now I still believe our country has got to move toward providing health security for every American family, but I know that in 1994, we bit off more than we could chew. So I'm asking you that we work together . Let's do it step by step. Let's do whatever we have to do to get something done.

We ought to make sure that self-employed people in small businesses can buy insurance at more affordable rates through voluntary purchasing pools. We ought to help families provide long-term care for a sick parent to a disabled child. We can work to help workers who lose their jobs at least keep their health insurance coverage for a year while they look for work, and we can find a way—it may take some time, but we can find a way—to make sure that our children have health care" (*January 1995, State of the Union Address*).[11]

"For all Americans, I propose lower-cost insurance for groups of self-employed and small business people." (*June 13, 1995, five-minute televised address*).[12]

"We must not, however, abandon our fundamental obligations to the people who need Medicare and Medicaid. Americans cannot become stronger if they become weaker" (*January 1996, State of the Union Address*).[13]

"Last year, I vetoed the Republican budget plan that was sent to me by Congress. The Republican budget would cut Medicaid by $163 billion. It would repeal the guarantee of health care for poor children, people with disabilities, pregnant women and older Americans. Now, this repeal was not an afterthought or an unintended consequence. The congressional Republican majority is actually insisting on it. What would this mean?

Well, in 2002 alone, the year the budget is supposed to be balanced, the Republican budget could deny quality health coverage to nearly 8 million people; deny meaningful health care to over a million people with disabilities, even to 150,000 veterans, and to tens of thousands of people with AIDS, many of whom are able to keep working , or who can get the help they need without their families being forced into poverty because of the assistance they get from Medicaid.

If the Republican cuts in Medicaid take effect, the blunt reality is that as many as 4 million children will simply be denied needed medical care. They'll either be turned away from medical facilities, denied preventive care, or be turned out too soon. That is unacceptable in a country that cares about its children. And I will not permit it to happen.

My seven-year balanced budget plan trims Medicaid and keeps costs down. It cuts federal spending, lets states be more efficient, and targets the money more wisely. But it doesn't end the guarantee of health care for millions of Americans who depend upon it now" *(December 9, 1995, Radio address by the President)*.[14]

"Specifically, my Medicaid plan saves $59 billion in Federal expenditures over seven years. Under a per capita cap, the federal guarantee of coverage would be retained, and spending per beneficiary would be federally matched up to a set level. The cap would be set using spending per beneficiary in a base year, increased by an annual growth limit. My plan would also no longer require states to seek and be granted a federal waiver to establish managed care delivery systems.

My plan to preserve and strengthen Medicare saves $124 billion over seven years, extends the solvency of the Medicare Hospital Insurance Trust Fund, and does not impose new costs on beneficiaries. It further expands Medicare managed care options by authorizing the participation of a range of health delivery plan options, including preferred provider organizations (PPOs) and provider sponsored organizations (PSOs). The plan would also develop information to help Medicare beneficiaries become more informed about their choices, and level the playing field for Medicare managed care plans and Medicare supplemental coverage. It also strengthens the Medicare benefit package by expanding coverage for important preventive care" *(March 25, 1996, "President Clinton's Balanced Budget: Health Care Reforms")*.[15]

"It's time for men and women of both parties to put aside their narrow interests and extreme ideology and together pursue the national interest. We expect every family to pay its bills and to care for its children. Well, our country can do the same. We don't have to hurt our children to balance the budget" *(December 9, 1995, Radio address by the President)*.[16]

"The Health Insurance Portability and Accountability Act of 1996 shows what happens when we work together, when we cross party lines and put the interests of the American people first. This bill is a clear boost to our values as Americans. It offers opportunity by allowing people to take their health insurance from job to job. It rewards responsibility by helping people to work who desperately want to work. It brings us together in a common community to do what's right by all of our people, saying that we ought to make it possible for more and more people to succeed at work without losing the security of knowing that when they need health care it'll be there. No longer will you live in fear of losing your health insurance because of the state of your health. No longer need you hesitate about taking a better job because you're afraid to lose your coverage. And no longer will small businesses be denied access to insurance for their employees.

The bill also addresses other problems in getting more affordable insurance to our workers. Briefly, the bill,

1) Makes it easier and less expensive for the self-employed to purchase their insurance. It phases in a tax deduction of 80 percent for the self-employed and helps to even the playing field with bigger businesses.
2) Prevents fraud and abuse. It toughens penalties and helps us to go after bad apple health care providers who bilk the system of billions of dollars from Medicare, from Medicaid and from private insurance companies.
3) Makes the health care system more simple. It will modernize, streamline and cut the cost of insurance paperwork by devising a uniform electronic system for paying health care claims.
4) Allows the establishment of a limited number of medical savings accounts to allow us to determine whether this new approach can make a positive contribution to health care coverage and to affordability.
5) Helps with long-term care. It provides consumer protections and makes long-term care insurance more affordable.

I wish this bill had also contained the provision to eliminate the differential treatment of mental health coverage. We must also find a way to provide coverage for workers and their families who are in transition. I have proposed a plan which we put in our balanced budget to cover 3 million workers and their families, including 700,000 children, who today have nowhere to turn for affordable health care because the worker is changing jobs.

Our mission in pursuing health care reform from the start has been to provide more fairness and quality for the American people. We can do things when we work together and put the American people first. And whenever we work on behalf of our families and our children, as we do with the Health Insurance Portability and Accountability Act, America always wins. I look forward to working with Congress when they come back in September and to continuing this effort. We must not let this be a temporary development. Now we need to build on what we have achieved" (*August 21, 1996, Remarks at the signing of the Health Insurance Portability and Accountability Act*).[17]

Additional material from "The President's Health Security Plan: The Draft Report"
compiled by Anand Parekh

The American Health Security Act

Summary:

The American Health Security Act guarantees comprehensive health coverage for all Americans regardless of health or employment status. Health coverage continues without interruption if Americans lose or change jobs, move from one area to another, become ill or confront a family crisis.

Through a system of regional and corporate health alliances that organize buying power of consumers and employers, the American Health Security Act stimulates market forces so that health plans and providers compete on the basis of quality, service and price.

The American Health Security Act creates an independent National Health Board responsible for setting national standards and overseeing the establishment and administration of the health system by states. The Board interprets and updates the nationally guaranteed benefit package and issues regulations.

A sample of the health services specified by the Act include: hospital services, emergency services, clinical preventive services, mental health and substance abuse services, family planning services, pregnancy-related services, and hospice. Elderly and disabled Americans receive coverage for outpatient prescription drugs under Medicare for the first time.

Under the Act health plans must meet national standards on benefits, quality and access to care but each state may tailor the new system to local needs and conditions. Thus the program encourages local innovation within a national framework.

Creating Security

The American Health Security Act enhances the security of the American people by extending universal coverage in an environment that improves quality and controls rising costs:

- All employers contribute 80% of the weighted-average premium for health insurance coverage in the regional alliances that serve their

employees. Families and individuals pay the other 20% of the weighted-average premium.
- Limits on out-of-pocket payments protect American families from catastrophic costs, while subsidies ease the burden on low-income individuals and small employers.
- A comprehensive benefit package with no lifetime limits on medical coverage guarantees access to a full range of medically necessary or appropriate services.
- Guaranteed choice of health plans and providers enhances choice for many Americans.
- No health plan may deny enrollment to any applicant because of health, employment or financial status nor may they charge some patients more than others because of age, medical condition or other factors related to risk.

Controlling Costs

The American Health Security Act brings growth in health care costs in line with growth in Gross Domestic Product by 1997. It accomplishes this goal by increasing competition in health care, reducing administrative costs and imposing budget discipline:

- A standard, universal package of health benefits and reliable information about the price and performance of health plans encourages informed choices.
- Consumers pay less for low-cost plans and more for high-cost plans, creating incentives for cost-conscious choice.
- Health plans receive fixed premiums based on risk characteristics or their patients. Working under a fixed budget, they have incentives to spend resources cost effectively.

If savings attained through effective competition and reductions in administrative costs do not achieve the spending goals, the national health care budget provides a backstop, ensuring that health care spending is in line with economic growth.

Enhancing Quality

The American Health Security Act improves the quality of health care by creating standards and guidelines for practitioners, reorienting quality assurance to measuring outcomes rather than regulatory process, increasing the national commitment to medical research and promoting primary and preventive care.

- Health plans are held accountable for quality improvement
- Regular publication of accessible information about quality and cost allows consumers to make informed choices among health care plans.
- Increased investment in research and public health enhances the level of protection for all Americans.
- Preemption of state laws limiting the scope of practice and new funding for the education of health professionals who are not physicians enhances opportunities for nurses, social workers and other non-physician providers.

Expanding Access to Care

The American Health Security Act invests in the development of an adequate health care system in areas with inadequate service. Those investments hold the promise of improving the availability and quality of health care in rural communities and urban neighborhoods.

- Health alliances assume responsibility for building health networks in rural and urban areas with inadequate access.
- National loan programs support the efforts of local health providers to develop community-based plans.
- Investments in new health programs such as school-based clinics and community clinics expand access to care for underserved populations.

Reducing Bureaucracy

The American Health Security Act reduces the burden of paperwork and administration; regulatory, billing and reporting requirements decline, and consumers experience a streamlined and simpler system:

- Administrative costs caused by multiple policies with different benefits and risk selection disappear.
- Standard forms for insurance reimbursement, the submission of claims and clinical encounter records simplify paper work and reduce administrative costs.
- Federal regulatory requirements for Medicare, Medicaid and other programs are simplified.
- Malpractice reform reduces incentives in the currents system to perform excessive tests or unnecessary procedures.

Reducing Fraud and Abuse

The American Health Security Act cracks down on health care providers and institutions that impose excessive charges or engage in fraudulent practices, setting tough standards and imposing stiffer penalties including:

- New criminal penalties for fraud related to health care and for the payment of bribes or gratuities to influence the delivery of health services and coverage.
- Tighter restrictions eliminate referral "kickbacks" in the private sector, and new standards prohibit physicians from prescribing services delivered at institutions in which they hold financial interests.

Notes

1. President William Clinton, 10/27/93, letter in *The President's Health Security Plan* (New York: Times Books, 1993), p. xiii.
2. Clinton, State of the Union address, January 1993.
3. Clinton, *Putting People First* (New York: Times Books, 1992), p. 107.
4. Clinton, State of the Union address, January 1994.
5. Clinton, Address of the President to the Joint Session of Congress, September 22, 1993, in *The President's Health Security Plan*.
6. Clinton, *Putting People First* (New York: Times Books, 1992), p. 107.
7. Clinton, *The President's Health Security Plan*, p. xiii.
8. *Ibid*, pp. 108-118.
9. Clinton, Radio Address by the President, October 30, 1993.
10. Max Heirich, *Rethinking Health Care: Innovation and Health Care in America* (Ann Arbor: University of Michigan, 1996), pp. 159-161.
11. Clinton, State of the Union address, January 1995.
12. Clinton, June 13, 1995, five-minute televised address.
13. Clinton, State of the Union address, January 1996.
14. Clinton, Radio Address by the President, December 9, 1995.
15. Clinton, "President Clinton's Balanced Budget: Health Care Reforms," March 25, 1996.
16. Clinton, Radio Address by the President, December 9, 1995.
17. Clinton, Remarks by the President at the signing of the Health Insurance Portability and Accountability Act, August 21, 1996.

28

The Politics of Health Policy Reform: An Inside View from the Clinton Administration

Judith Feder, Ph.D.

President Clinton is committed to health reform for two critical reasons: (1) so that all Americans have coverage that assures them access to health care when they need it and (2) to establish a stable health financing system in which everyone pays their fair share. His proposal, however, is under serious challenge. My remarks will lay out the kinds of challenges we face and the way the President's proposal aims to overcome them.

The first set of challenges to comprehensive health reform reflects broad philosophical points of view. There are many who question the role and the capacity of government to institute an effective reform —despite the evidence that an unfettered private market with few, if any, rules is producing unacceptable gaps in coverage and shifts in health care costs. Many also question whether we can afford to guarantee health care coverage for all people — despite the fact that we are already paying for people without coverage and often providing inappropriate and inefficient care. And many question whether we can slow the rate of increase in health care costs without threatening quality or choice — despite the fact that in our current system rising costs mean declining choices and threats to the continuity of care on which quality depends.

These are the big picture challenges. Equally important, however, are the specific concerns of the many powerful interest groups who are involved and have a stake in the health policy reform debate. We know that insurance companies are concerned that they will lose more from new rules affecting the way they operate than they will gain from an expanded market for insurance. We also know that providers fear that they have more to lose

---

This presentation was delivered at the University of Michigan on April 26, 1994.

from efforts to slow cost growth than they have to gain from the fact that, under reform, every patient they see would be a paying patient. And we know that big and small businesses are concerned that obligations to pay under reform will exceed or outpace efforts to contain the cost increases from which they are now suffering.

Addressing these concerns is a primary focus of legislative design efforts by the Administration and the Congress. But no attention to design can eliminate the sizable political threat that these concerns pose — or that interest groups pose: that is, their capacity to undermine Americans' commitment to reform. We know that the public is frightened under the current system, afraid of losing their health care coverage; but we also know that they are concerned that reform might make things worse rather than better. Interest groups are provoking these fears in order to forestall reform. In the face of this activity, the real political challenge for those of us who are committed to reform is to give voters confidence that reform will provide them with the security they are seeking and will preserve, rather than threaten, the high quality medical care that Americans value.

Let me now review how the President's proposal aims to achieve this objective. Overall, the President's bill builds on the coverage most people have in the current system and legislates a framework that enables them to keep it. That means that we would retain an employer-based financing system and a private insurance market, but take significant steps towards making those systems work effectively. Let me explain how.

The first question is: What do you get under the President's health reform program? You get a guarantee of private health insurance coverage for a comprehensive set of benefits — similar to those that are provided by major businesses today. The proposed benefits are broader, however, in one important respect: they include coverage for a specific set of preventive services (like mammograms) without any cost-sharing. The goal is to eliminate barriers to use of preventive services that promote health.

As people evaluate the President's proposal, they are looking to see how the set of benefits and coverage in health reform compares with what they have today. They are afraid that they will lose what they currently have and are looking to ensure that, under reform, they will have a clearly-defined comprehensive set of benefits that secures, rather than diminishes, their current protections. It is our view that the package has to be comprehensive in order to promote adequate access to appropriate health care and to assure that current benefits are secure.

The second question is: How does everybody get coverage? Under the President's bill, all workers get coverage through their jobs. Government would help sustain that coverage for nonworkers. It is generally known that most Americans who have insurance get it through the workplace. It is less widely known, however, that most people who don't have insurance work. About 80% of the people without insurance coverage are workers or in the families of workers — most, though not all, of them working full time. If all employers and working families were contributing toward insurance premiums, we would go a long way toward financing universal coverage.

Just as we have pursued a strategy that says that every job should provide insurance, we have pursued a balance of affordability and responsibility. In today's environment, when not every job is offering coverage, we have some employers covering other employers' workers. Small employers of low-wage workers are less likely to contribute to their own workers' coverage. When we expect every employer to bear responsibility for coverage, we have to pay particular attention to the burden of this responsibility on employers of low-wage workers for whom new costs could, if excessive, threaten jobs. To avoid this threat, the President's plan offers a discount in the premium to all employers of low-wage workers, with a special discount for small employers. All employers who participate in the pools that we call alliances would pay an insurance premium limited to 7.9% of payroll. Employers with fewer than 75 employees would face a lower cap, ranging downward from 7.9% to 3.5% for the smallest employers of the lowest wage workers. That means that if you are a small employer of minimum wage workers working a 40 hours week, you would pay no more than 15 cents an hour in order to guarantee your workers and their families comprehensive coverage. That is how we propose to balance affordability and responsibility for employers.

For families, the balance is achieved as follows: The employer contributes to a credit of 80% of the average costs of the plan in their area for each worker. Families bear responsibility for the difference between the employer's contribution and the cost of the plan they choose. Employees' contribution for their share of the premium is limited to 3.9% of their income. If people lose their jobs, they can keep their coverage but will be obligated to pay for the family share of the premium, with government help toward the premium share the employer would have paid. The government will also help early retirees by paying the share of the premium that employers would have paid on their behalf.

This is the way everybody will be included in health care coverage. We are extending the employer-based system, with additional protections, to all employers and to all families, working or not, in this country.

Third question: how does the insurance market work? There is a great deal of agreement that we have got to change the rules for insurance companies. We all know that individuals, small businesses, and not-so-small businesses are at a terrible disadvantage in today's insurance market, with its incentives to compete to avoid risk. It is the President's commitment, shared by many in the Congress, to bring an end to — and virtually outlaw

— discriminatory practices by insurance companies. We must promote choice of provider and health plans for families.

Under the President's plan, we will do this through a federal/state partnership in which the federal government establishes the ground rules and states put most of them into effect through the private sector. If they wish, states have the option of pursuing a single payer plan, but we expect most states to stay with the current market-based system. This system has several pieces. First, we have to re-establish the community pool of risk spreading that insurance was intended to be. This will be accomplished through alliances. In TV ads, the insurance industry's "Harry and Louise" have maligned alliances. Let me tell you what they're really about. Their fundamental purpose is to re-establish an insurance pool. Alliances are not about forcing people into pools, but rather about forcing health plans into pools so that there is a central place of enrollment at which every family has access to every health plan. This way insurers cannot avoid bad risks or pick off good ones by selecting and choosing to whom they wish to market. We will make these pools relatively large in order to spread risk as broadly as possible and to allow a maximum of family choice rather than employer choice. In these pools insurance is not only community-rated — charging the same amount to every applicant regardless of age, gender, or health-status — but also available to the whole community. We are committed to community-rating and open enrollment, not only by making rules for insurance plans, but also by setting up a marketplace that makes those rules work. That is what alliances are all about: choice, community rating, and competition among plans. That is how we would change the marketplace.

Finally, let me spend a moment talking about seniors. Despite Medicare, seniors face serious gaps in protection. Comprehensive reform should also address these gaps — in particular, the lack of protection for the costs of prescription drugs and the costs of long-term care. The President's bill preserves and strengthens the Medicare program by adding prescription drug coverage. It also establishes a new program which is largely federally funded but state administered to address the biggest gap in long term care services — services at home and in the community for people of all ages with serious disabilities.

These key elements of reform are the focus of the legislative process. As you watch this process, it is easy to be distracted by the "horse race." The press enjoys nothing more than commenting on whether the President's bill seems to be winning or losing on any given day. But let me caution you to keep your eye on the real issue — that is, whether the President's goals are being achieved. In both houses of Congress, the major committees of jurisdiction are developing the components of reform I have outlined for you. Each of those committees is working to come up with the best bill it can within the political limits of its committee. We will see this bill rewritten, and rewritten, and rewritten as we go through the process. Sometime next August, or September, they will be writing the final bill. As you look at the final legislation, be sure to check for the key components: a guarantee of affordable private health insurance for all Americans, an end to discriminatory insurance practices, choice of health plans and providers, and a strengthening and preservation of the Medicare program for the nation's seniors. That's what health reform must be about.

29

Political Strategies in the Long Run: Decades of Efforts at Health Care Reform

An Interview with John Dingell

Q: Since the enactment of Medicaid and Medicare, what have been some of the successes and stumbling blocks in efforts to reform health care?

The enactment of a major, significant piece of legislation always has required a commitment to work toward the goal with minimal interference from partisan politics or the common power wrangling between Congress and the Administration. The enactment of Medicare and Medicaid 30 years ago exemplified this fundamental principle. It was an exercise in bipartisan, negotiated compromise, and a cooperative and positive working arrangement between the Congress and the President. The Congress recognized the President's desire to establish these programs, and the President respected the right and the ability of Congress not only to write appropriate and acceptable legislation but also to engage in positive bipartisan compromise to achieve enactment. This was an historical period during which the American people themselves were receptive to the concept that the government ought to be responsible for its vulnerable citizens. Knowing that the public could be persuaded that his ideas were good ones, however, did not result in the President's complacency, and he did an excellent job of arguing for the need to provide health care for poor children and for seniors. In addition, experts projected that spending for such programs could be anticipated to be reasonable and manageable. This was before the days of disputes between "CBO numbers" and "OMB numbers;" before the days of rapidly escalating health care costs, and before the days of the debate over managed care vs. fee-for-service medicine.

This interview took place on Mach 13, 1996.

The programs have been extremely successful. Today, every senior citizen in America knows that he or she can count on Medicare as a health insurance policy. Whether they have worked for companies with health insurance or not, and irrespective of whether that insurance continues beyond retirement, our senior citizens do not need to worry about health care. Before Medicare, fewer than half of our senior citizens had health insurance. Today, almost every senior has insurance. Medicare and Medicaid also provide a guarantee of care for disabled people — whether they would be eligible for private health insurance or not. Medicaid has served the health care needs of millions of women and children who cannot afford health insurance, and who cannot afford to visit private physicians or pay hospital bills. And — perhaps most significant — Medicaid has helped millions of middle-income families ensure that their elderly parents and grandparents can have nursing home care when they need it, even though those hard-working families cannot afford the $30,000 or more per year that such care can cost. In fact, more is spent by Medicaid for nursing home care for the poor and near-poor elderly than for any other program beneficiaries. So Medicaid is much, much more than a "welfare" program — it truly has been a safety net for our fragile senior citizens and for our hard-working, middle-class families.

Over the years, we have learned three general and important lessons from Medicare and Medicaid. First, the programs have worked. And this is the most important lesson. Second, they original structure was not perfect, and they have needed to be modified to meet the needs of the times, the changing health care marketplace, and the nature of the beneficiary population. We have made such modifications, and they have helped the programs work more effectively. And finally, we have learned that predicting the costs of health care is not easy. The knowledge about health and disease that we have gained through medical research has driven incredible changes in health care. Medical progress has been enormous over these 30 years, and the consequences of that progress have benefited our people. But they have thrown a major monkey wrench into cost predictions.

In short, we've learned that the government can ensure good quality health care for our citizens. But we've also learned that sometimes programs don't work in practice quite the way intended, requiring consequent oversight and a willingness to make targeted changes. Finally, we've learned that health care is a huge business with many participants who believe that their needs should be at least equal to the needs of the program beneficiaries. We've learned that we need to listen to both those participants and to patients.

Some of the most significant pieces of health care legislation since enactment of Medicare and Medicaid have been changes in those two programs — to improve benefits, based on increased knowledge about health and medicine, such as the importance of preventive care; to change the nature of the beneficiary population, based on demographic changes, economic factors, and increased understanding of the needs of specific populations; to improve program administration, to reduce fraud, to control costs, etc. Over these 30 years, Congress and Administrations both Republican and Democratic have recognized the need for change. We've seen what's worked and what hasn't, and we've been ready and willing to make necessary changes. One of the hallmarks of these efforts over the years, though, has been that we've never declared the programs completely unworkable, we've never pronounced them dead. We've always believed, as we do now, that incremental, targeted, careful change could result in improvements without placing people in jeopardy. That has worked for 30 years, and it can work now.

Q: What political strategies could be useful in getting health care legislation passed?

In general, although it is important to look for new and improved ways to make structural changes to health care programs, we know from past experience that it is often more successful to tackle discrete aspects separately rather than taking on too much. Our experience of last year illustrates this. But it is more than that. Any time you try to make major changes in health programs as large as Medicare and Medicaid, or, on an even broader scale, in the case of health care reform, it can have a dramatic impact on large sectors of the economy, with obvious political implications. Health care is a major portion of our economy. Millions of people and companies depend on it for their income. If you try to change the health care system too dramatically, the results can have a domino effect — with implications beyond the intended policy for many sectors of the economy.

Q: What is your opinion of the Clinton plan for health care reform?

President Clinton had a vision with which the majority of Americans agreed: a vision of an America in which every person, regardless of age, health, or socioeconomic or employment status, could have access to appropriate health care services. His vision was rooted in the knowledge that every other country in the industrialized world has founds its way to "universal health care." He believed that for America to do less was not in keeping with this country's proud tradition of serving its citizens, and was not acceptable for the wealthiest country in the world. I believe that initially, America was with President Clinton on this.

However, other important activities intervened on the President's time, and it was many months before he was able to be more specific with the public about his goals and how he would achieve them. In the interim, the Administration engaged in a complicated process for developing a health care reform proposal, and a number of sectors of the health care industry began to set a stage for opposition. By the time the President's plan actually was offered, there was a well-organized public relations campaign designed to alarm people about the potential results of fundamental health care reform. Thus, the Administration was in a defensive position before they even had had an opportunity to explain their position to the public.

Secondly, the President's comprehensive proposal was complicated and difficult to explain. In fact, it was easier simply to dismiss it than to attempt to sort through it. Thus, its opponents merely could say this is much too complicated to work. They merely had to say that this approach would mean more bureaucracy, would disrupt what people had become accustomed to, could be so complicated that even your own doctor might not be able to figure it out. By doing this, they were able to plant significant seeds of doubt in the minds of the public.

In addition, virtually every segment of the health care industry scrutinized the proposal for any granule of adverse effect. When they found these provisions, which might mean they would have to change their customary ways of doing business, they went about trying to change them. So Congress was besieged by literally thousands of special interest representatives, each arguing for this change or that. If all of those changes were made, the legislation would have been nothing like what had been envisioned originally.

In short, the plan failed because it tackled one of the largest and most profitable industries in America and tried to rein it in. It was almost too complicated to explain. It was presented in the second session of the Congress, thus allowing only a relatively short time for deliberative debate and negotiation. And it was presented to the public before the President had had time to market it strategically and after its opponents were well into their public relations campaign.

Individually and collectively, Members of Congress had many of the same concerns as those mentioned above. They also had numerous specific local concerns about such matters as the consequences for particular health care and academic institutions, medical specialties, companies, and others. These concerns were heavy baggage — especially in an election year. In the end, that baggage weighed more heavily than the need and desire to reform the health care system. That, purely and simply, was why health care reform legislation was unsuccessful.

Q: What are some of the central issues around Medicare/Medicaid.

In general, I think both sides have agreed that these programs need some reforming to assure Medicare's solvency, but there are fundamental, philosophical differences about how this should be accomplished.

As to Medicare, both sides have agreed to a reduction in spending. However, Republicans want to take money out the program to pay for a tax cut for the wealthy. Many Democrats are concerned that if Medicare reductions are too large — as those originally proposed in the Republican budget — the program could be seriously damaged. Democrats also believe that people should be able to see their own doctors. Under the Republican plan, Medicare reductions are so deep that many physicians will be forced either to join a managed care plan or to move to other situations where they can charge beneficiaries what Medicare doesn't pay in order to stay financially viable. Many seniors won't be able to afford this extra amount, so they will be forced either to leave their doctors or move into managed care. Democrats object to limiting seniors' choices.

With respect to Medicaid, the philosophical differences are even greater. Medicaid originally was established as a joint federal/state shared program. The intent was to ensure that there was enough money to assist the people most in need. However, it also was intended that there be equal investment. The States were required to share in the expense so that they would manage the program carefully. The federal government's role was to provide half of the money and set federal standards for who should be eligible and for what benefits. Over the years, States have tried to achieve more flexibility in the program, and both Republicans and Democrats agree that they should have more. However, the Republicans believe that the Federal government should have no say in how States manage the program, who is served, or what services are provided. I don't know of any business partnership where the chief financing partner doesn't have a role in determining what and how the product is produced by the managing partner. It isn't that the Democrats don't trust the Governors or the States, but we do feel a responsibility as managers of the federal trust to ensure that the federal dollars for which we are responsible are being spent the way we intended. The federal government also has a role in ensuring that the elderly, the poor, and the disabled are treated equally in all 50 states.

Q: Why has it been so hard to get health care reform legislation passed?

Many of the answers can be seen in our recent experience. Health care makes up a very large percentage of the economy. Any time you are trying to change such a large sector of the economy, as we learned last year, you have an increasing number of political interests involved. Any time you have major businesses and millions of people who are going to be affected by such major changes, you run into political dynamics that make it impossible to reach compromise and pass legislation. We learned last year that we should move slowly and allow some of the changes to take effect before we make the next set of changes.

Q: What do you see as the role government should play, as opposed to letting the Market rule?

We ask government to do many things the private sector will not do. The government thus plays unique roles on which many people in this country depend; roles played by no individual business or component of the marketplace. For example, seniors who are enrolled in Medicare and Medicaid and are treated in nursing homes can trust that the services they receive will be safe. Because of federal rules relating to Medicare, seniors also know that the amount of money that will have to pay for health care will be within certain boundaries. Although market competition may help to drive the costs of services down, there is evidence that the market doesn't always ensure safety and quality of services. I believe it is the role of the federal government to provide guidelines for safety and quality and to provide security for people in the later years of their lives.

One final point about letting the market rule, particularly when it comes to health care. Health care in this country is unlike any other product in one major respect. Generally, if an individual doesn't have the money to pay for a product, the business simply does not provide that product. However, inability to pay for health care does not necessarily deny services to people. Eventually, when they become seriously ill, even those who cannot pay *will* receive health services. They will receive them, however, in the most costly way — by admission to a hospital emergency room. Neither market forces nor reforms can stop this from happening, and we as a society are not willing to deny this care. So, in the end, somebody does pay. The questions then become: Do we continue to provide access to early intervention only to those who can afford to pay for it and then spend everyone's money to provide the most expensive kinds of care for the rest of the people? Do we treat health care truly as a market commodity, and deny care entirely to those who cannot pay? Or, do we take the money we are going to spend on health care anyway and try to direct it into more appropriate forms of care? I hope our answer is the last.

Q: What would you do differently?

With hindsight being 20/20, it's easy to identify where past efforts to get health care insurance for every American went wrong. I'm not sure it's a question of doing something different as much as it is a question of doing things better. Harry Truman, Lyndon Johnson, Bill Clinton, and even that well-known Republican Richard Nixon endorsed and presented plans to provide every American with health care coverage. Truman was defeated by what was at that time an unprecedented $25 million lobbying effort ($25 million being a substantial sum in that era). Johnson's efforts were sidetracked by strains over the Vietnam War. Ironically, Nixon introduced a health care plan remarkably like the Clinton plan; unfortunately, it was quickly overshadowed (as was his Presidency) by Watergate.

We have developed in America a marvelous health care system that works quite well for many of our people. But the harsh fact is that nearly 40 million Americans without health insurance are not part of that system. Sadly, those numbers will only rise if the current wave of corporate downsizing continues. The need for universal health insurance remains, but up to this point the political climate has never been right. What may be needed more than anything is a clear expression from the American people that health care for all should be one of the goals of a civilized society.

30

Inside the Senate Finance Committee

An Interview with Katherine Hayes

Q: What, in general, is the job of the Senate Finance Committee? How difficult is it to get an appointment on the committee? Can you make any generalizations about who tends to get appointed to the Committee? What their political goals might be?

The Senate Finance Committee has within its jurisdiction the vast majority of federal spending. The Committee is responsible for the Internal Revenue Code and the Social Security Act (Medicare, Medicaid, the Supplemental Security Income program, and welfare programs). The Committee also has jurisdiction over international trade issues. Thus, it is a very popular committee assignment and most Senators are eager to be appointed to the Finance Committee.

During the 103rd Congress (1993-1994), the Republicans were appointed to committees on the basis of seniority. Thus, a Senator's political leanings —conservative or moderate—played no role in whether or not they were appointed to the Committee. Several moderate Republicans, elected during the 1970s were, by the early 1990s, among the senior members of the Finance Committee.

Democrats, on the other hand, were assigned to committees by their leadership in the Senate. Thus the leadership could appoint Senators to the Committee who would be amenable to the leadership's (or the Chairman's) political agenda. The two previous Chairmen of the Finance Committee on the Democratic side were Lloyd Bentsen (Texas) and Russell Long (Louisiana).

Clearly, this is speculation on my part, but since both Long and Bentsen were from states with oil and gas interests, one might assume that it would have been in their best interests to assure that there were a few other Senators on the Committee that would have shared their interests in protecting

---

This interview took place in November 1996.

that industry under the tax code and through trade policy. Or perhaps, more generally, these Chairmen influenced the leadership to appoint some Democrats to the Committee that shared their conservative views.

Two keys to the outcome of the Clinton plan in the Finance Committee were the relationship between the Chairman, then Pat Moynihan (New York) and the number of conservative Democrats and moderate Republicans on the Committee.

Q: What were the specific issues that the Committee was to address concerning the Clinton health care proposal? Was this the starting point of their discussions? Did other members of the committee have proposals from the beginning or did some (e.g., Chafee's proposal) emerge later in the process?

The Finance Committee had broad jurisdiction over the health care reform issue. The Clinton health care proposal was financed through an employer mandate to provide health care coverage to employees (enforced through the tax code), and through savings in the Medicare and Medicaid programs. Democrats controlled the Senate and thus they made the Clinton bill the starting point for health care reform. Other members of the Committee also had made proposals in previous years. Among them were the Ranking Minority Member of the Finance Committee, Senator Bob Packwood (Oregon), and the Majority Leader, George Mitchell (Maine).

Interestingly, Packwood had, in past years, introduced health reform proposals that included an employer mandate, but by the 103rd Congress he had abandoned that proposal. At the start of the 103rd Congress, the only other major proposal introduced by a member of the Finance Committee was the one Senator Chafee introduced on behalf of the Republican Health Care Task Force, which he chaired. A majority of the Republicans in Congress were cosponsors of that proposal. Much later in the process Dole and Packwood introduced their own proposal.

A major proposal that emerged later in the process was one drafted by the so-called Mainstream Coalition, a group of moderate Republicans and conservative Democrats, some of whom were on the Finance Committee. That group was led by Chafee and Breaux.

Q: What were the original major different positions on the committee? What were the different goals of committee members? How did they evolve over time?

Although there were myriad provisions in the Clinton bill which proved controversial, the major sticking point was the employer mandate.

Inside the Senate Finance Committee

The Committee was polarized along party lines at the start of the process. The Democrats, under the leadership of Mitchell and Chairman Moynihan, tried to bring the Committee Democrats together around the Clinton proposal. Their goal was to try to get the Clinton bill through the Committee and onto the Senate Floor. The Committee was comprised of 11 Democrats and 9 Republicans, so if they could hold all the Democrats together, they would not need any Republican votes.

That strategy proved impossible when Senator David Boren (Democrat from Oklahoma) refused to go along with an employer mandate. He was rumored to have told Moynihan and Mitchell that he would support them if they could get a Republican on the Committee to vote for the mandate. They held out hope that at least one Republican would ultimately vote for it. Packwood had at one time supported the concept, and Chafee never took a public stand in opposition to the mandate.

When it became clear that they didn't have the 11 votes that they needed to get the bill through the Committee, moderate Republicans and conservative Democrats on the Committee began working together to find a compromise. The coalition consisted of Chafee, Jack Danforth (Missouri), Dave Durenburger (Minnesota), Breaux, Max Baucus (Montana), Bill Bradley (New York), Boren, and Kent Conrad (North Dakota). (Before Committee consideration of health care reform, however, Baucus left the group.)

President Clinton called each member individually to the White House and asked them to work out a compromise that could make it through the Committee. He told each of them that an employer mandate did not have to be a part of that package for him to support it. (Weeks later the President said publicly that he would support a bill without an employer mandate, but outrage from allies caused him to retract that statement.)

Q: Who were the people who played key roles among Committee members and among key staff? Who were the leaders that emerged? Did some Committee members play special roles (e.g., Dole)?

The key player on the Finance Committee shifted during different points in the process. Early on, Mitchell and Dole were the spokespersons for their respective parties and were setting the agenda. On the Democratic side, Senator Jay Rockefeller (West Virginia) was the most outspoken proponent of the Clinton bill and the most resistant to compromise. Senator Don Riegle (Michigan) was a strong supporter of the President's proposal, particularly the employer mandate, but seemed more willing to seek compromise.

Chairman Moynihan was a vocal critic of the Clinton bill. The Administration had not consulted him in developing the proposal, which was a critical mistake since they needed him to move the bill through the Committee. In fact, a White House staffer was quoted in *Time* magazine, saying that if Moynihan didn't go along, they would roll over him. Had he been an ally in the beginning, they may have been more successful. In the end, however, Moynihan fell in line and worked to get the Clinton bill through the Committee.

The role that Bob Dole played was less clear. Early on in the process he seemed willing to compromise, but when it became obvious that the Administration would not compromise on the employer mandate, he developed his own proposal.

Toward the end of the Committee process, Chafee and Breaux assumed leadership roles among the moderates on the Committee. They worked together through the Mainstream Coalition to get a bill through the Committee.

A handful of staff played key roles throughout: Sheila Burke from Dole's staff; Christy Ferguson from Chafee's office and Moynihan's Lawrence O'Donnell. These three had extensive knowledge and strong political instincts. They not only influenced their own Senators but also other Senators and their staffs. They were highly regarded across party lines.

Q: Who were the "consensus builders"—the people who understood each member's underlying agenda and understood where there might be agreement?

By the end of the Committee process, the Committee seemed to be driven by the small group of moderates in the Mainstream Coalition led by Chafee and Breaux. Although some Members within each party were angered that Chafee and Breaux, as well as the other members, were bucking party leadership to develop a consensus, the respective leadership of both parties allowed it to move forward. Neither Dole nor Mitchell seemed willing to step in and ask their side not to work with the other.

Among this small group it is difficult to say that any of them really had an agenda other than getting a bill passed. Although the majority of the members, Democrats and Republicans alike, opposed the employer mandate, their major goals seemed to be to lower health care costs and increase coverage. Chafee and Breaux as leaders of the group were more facilitators and the official spokespersons. The members of the group were all equal partners, and these roles continued as the bill moved out of the Finance Committee and onto the Senate floor. Over time, the number of Coalition members expanded.

Q: Given that there were continuing differences, how was consensus reached so that the committee could report out?

Once the Coalition reached a consensus on major issues they agreed to vote as a bloc. Since the Chairman and Majority Leader wanted to get a bill through the Committee, they had no choice but to accept the Coalition's position on various issues. Some might go so far as to call it blackmail. None of the Coalition members were under any illusions that the leadership would continue to support their positions once the bill was reported from the Committee. In fact, both Mitchell and Moynihan stated on several votes during Committee consideration that they were voting with the Coalition only to get a bill through the Committee. Coalition members knew they would have to fight the same battles again when the bill came to the Senate floor.

Q: How did staff get chosen? How did they work out (or not work out) relationships among themselves? How did this affect the work of the committee?

Staff choices are based on many factors. Having expertise on an issue or area is probably the most critical aspect for a legislative assistant, particularly for those who work on issues within the Committee. For example, if a Senator is on the Finance Committee, it is important for his or her health staff to have expertise in Medicare, Medicaid, as well as insurance market reform issues. Since public health is not within the jurisdiction of the Finance Committee, a background in public health is not as critical as it would be for a Senator on the Labor and Human Resources Committee which has jurisdiction over public health programs.

It is also useful to be from the Senator's home state and having political connections doesn't hurt. It can really vary from office to office and from one position to another within the same office.

The relationship among staffers can play a role in how policy is set. Although most professional staffers advise their Senators based on policy and political considerations, it is not unheard of for a staffer's ego to color that advice. Relationships among staff can certainly have an effect on policy decisions.

During the health care reform discussions, many staff relationships developed based on a combination of the role the Senator took during consideration, the staff's leadership abilities and political instincts, and the expertise of the staff in a particular issue area. Among Republicans during the health reform debate, Sheila Burke was the obvious leader. Not only was she the staff director for Minority Leader Dole, but her area of expertise was health care.

Another leader was Christy Ferguson, Chafee's legislative director, although there was considerable tension. A number of staffers wanted their Senators to be the recognized leader in health care. Over time, as Chafee emerged as a leader among the moderate wing of the Party, in part due to Christy's efforts, she emerged as a staff leader both among Republican staff and the bipartisan Mainstream Coalition staff.

Q: Who were the major interest groups? What did they each want? And how did they work?

Interest groups played a considerable role in the health reform debate. While some were influential among Senators from both parties, some were clearly counting on one party or the other to look out for their interests.

Since the employer mandate was one of the most controversial issues, special interests seemed to line up on either side of the issue. For Democrats, the most vocal special interests were the unions and large companies that had unionized employees such as Chrysler and GM. Conversely, small businesses tended to look to Republicans to look out for their interests in the debate.

Other special interests that played key roles in the debate were: the American Association of Retired Persons, the American Hospital Association, the Federation of American Health Systems (for profit hospitals), the Health Insurance Association of America, the Group Health Association of America (managed care plans), the American Medical Association. Nurses, other non-physician provider groups, and countless others were also active.

Their roles were different. Some had a key issue that was important to them and they were not concerned with the overall structure of the bill. For example: some wanted mandatory coverage of a specific benefit which they provided. Others were interested in overall structural issues—whether the final proposal included an employer mandate, or whether costs would be controlled through market forces or by the government.

Those in the moderate camp tended to get advice and information from a cross section of organizations and individuals. Some lobbyists were consulted because of who they represented while others were consulted because of expertise on issue areas or their political experience—often a combination of the two were desirable. Some had clear Republican ties. Debbie Steelman and Gail Wilensky had been health policy advisors to President Bush. Tom Scully and Don Moran were current and former officials with the Office of Management and Budget. Mike Bromberg from the Federation of American Health Systems was also consulted frequently. Other experts had Democratic ties. Stan Jones, affiliated with George Washington University and Richard Froh with Kaiser Permanente, both former Kennedy staffers, were well respected by Democrats and Republicans alike. Many of these folks, while representing a specific interest, could also be trusted to step out of their roles as representatives of groups or companies and give neutral policy and political advice.

Q: *Describe the final committee report. What did the committee achieve in the end? Not achieve?*

In theory, the health care reform proposal that was reported out of the Finance Committee was a proposal that represented a compromise between the Clinton Bill and the more conservative Dole/Packwood proposal. It was a variation of the managed competition theory developed by Alan Enthoven. Where the Clinton proposal took managed competition and added government regulation, the Mainstream Coalition proposal removed a few of the most controversial provisions in an attempt to address some of the biggest criticisms of the Clinton plan.

If the sign of a good compromise is that neither side is happy, the Mainstream Coalition had the perfect bill. Everyone hated it. After the Finance Committee reported the bill, the Majority Leader attempted to blend the proposal with the bill reported out by the Committee on Labor and Human Resources. By the time the bill came to the floor, it was so similar to the Clinton proposal that none of the Coalition members could support it.

After Committee markup, the Mainstream Coalition expanded. As it became clear to Mitchell that he did not have the votes to pass the bill that he brought to the floor, he made overtures to the group seeking a compromise. Shortly thereafter, unions and consumer groups sent a letter to the Majority Leader stating that the proposal was unacceptable because it did not go far enough, and that health care reform should be abandoned for the year. This was a bill that, according to the Congressional Budget Office would spend over $700 billion in federal subsidies over 10 years for low- and middle-income families to purchase health insurance. CBO estimated that by the end of that ten-year period, approximately 90% of Americans would have had health insurance coverage. On the other extreme, the business and insurance community had decided to oppose the proposal because it went too far.

As the days wore on, in fact, some of the moderate Democrats in our group started moving to the right of many of the group's Republicans. There were some conservative southern Democrats that would have voted with Dole in opposition to our proposals had it come to the floor.

In reality, by the time the Finance Committee reported a bill, it was already too late to enact a health reform proposal. The Committee finished its work in July, four months before the mid-term Congressional elections.

The Clinton bill was becoming increasingly unpopular and the extremes of each party were convinced that it was time to abandon the issue and use health reform as a campaign issue instead.

31

The Politics of Health Care Reform

Julie Kosterlitz

Last September, about the time the health care reform issue went into a political free fall, a U.S. Air flight plowed into the earth, killing all those on board. When the press corps, on behalf of a understandably jittery public, pressured a federal investigator for the cause of the accident, he cautioned them to be patient. The early answers, he told, them, often turn out to be wrong.

In politics, however, analysts show little such forbearance. Indeed, many commentators were already declaiming on the causes of health care reform's demise well before the patient had been officially pronounced dead—a "pre-post-mortem" if you will.

But we, too, should be careful about our conclusions. What we take away from this episode will shape our attitudes about what can and ought to happen next. Unlike the airplane investigator, we will likely never have a definitive answer: no flight recorder, no jammed wing flaps. When it comes to history, all we have are collective judgments, and these can prove both malleable and volatile. We must scrutinize the pronouncements all the more when they are rendered in Washington—that most political of towns, around election-time—that most political of seasons. Most of the pronouncements we read in the newspapers are intended more to influence the collective view that to reflect it.

Thus, for example, Republican strategist William Kristol declared in a September memo that the demise of health care reform reflected the fact that "the goals driving a government-directed overhaul of American health care were essentially flawed...and were conclusively rejected by an informed American people." First Lady Hillary Rodham Clinton and some pro-reform advocates counterclaim that this was a case in point of special interests frustrating public aspirations to "health care that's always there."

This presentation was made on November 18, 1994, at the University of Michigan Forum on Health Policy.

But in the collective judgment of the public—to the extent this is reflected in opinion polls—both Kristol and Mrs. Clinton are right. In a September 12 CBS/New York *Times* poll that allowed respondents to pick several answers in a multiple choice question about what they blamed for health care's demise, "too much government" and "special interests" tied for first place.

Even a dual explanation, however, ignores the complexity of this debate. It ignores, for example, the profound public ambivalence that surrounded the debate. The Clinton plan may have been rejected in large part for its reliance on big government. But a large dose of government may have been inescapable to achieve what the public resoundingly said it wanted: universal coverage and lower costs. "Health Care That's Always There" sounded good to a public made jumpy by the recession of the early 1990s. But income redistribution, and restraints in health care spending that might change or put a crimp in the kind of care most Americans were accustomed to did not.

The Administration seems to have believed that a popular end would exonerate unpopular means, and that the short-term dislocation would be more than offset by the long term gains. Constraints on runaway health care spending, they argued, would eventually ease the pressure on family, corporate, as well as state and federal budgets, and free up money that could be spent on other priorities.

But this was bound to be a tough sell. Americans and their institutions are not known for their propensity to take the long view. Their demand for short term results has been duly noted by their elected representatives.

The payoffs, however, were not only distant but subtle to most people. Remember, reform advocates weren't promising to actually roll back health care prices, or the share of gross national product consumed by health spending—they were only promising that prices, or spending would *rise less than it otherwise might have*. That may elate economists, but it's hardly a rallying point for the middle class. Moreover, under the Administration's scheme, 30 per cent of the already insured would have had to pay more. Most of these would have received better benefits, but some would be paying more for roughly the same benefits. The public didn't have the statistics, but they caught and amplified the rumblings: an ABC News/Washington *Post* poll from November of 1993 showed that 60 percent of the public believed they would pay more for health insurance under the Clinton plan.

The potential pitfalls, by contrast, were easily grasped. Even a hint of more government, at a time of unusually high disenchantment with government, was bound to raise hackles. So too would a whiff of "government rationing," and the threat of being shepherded away from traditional fee-for-service medicine into the alien world of "alliances" and "accountable health plans" that opponents could tar as "K-mart care". No matter that the status quo was rife with failings, or that additional rationing and reorganizing of health care were likely from the private sector even in the absence of reform. By devising a blueprint for the future, the Administration became the target for all of the public's anxieties about change.

Public misunderstanding of the tradeoffs for universal coverage and health care cost control made reform a tough sell. But the Administration only made things worse by pandering to these unrealistic expectations. Instead of acknowledging and making a straightforward case for the sacrifices entailed in their plan, the Administration reformers, led by master architect and Clinton's Oxford buddy, Ira Magaziner, poured most of its creative energy into concealing them.

Faced with the public's unwillingness to pay more taxes, the Administration plan mandated all employers to contribute to the cost of workers health insurance—a cost that would be made up out of workers' wages and in some cases, their jobs—and devised an intricate system of hidden cross-subsidies within their health care alliances. Confronted with the public's mistrust of government, the Administration plan created "health care alliances" which were elaborate new, quasi-public superstructures that—as best anyone could tell—would function like and have its budgets set by government. Confronted by public fears about rationing, the Administration claimed that its plan would, with surgical precision, excise only waste, fraud and abuse.

To be fair, Magaziner was only attempting to deliver what Clinton had promised during his presidential campaign: high-quality, guaranteed comprehensive care that built on the current private system, without an upfront tax increase ... in short, something for nothing or for almost nothing. Moreover, it's not clear that the Administration would have fared any better had it been open about the sacrifices involved: the ghost of the failed 1982 candidacy of Walter Mondale still haunts the Democratic party.

It is clear, however, that trying to gloss over the sacrifices did not work. The Administration's architects had to go through massive contortions to achieve reform's goals while simultaneously maintaining the illusion of a taxless, privately-run system. The result was a system so complicated it was never possible to explain to the public. No one was fooled by the artifice. The public fervently wanted its leaders to deliver the impossible—but it rather quickly came to disbelieve them when they promised to comply. The plan's complexity and a public climate of suspicion created fertile soil on which opponents could cultivate active opposition.

The failings of the plan were compounded by the Administration's alternately high-handed and ham-handed public relations techniques. From the outset, it seemed bent on alienating whatever key constituencies it didn't simply ignore. Attempting to smuggle 500 people into Washington to secretly restructure the nation's health care system wasn't merely futile, but needlessly created ill will with the Washington press corps, the U.S. Congress and the medical-industrial complex. Belated and token consultations and briefings by top White House officials ended up merely adding insult to injury. Disappointed lobbyists sported buttons that read "But Ira promised"—complaining that Magaziner in private audiences repeatedly offered empty assurances that their top concerns would be addressed. Alarmed, they began to fight back.

After the plan's release, the public relations and tactical errors seemed to proliferate. Disorganized aides failed to keep pace with public and congressional demand for speakers knowledgeable about the plan; the top salesman himself was beset by distractions from Bosnia to bimbos. And the Administration began shifting its emphasis away from security for the middle-class insured, and towards helping the uninsured, allowing the opposition to insinuate—erroneously—that health care reform was another welfare initiative.

Finally, repeated delays in devising and handing off the plan to Congress meant that by the time it faced serious consideration, the President had already used up many of his political chits. He watched his personal popularity decline dangerously as the debate was pushed into a volatile election year.

These tactical blunders, however, still beg the question: could a more skillful politician have won over the public? A variety of opinion polls from the past two years suggest that the public climate that would have made life difficult for any reformer. There was frustration that government hadn't done more to solve pressing social and economic problems on the one hand, and a deep and abiding mistrust of government's ability to do so on the other.

This public ambivalence dogged the health care debate even before it got going. It helps account for Clinton's 43 percent share of the popular vote, which in turn helps account for the difficulties he had pushing through most items on his ambitious agenda.

The ambivalence also exacerbated splits within political parties, and meant that Clinton couldn't rely on the Democratic majority in Congress to enact his plan or some derivative. Indeed, conservative Democrats were initially the most effective opponents of the Clinton plan. Conservative Democratic Rep. Jim Cooper, D-Tenn., came up with a centrist alternative to the Clinton plan which—whatever its feasibility or public popularity—gave large insurers and large employers something to rally around and to shield themselves from charges of being anti-reform. Cooper, along with his like-minded colleague Jim Slattery, D-Kansas, who were both embroiled in tough races for statewide office—were also critical swing votes on the House Energy and Commerce Committee, whose defections doomed the

The Politics of Health Care Reform

committee's ability to pass out a bill. Over in the Senate, the Democratic chairman of the all-important Finance Committee, Daniel Patrick Moynihan of New York, was ambivalence personified—alternately promising to help the Administration achieve its goals and publicly casting aspersions on the effort. In the end, he chose to sit out the debate, leaving a leaderless, ad hoc group of centrists from both parties to try, vainly, to engineer a compromise.

Election year politics further polarized the debate. Emboldened by their gains in special elections in May 1994, Republicans became persuaded they could win—big—by capitalizing on Americans' unusually high level of disaffection with government. William Kristol himself took the lead in exhorting party members to abandon compromise efforts on health care reform, arguing they would be better positioned to win if they cast health care reform as a symbol of big government, and campaigned against it.

Kristol argued Republicans should abandon reform efforts because they were wrong-headed. But it seems clear that Republicans knew that their opposition would force gridlock, thus fanning anti-government sentiment. The resulting backlash, moreover, was likely to disproportionately hurt Democrats, who comprised the majority of incumbents and the party in power.

Kristol's argument not only resonated with the party's right wing, but had a decided impact on a key moderate: then-Senate Minority Leader (now Majority leader) Robert Dole of Kansas. As a likely presidential candidate in 1996, he couldn't afford to be outflanked by the party's right. By June, Dole had abandoned his long-standing support for a moderate Republican bill that included a mandate that individuals buy health insurance, as a way to reach universal coverage, a bill widely seen as a basis for compromise with the Democrats. Dole also pulled other key moderates with him, most notably Sen. Bob Packwood, of Oregon. Having been on record supporting an employer mandate for 20 years, Packwood, enmeshed in political troubles stemming from sexual harassment allegations against him, dropped his support of mandates and sided with Dole against compromise.

Interest groups representing those with a financial stake in the status quo also exploited public mistrust of government. The small-to-midsized insurers in the Health Insurance Association of America and insurance brokers that had flourished under the status quo were concerned that the Clinton plan would put them out of business. But their multi-million dollar advertising and grass-roots organizing campaigns were aimed at persuading people that government involvement would mean rationing of care, large bureaucracies and less freedom of choice in how they received care. The Annenberg School of Journalism has estimated that interest group spending on television commercials on the health care reform issue outstripped the campaign expenditures of the Presidential candidates in 1993. Taking no chances, interest groups also dramatically increased their contributions to congressional campaigns: an analysis by Citizen Action, an unabashedly pro-reform consumer group, found that in the 21 months ending September 20, 1994, health and insurance businesses and trade groups had upped their contributions by 65 per cent over the same period during the previous election cycle.

If it does nothing else, the forgoing should reinforce the warning I made at the outset: when it comes to explaining the cause of health care's demise, beware the simple and speedy conclusions.

Some of them contain just enough truth to be seductive. But they are often selective and self-serving. When Kristol suggests that reform's demise reflects public rejection of big government, we must remember that much of public's disgust with government comes from its inability to get things done. We must also remember that it was in some part due to calculated intransigence by Republicans that compromise was not reached.

Similarly, when Hillary Clinton points a finger at "special interests" for subverting the interests of the people, it's worth remembering that the White House, with the best bully pulpit in the land, did a third rate job of explaining to people why the plan was in their best interest. And it's worth noting that the distinction between special interests and the public has become increasingly blurred in recent years as people define their self interest more narrowly. Individuals looked at health care reform in terms of their individual status—as Medicare recipients, insurance brokers, hospital employees, or the already well-insured—and found it wanting. There was, seemingly, no constituency for a bill that promised broad societal benefits over time. Special interests, it turns out, aren't just the top brass and shareholders in the health care industry—special interests are also "us."

The crashing and burning of health care reform is going to make a lot of politicians either take the train next time or just stay home. But only sifting through the wreckage carefully will give us the clues we need to prevent a political nose-dive the next time the debate takes wing.

32

The Politics of Comprehensive National Health Care Reform: Watching the 103rd and 104th Congresses at Work

Sallyanne Payton, L.L.B.

The failure of comprehensive health care reform in the 103rd Congress was, in the language of social science, "overdetermined": it seems that almost everything that could have gone wrong did. The effort had a star-crossed quality from the beginning. In addition to the usual difficulties that attend any attempt to enact legislation reorganizing an entire industry, the unique burdens of comprehensive health care reform included an inexperienced White House headed by a President who had not received a majority of the popular vote; a mammoth White House Task Force[1] summoned to work in extensively-trumpeted "secrecy"; the illness and death of the First Lady's father in the Spring of 1993 just at the point when critical decisions had to be made; the diversion of the President's attention because of crises abroad; the indictment of the Chairman of the House Ways and Means Committee; and the skepticism and uncooperativeness of the well-respected Chairman of the Senate Finance Committee. Any one of these conditions by itself might have been fatal. Collectively, they created difficulties that could not be surmounted given the procedures, the policy issues and the politics that structured the environment in which comprehensive reform was proposed and considered.

Procedure

Comprehensive reform was in jeopardy simply because of the magnitude and complexity of the legislative effort required to enact it. There was a mismatch between the comprehensiveness of the President's proposal

---

This chapter developed from the author's presentation at the April 1, 1995, University of Michigan Forum on Health Policy. It was written in June 1997.

and the fragmented nature of the process of congressional consideration. The President's proposal, though gargantuan, was finely crafted and its parts coherently interrelated, to the point of its being vulnerable to the criticism that it could not easily be disassembled and its parts considered separately. However, the Senate and House Democratic leadership declined to create joint or special committees to consider health care reform, with the consequence that the President's proposal had to be referred to five committees in the House and three in the Senate. Each committee was empowered and inclined to act independently. The congressional procedure called for the leadership of the respective houses to craft at the end a composite bill from the work of the various committees. Those bills would have to be steered into enactment by the House and Senate and resolved in conference, resulting in a piece of legislation that President Clinton would be willing to sign.

This procedure might simply have run out of time even under the best of circumstances. A single Congress lasts for only two years and congressional elections are held in November of even-numbered years. In order to enact legislation as enormous as comprehensive health care reform, with its unique complexity and complicated procedural situation, a majority coalition should have been coalescing around a politically and technically viable approach to reform by the time of the Memorial Day recess of 1994.

This turned out to be unachievable. For a variety of reasons, many of them unrelated to health care reform, the Congress did not receive the President's bill until November 1993. The process of congressional consideration did not commence in earnest until the Congress reconvened in January 1994. What happened to health care reform in the 103rd Congress must be understood against the background of this impossibly compressed time frame.

Policy

The attempt to enact comprehensive reform must also be understood against the background of the larger policy issues that were shaping the general politics of the 103rd Congress. National health insurance as an idea is strongly associated with social democracy and the ideal of the welfare state and consequently with conventional liberalism, which itself has been under continuous fire since the late 1960s. By 1993 the conventional liberals could not muster a majority in either house of Congress even though Democrats nominally controlled both the House and the Senate. Any national health insurance scheme proposed in the Clinton years would, in order to succeed, have to gain the support of some number of centrist Republicans willing to form a bipartisan coalition.

For purely political reasons, quite apart from the details of program design, achieving bipartisan consensus on a tax-financed universal national health insurance system was at best unlikely. President Clinton's election marked the first time since the Carter Administration that Democrats would control both the White House and the Congress, ending a long period of "divided government" and potentially ending the state of governmental paralysis known as "gridlock." President Clinton had defeated President Bush partly on the strength of his promise to reform the health care system, and it seemed likely that his success in doing so would make his own re-election and continued Democratic majorities in the Congress more probable.

Health care reform thus had the potential to revive conventional liberalism, which had appeared to have lost favor with the public. Over the preceding 20 or so years a large number of the people most likely to vote in American elections, encouraged by the conservative political movement, appeared to have become persuaded that government social programs, particularly those associated with the federal government, were mainly means of distributing assets from themselves to poor people and members of racial minorities. The middle-class demand for health care reform could be interpreted as a change in attitude, an acknowledgment that government, even the *federal* government, might be able to do something about a problem that the middle classes regarded as being at the heart of their own interests. If President Clinton could succeed at health care reform he might have an opportunity to cement middle-class loyalty to the federal government. This was a moment to be seized, and the high-profile Clinton health care reform effort was designed to secure President Clinton's place in history by seizing it.

Sensing the same historic moment that the liberals perceived, however, conservative strategists were equally determined to seize it for themselves. In their finely-observed account of the health care reform effort[2] Haynes Johnson and David Broder report that Newt Gingrich, then an obscure congressman from Georgia, had anticipated before the 1992 presidential election that the liberals would try to create a national health insurance system, that he would thwart their effort and that the consequence would be that the Republicans would become the majority party and he would become Speaker of the House.

That both sides could have seen this as "their moment" is a reflection of the fact that Democratic control of both the White House and the Congress was fragile. Mr. Clinton had been elected with a plurality, not a majority, of the popular vote in the three-way race of 1992: the majority of voters had chosen either President Bush or Ross Perot, a fact that led the Republican leadership to hope from the beginning of the Clinton presidency that if they could successfully represent the views of the majority of the electorate that had voted against Mr. Clinton, and deprive him of success, the Republicans might aspire to regain the presidency in 1996 and perhaps control the Senate. Notwithstanding the results of the 1992 elections, the long-term tide was running against the congressional Democrats. The liberal base was shrinking; the continuing Democratic congressional ascendancy was arguably already the artifact of the power of incumbency and Democrats' ability to reach a stable working arrangement with major business interests. Many Democratic centrists and conservatives represented districts in which conservative forces were gaining ground. They were therefore under pressure to resist supporting programs that could be characterized as conventional, "big government" liberalism.

The Republican strategy of using the Democrats' own ideological divisions to block the President's program became apparent when President Clinton submitted his first budget proposal. The Republicans refused to provide a single vote for the Clinton budget, thus forcing President Clinton to satisfy the most conservative members of his own party in order to gain a legislative majority. The budget plan succeeded by only one vote, signaling, among other things, that the President would have difficulty persuading the Congress to enact any ambitious health care reform scheme.

The drama of comprehensive health care reform in the 103rd Congress was played out against this backdrop. Republican passive non-cooperation could shift Mr. Clinton to the right, away from a "comprehensive" national solution, or force reform to fail altogether. Among Democrats, only liberals favored the most comprehensive approach, which would have involved creating a single-payer system with near-complete federal control of the health care sector; Democratic centrists, like Republican moderates, tended to prefer reforms designed to rectify by regulation some of the shortcomings of the private market without creating a new system of government-backed entitlements; and Democratic conservatives stood with their Republican counterparts in their determination to prevent the "crisis" of the health insurance system from becoming the predicate for an expansion of federal power. Given this range of opinion in their ranks, it is probable that congressional Democrats could not have enacted a comprehensive national health insurance scheme even if only Democrats had been voting.

While centrist and conservative Democrats were unwilling to create a full-scale national health insurance system, the most devoted advocates of the comprehensive approach, mainly liberals, were disinclined to squander on partial measures this rare moment when creation of a national health insurance system seemed finally possible. They were willing to extend the middle-class frustration that was creating the moment if that was the price of sustaining public demand for reform.

The liberals' insistence on comprehensive reform was soundly supported by technical considerations. Among those who had studied health policy closely enough to understand the relationship between insurance underwriting and risk pooling and the financing of provider institutions, it was conventional wisdom that the growth in the number of persons without health insurance was causing much of the crisis in the financing and delivery systems and that a significant fraction of the apparent "cost" of health care was attributable to the cross-subsidies by which provider institutions, most of which were nonprofit charitable organizations, were charging off to their paying customers the cost of uncompensated care that they were rendering to the uninsured and under-insured. It was also understood that persons who lacked insurance coverage tended to underconsume primary and preventive care and therefore sometimes to require much more expensive care for preventable illness. In the end, lack of insurance coverage might well lead to more, not less, consumption of medical services. Comprehensive reformers therefore insisted that reforms ought not be undertaken that would have the net result of shrinking the market for private health insurance and therefore of increasing the numbers of the uninsured.

Unfortunately, many popular incremental reforms would be likely to have such a result. Middle-class voters were demanding that health insurers (including self-insured employee benefit plans) be forbidden to exclude "pre-existing conditions" from coverage, and they wanted rates to be lower. It was being observed that numerous Americans were suffering from "job lock," the perception that they could not change jobs (or become self-employed) because they or their family members would not be able to obtain insurance coverage in their new circumstances.

However, to fix the private insurance market by compelling insurers to take or retain high-risk customers would result in raising the price of insurance, thus forcing some customers out of the market. Conventional wisdom was that those most likely to go without insurance when prices rose would be, in addition to those for whom the prices would be actually unaffordable, those who did not expect to experience illness. These would mainly be the younger customers, for whom health insurance would increasingly seem to be a bad bargain. In joining the ranks of the uninsured, they would increase the average riskiness of those buying insurance, forcing insurers to raise rates even higher, making insurance less affordable and contributing to the growth in the number of the uninsured.

For comprehensive reformers, then, the importance of eliminating uninsured status, that is, achieving universal coverage, was not just a matter of distributing a benefit by creating a new entitlement; it was also a determination to eliminate the "free rider" effects in the current system. Because health care institutions try to maintain a formally equal standard of care for all patients regardless of their insurance status or ability to pay, a person's lack of insurance throws the risk that that person might need medical care onto someone else, typically onto the providers and other payors whose bills include the cost of uncompensated care. A great many of the uninsured are relatively healthy persons, many of them young, many of them working part-time or for small businesses that do not pay health benefits. Their lack of coverage means that they do not contribute to the common funds out of which the community's health expenses are paid. Their absence from the insurance market also raises the average riskiness of the persons seeking coverage, therefore forcing insurers to raise rates to compensate for the greater risk. For this reason, advocates of comprehensive reform insisted that coverage be not only universal but mandatory. Because the reformers had decided to fund the system through premiums collected through payroll withholds, universal coverage also implied an "employer mandate" that would require many businesses to offer health benefits for the first time. Mandates imply subsidies for those who cannot afford the full cost of coverage, but for comprehensive reformers the idea that everyone should be in the system was a bedrock value.

Although many centrist Republicans were willing to look for methods of expanding private health insurance coverage, and were willing to find resources to support coverage for persons with low incomes, centrist Republicans have for the most part not been willing to support health care reform schemes that would create uniform national entitlements and authorize full government control of the medical industry.[3] Moreover, even those Republicans who might in other times have gone along with a competently-designed moderately statist plan were this time alert to the possibility that by stiffening their posture just a bit they might help achieve a Republican majority in Congress. In the Senate, the Republicans were led by Robert Dole, who intended to contend for the 1996 Republican presidential nomination and therefore was not disposed to help Mr. Clinton achieve a great success. The likelihood of bipartisan cooperation on a national health insurance scheme of the magnitude envisioned by liberals was therefore small. On the other hand, there was a history of bipartisan cooperation on health matters and, at least in the Senate, considerable sophistication about the need to restructure the health insurance function in both private and public sectors.

The challenge for the Clinton Administration was therefore to overcome Republicans' inclination to withhold their cooperation and instead to build on the history of bipartisanship already achieved. If anything was to be enacted in the end, it would have to be bipartisan; and the more comprehensive it was the more hugely bipartisan it would have to be. It did not, however, follow from that observation that the Clinton Administration's own proposal ought to be the product of bipartisan cooperation or that the President ought to propose reforms on which there might be initial bipartisan agreement. The Administration decided that in view of the magnitude of the effort required to restructure the entire health care industry what was required was a proposal that would generate enthusiasm coupled with will, drive, savvy, power and the willingness to use it. The hope was that the idea of reform, backed by its most committed supporters, would develop irresistible momentum and that more reluctant constituencies and stakeholders would come along if only to be included in the group at the table during the final bargaining. Indeed, at the beginning this seemed to be a plausible scenario. The prevailing political wisdom was that the middle class was demanding action and that part of the reason for President Bush's defeat had been his inability to persuade middle-class voters that he would act on their health care concerns. The fate of President Bush's Attorney General Richard Thornburgh in his Pennsylvania senatorial contest with the previously-obscure Harris Wofford was still fresh in political memory.

Republican enthusiasm did not extend, however, to anything as ambitious as the program that the Clinton planners were inclined to put together in the service of comprehensiveness. Middle-class voters were mainly interested in reforms that would enable them to buy stable, portable coverage at affordable prices. The complexities of the health care system and of health care financing were quite beyond the public debate. Some moderate Senate Republicans who had studied the health issue understood, however, the central importance of achieving universal coverage, and at the outset were willing to impose a combination of employer and individual mandates to achieve that goal.

Was there a moment, perhaps in the Spring of 1993, when it would have been possible to have enacted a bill that would have provided universal coverage if, for example, the Clinton Administration had simply thrown its weight behind a centrist Republican bill? Perhaps. If so, the moment passed. At the White House, a reform proposal of very ambitious architecture was taking shape under the direction of Ira Magaziner, one that was substantially beyond the ability of most moderate Republicans to support.

A word may be in order here about the essential differences between conservatives and liberals as those differences were manifesting themselves in the 103rd Congress. Because they are concerned with tax burdens, representing mainly the persons taxed rather than those who are visibly dependent on tax-financed expenditures, conservatives tend to seek minimalism and efficiency in government operations, and to oppose proposals for government programs that create direct bonds of patronage between individuals and the federal government, since patronage increases the constituency for government itself. As of the time when national health care reform was being debated, only the elderly and the poor enjoyed comprehensive patronage relationships with the federal government: elderly persons received income transfers through Social Security and medical coverage through Medicare; many poor persons received some form of federal income support and a somewhat larger group that included the working poor was eligible for medical coverage through federally-assisted state Medicaid programs. A program of universal mandatory national health insurance would expand this relationship drastically, creating direct patronage bonds between the federal government and virtually every person in the nation, and would bring the entire health care sector within a system of federal regulation and funding. A very large number of new institutions would be required to operate such a system; each of those institutions would become part of the infrastructure of government and part of the constituency for this function of government. Regardless of the technical justification for taking this course, conservatives would view the result with the greatest suspicion.

Viewing the same possible range of outcomes, liberals would have reason to applaud. For the advocates of national health insurance, comprehensive reform meant moving from the current "fragmented" health care system to one more centrally managed that could administer and enforce government policy. Both ethical and technical considerations reinforced conventional liberals' historic preference for a large-scale tax-financed, government-administered social welfare program of the type associated with other industrialized countries such as England, Germany and Canada, and in this country with the New Deal and the Great Society. The stage was therefore set for a clash over the principles of organizing government and its relationship to the private sector, as a counterpoint to conflict over the technical and ethical issues surrounding health care, which were by themselves difficult enough.

Health care reform was being considered, however, at just the time when even proponents of government systems were beginning to appreciate the benefits to be achieved by allowing internal markets in the actual delivery of services. Indemnity insurance was in decline generally, and fee-for-service medicine was blamed for much of the overconsumption that had driven the American system into crisis. The solution seemed to lie in "managed care," which was an integration of insurance and service delivery functions, placing providers at financial risk and giving the payor control over the delivery of services. Managed care enjoyed a good reputation among health policy experts of both liberal and conservative political shades. For liberals, managed care was attractive because it tended to promote medical efficiency, allowing a redirection of resources away from high-cost acute care for diseases and toward primary and preventive services; for conservatives, managed care promised to reduce the amount of economic waste that seemed to characterize the medical services industry and to give consumers choices as to how much they wanted to spend on health care and how they wanted that care to be organized. Common ground was the perception that managed care organizations could engage in and stimulate price competition in the industry, and thereby aid in the cause of cost containment.

There was the further possibility that managed care would allow an organization to run a large health benefit program without having to create a large bureaucracy or exercise tight regulatory controls. Already a number of employers, including both private employers and federal and state government employee benefit plans, were procuring their health benefits through a form of competition: they operated internal markets for their employees where the employees might choose among approved plans and carriers. The employer's role was limited to selecting the plans to be allowed to compete and managing the competition among them as by, for example, requiring certain benefits or limiting prices or enrollment practices. Some private market reformers were arguing that smaller employers ought to be empowered to create health insurance purchasing cooperatives that would operate on similar principles. This technique became known as "managed competition," and it was generally understood that the most successful competitors on price would be managed care plans that could control their costs, partly by controlling the patients' consumption of medical services. Managed care and managed competition would therefore allow care to be rationed by the market, as an incidence of cost control, rather than as a function of articulate public policy.

The idea of blending government control of revenue collection, risk pooling and overall program management with price competition among service providers for the patronage of individual program beneficiaries was catching on even in Europe, where the trend in health care reform seemed to be toward internal markets under government-controlled financing schemes, principally single payer systems. This distribution of functions was thought to afford the government power to control the total resources flowing into medical services while stimulating greater efficiency in the delivery of care and greater responsiveness to consumers on the part of providers, which have historically tended to hold government monopolies. In the European systems, however, the decisions to have universal coverage, rationing and overall budget controls were already made and were not being reconsidered; the adoption of internal market techniques is a matter of improving the efficiency of the production of services.

In the United States, by contrast, the questions *whether* to create a tax-financed national health insurance system, *whether* to make it universal and mandatory, *whether* to subject the medical services sector to overall resource consumption constraints and *whether* to adopt an internal market system for the procurement of services were all on the table simultaneously in the 103rd Congress. Liberal advocates of national health insurance might well have answered "yes" to all four questions without significant hesitation, leaving for negotiation the details of *how* to design the program. Conservatives would surely answer "no" to all four questions. The question was where the center lay, because that would be the terrain on which bipartisan consensus might be achieved. Moderates might be willing to answer "yes" to the question *whether* a program with these general features should be developed if the *how* was acceptable in the context of their general preference for market-based solutions and did not do violence to other values that they held dear, such as maintaining the national pre-eminence in medical technology. There was thus a mismatch: for the committed advocates of national health insurance the question of technique was a matter of detail, even detail that could be adjusted in the light of experience once the principle of universal coverage was established; for the more skeptical, technique was a major element that would make the program acceptable or objectionable.

The Clinton Administration gambled that it could design a technically feasible national health insurance system with universal coverage and sufficiently robust internal markets to deflect any suggestion that it intended comprehensive reform to result in a nationalization of the health care industry. Managed competition could be the bridge connecting public and private sectors, liberals and moderates. In its main features, therefore, the Clinton Plan was designed to emulate the existing private systems operated by large employers: consumers were to be organized into large purchasing cooperatives, eventually called Health Alliances; approved health plans would bid for individual customers; the federal government would control enrollment so as to avoid risk selection; prices would be determined by competitive bidding subject to a price control cap. It was to be the Federal Employees' Health Benefit Plan, scaled up dramatically and covering everyone except the very largest employers who would be able to continue to operate their own plans. Other employers would pay premiums on behalf of their employees, subject to some cost-sharing with the employees, and individuals without employers would be required to pay for themselves. There would be subsidies based on ability to pay. Regulatory and enforcement duties were to be distributed among state and federal agencies.

Politics

Notwithstanding the opportunities presented by the "managed competition" technique, on any objective appraisal the political base supporting universal coverage was thin, the opposition to comprehensive reform intense and the likelihood of success low. The most reliable supporters of universal coverage were the large industrial labor unions; the other reliable backers were, or should have been, health care providers that would have seen effective demand for their services rise if patients had a source of payment. This would be particularly true of those providers, such as nonprofit hospitals, that were giving large amounts of uncompensated care to uninsured persons. Providers, however, could expect to suffer some disruption of their markets and increase in government control as a consequence of the creation of a national health insurance system, and they would need to protect their corporate interests even while they might advocate universal coverage as a matter of principle.[4] They therefore tended to be ambivalent and self-protective.

The apparent public support for what was being described as "health care reform" was a weak reed. Middle-class dissatisfaction with the present state of affairs did not assure informed and vigorous support for universal coverage, come what may. As Karlyn Bowman[5] points out in her paper in this volume, the public opinion pollsters were consistently producing information tending to suggest that the public that supported health care reform would not necessarily support government price and consumption controls of the magnitude that would be rendered necessary by a rigorous implementation of the idea of universal coverage, even as mitigated by the techniques of "managed competition." The public said that it supported universal coverage but it said just as clearly that did not want Big Government and was worried that a national health insurance program might result in a lowering of the quality of care.

Moreover, the "public" in the health care reform debate was not the classically diffuse constituency described by political scientists: individuals were stakeholders in the debate over health care reform quite as much as providers and insurers were. Persons likely to vote tend to be employed and are therefore likely to be covered by private health insurance, and the middle class had something to lose in reform because of the redistributive effects of universal coverage. The danger was that the middle class would see Big Government in the regulatory scheme, would see universal coverage as a liberal social program for the poor and minorities, and would not see the proposed new system as the necessary foundation for the coverage security and price restraint that it wanted for itself. The public would have to be persuaded that the Clinton Plan was what it actually wanted. Since it was only public support for health care reform that was making the idea politically thinkable, a falling off of that public support would doom the reform effort.

With the political situation so fragile, what wants explaining is why the Clinton Administration, as it appeared at the time, staked the Presidency on the success of its health care reform initiative. Some of the answer is supplied by the workings of simple "politics": the President was anxious to make a place for himself in history and by so doing secure his re-election. There was, however, and continues to be, more to the health care issue than the satisfaction of interest groups or the pursuit of political career. In the health care arena, government itself has interests. Governments, like other large employers, bear the escalating costs of care and assume some of the cost of serving the uninsured through the "cost shifting" that occurs when providers charge their paying customers an amount designed to cover bad debts incurred in rendering service to persons who do not pay.

Government-run (mainly county) hospitals take care of large numbers of uninsured persons, whose costs are borne by the taxpayers. Most urgently, government health benefit programs are the insurers of last resort. In addition to covering the elderly, the poor and the disabled they also cover many low-wage persons whose employers do not provide health benefits. Much of the most acute distress in the health care system was consequently being felt by government: the crisis in government finance is caused mainly by the cost of Medicare and Medicaid, which are the largest uncontrollable expenditures. From the perspective of government as insurer and provider of last resort, a chief attraction of a national health insurance program providing universal private coverage was that it might both bring new revenues to pay for the currently uninsured and shift some of the burden of finance into a privatized rate structure. Such a system could be comprehensively cost-controlled as well, which would deal both with the government's problems in financing its own programs and with the larger economic problem that the health sector generally was absorbing too much of the gross domestic product. It was plausible to trace a number of domestic problems to the rising costs of health care. Corporations were spending money on employee health benefits that could be used to finance an economic expansion; workers were not experiencing real wage gains because so much of the gain was being devoted to paying for rising health care expenditures. Many students of the economy of the medical services industry believe that the pattern of national expenditures on health care represented wasteful overconsumption stimulated by poorly-designed third-party payment systems and that some of the labor and capital devoted to health care constituted economic waste that could have been put to more productive use. President Clinton, who has an impressive ability to understand the interconnectedness of things, appreciated the urgency of dealing with this situation and was determined to reach a solution that was not just a quick political fix, but rather would deal with the actual problem. His background as a former governor also led him to commit strongly to a state-run program instead of direct federal administration as in Medicare.

Creating in one legislative gulp a system with universal coverage, internal markets, cost control and a federal structure presented a daunting technical challenge, hence the decision to form the President's Task Force on National Health Care Reform. As a candidate, Bill Clinton had committed to design his health care reform plan as a system of managed competition under a global budget and had moreover promised, gratuitously, to have a program in the first 100 days. The Clinton Administration thus committed to a program design that would necessarily have a staggering level of complexity and that could not be designed in the time allotted. It would thus always be open to the charge of being behind schedule, even when it was doing as well as reasonably might be expected.

The design task the President set for his people was impossible; but it was either more or less impossible than it seemed, depending on the definition of the real task. How much did the White House actually have to do? Since the point is to have an enacted statute in the end, one needs to think backwards from the final result one wants to achieve. Legislating is done in the legislature: the president's allies in the Congress manage the president's program in the legislative process. The executive branch may help in assembling the legislative coalition, which may involve dealing with interest groups; but the action takes place in Congress.

Because enacting a president's program requires cooperation between the branches, it is extremely rare for an administration to try to handle the drafting and political coalition-building functions itself without consulting or cooperating with its congressional allies. Sometimes there is an "administration bill"; but just as frequently the executive will provide political and intellectual support but not have a bill. The President may issue a message on a subject, or have a proposal that consists of some presidential objectives not yet addressed in legislative language. The executive agency that will be involved in administration typically collaborates with the administration's congressional allies and provides technical assistance to the legislative process.

From the time when the composition and conduct of the President's Task Force signaled that the Clinton Administration was going to attempt to draft a bill without the close involvement of its congressional allies, assemble the supportive interest group coalition in the process of drafting its own bill, and then simply present the completed product to the Congress, there was reason to doubt that an enactable bill was likely to be produced. The doubts were exacerbated by the "secrecy" of the Task Force, which generated criticism on the grounds of its process without actually achieving even ordinary levels of confidentiality.

The isolation in which the White House was working contributed to its experts' inclination to seek in the design of the program a high level of intellectual comprehensiveness and coherence rather than allow the much looser design processes that occur in the congressional process. As John Dingell, then Chairman of the House Commerce Committee, points out in his interview in this volume,[6] the Congress is accustomed to creating programs without thinking through all the problems and implications. Legislating is a continuous activity: the committee that creates a program maintains continuing legislative power over it, and authority to oversee administration; between them the committee and the agency (sometimes contentiously) work out the problems and issues uncovered in the course of administration. The first statute enacted on a subject is the beginning, not the end, of a legislative story; details can be adjusted over time.

The alternative approach is to try to achieve comprehensive rationality before committing an idea to law. Comprehensive rationality requires that the reasoning that goes into the construction of proposal be state-of-the-art and that its architects try to think of all alternatives, anticipate all effects, deal with every adverse result that can be foreseen. Where analytical rationality is the norm, data analysis and economic theory are the languages of public policy. The often-ridiculed dimensions of the Clinton Plan as it was submitted to the Congress was a consequence of the Clinton planners' attempt to achieve comprehensive rationality within the logic of their goal of universal coverage.

Achieving comprehensive rationality takes time: the task of constructing the Clinton Plan would have consumed many months even under more favorable circumstances. The circumstances in 1993-94 were uniquely poor for the creation of a major new federal program that relied on new techniques and institutions. Although the Congress does not aim for comprehensive rationality in program design, since the 1970s the Congress has increasingly constrained its own deliberations on budget and tax policy by requiring that proposals for new spending or reductions in revenues that might increase the deficit be identified and offsetting funds be found. The Congressional Budget Office, keeper of the disciplines of the budget process, thus stood astride the political process leading to health care reform. All of the maneuvering required to achieve a legislative majority in favor of creating a national health insurance program therefore had to be carried out within the budget rules.

On top of it all, the President had promised that the overall impact of the program would be to reduce the federal budget deficit, which meant that some persons presently getting federal money would lose it, and resources would be shifted away from existing programs, mainly Medicare and Medicaid, to this new one. Health care reform was thus to be at the opposite pole from ordinary logrolling, pork barrel politics. Major costs and rearrangements of benefits would be required by the discipline of the budget process to be estimated candidly and revealed during the deliberative process. The pressure on the numbers was intensified by the CBO's entire skepticism about the likelihood that the competition to be engendered by managed competition would moderate health care inflation. The CBO demanded backup price controls, which were immediately assumed to be the real numbers.[7]

Because the process of putting together a proposal sufficiently detailed to satisfy the White House's taste for comprehensive rationality and to be "scored" by the CBO began in the White House, the winners and losers in Clinton-style managed competition under a cap were identified before the plan was transmitted to Capitol Hill. While the White House process did not succeed in building a committed majority coalition in favor of the plan, the most dedicated opponents, mainly conservative political strategists and the more radical elements of the small business community, had time to mobilize against it. Opponents developed a grassroots strategy to turn the appearance and reality of public opinion against the Clinton Plan. The strategy of the opponents was to make the public aware that the "employer mandate" would mean declining wages and job loss in the small business sector; and the opponents also pointed out the degree to which the complex administrative machinery required to operate managed competition corresponded to the public's image of "big government." Opponents were careful not to express opposition to the goal of universal coverage; but they did point out the degree to which the means selected to achieve universal coverage placed at risk the interests and values of a large middle group of voters.

As of November 1993, when the Clinton Plan was officially transmitted to the Congress, the political weather was already heavy and the opposition massing. The intellectual communities associated with the political right, represented in this collection by William Niskanen of the Cato Institute,[8] were ready to do battle over fundamentals - the *whether*, not just the *how*, of national health insurance, while the community of larger employers could begin to see exactly how the proposed system would affect them. Most larger employers pay health benefits and operate their own employee benefit plans under the self-insurance provisions of the Employee Retirement Income Security Act of 1974 (ERISA). These larger employers had to decide whether they thought that they would be better served by a government-controlled program than by the ones they were running themselves. It was at this point, when the business community had to decide what to do, that the real dimensions of the policy disagreements became apparent.

Of all the participants in the health care reform effort, governments and their allies in the health policy profession had brought to the table the greatest amount of intellectual capital and the greatest clarity about what needed to be done. Within the health policy profession, which is an international specialty, the United States has long been regarded as anomalous among industrialized nations because of its willingness to tolerate a situation in which many of its people do not have reliable access to medical care. For the health policy experts the moment had come to bring the United States to respectability. Universal coverage was the touchstone of traditional health policy.

Traditionalists had had the debate over health policy largely to themselves until the 1970s, when the cost of Medicaid created a crisis in state government finance and the Arab Oil Embargo created a general interest in reducing the cost of employee health benefit programs. These systemic difficulties attracted the attention of mainstream economists and regulatory policy experts, who have argued for improving the state of the medical economy by improving the economic efficiency of the markets for medical services, viewing the individual as the ideal consumer, as in other markets. Mainstreamers have emphasized the market failures of the existing health care markets: the overconsumption of health insurance caused by the income tax exclusion for employer-paid health benefits, and the overconsumption of medical service caused by third-party payment.

Some mainstreamers have even, radically, suggested that the consumption of medical care ought to be thought of as being like the consumption of other goods and services, so that people ought to be able to buy only what they want, and receive only what they buy. The mainstream view tends to be a radically different view from that of traditional health policy. Traditionalists tend to assume the desirability of providing care from pooled resources, distributed according to criteria of medical need rather than income or contribution; while mainstreamers tend to assume the desirability of individual purchase of care, with pooling of resources and collective provision of care handled according to practices that make sense from the perspective of individuals who create voluntary institutions for these functions. The paradigmatic institution for the public health traditionalist is a government or a private institution with community rating such as the Blue Cross; the paradigmatic institution for the mainstreamer is a voluntary health insurance purchasing cooperative. The "managed competition" idea of constraining prices by engendering price competition among managed care organizations, as distinct from imposing government price controls, was first advanced by Alain Enthoven, a mainstreamer, in the 1970s.[9]

The policy argument over *whether* to create a national health insurance system is largely an argument between traditionalists and mainstreamers. Traditional health policy experts assumed that third-party payment was good, and ought to be expanded into a national health insurance system, and that the regulatory mechanisms required to moderate its tendency to encourage overconsumption ought to be created and made a permanent feature of government. Mainstreamers argued for reducing the role of third-party payment at the point of the consumption of services, and were entirely skeptical about the ability of the managed competition mechanism, as proposed by the Clinton planners, to hold down consumption and prices sufficiently to obviate the need for the "backup" price controls. To mainstreamers, price controls are anathema.

Both sides agree that there is public support for universal access to medical care. The question the mainstreamers have set for themselves is how to achieve universal access to care at the lowest aggregate cost consistent with the amount of money Americans are willing to spend in order to get the service they want. For some mainstreamers, that means reforming the markets to make the purchaser, the consumer and the patient the same person (or the same family unit), reforming the tax system to eliminate the bias in favor of employer-paid health benefits instead of cash wages, eliminating the bias in favor of using the proceeds of insurance instead of other resources to buy medical services, and decoupling the health insurance relationship from the employment relationship by allowing health benefits offered by other aggregations of persons (*e.g.*, unions, churches) to enjoy tax-favored status equivalent to that enjoyed by employer-paid insurance. The conservative brand of mainstream thinking has invented the Medical Savings Account, which made its first appearance in several of the Republican health care reform bills introduced into the 103rd Congress and is getting a trial as a result of a demonstration program authorized in the Kennedy-Kassebaum Act, officially known as the Health Insurance Portability and Accountability Act, enacted in the 104th Congress.

Mainstream thinking did not triumph in the 103rd Congress; rather, mainstream thinking offered a critique of the traditionalist approach and pointed toward the possibility of further intellectual development of health policy in mainstream directions. In the 103rd Congress, the contest was for the allegiance of the community of larger employers, which had seen themselves become the principal providers of private coverage and the payors of last resort for hospitals. In paying their bills to providers, major employers' health plans found themselves picking up the cost of bad debts incurred by uninsured persons and paying the shortfall between what government programs such as Medicare and Medicaid paid and what the hospitals said they actually expended to provide the service. This system of "cost-shifting" was consistent with the medical industry's historic practices; however, the magnitude of the application of the Robin Hood principle was leading major corporate employers to seek, by the late 1980s, a more broadly-based source of revenue for health care providers. The Clinton Administration's choice of an "employer mandate" that would amount to a payroll tax on all employers virtually guaranteed the opposition of businesses that had not previously been paying health insurance benefits but was broadly consistent with the interests of larger employers, whose load it would distribute.

Large employers are also, however, large corporations that have general institutional interests and attitudes that come into play when an expansion of federal power is proposed. From the point of view of corporate officers who manage employee health benefit programs it might be reasonable to conclude that, all things considered, the corporation would be better off if the government were to institute national health insurance if the taxes that the employer would pay as part of a broad-based tax to support the government's program would be less, in the aggregate, than the cost of paying for the existing health benefit plan. Thus the business organizations, such as the Washington Business Group on Health, that were composed mainly of corporate officials concerned with health benefit programs, had generally understood the issues in the same frame that was being used by traditional health experts and were generally friendly to reform that would spread the cost of care and relieve them of the cost of their retirees, which the Clinton Plan promised to do. Business organizations such as the United States Chamber of Commerce and the National Association of Manufacturers began as supportive of comprehensive health care reform in general and were friendly to the Clinton Plan in particular.

The Chamber's leadership was pulled away from its support of the Clinton Plan by intense pressure from other organizations representing small businesses. The reaction to the employer mandate of the small business community and the low-wage service industries, led by the restaurant owners, was intense opposition. To the surprise of the Clinton forces, the NAM, representing the larger businesses, announced its own opposition in February 1994, as did the Business Roundtable. This was, in a word, fatal. From that point forward, as chess players would say, the position was lost and the rest was a matter of technique. National health care reform could not succeed without the support of either the physicians or the business community, and in the end it was not to receive the support of the principal physicians' organizations.

What happened in the large business community? The short of it is that corporate managers at the CEO level did not believe that it was in their own long-term interest to trade away control of their own employee benefit programs for a government system based on the principles and structures being built into the Clinton Plan or any of the other managed competition plans. They thought they could do better. To an eye trained in mainstream economics, the managed competition design seemed unlikely to achieve its purposes. In large parts of the country there could be no competition because there were monopoly hospitals or physicians; and in the areas in which there was competition it seemed that the structure of a monopoly/monopsony Health Alliance facing what seemed certain to become a local insurer/provider network oligopoly would lead to stagnation in price and quality competition. In the business community, by contrast, there was a strong move toward managed care, which was driving down prices (quality was not yet being addressed); and provider networks were forming to serve a more demanding and sophisticated market. These developments were in an early stage; but they had behind them the robustness of the private sector while the proposals for national health insurance promised a politicized, regulated health care sector with numerous opportunities for familiar types of regulatory capture and other failings of public systems.

Into the gaps left by the intellectual opposition of mainstreamers and the withdrawal of the support of the large employers there poured the combined forces of small businesses and political conservatives determined not just to oppose comprehensive health care reform but to drive a stake through its heart. At the Michigan Health Care Forum, we were fortunate to capture the thoughts of participants in this process while it was happening, during the winter and early spring of 1994. John Dingell spoke to us, for example, in the week before he decided that he could not report a bill from his Energy and Commerce Committee; he spent some time with us wrestling with the question of how to redistribute the powers of the Health Alliances to other governmental entities. At the end, our session was held in November 1994, just a few weeks after the Republicans had won the Congress, in what was universally regarded as a repudiation of the Clinton Plan. As Len Nichols said, finally, in his delightfully candid review of the policy decision-making that went into the Clinton Plan, "the details of the exact managed competition framework finally proposed could be and were thought of as rather technical details designed merely to minimize the transitional pain, i.e., the rationing, that is implicit in the premium caps, by encouraging competitive forces underneath the caps. Unfortunately for the Administration, as wiser heads have concluded before, both God and the Devil really are in the details. For it was precisely in these relatively technical details regarding alliances and their rules about standard benefit packages, community rating, risk adjusting, etc., it was here that the absolutely crucial battle over the public characterization of the President's plan was lost...".

In the Congress, senior legislators who would have viewed the enactment of national health insurance as the capstone to their careers made valiant and doomed efforts throughout the spring and summer of 1994 to put together a plan that might command a majority. Whether things might have gone differently if Dan Rostenkowski, Chairman of the House Ways and Means Committee, had not been forced to resign his chairmanship in the face of indictment on corruption charges, is an open and interesting question. In the end, although three bills were reported out of committee in the House, no reform bill reached the floor of either house in the 103rd Congress. Republicans dug in their heels, secure in the expectation of winning the Senate in the fall elections. The Democratic leadership was unable to put together a composite bill that could pass the House. The bipartisan group in the Senate in the end admitted defeat. Time ran out. The moment passed.

The effort to achieve comprehensive health care reform did not just fade away, however; it became a kind of defining political experience for the nation, an event that lit up the political landscape and precipitated changes that had been long in the making. The political forces that had organized to oppose health care reform carried their momentum into the 1994 elections, vowing to change the composition of the Congress, particularly the House of Representatives, in which all revenue measures must originate, forever. Conservatives had been right: the Clinton Plan had given them their moment.

The 104th Congress and the Conservative Revolution Health Policy

In the 1994 congressional elections, Republicans gained control of the Congress for the first time in 40 years, in large measure on the strength of adverse public reaction to the prospect of national health insurance along the lines proposed in the 103rd Congress by the Clinton Administration and the Democratic congressional leadership. All across the country, in races that were genuinely contested Democrats were swept decisively from office. The Democratic Speaker of the House, Tom Foley of Washington, lost his own seat. Newt Gingrich, in accordance with his own prediction, became Speaker of the House.

The new Republican majority, spurred by the radical House freshmen, came with an agenda, only partially encompassed by their Contract With America: they wanted a smaller and less dominant federal government, less federal regulation, devolution of power to states and local governments, overall reductions in social programs and in individuals' access to and reliance on resources held in common and controlled politically, and an increase in "personal responsibility." Above all they wanted to reduce taxes in order to shrink government, grow the economy and empower those who earn incomes or create wealth. This agenda called for taking radical legislative action to reduce the revenues and powers of the federal government. The heart of their program was to be the tax cut.

Reducing taxes, however, means reducing the size of the budget, which means taking away from those who have favorable relations with the government the flow of resources that derive from those relationships. The rhetoric of the contemporary conservative attack on government relies on mobilizing people who think of themselves as "taxpayers" and "working families," who are the payors into government against other, less worthy categories of persons who are the payees of government and therefore can be characterized as parasitic on the productive classes. Opponents of government thus try to associate government spending with financing racial minorities, idle or dissolute able-bodied adults, women who have children out of wedlock and neglect them, lazy and inefficient bureaucrats, corrupt and wasteful defense contractors and other types of persons who can be demonized and made to stand symbolically for government itself, for the inevitable tendency of government to ally with the unproductive and undeserving in order to enhance its own illegitimate power.

Reality, as was discovered during the course of the 104th Congress, is something different. The government's money actually flows out mainly to racially majority members of the middle class who are, once were, or can be expected to become, workers and taxpayers. In terms of both numbers of persons and numbers of dollars, most of the persons who receive benefits from the federal government are senior citizens who receive Social Security and Medicare. Social Security and Medicare are not popularly perceived as "welfare"; if they are regarded as "entitlements," they are also regarded as having been earned and therefore as being deserved. The illusion that Social Security is like a publicly-organized annuity plan has worked to produce a politics of righteous support for it, since people who are receiving it have paid during their working years. Universal availability of Medicare to the over-65 population has made that program an essential element in the financial planning and security of middle-aged and elderly persons since health insurance is effectively unavailable on the private market to great numbers of elderly persons. Conservative anti-government rhetoric therefore does not reach Social Security and Medicare, which are regarded as among the few unequivocally good things that the federal government does.

Under these circumstances, and in light of the fact that their victory over the Democrats had been partly the result of an alarmed public's reaction to the prospect of radical changes to health insurance programs on which they rely, Republicans might well have tried to skirt the issue of Medicare while they tried to reduce other federal government operations. A large tax cut was essential to their agenda, however, and Medicare is where the money is. Under the rules of the Congress any proposal to reduce federal revenues or increase federal expenditures must be accompanied by proposals for offsetting increases in revenues or reductions in expenditures so the measure as a whole will be "revenue neutral." It is therefore impermissible to cut taxes without reducing spending and impossible to reduce (domestic) federal spending to any significant degree without reducing spending on Social Security or Medicare. Cutting back on discretionary federal activities and eliminating dozens of small programs and agencies will not in the aggregate save much money even though it may generate an impressive list of federal authorities removed. The big money is in the entitlement programs, which are mainly Social Security and Medicare. Attacking Social Security was out of the question; and so the Republican Congress took on Medicare. Unlike the Clinton administration's attempt to create a national health insurance system, the Republican initiative with respect to Medicare was not the product of a lengthy, publicized, articulate process of policy development and was not presented as the culmination of a century-long development of a particular political philosophy. Speaker of the House Newt Gingrich put together a package of Medicare reforms quietly, without inviting a blaze of publicity such as the one that had accompanied the creation of the Clinton Plan. He invited stakeholder groups into his councils, and adopted for the structural reform parts of his proposal many ideas that had wide bipartisan currency, some of which had been considered or proposed in the Clinton Plan. In addition to reductions in provider payments, mainly he proposed managed care, a familiar idea. Speaker Gingrich explained his proposals, as President Clinton had explained his, as giving seniors more "choice," by which was meant choice of health plan. Mr. Gingrich explained that his program would let beneficiaries choose from a variety of health plans, from the existing fee-for-service-style system, to managed-care plans, to a medical savings account system that would allow senior to share in savings generated by controlling their utilization, review their own medical bills and be rewarded with a rebate if they discovered waste, fraud or abuse.

The idea of converting Medicare from a defined benefit program to a defined contribution program was shared across party lines; and the idea that actual costs could be lower if Medicare beneficiaries were in managed care was conventional wisdom. Saving money for the program by cutting back on provider payments is standard practice. Speaker Gingrich presented his program as an effort to "save" Medicare by modernizing its structure to allow more options and to reduce program costs. The conservative proposal was nonetheless greeted with deep skepticism by liberals, who pointed out the close correspondence between the size of the proposed tax cut and the amount of the proposed reductions in Medicare spending and argued that the motivation for proposing reductions of very large magnitude did not stem from health policy considerations but from an ideologically-motivated determination to reduce the size of government regardless of the effect on the Medicare program or the well-being of its beneficiaries. That the Republicans wanted to gut Medicare to pay for a tax cut for the wealthy was an easy charge, easily believed. The Republicans protested that they wanted only to save Medicare from going into the red in the short term and in the longer term not being able to pay for the expenses of the baby boom generation that will begin to retire in 2010.

As usual, both sides had merit. Knowledgeable persons agree that something must be done to restructure Medicare in order to control its costs and procure better value for beneficiaries and the government. The question was trust. The conservatives lost the trust issue because the argument over their Medicare proposal was not cast in terms of the wisdom of specific measures for instituting managed care but rather focused on the degree to which their proposal was motivated not by a desire to "save" Medicare but was part of the general conservative effort to reduce the influence of government and to loosen the ties that bind individuals to collective resources in general and to the federal government in particular.

Recognizing the constant fragility of the constituency for social welfare programs, supporters of the programs recognized that the way to erode public support for Social Security and Medicare is to reduce their basis in principles of universality, indivisibility and equality and to undermine the perception of the federal government as a competent and trustworthy manager of a collective resource that is critical to the well-being of individuals. Proposals to increase the amounts that seniors pay for Medicare or to means-test or tax their benefits are consistent with a strategy of reducing the allegiance of the more affluent to the program. Converting the program from fee-for-service, in which all Medicare beneficiaries participate equally according to their medical needs, to managed care in which the government supplies a voucher that allows seniors to shop for a private plan, and even authorizing medical savings accounts, encourages individuation of the resources, distribution of seniors into plans differentiated by income and class, and privatization of decision-making. The overall impact of these changes would be to convert Medicare from a collective resource on which a person might draw in time of need to a cash distribution with which a person might buy into a collective resource organized privately.

Although on their face the proposed conservative reforms of Medicare (apart from the medical savings accounts, which were opposed vigorously by the Clinton Administration) were not greatly dissimilar from those proposed in the Clinton Plan, the overall direction of Republican reform would have been very different. For the Clintons, managed care would have been a technique of cost control within a structure of entitlements and a vigorous role for government. The Republican proposals in the 104th Congress, by contrast, were part of a strategy of curtailing entitlements, reducing reliance on collective resources and turning power away from the government and to the private sector. In the 104th Congress, consequently, conservative proposals that might have been viewed as reasonable if they had come from parties generally friendly to Medicare were greeted by liberals as an attack on the very essence of the program. Conservatives responded that they had been accused unfairly of trying to destroy Medicare when they were only trying to save it.

Public perception took the Democratic side of the argument: when in the winter of 1995-96 President Clinton closed down the federal government rather than approve the continuing budget resolution that would have reduced the Medicare budget and restructured the program along the lines desired by the House Republican leadership, the public stood overwhelmingly with the president.

The closure of the federal government brought the country up short in a reality check on the question of who was benefiting from federal expenditures. Anti-government rhetoric had created a world in which the people who got money from the government were in some sense "not us," where "we" were "taxpayers" and "working families." When the government closed, the public found out who really received the flow of federal funds, because the money stopped. When the federal government ran out of spending authority it stiffed its creditors, defaulted on its obligations. The people who were affected included employees who were prevented from working, businesses large and small with government contracts who were not paid for work already done, health care providers that were not paid for the patients whom they were taking care of and could not abandon, states and local governments that did not receive the expected federal contribution to the programs they continued to be obligated to provide. The hardship of federal government shutdown fell surprisingly, and widely. Taxpayers and working families got laid off, defaulted on their mortgages, could not pay their bills. Businesses could not get licenses, clearances, contracts. People who had planned vacations abroad could not get passports. The country found out what the federal government actually does.

This was not the only conservative miscalculation. The Republicans had badly misunderstood the true nature of the Medicaid program. Conservatives came to power determined to eliminate the federal entitlement to income support for poor people. The main program in this category is Aid to Families with Dependent Children, commonly known as "welfare." AFDC is a state grant-in-aid program to which the federal government makes a contribution inverse to the wealth of the state being aided. When Medicaid was enacted in 1965 it created a health benefit program to complement AFDC: all persons eligible for AFDC are also eligible for Medicaid.

The converse is not the case, however: Medicaid covers more than AFDC recipients, and indeed as of 1995 about two-thirds of Medicaid funds were going for the support of the chronically disabled and the elderly medically indigent, many of whom were in need of institutional care. With respect to these categories, Medicaid acts as a social safety net for middle-class families. The Republican proposal to eliminate AFDC and Medicaid entitlements and to convert these programs to block grants administered by the states thus struck, unexpectedly, at middle-class self-interest. By the spring of 1996 Newt Gingrich was the most unpopular elected official in the United States.

Meanwhile, in the midst of all of the ideological battle the bipartisan coalition of Senators that had set out years before to achieve private health insurance reform decided that they were going to succeed in getting a bill enacted into law in the 104th Congress. When the Republicans won the Senate in 1994, Nancy Kassebaum of Kansas succeeded Ted Kennedy of Massachusetts as Chair of the Senate Labor Committee. The two of them patiently put together a bill that incorporated only provisions on which virtually unanimous bipartisan agreement could be achieved; and they vigorously beat back efforts from both sides of the aisle to include provisions to which there would be bitter opposition. On the face of it, consequently, the Kennedy-Kassebaum Act, officially known as the Health Insurance Portability and Accountability Act (P.L. 104-191) does not amount to very much. It provides a bit of portability, some tax breaks, and mental health parity.

And there is one genuinely new idea, the medical savings account, insisted upon by the conservative leadership. The MSA is a variant of the Individual Retirement Account. It aims to allow the individual to accumulate first-party funds through tax-favored savings accounts the contents of which might be withdrawn and used for medical expenses. The accumulations in the MSA allow a person to take high-deductible backup health coverage. The money in the MSA might be used for any expenses that qualify as "medical" under the Internal Revenue Code, which could include deductible and co-insurance payments associated with the insurance plan, or items and services not covered by the plan. Since expenditures would be controlled entirely by the patient there should be a market for fee-for-service medicine in items and services that could be financed with the proceeds of MSAs. After a protracted battle, in which President Clinton threatened to veto any insurance market reform bill that included MSAs and the Republican leadership threatened to block the Kennedy-Kassebaum bill if it did not include them, the compromise reached was that MSAs would be authorized on a four-year demonstration basis for persons who are presently uninsured and for no more than 750,000 persons who are presently insured.

MSA supporters think that the MSA is a revolutionary advance in promoting individual control and responsibility; its detractors think that it could destroy health insurance as we know it. Because MSAs are the antithesis of insurance, encouraging the individuation and privatization of resources rather than the development of collective resources, they are greeted with suspicion by the advocates of expanding guaranteed access to care and by those who presently are in the marketplace occupied by large group plans. MSAs are most attractive when they serve the purpose of expanding access to coverage among those who do not have it, who are chiefly the self-employed and employees of small businesses. For those who have adequate incomes and expect to have relatively low utilization of medical services, it is realistic to build resources through savings. These are the (relatively) healthy and the (relatively) wealthy who are also (relatively) self-confident and self-reliant; the favorable risk selection represented by this group means that they are attractive to insurers writing high-deductible policies. At the end of the 104th Congress, it could be said that the conservative approach to health care reform, which involves reducing collective resources and individual reliance on them, was put forth very strongly and did not succeed. In the 1996 elections, Mr. Clinton was re-elected and the Republicans retained control of the Congress. The electorate appears to have rejected the most vigorously liberal and rigorously conservative solutions to the health care problem; the question is whether there is or ought be a middle ground and whether it can be found. The answer to that question will be pursued in the 105th Congress, and, doubtless, beyond.

Notes

1. Technically, the Task Force itself was a group of government officials headed by the First Lady. It had, however, a staff of several hundred persons drawn from government and academia, who became known colloquially as the "Task Force."

2. Haynes Johnson and David Broder, *The System: The American Way of Politics at the Breaking Point*, Little, Brown, 1996.

3. In 1990, the bipartisan, congressionally-created Pepper Commission had been unable to agree on a health insurance plan that would include an employer mandate; the final report of the Commission was adopted by a bare, partisan majority of Democrats. See Theda Skocpol, *Boomerang: Clinton's Health Security Effort and the Turn Against Government in U.S. Politics*, New York: W.W. Norton, 1996, at 34-35.

4. See Monique Jerome-Forget, Joseph White, Joshua M. Wiener (eds.), *Health Care Reform Through Internal Markets: Experience and Proposals*, Washington, DC: Brookings Institution, 1995.

5. See Chapter 12 in this volume by Karlyn Bowman.

6. See Chapter 29 in this volume by John Dingell.

7. See Chapter 3 in this volume by Len Nichols.

8. See Chapter 1 in this volume by William Niskanen.

9. A.C. Enthoven, "Consumer choice health plan: A national health insurance proposal," (Memorandum to HEW Secretary Joseph Califano, 22 September 1977), reprinted in R.D. Luke and J.C. Bauer, *Issues in Health Care Economics*, Rockville, MD: Aspen, 1982; and A.C. Enthoven, "Consumer choice health plan: A national health insurance proposal based on regulated competition in the private sector," *New England Journal of Medicine*, 23 and 30 March, 1978: 650-658 and 709-720.

SECTION FOUR

Change Without Legislation: The Managed Care Revolution

Section Four
Introduction
Managed Care

John E. Billi

During his first term, President Clinton attempted to enact comprehensive health care reform at the national level. The dual goals of that reform effort were to provide universal access through expanded insurance coverage and to rein in health care costs through increased use of managed care. The Clinton team viewed these two goals of universal access and cost reduction as complementary and interdependent. In Clinton's view, both goals were necessary for comprehensive reform, to lessen the risk and impact of cherry-picking, benefit reductions, insurance non-renewal, pre-existing condition exclusions, uninsurability, adverse selection and other tactics and consequences of piecemeal insurance reform.

Had it succeeded, the single most important effect of the Clinton health reform effort would have been the coverage of the 35-40 million Americans who are currently without health insurance. The linkage of the two goals, cost and access, was critical, for without controlling costs the price tag of covering the uninsured would likely have been unacceptable to the American people. But the Clinton plan for comprehensive, nationwide health reform was not enacted. It was "dead on arrival" in Congress, labeled as a huge intrusion of the federal government into the personal lives of the people. Even as late as the 1996 Presidential Campaign, Bob Dole labeled Bill Clinton as the person who wanted to impose federal government regulation on the entire health care system, one seventh of the economy. Such allegations raised the fear of bureaucratic intrusions into the individual decisions made between doctors and patients, and of strict, cost-oriented regulation over access to services. The Clinton plan was defeated, so instead of government imposed regulation of health care, the people got purchaser driven "managed care."

The failure of the Clinton effort left those entities who pay for health care (corporations and state and federal governments) to enact their own version of health care reform. Unlike the comprehensive efforts under

Clinton, the reforms enacted by employers and government primarily sought the goal of cost reduction. These efforts did not address expansion of access to the uninsured. The linkage between cost and access was lost. The goal became saving money, to increase profits or to lower taxes, rather than to be able to afford universal coverage.

To accomplish the goal of cost reduction, corporations and state and federal government turned to managed care. Loosely defined, managed care is a system of health care financing and delivery in which a limited group of providers deliver health care to a defined population, in which the process of health care is measured and improved. While managed care has demonstrated its ability to control costs (primarily through reduced hospitalization), much work remains to be done with respect to understanding the implications of managed care on quality of care. Four papers in this section address these trends. Gabel provides an overview of the HMO industry, including growth in both the number of managed care plans and in enrollment. He describes Point of Service plans as the most rapidly expanding segment of the HMO market, and predicts how managed care will be incorporated into the Medicare and Medicaid programs. Billi brings these national trends to the local level through a discussion of the Michigan market. In Michigan the influence of the large employers, large unions, and a dominant Blue Cross payer all lead to a unique local variation on the national trends. Pryde speaks from the perspective of a large employer who believes that well-designed managed care plans are key to controlling the spiraling costs of health care. Gold addresses the important question "what forms of managed care can be credited with producing cost savings?" She argues that superficial analyses cannot be used to understand how much of cost savings is real and how much attributable to favorable insurance selection.

State governments are among the most aggressive entrants into managed care at the current time. Most states either have moved significant percentages of Medicaid recipients into commercial managed care plans, or intend to do so over the next few years. Most states are motivated by the lure of huge financial savings in their Medicaid budgets, which budgets consume more tax revenue than any other program in most states. Only a few states have coupled this move with an expansion of coverage to the uninsured.

Many physicians were critical of the Clinton proposal because of their fear of bureaucratic imposition upon their autonomy and their relationship with their patients. In the end, they traded the fear of government intrusion for the reality of managed care health plan intrusion into their clinical decision-making. Since it is the private sector, rather than the government, intruding on the physician's autonomy, this is perceived favorably by

Section Four: Introduction

business interests as the normal workings of the free market, which will ultimately provide society with the best services at the best price through competition. Ironically, physicians are increasingly the target of the micromanagement they feared, but without having accomplished the goals of universal access for the uninsured.

While there are a myriad and expanding number of models of managed care across the country, one feature dramatically differentiates most new managed care arrangements from the traditional insurance plans they replaced: the sharing of financial risk with the providers. This fundamental shift in financial incentives holds the most promise for physicians who fear micromanagement, but also raises the most serious ethical dilemmas under managed care. Will the physician who has financial incentive to withhold care still provide all appropriate care? Indeed, can such a physician objectively judge what the patient needs, when under what Himmelstein and Woolhandler have described as "extreme financial risk"? The paper by Morreim tackles troublesome ethical issues of managed care, discussing how the changing economics of health care affect the patient-doctor relationship. She comments on controls vs. incentives as a cost management strategy, and cautions on the danger that patients could be marginalized from participating in decision-making about how health care dollars are spent on their behalf.

Another side of this balance of trust and responsibility is provided by Reardon who speaks as a representative of organized medicine. While recognizing that managed care has been successful in reducing the cost of medical care and that many patients and physicians are satisfied with managed care, he expresses concerns about preserving the positive aspects of the pluralistic U.S. health care system and traditional patient-doctor relationships. He reviews a "patient protection act," antitrust reform for physicians and the Medicaid waiver process. Payton speaks from the vantage point of a legal scholar on the issues of contract and antitrust in the changing health care market.

But what has happened to the quality of care under these cost-focused changes? In his paper, Simmer discusses quality management approaches within the health maintenance industry, and the state-of-the-art with respect to measuring quality. He effectively argues that quality must be defined within balanced input from patients and purchasers (employers) as well as the medical profession. In her contribution, Goon provides the HMO industry's perspective on patient access to quality care. She reviews six principles for the insurance industry, to provide a level playing field. Where is managed care going? What models can be used to rebalance the effort to integrate cost and quality efforts? In an interview, Warden debunks widely held "myths" about managed care. He cites the need for health care organizations and physicians to work as colleagues to take responsibility for the health of a population. He expresses the view that quality can actually reduce costs.

What are the key observations that unite these diverse presentations? Managed care is associated with lower costs, due to utilization management and possibly also favorable selection of members. Models of managed care are heterogeneous and the industry is evolving very rapidly. This makes it difficult to conduct or to correctly interpret studies of cost and quality outcomes in managed care. The rapid transformation of health care delivery under managed care will pose intense challenges and opportunities for patients, physicians, payers and society. New ethical dilemmas will continue to appear, and will test our vision of health care as a public good, rather than as a market commodity. Purchaser-driven health care reform has almost no impact on the tragedy of the uninsured.

33

Some Thoughts About Managed Care

An Interview with Gail L. Warden

There are a lot of myths about managed care in our country. Part of the problem is the way managed care has grown; part of it is the way it has been organized in many communities. I would like to dispel three of those myths.

First myth: Managed care means a loss of autonomy. Autonomy means being able to control one's destiny. We have so many plans operating in a single community that in order to control costs each one ends up micromanaging processes such as utilization review and precertification.

All this is aimed at trying to impact your relationship with your patient. Instead, we should be concentrating on how a population of patients is cared for and then try to draw some conclusions. I am convinced that physicians do not want to be overutilizers. They do not want to increase health care costs. We have to find a way to organize managed care so that physicians feel they are in control of their destiny.

The myth that managed care equals a loss of autonomy can be turned around. Perhaps under the right set of circumstances, it could actually mean more autonomy than many physicians now have in managed care contracts.

Second myth: For managed care to be successful, physicians have to work for the managed care organization. I don't believe this, either. It's been shown that many organizations are successful because the physicians are employed and connected with a managed care organization. But any type of arrangement will work as long as the physicians and the hospital are willing to share risks and to think in terms of a given population—not just individual patients or individual services. Local factors have to be taken into consideration in designing each of these managed care networks or what will eventually become the accountable health plans.

This article is excerpted and reprinted with permission from Hospitals & Health Networks, August 5, 1993.

Third myth: The cost controls that come with managed care result in reduced quality. The Rand Health Insurance Experiment and various efforts at my own organization have shown that quality actually can reduce costs.

When an organization and physicians work as colleagues, taking responsibility for a population and improving the process of care, we really can accomplish what we need to.

Q: What was your experience with the Clinton Health Care Reform Task Force?

In January, I was part of what was called "the health care delivery task force," which was a group of providers brought together to react to the initial plan developed during the transition period. Much of the current plan took shape during that period.

It's interesting that the issues unanswered then are the ones that are unanswered today: Namely, what is the short-term cost-control mechanism, how do we pay for it, and just exactly what is the role of the alliances or HIPCs. Later, I was a panel member for one of four town meeting forums sponsored by the Robert Wood Johnson Foundation and Mrs. Clinton. Most of the speakers wanted an expanded benefits package and addressed their specific concerns, such as mental health coverage, long-term care coverage, etc., all of which are legitimate concerns. But I felt that those sessions would have been a good opportunity to educate the public and the press about some of the tough issues and tough choices that we face.

Recently, I was asked to react a second time to the proposal, but I declined because it meant resigning my position on the AHA board. I felt that I could do more good on the outside because I basically support what the task force is doing.

The people I dealt with were very bright, quite well-informed and committed to doing what was right.

Q: What are some of the common barriers to bringing physicians and hospitals together?

Number one is to accommodate the pluralistic nature of medical practice. Secondly, physicians and hospitals must view the marketplace in the same way. If they don't, then it will be very difficult to work out a networking relationship.

For example, if physicians believe that managed care is never going to come to a community, it's pretty hard to hospital administrators to convince them that a network is necessary.

Some Thoughts About Managed Care

I find this when I talk in various places all over the country. Either the hospital administrator or the physicians, one or the other (and sometimes both), don't really understand the changes taking place.

Sometimes cultural issues stand in the way. We ran into that while working out our collaborative relationship with Mercy [Health Services]. However, by keeping our focus on our goal, we have been able to work through these differences.

Another barrier is aligning incentives in such a way that both feel they are benefiting form the relationship.

And finally, one of the big barriers related to leaderships and decision-making. Physician partnerships will not work if the decision-making process is not consistent and predictable. If it isn't, people become insecure and they bolt. We need to be very clear about how decisions will be made concerning payment and how quality will be monitored. And when the issues come up, it must be very clear how an assessment of the problem will be made and how decisions will be reached.

Q: Are today's information systems capable of true integration? What are some of the deterrents to using data?

The technology is here now; it's just arrived in the last few years. The main missing link was the networking technology to allow various databases to interface.

However, we still have to overcome our fear of data getting into the wrong hands. The fact is that we will have to share data. We will be able to protect the individual patient, but the data has to be available if we want to make quantum leaps in information services.

Another deterrent to effectively using information systems is the black box of the doctor's office all over the country. Linkages to those offices don't exist, and so there's no real information online about the outpatient encounters that take place there. It makes it very difficult in most settings to gather the type of information that one could with a total health care information system.

The technology exists to link the doctor's office, the hospital, the home care facility, and everything else. One of the obligations of the people organizing networks should be to see that these linkages are made available. But to get to this point it has taken a lot of time, and an unbelievable amount of money was spent because everybody thought they were unique.

Q: What do you think needs to be accomplished in the area of chronic care?

There's tremendous potential to improve the quality of life of individuals with chronic diseases if we would just address the issue. But not much progress has been made in this area because the traditional insurance model doesn't pay for the regular and predictable expenses of maintaining chronic disease patients. The potential for improving productivity, for improving functional status, for improving quality of life for these individuals is significant.

The implications of the age-wave when the baby-boomers become elderly are enormous. Health care institutions must pay attention to this and recognize the contributions that they can make in this area.

Q: How do people begin to look at a health delivery system as a whole?

The first point is that any organization—a group of physicians, a hospital, an insurance company, a community agency, or an individual—can become the integrator. Any one of them can take the lead.

If you begin to think in terms of the entire system and the scope of services that can be delivered and how they can be linked, it begins to make sense. Add to that the benefit the patient receives from being able to enter a seamless system and have access to a full range of services, and the pluses of integration become obvious.

Q: Other than better-coordinated care, what will integration mean to patients?

Consumers need to understand that integration means changes for them, too. Choice of physician will become a two-step process. First they will select an organization, and then they will be given an opportunity to select a physician. That's one of the reasons why I think integration will be more cost-effective.

And, similarly, purchasers will have to make the same kind of transition.

Q: How will integration affect human resources?

People who come to work for organizations like ours and the organizations that will evolve in the future are probably going to view it as a lifetime job instead of just a temporary stopping point. Organizations will have more responsibility for the entire work life of an individual. For instance, our organization is very interested in management development. We must give employees opportunities to be promoted, but we also must give them opportunities to be exposed to all aspects of the organization.

I envision us moving toward a system in which management is less hierarchical, and much of the work is performed by multidisciplinary teams. Cross-training is already occurring in many organizations. But it's important to remember that work should be focused on what the patient needs, not the organization.

Health care must also come to grips with demographic trends that point to a much more diverse work force by the year 2000.

Q: What does it mean to add value to health care?

Many people talk about the right ingredients of cost and quality as equaling value. But I look at it a little bit differently. I assume that cost-effectiveness and delivering high-quality care is a given. The real value, I think, is achieved by being customer-oriented, having a health care system that's community-based, highly accessible to the patient, and one committed to being a good place to work. If it's a good place to work, it'll be a good place to get care.

Q: What is the most urgent task facing the health care community?

There are two, and they are equally important. One is achieving integration of physicians, hospitals and other providers into networks.

The second is making the transition from what I call cost containment to economic discipline. The difference is that, in the cost-containment era, we reduced the cost of services but not the volume. We did not control utilization. We did not control capacity, and we did not assume risk for caring for a given population for a given capitation. And that will be required if we're going to moderate the rate of increase in health care costs.

34

The Politics of Managed Care: The Regulatory Issues from the American Medical Association Perspective

Thomas R. Reardon, M.D.

The rapid transformation of the American health care delivery system raises important public health concerns that the American Medical Association (AMA) continues to press before Congress and federal agencies. The current trend toward consolidation and the emergence of large, corporate for-profit health care systems potentially reduces patient choice and threatens to remove medical decision-making from the practitioner.

The AMA does not oppose managed care; it recognizes managed care as a method of delivering care in a pluralistic health care system. The AMA has, in fact, developed a wide range of products and services to help physicians adapt to managed care, including an extensive publications series, managed care workshops and the Physicians Capital Source which assists physicians in forming their own managed care networks. The AMA also recognizes that managed care has been successful in reducing the cost of medical care and that many patients and physicians are satisfied with managed care. The AMA's primary concern is accountability in managed care, and we believe that some regulation is necessary to prevent bad managed care that compromises patient health.

The AMA is concerned with a broad spectrum of regulatory issues that affect patients and physicians in the new environment. This paper focuses on three. First, the American Medical Association supports regulation of private health benefit plans to ensure patient choice, patient fairness and physician fairness. The centerpiece of current AMA federal legislative efforts in this arena is the "Patient Protection Act of 1995" (PPA95). Second, the AMA seeks antitrust relief to permit physicians to form their own networks. Third, the AMA seeks to ensure that as Medicaid moves increasingly toward managed care, its vulnerable patient population is adequately protected.

The Patient Protection Act of 1995

1. Background

Physicians and patients report insurance companies and managed care plans making inappropriate treatment coverage and treatment decisions and aggressively dropping physicians from their networks. These incidents demonstrate an imbalance of power between plans and patients and the physicians who ethically must serve as advocates for those patients.

The AMA is concerned that lack of adequate disclosure of coverage and utilization review protocols keep patients and physicians in the dark and allow some plans to make decisions selectively and arbitrarily. Some plans do not offer an appeals process which the AMA believes is paramount and also avoids expensive litigation to enforce benefit rights.

Some plans also lack a mechanism for involving physicians in the most critical decisions involving patient care — including utilization review and quality assessment of outcomes. Without access to these guidelines and peer review information, many physicians must rely only on their best judgment, not knowing if they will be branded as "overutilizers" if their patients are older, sicker or outside the norm.

2. The Nuts and Bolts of PPA95

PPA95 is designed to work within marketplace realities and to empower patients with certain basic protections when they enroll in a health benefits plan. The PPA95 does not require a huge bureaucracy. Instead, PPA95 is tied to the tax code; a plan must satisfy the requirements of PPA95 to be eligible for a tax deduction under the Internal Revenue Code. **PPA95 explicitly states that it is not to be construed as an any willing provider law** and does not seek to regulate self-insured plans currently regulated by the Employee Retirement Income Security Act.

PPA95 is based on the following five principles: 1) Information Disclosure; 2) Freedom of Choice of Plan and Physician; 3) Access to Physicians; 4) Fairness to Physicians; and 5) Physician Involvement

The passage of PPA95 will significantly alleviate current problems by providing patients and physicians with clear, specific plan information and by helping physicians protect the interests of patients through the establishment of uniform industry-wide standards.

Antitrust Reform: Leveling the Playing Field

Antitrust reform continues to be an AMA priority. The AMA has asked the 104th Congress to reform the antitrust laws to eliminate the disadvantage physicians have in comparison to insurers, hospitals and other non-physicians in the development of health care delivery networks and health plans. The object of AMA efforts is not to prevent price competition or enable physicians to unionize, but to enable physicians to compete. The current antitrust structure which views physicians as individual entrepreneurs is out-of-step with a market that requires physicians to form alliances in order to survive.

Medicaid: Ensuring Access for the Underserved

While much remains to be done to improve care for the needy, Medicaid has made significant progress in improving care for America's most vulnerable population. Medicaid laws are designed to ensure that state programs are adequately funded, that they offer sufficient and timely payment to providers and that they assure the quality of medical services. States that adopt capitated systems of payment must establish rates that are adequate to cover the health needs of the population served.

HHS "Streamlines" Waiver Process

Across the nation state government leaders are attempting to control state Medicaid expenditures, which have soared in the past several years to the point that in some states, they surpass expenditures for education. Under federal law, the Secretary of Health and Human Services (HHS) may waive compliance with some Medicaid Act requirements for any experimental, pilot or demonstration project, which in the judgment of HHS is likely to assist in promoting the objectives of the Medicaid program.

Between 1993 and 1994, the percentage of the 34 million Medicaid beneficiaries enrolled in managed care plans jumped from 14% to 23%. Half of the increase is attributable to the increase in Medicaid managed care demonstration programs.

Beginning in October 1993, HHS announced that it was "streamlining" the process for waivers and was prepared to approve large-scale statewide reform programs for five-year tests. Since the new policy principles were adopted, HHS has approved six demonstration projects (Tennessee, Oregon, Rhode Island, Hawaii, Kentucky and Florida), and eight currently await approval.

While the AMA supports Medicaid waivers and other programs to cost-effectively improve Medicaid access and quality of care, it has serious concerns that the waiver process is being implemented in a manner that erodes the fundamental patient protections embodied in the Medicaid Act.

The Oregon Health Plan had the key to success: an existing infrastructure. The TennCare approach is a textbook example of waivers gone wrong.

Faced with a budget crisis, the state forced patients and physicians to make TennCare enrollment decisions without sufficient time to make an informed decision. When TennCare took effect January 1, 1994, chaos ensued. Patients were denied access to hospitals and transferred back and forth between institutions. Managed care plan listings of participating providers included names of physicians who were deceased or who had left practice. Physicians and their staffs were required to spend many hours on the telephone to assure their patients access to specialty care.

TennCare is an example of state and federal officials pushing through a quick-fix solution to a complex problem, thereby threatening the health of the population it seeks to assist.

The waiver process should ensure improved access to quality medical care. The AMA believes that all statewide demonstration programs must comply with the following principles.

1. They must assist in promoting the Medicaid Act's objective of improving access to quality medical care by
   a. ensuring that the program is adequately funded;
   b. ensuring an adequate infrastructure;
   c. ensuring sufficient provider reimbursement levels to secure adequate access to providers; and
   d. eliminating any provisions designed to coerce physicians and other providers into participation, such as those that link participation in private plans with participation in Medicaid.
2. They must be preceded by a fair and open process for receiving public comment on the program.

Conclusion

The AMA does not seek special protection for physicians in the evolving health care market. However, the AMA does seek to ensure that physicians can compete with other players in the market and that the rights of physicians, patients and particularly the most vulnerable members of our society are adequately protected in a pluralistic system.

35
Ford Motor Company's Perspective on Managed Care

Charles T. Pryde

I appreciate the opportunity to be a part of this panel and present before such a distinguished audience discussing the politics of managed care. As I am sure you all are aware, Ford Motor Company is a major employer in the state, directly employing about 80,000 employees in Michigan. As Ford's Health Policy Manager, I am here today to discuss the important role managed care plays in helping control Ford's health care costs.

My main message to you is that as employers, such as Ford, continue to seek ways to curtail ever increasing health care costs, health maintenance organizations and other managed care organizations play a key role in efforts to control these rising costs.

Controlling rising health care costs is important to employers like Ford for several reasons:

1. *Their effect on international competitiveness*: The auto industry operates in an intensely competitive market. We are convinced there will be a huge consolidation resulting in 5 or 6 surviving auto makers in the entire world. We want to be one of them, and we want to continue to produce high quality cars and trucks in Michigan. Controlling all of our operating costs is critical to Ford being one of the survivors. But in the United States in 1994 we spent about 20% of payroll to purchase health care. For our employees at Ford of Japan (a country with a national health care system) the cost is about 2% of payroll — and this holds true for our Japanese competitors.

This presentation was made on April 1, 1995, at the University of Michigan Forum on Health Policy.

2. *Rising health care costs force businesses to change or drop coverage*: There is a lot of debate right now on how health care is changing in America — one point of agreement is that fewer businesses are providing health coverage for their employees. And they drop coverage because health costs are too high. While businesses drop coverage the number of people without health insurance is increasing — this growing uncovered population presents a problem for all, be they business, government, or the provider community. A shrinking base of payers means the remaining payers will have to shoulder more of the costs. If unchecked, we expect this unfortunate cycle to continue — fewer businesses providing coverage and growing numbers of people without insurance.
3. *Absolute costs are too high*: In 1993, Ford purchased health care coverage for about 350,000 people in Michigan. The cost of this coverage was about $750 million. But this is only part of the story — from 1988 to 1993 the per contract cost of our health care rose on average about 6% year nationwide. While high, these cost increases were less than national averages of 9.9% a year for business.

We believe managed care is a key component of our past successes in controlling health care costs and key to future efforts.

First, let me briefly review why health care costs are so important to Ford. I mentioned that Ford spent about $750 million for health care in Michigan in 1994. Nationwide the Company spent $1.4 billion to provide health care for our employees — an increase of almost $1 billion from 1980 health care costs of $552 million.

These cost increases led Ford to purchase health care from managed care organizations over a decade ago. Given this experience let me tell you why Ford believes managed care is a key tool for controlling health costs:

1. *Managed care helped us control our health costs:*

    - Ford, in cooperation with the United Auto Workers, has actively pursued cost containment programs like managed care, case management, and wellness programs. The managed care efforts alone helped Ford save about $110 million nationwide in 1994.
    - A specific example of the effectiveness of a network managed care program is our national managed care drug program, implemented in 1994. Prescription drugs were the fastest growing segment of our health care benefits program with annual increases of up to 15%. After implementing the program

the Company experienced a decrease in the per contract cost of outpatient drugs.

2. *Managed care has helped us in our efforts to improve the quality of health care.*

- Ford and the UAW carefully review each HMO prior to approval and implementation. The review covers virtually all aspects of an HMO's operations. And we are requiring all of our HMOs to obtain accreditation from the National Committee for Quality Assurance by 1996.

3. *Managed care has allowed Ford to both preserve choice and offer new options for our employees.*

- We presently provide a choice of traditional indemnity insurance, and quality managed care organizations for our employees — and people like that choice. For example, under traditional indemnity insurance, office visits and preventive care are not covered for our hourly workers — whereas under HMOs they are covered. Presently, about 50% of Ford's active employees and dependents, nationwide, have chosen managed care programs.

The Ford Motor Company believes that well designed managed care plans are a key component in our efforts to control spiraling health care costs. Thus, we are concerned about maintaining the effectiveness of the managed care plans we provide to our employees.

Any willing provider, patient protection acts and similar laws affecting managed care organizations, arise from good motives — the desire to preserve existing patient-provider relations and to safeguard patients' access to care or choice of providers. These are legitimate goals that need to be addressed. But if we undermine the effectiveness of managed care organizations by restricting their ability to contract with quality providers, or require other provisions that hinder their ability to compete effectively in the market place — we will be deprived of an effective tool in our efforts to provide quality, cost effective health care to our employees, our retirees, and to their dependents.

While I am not an expert in managed care plan design, and I cannot tell exactly where to draw the line on anti-managed care legislation, we hope that legislation does not erode the cost, quality and access advantages that well designed managed care plans can and do provide.

36
Will Managed Care End the Need for Managed Competition?

Richard Kronick, Ph.D.
Max Heirich, Ph.D.

The market has changed remarkably since 1993, and a number of reforms are occurring through private initiative which echo some of the key proposals of the Health Security Act that the Clinton Task Force on Health Insurance Reform recommended. We have a market that is not very much managed, although there are pieces of it that are being managed by large employers and some small market reforms are occurring. At least in some parts of the country, providers of health care are beginning to respond in desired ways. Does this mean that we do not need any kind of public management of competition in health care?

Events sometimes provide their own correctives to assumptions of the past and we, like many other observers today, find ourselves re-examining earlier assumptions. It seems clear that not every detail of the task force blueprint for managing competition in the public interest would be necessary now. Some positive changes are occurring through private initiative. It seems equally clear, however, that the reforms which are occurring without legislative mandate are leaving the most vulnerable parts of the market and growing numbers of the public severely at-risk. It also seems clear that some of the most important recent reforms of the private market that we have seen recently came as responses to expected legislative change. In some cases special interests innovated to reposition themselves more favorably to take advantage of expected changes in rules for competition. When enough key players did this, some of the rules did change, without legislative action. Note, however, that they did not change simply from

---

This paper grew out of conversations between Richard Kronick and Max Heirich, during the process of editing Kronick's November 19, 1994, presentation for publication in this book. Final editing of this paper was completed in June 1997.

dynamics of normal market activity. They came in response to public agreement about ways the market conditions needed to change.

Other important changes occurred because key purchasers in the health care market began to recognize public needs and their ability to "manage" the rules of competition for their share of the market. Thus they began to take on some of the roles that the task force said needed to be played in order to protect the public interest. From the public debate about how the market needs to change, in short, has come a striking private response. Some key aspects of health care market dynamics are changing because of this public discussion. Some private interests have begun to recognize that there are areas where their interests and the interests of the public at large are identical and that they control access to enough of the market to be able to force some changes.

The market has been restructured quite fundamentally, with the creation of large provider networks and the shift of much private insurance into capitated payment plans. Public insurance, for Medicaid and Medicare, also is moving rapidly toward capitated payment. Ironically, these developments were recommended as a central component of the Health Security Act's restructuring of the health plan market. In the thinking of the Clinton task force on health insurance reform, provider network consolidation would be needed in order to make it possible for health care providers to remain financially healthy as they extended services to poor Americans and to those who live outside the metropolitan areas—i.e., to those with least access to services at present, and who may prove to be more expensive to serve. Network consolidation would enlarge the risk pool of paying customers, making it easier for capitated payment plans to absorb the costs of caring for those who need more expensive care. Network consolidation, thus, began in response to the Health Security Act's proposals, as a way to guarantee financial stability if providers had to provide services to all Americans. In the absence of a financing mechanism to provide health services to all, which was part of the managed competition proposals, however, this consolidation has not led to greater access to care for Americans previously left out. Instead, the number of uninsured who have only marginal access to health care services has grown, and the needs of poor Americans have been largely ignored. This is, indeed, an ironic outcome of attempts to reform health care more fundamentally.

Large employers and employer coalitions have implemented some of the strategies needed to manage competition. They require, as they have historically, each health plan serving their employees to guarantee issue to all employees and dependents, regardless of health status. They provide, as they have historically, community rating of premiums for their employees, and large subsidies for health insurance purchase, effectively encouraging both the healthy and sick to purchase coverage. In a break from the past, however, large employers are increasingly making their employees 'cost-conscious' consumers- that is, the employer makes a contribution at approximately the premium price of the low-price plan, and employees choose whether a more expensive plan is worth the extra premium. And, increasingly, employers have standardized the benefits offered by competing plants, reducing the opportunity for plans to tailor the benefit package in an attempt to segment the market or attract good risks, and simplifying the choice environment for employees. Some employers have also begun to provide information on satisfaction and quality, although very little information to judge quality is currently available.

These actions by employers, and the resulting pressure created by consumers on health plan price, appear to have fundamentally changed the dynamic faced by health plans and providers. In markets characterized by excess provider capacity, little information on quality, and capitated payments to large groups of providers, providers have been forced to accept capitations at or below the previous year's level. Provider groups that might try to price their services at a higher rate would find themselves losing patients. And in the absence of knowing whether a lower price means poorer quality, many consumers- particularly those who do not have chronic medical problems- are happy to choose a lower priced plan when given the opportunity to do so.

The theory of managed competition suggests that large employers could act as sponsors for their employees, but that a public sponsor (or 'health alliance' in the language of the Health Security Act) was needed to organize the market on behalf of many Americans who do not work for a large employer. We are currently conducting an experiment in which increasingly active sponsors are performing some of the functions of managed competition for perhaps 20% to 30% of the private market, and observing whether a change in demand from a segment of the market is enough to change provider behavior throughout the market. Although the results are far from complete, it appears that the answer is 'yes'.

It is not clear, however, whether an only partially managed market will produce high quality care for those who are most in need, or how consumers without benefit of an active sponsor will react in an environment in which they find themselves powerless in the face of strong HMOs and provider groups. The anti-managed care backlash finding expression in both state and federal legislatures is, in part, supported by provider associations attempting to stem the tide of managed care. But it also finds support from the very real fears of voters that managed care organizations will not do a good job of providing care when it is most needed, and that voters have no recourse other than turning to their legislators. Although we have not seen any polling data on the issue, we suspect that support for anti-managed care legislation is stronger among the self-employed, employees of small businesses, and the elderly than it is among the employees of large businesses who at least have the employee benefits manager as a potential ally in a triangular relationship between consumer, sponsor, and health plan. But for all those consumers without an active and effective sponsor, the legislature or the State Department of Insurance is their only recourse. And while some of the anti-managed care legislation may lead to improved delivery of care, particularly for those most in need, much of it will not. Bad cases typically make bad law. It is difficult to manage competition effectively through the legislative process; what is needed is an active and intelligent agent to respond creatively the changing market conditions.

If the effects of an only partially managed market on care for the insured are unclear, there is not uncertainty about the effects of our current financing arrangements on the most important problem of resource allocation in our health care economy.

The most important part of better resource allocation does not involve getting more efficient services to employees of large companies, or even to the 83 percent of the public that now have health insurance. The most important part of resource reallocation involves getting services to the 17 percent of the population who have no insurance. As each day goes by the number of Americans without health insurance is rising. In Los Angeles County, California, for example, 25 percent of the population now has no health insurance. To address resource allocation in ways that get access to health care for all requires political legerdemain.

It seems clear today that market-driven reforms in the private sector, combined with legislative pressures to reduce public commitment to health care expenditures for the poor and aging sectors of the population, are doing little to make health care available or affordable to those who now are left out. It also is clear that the number of people without health insurance is growing. Managed competition proposals included keys to giving all Americans access to health care. The employer mandate, universal coverage, community rates for insurance premiums (or some equivalent that shares costs evenly and fairly) and health purchasing alliances that give all Americans access to health care at roughly comparable prices, regardless of the size of their employer's business—or at least some functional equivalent for these "managed competition" solutions—are sorely needed in order to provide access.

Interest groups, acting on their own behalf, can provide part of the solution that is needed. Industry-wide managed care organizations, for example, are making information about capitated payment plans available to the public so that better informed choices will be possible. This strengthens the market at the same time that it furthers their own interests and helps enlarge their share of the health care market; but it does not address the concerns of those who are left out of the market altogether. Some altruistically-focused institutional interests, such as African-American churches in the inner city, despairing that the legislative process will give higher priority to health needs of the poor, are forming non-profit corporations to redirect cash flows that now go out of poor neighborhoods back into them, to be used for health services and other neighborhood needs. It remains to be seen whether sufficient private funds can be redirected to serve those now ignored in public budgeting. It also remains to be seen whether health services directed specifically to the poor can be of high quality, and if so, whether they can be affordable without public investment. Far better to be doing something, however, than to do nothing.

The invisible hand of the market innovates constantly, and some of the innovation is in the public interest. Despite the changes that have occurred, however, the "free" market still is leaving many Americans unserved. We must sponsor better competition among health care providers so that all Americans get the services they need, at a price we can afford. As we survey the unmet problems still plaguing American health care, it is clear that publicly managed competition, in some form, still is needed. The details of management change as private players adapt to changing conditions, but the need remains, as do the issues which need attention and the larger parameters for choice.

37

Managed Care: The Legal Viewpoint

Sallyanne Payton, L.L.B.

I speak about the problem of managed care from the vantage point of the law. Managed care is forcing courts and legislatures to rethink virtually the entire body of law that governs medical care, because it has made obsolete many of the assumptions about the practice of medicine that have informed legal doctrine for centuries. In this discussion I am going to try to outline the major conceptual issues that arise out of managed care. I shall try to make this discussion brief and not very technical.

For hundreds of years physicians and other learned professionals have been special people in the eyes of the law. The relationship between physician and patient is understood to be not fundamentally commercial, not a transaction in which the rules of *caveat emptor* apply or the patient gets only what the patient pays for. Once the physician has entered into the physician-patient relationship the physician has a duty to render care that is within the professional standard of care: the professional's duty to the patient is in the nature of a fiduciary duty, ruled by high standards developed by an autonomous, self-governing profession that has controlled the practice of medicine in hospitals and other medical institutions. On this base of professional trustworthiness have been erected the edifice of modern American medicine and the law governing medical care.

Managed care, however, has brought to the delivery of medical care considerations of cost and even of profit that historically have not been regarded as legitimate influences on clinical decision-making. In introducing financial considerations into the heart of medical practice, managed care has precipitated a decline in the autonomy of the individual professional and the independence of the medical profession itself. Increasingly, the care that patients receive is not a function of the medical judgment of their physicians but rather is determined by the terms of their managed care contracts.

This presentation was made April 1, 1995 at the University of Michigan Forum on Health Policy and was subsequently edited in June 1997.

Ordinarily the law protects contracts and holds people to the bargains they have made voluntarily. The move from professional standards to contract as the measure of provider responsibility to patients is not a theoretically difficult leap to make. The history of modern law has been a movement from status to contract as the basis of relationship. The historic duties and rights of the physician-patient relationship are based on status; the transition to managed care can be considered a move in the direction of contract and therefore of greater autonomy on the part of the patient, who can bargain for what the patient wants. Considered as contracts, however, managed care contracts are problematic because of the information problem. The explanatory documents that are given to individuals generally specify that the patient is entitled to certain categories of medical care (e.g., inpatient and outpatient services, prescription drugs, home health care services), subject to certain categorical exclusions such as for investigational or experimental treatments, and subject to the overall condition that the service be "medically necessary" for the individual patient. There may also be procedural requirements, as for example that the patient use only authorized providers, consult a gatekeeper in order to obtain a referral to a specialist, obtain prior approval for a visit to a hospital emergency room. However, the documents furnished to the individual almost never describe the utilization controls that are the soul of the contract, even though the patient's coverage in reality consists of what the utilization controls allow. And where patients and providers are aware of the restrictions on utilization under the patient's managed care plan, and do not intend to incur expenses that are not consistent with the cost controls, the plan's utilization constraints determine what care is realistically available.

The information problem is exacerbated by the agency problem. The true customer of the managed care organization is generally not the individual consumer but is rather a corporate sponsor of a group health plan, typically an employer or, increasingly, a government health benefit program. The plan sponsor's interests lie generally in avoiding medical costs, and therefore the plan sponsor may share with the beneficiaries an interest in keeping the beneficiaries healthy, since health is preferable to disease from the beneficiaries' point of view. When an individual becomes ill, however, interests diverge. Necessary medical care is a benefit to an individual and the individual is interested in having high-quality care while the price of the care is a cost to the plan sponsor, a "medical loss" in the terminology of the insurance business. Plan sponsors therefore have an urgent interest in keeping down the cost of treatment, and therefore a much less intense interest in assuring that the plans provide high quality care if higher quality means more expense.

In terms of economic theory, this agency problem means that corporate plan sponsors may make suboptimal choices of plan. Insofar as the quality of medical service for patients who become ill is relevant to an assessment of the quality of a plan, and the quality of the service turns on the actual experience patients have with illness and treatment under the plan, purchasing decisions that ignore patients' experiences will result in the making of choices that individuals would not have made for themselves. The plan sponsor may be a poor agent for the beneficiaries. If it is the theory that the market is most efficient when it is producing what individuals would buy if they were spending their own money, the agency problem leads also to choices that may not promote economic efficiency as completely as they otherwise might. The structural adversity of interest between individual beneficiaries and plan sponsors is present even if, as is true of many employers, the sponsoring organization has an interest in providing an attractive plan in order to recruit or keep its members or employees. All of this means that even as a theoretical matter the managed care contract as it is presently created is probably not entitled either to the dignity that the law accords to bargains freely made between parties whose eyes are open, or the deference due to bargains that promote efficient allocation of resources.

This brings us to the next point, the question of liability for injuries to patients. One of the consequences of aggressive management of patient care in the interest of reducing costs can be an increase in risk to the individual patient. Who should be responsible when injury occurs because of these deliberately increased risks? One might argue that if a patient had decided that she was willing to buy a managed care plan that provided, say, medical service at the 75th percentile because the plan that provided service at the 90th percentile was too expensive, that would be her choice and she might well be held to it if the 75th percentile treatment did not result in an adequate outcome. But what is she was told by both plans that she would receive "all medically necessary" services within the covered categories and the more stringently managed plan gave no hint that it had reduced medical services to the bare minimum? Should it be a complete answer to a malpractice complaint that she bought the cheaper plan? What if she had no choice because the plan had been selected by her employer? Should the employer bear responsibility for having selected a plan that skated too close to the edge? Should the plan be held liable when it has made coverage decisions that throw excessive risk onto the patients? What is excessive in this environment? Where is the edge? Who sets the medical standards when managed care becomes the dominant mode of medical care delivery? Are these questions properly thought of as problems of professional malpractice? Is it possible that the providers, giving treatment in accordance with the patient's coverage, are not guilty of malpractice while the managed care company and the plan sponsor are liable, and if so for what, on what theory? How should ERISA, the Employee Retirement Income Security Act of 1974, under which many self-insured employee benefit plans operate free of state regulation but have federally-imposed fiduciary duties, be interpreted in light of the problems of trust and agency that have developed in the managed care marketplace?

While the courts may struggle with the liability implications of managed care, the tort liability system was never intended to be a primary technique of quality control the medical services sector; it has always looked to the medical profession to set its own standards and has always assumed that patients will be well-served if the medical profession and medical care institutions simply act in accordance with the trust reposed in them. Some of the issues of agency and information can be overcome, and the marketplace be made more diverse and robust if at least some of the purchasers of health plans are organizations representing consumers and some of the managed care plans are organized by providers who have an interest in maintaining high standards of care for persons who are ill. Any employee health benefit plan can be made into a more consumer-oriented purchaser, and with a few changes in relevant legislation many other types of institutions, such as small business purchasing cooperatives, can participate effectively in the market. There is nothing to prevent providers, including physicians, from creating networks and even managed care plans. The antitrust laws allow cooperation among competitors as long as the relationships do no amount to simple price-fixing or cartelization but instead tend to promote efficiency, open up new markets, put new products into the market, and so forth. The antitrust enforcement community has been bending over backwards to accommodate physicians' desire to form organizations to compete in the managed care marketplace while not giving up the autonomy of private practice. All they ask is that the agreements not be anti-competitive. The Justice Department and the Trade Commission have gone so far as to issue guidelines and create 'safe harbors' for arrangements the legality of which they will simply presume.

Managed care is an infant industry, not a mature one. It has virtually eliminated fee-for-service indemnity insurance and the cottage industry style of organizing medical services. The institutions that were best positioned to enter the new market for integrated health services were institutions with access to capital. It has not taken long, however, for the public to discover that the behaviors that have been unleashed in this new marketplace challenge ideas and practices regarding the relationships between professionals and their patients that are deeply embedded in the culture and the laws, and threaten values that the public and the profession are unwilling to abandon. If I may tie together the two themes of this rumination, the patients who are having such difficulty with their managed care organizations might be better served by physician-led, professional responsible, disciplined medical care organizations that could provide high quality at reasonable prices. A new form of alliance between physicians and patients needs to be forged in this new era of economic integration and cost consciousness. It can be created if organizations representing patients and organizations representing physicians turn their collective intelligence to the task of designing and managed institutions for the world in which cost control, professionalism and quality can be viewed as complementary rather than oppositional. The future of the medical profession, indeed the entire concept of professional autonomy and self-governance, is at stake in this effort.

38

Managed Care: Reform Without Legislation

Jon R. Gabel

Only in America could there be national health care reform without any legislation. In this paper I will report how the health care market has changed and will bring to your attention recent studies about the cost-savings achieved by managed care plans.

Let us not overstate, however, what Americans can expect from "reform without legislation." First, it will not provide coverage for the approximately 40 million Americans who are without any health insurance coverage. Second, it will not prevent insurers or health maintenance organizations (HMOs) from pursuing underwriting practices that will deny coverage to those Americans who need the financial protection of health insurance most. Third, it will not change the incentives that health plans face — to enroll an unhealthy individual is not good for the bottom line. Only "reform through legislation" can correct these problems.

What reform without legislation can do is to improve the value of health care received by insured Americans. This means improved quality of care at a more affordable price. Reform without legislation will also bring improved customer service and modern business practices to a sector that has historically resisted such change.

Growth of Managed Care

In 1988, nearly 71 percent of the 140 million Americans who receive their health insurance through their employer were covered by an indemnity policy. By 1994, that figure had fallen to 35 percent.[1] HMOs share of the market grew from 18 to 25 percent. Preferred provider organizations (PPOs) and point-of-service (POS) plans experienced the biggest growth in market share.[2] Combined PPO/POS enrollments increased from 18 percent to 40 percent between 1988 and 1994.

This presentation was made on April 1, 1995, at the University of Michigan Forum on Health Policy. It was subsequently edited in June 1997, by the author.

Different metropolitan areas are in different stages of development. The National Research Corporation's survey of 132,000 U.S. households in the spring of 1994 shows that in some metropolitan areas such as San Antonio, Charlotte and Canton, Ohio, about 15 percent of the population is enrolled in HMO plans. Metropolitan areas with medium levels of penetration include New York at 38 percent, Chicago at 32 percent, and Cleveland at 33 percent. The future of the American health care system may look more like the high HMO penetration metropolitan areas such as Buffalo (58 percent), Los Angeles (55 percent) and Tucson (56 percent).

Why are enrollments in managed care growing so rapidly? Purchasers are convinced that managed care plans can provide more financial protection against the cost of health care than indemnity plans. Consequently, employees today are far less likely to have a choice of an indemnity plan than they were in 1988. Figure 38.1 shows that in 1988, nearly 90 percent of workers who received their insurance through their employer had the option of choosing an indemnity plan. In 1994 that figure had fallen to 51 percent.[3] However, fewer employees now can choose an HMO plan. In 1988 about 70 percent of employees had a choice of an HMO plan, but by 1994 that figure had fallen to 62 percent. It is the PPO and POS plan that are now more available to workers—nearly 40 percent may choose a PPO plan, and 30 percent may choose a POS plan. POS and PPO plans are in the jargon of the insurance industry, often "replacement products." Previously an employer may have offered both an indemnity and HMO plan; now it offers only a POS plan (or PPO plan). Hence, if workers today "are forced" into any plan, it is probably a hybrid-type plan — PPO or POS.

Figure 38.1   Fewer Americans Can Choose Indemnity and HMO Plans, 1988-1994

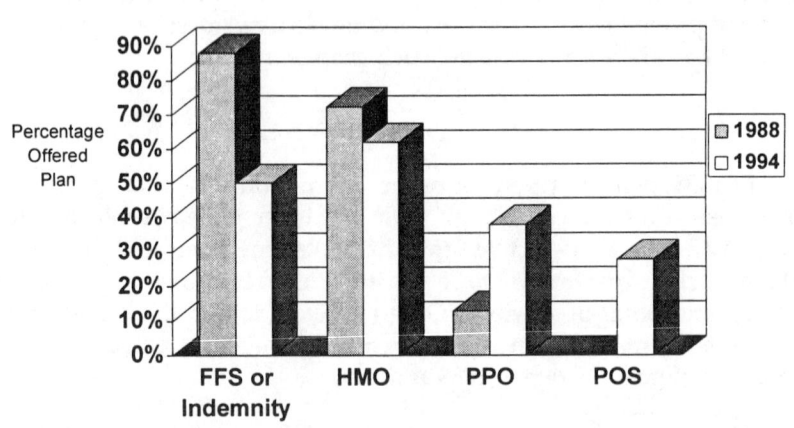

Sources: HIAA, KPMG

Managed Care: Reform Without Legislation 269

Nevertheless, HMO enrollment grows because American workers are as satisfied, or more satisfied with them, than they are with indemnity coverage. As Figure 38.2 shows, Americans, who receive their coverage through their employer, regardless of their health status, rate their HMO plans more highly than their peers in indemnity plans. HMOs score higher with regard to out-of-pocket costs and time spent with paper work. Indemnity plans score higher concerning quality of care, and access to specialists.

Figure 38.2 Percent of Americans with Employer-Based Coverage Who are Completely Satisfied with Their HMO and FFS Plans, by Self-Reported Health Status

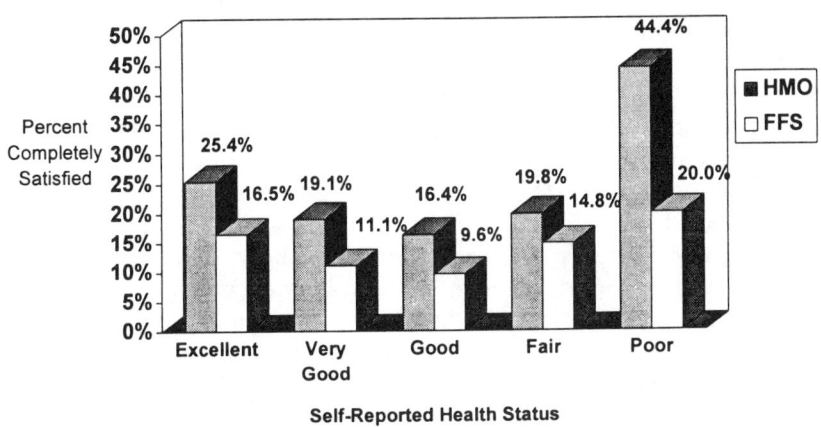

Source: National Research Corporation Survey Data

HMO Performance Survey: Future Market Directions

GHAA surveyed its membership in November, 1994, interviewing 71 HMOs about a host of issues. The survey provides some important indicators of the future direction of the market.

Fifty-eight million Americans in 1995 were enrolled in an HMO plan, a figure roughly double the number of enrollees in 1986.[4] During the past year, HMO enrollment grew at more than 14 percent, and in absolute terms, nearly eight million people. In 1980, there were fewer than 10 million Americans enrolled in HMOs.

Sixty-three percent of HMO plans now offer POS plans. As recently as 1990, only about 36 percent of HMOs offered POS plans. According to GHAA data, only about 10 percent of people enrolled in POS plans ever use their out-of-plan benefits.[5] Yet, many Americans gain a sense of security knowing if they want to use an out-of-network physician, they can do so. A POS plan costs about 15 percent more than a close-ended HMO plan, offered by the same HMO in the same state.[6]

Medicare is the last bastion of fee-for-service, but that is changing. The 1994 Congressional elections have shifted the priorities of the Congress in the health care arena from universal coverage to reducing federal outlays. If America is to balance the budget by the year 2002, we will need to reduce expenditures by $1.2 billion dollars below current trends. To achieve these budgetary goals, the greatest savings must come from Medicare. When Senator Packwood spoke to GHAA in February 1995, he said, "We need to cut Medicare spending by $450 million dollars. To put this in perspective, the current cost of the Medicare program is $170 billion. Hence, we are talking about extraordinary reductions in the rate of increase in the cost of the Medicare program.

One way to control the rate of increase in the cost of Medicare is to introduce into Medicare financial incentives similar to those found in some employer groups. A politically controversial way to do so is to change Medicare from a defined benefit to a defined contribution program. Thus, if the expected cost in a county is 20 percent more for the traditional Medicare fee-for-service program than an HMO, the beneficiary should pay for the difference out-of-pocket. Even without these incentives, enrollment in the Medicare Risk program has doubled over the past few years.

GHAA's survey indicates that more HMOs intend to enter the Medicare Risk market than are currently participating in the market. I believe within the next few years, you will see another doubling of enrollment in Medicare Risk HMOs, from the current 8 to 16 percent. Already, in a few western states, nearly a quarter of the state's elderly population are enrolled in the Medicare risk program. In contrast, in Michigan, virtually none of the elderly are currently enrolled in Medicare Risk plans. I believe in the future, Michigan will look like Arizona or California do today.

One reason that the Medicare Risk program grows is that some large HMOs have demonstrated their ability to serve the elderly effectively, and earn a profit. When I use the term "effectively," I am referring to the ability to satisfy their members. The elderly enrolled in HMOs now rate their overall satisfaction with their plan higher than those enrolled in the traditional fee-for-service program. This is not true just for the elderly in "excellent" or "very good" health, but also those in "poor" and "fair" health. A closer look at specific components of satisfaction reveals a similar pattern to the employed population. The elderly enrolled in the traditional program rate their access to care and quality of care more highly than the elderly enrolled in HMOs; HMOs receive higher ratings with regard to paperwork and out-of pocket costs.[7]

Another reason that the HMO industry looks upon Medicare Risk as a growing segment of the market is the opportunity to reduce inpatient hospital utilization from fee-for-service norms. Even within Medicare Risk programs, the number of hospital days per 1,000 members varies immensely across regions. For example, in the Northeast, Medicare Risk plans average 2,474 days per 1,000 members; in the West, they average 1,081 days.[8] Few would argue these differences are due to the East enrolling a much sicker population.

HMOs also view Medicaid as a growth market. Almost as many HMOs plan to enter the Medicaid market as plans that are currently participating in Medicaid. Many states now mandate that some components of the Medicaid population, such as the Aid to Families with Dependent Children (AFDC), must enroll in a Medicaid managed care plan. Some in the HMO community have concerns about the quality of care and customer service that some newly created plans —hastily built to serve the Medicaid population — will deliver.

Member Satisfaction Surveys

According to the HMO Performance Survey, about 97 percent of HMOs report undertaking member satisfaction surveys. For example, one large insurance company, centrally involved in the HMO business, is surveying 600,000 of their HMO subscribers. The large sample is made necessary to develop report cards on every single physician who participates in that HMO. The report card will be the basis of bonus payments to physicians.

The previous example illustrates the central use of member satisfaction surveys — continuous quality improvement. Many CEOs use member satisfaction surveys to identify weak areas of customer service. At the end of the year, management will then assess plan improvement. For example, how are we answering our phones? How many rings does it take before we answer? How polite are we? How polite are our administrative workers? How long do members have to wait for appointments? American business adopted the use of customer satisfaction surveys to improve service many years ago, and now the medical care sector is overcoming its historic resistance.

Patient satisfaction surveys represent a strong countervailing force in a capitated environment to provide necessary services, and to spend more time with their patients. There are, of course, other uses for member satisfaction surveys, such as marketing and understanding member disenrollment. Another potential use of member satisfaction surveys is to link information about member health status collected in the surveys, and use it to risk adjust payments to providers.

Falling Premiums

The most striking finding from the HMO Performance Survey is that HMO premiums declined between 1994 and 1995 (Figure 38.3). This decline is unprecedented and evidence that the market for health insurance has been transformed. Data from 1981 to 1993 shows that premium hikes swung between about five and 25 percent increases each year.[9] As HMO market share has grown, increasingly competition in local markets is between HMO plans, not HMO versus indemnity plans. There is extensive research showing that employees are highly sensitive to their out-of-pocket costs in selecting an HMO plan, particularly across HMO plans.[10] Perhaps the decline in premiums is an indication that society is now reaping the benefits of employees' sensitivity to differences in the cost of HMO plans.

Figure 38.3 Trends in HMO Premiums, 1992-1995

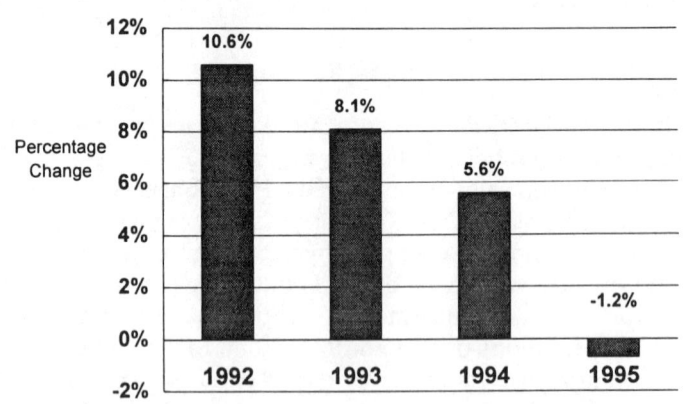

Source: HMO Performance Report, 1994, GHAA

Let me temper this optimism with some reservations. Historically, the health insurance market has experienced an underwriting cycle filled with peaks and valleys. For example, Blue Cross/Blue Shield Plans operating profits went through a cycle where three years of underwriting profits (profits before investment income) were followed by three years of operating losses.[11] The importance of this cycle to American businesses and workers is that this profitability cycle was linked to a price cycle.[12] When the health insurance industry earns profits, two years later premium increases are modest; when the health insurance industry loses money, premiums increase by 15 to 20 percent two years later. In 1992, the health insurance industry broke the underwriting cycle by earning profits for the fourth consecutive year. We now have six consecutive years of underwriting profits. In a few years insurers and HMOs may whittle away these profits through declining premiums, which in turn will be followed by double digit increases in premiums.

The HMO industry has been able to remain profitable, despite historically low premium increases during the past few years. By implication, underlying increases in health care expenses have been very low during recent years. This may be the true reason to believe that health care inflation will remain modest, and that the health insurance market has been transformed.

HMOs and the Congressional Budget Office (CBO)

The CBO scores all federal legislation with budgetary implications. Therefore, CBO profoundly affects any legislation that promotes the use of HMOs to control Medicare or Medicaid expenditures, as well as comprehensive health care reform, such as the President's now defeated Health Security Act. I wish to show data that calls into question recent CBO scoring concerning the savings of managed care.

In a February 1994 memorandum, CBO estimated that the most effective HMOs reduce the use of services by 22 percent, compared to an indemnity plan with utilization management. Group and staff models save an estimated 20 percent, and for IPAs/network models, only 1 percent.[13] GHAA data on use of hospital inpatient services is not compatible with CBO scoring. The differences in hospital days per 1,000 members under the age of 65 are lowest for network plans, and highest for IPA plans, with group and staff plans in the middle. They do not suggest utilization rates 20 percent lower for group/staff models over IPA/network plans. These data are not adjusted for differences in the population; however, we are unaware of studies indicating that IPA/network plans enroll a healthier mix of patients.

If IPA/network plans are more inefficient than group/staff models, one would expect IPAs/networks to have higher monthly premium costs. Figure 38.4 shows that between 1988 and 1993, IPAs/networks typically cost between 0 and 4 percent more. The rate of increase between group/staff and IPA/network plans is also similar. This analysis, of course, does not control for differences in the population or geographic distribution between the two groups.

Figure 38.4 Trends in HMO Premiums for Single Coverage, by Primary Model Type, 1988-1993

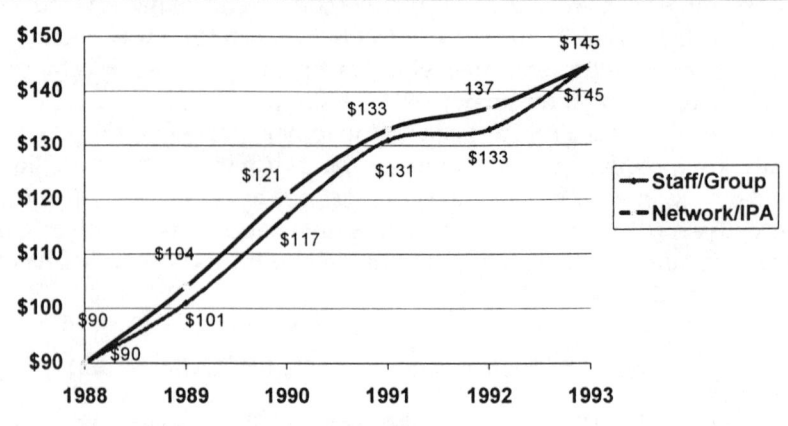

Source: GHAA's Annual HMO Industry Survey

CBO views managed care savings as one-time savings over indemnity coverage. Stated differently, savings from managed care plans do not alter the slope of the line relating cost to time, but shift the line to the right. I disagree. The Health Insurance Association of America (HIAA) and KPMG Peat Marwick LLP annual surveys of employers suggest (Figure 38.5, next page) that between 1987-1994, HMO plans realized annual rates of increase of 2.1 percent points less indemnity plans. This may not sound like much, but when 2.1% is compounded over five years, it results in double digit reductions in premiums.

Conclusion

In this paper, I have shown findings from a number of different surveys. Perhaps, even the critics of HMOs would concede that three facts are undeniable:

- HMOs and managed care are growing rapidly.
- Even without further legislation, HMOs will play an increasing role in the delivery of care in the Medicare and Medicaid programs.
- HMOs have brought about unprecedented reductions in the cost of health insurance in recent years.

If you are not enrolled in an HMO currently, chances are that you will in the future. Not everybody will be happy in an HMO. Nor should everyone be enrolled, for it is a different health care system than the one many of us grew up with.

So my concluding observation is this: Things don't always turn out the way we planned, but sometimes it is for the better!

Figure 39.5   Annual Increases in HMO and FFS Premiums, 1987 to 1994

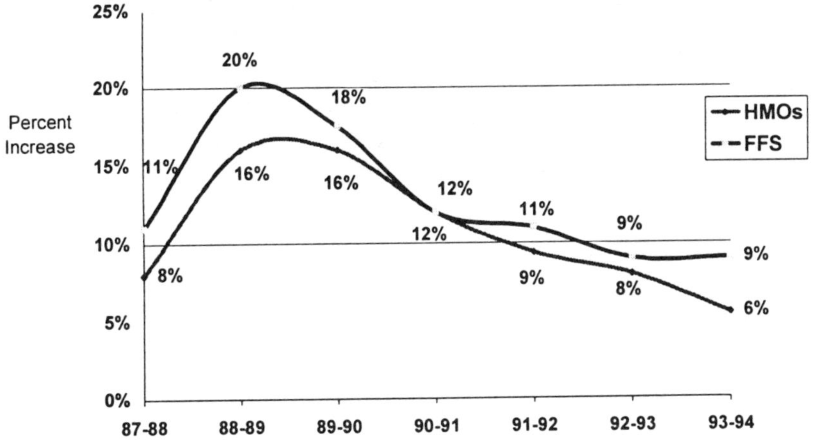

Sources: HIAA, KPMG

Notes

1. KPMG Peat Marwick LLP, *Health Benefits in 1994*, Montvale, New Jersey.
2. POS plans can be either HMO plans that offer out-of-network benefits or PPO plans with a primary care gatekeeper. Typically, the financial penalty to use out-of—network services is much stronger for POS plans than PPO plans.
3. KPMG Peat Marwick LLP, *Health Benefits* in 1994, Montvale, New Jersey.
4. These figures include members of HMO-type POS plans.
5. Unpublished data, GHAA Annual Industry Survey, 1994.
6. Unpublished GHAA data.
7. Unpublished ata from National Research Corporation, 1994.
8. Unpublished data, GHAA Annual Survey, 1994.
9. Data are from the KPMG surveys, 1991-1993; Health Insurance Association of America Surveys, 1986-1990; and unpublished data from the Bureau of Labor Statistics, 1980-1985, Employer cost Index.
10. Illustrative studies include: T.C. Buchmueller and P.J. Feldstein, "The Effect of Price on Switching Among Health Plans," original paper from the Graduate School of Management, University of California, Irvine, (May 1995). B. Dowd and R. Feldman, "Employers as HIPC Models: Premium Elasticities of Health Plan Choice and Premium Contribution Methods," original paper from the Institute of

Health Services Research, University of Minnesota, (July 9, 1993). S.H. Long, R.F. Settle, and C.W. Wrightson, "Employee Premiums, Availability of Alternative Plans, and HMO Disenrollment," *Medical Care* 26, no. 10, 1988, 927-38. W.P. Welch, "The Elasticity of Demand for Health Maintenance Organizations," *Journal of Human Resources*, 1986, 21:252-66. W.P. Welch, "The Elasticity of Demand for Health Maintenance Organizations," *Journal of Human Resources*, 1986, 21:252-66. For a review of the literature, see M.A. Morrisey, "Price Sensitivity in Health Care: Implications for Health Care Policy," NFIB Foundation, Washington, 1992.

11. See J. Gabel, D. Liston, G. Jensen, and J. Marsteller, "The Health Picture in 1993: Some Rare Good News," *Health Affairs*, Spring (1) 1994, p.331.

12. J. Gabel and G. Jensen, "Can a Universal Coverage System Temper the Underwriting Cycle?" *Inquiry*, Vol. 29, No 2, Summer, 1992, p.250-251.

13. Congressional Budget Office, "Effects of Managed Care and Managed Competition," CBO Memorandum, February, 1995.

39

How Well Does Managed Care Control Costs?

Marsha Gold, ScD

I want to focus on four questions. What forms of managed care should we credit as producing cost savings? More specifically, does managed care save money and, if so, which forms of managed care do so? Then I will ask what are "enough" savings? And, finally, What lessons have we learned?

1. Does Managed Care Save Money?

I don't think we have all the answers that we need, but we do know some things. Much of the early research on managed care up to the 1980s was based on the study of group/staff model plans. They showed that there were considerable savings, largely from reduced hospital admissions. Researchers, however, asked whether this could result from selection of who got enrolled in an HMO—was their population healthier to begin with than a comparison group? The Rand Study addressed that question, through their study of the Group Health Cooperative HMO.[1] They found that there are real savings, independent of selection factors.

Now, as the population enrolled in managed care plans becomes more prominent for the population as a whole, additional questions need to be asked. Is it still true that managed care plans produce considerable savings? And do other forms of managed care produce the kinds of savings seen for group/staff models? That's the current debate. An excellent article by Robert Miller and Harold Luft, in the *Journal of the American Medical Association (JAMA)*, reviews studies since 1980. It provides a meta-analysis of studies that met their quality criteria, looking across these studies at a variety of outcomes. They analyzed three major studies and a cluster of other ones, including the Medical Outcomes study, the Medicare Risk Contracting study and some others on social HMOs.

This presentation was made on April 1, 1995, at the University of Michigan Forum on Health Policy. It was subsequently edited in June 1997, by the author.

Randy Brown did the study on Medicare risk contracting HMOs.[2] It has decent results that seem to pass all methodological tests. The study has gotten tremendous attention in Congress. It is the first study I've seen in a while that people who do health care policy are having to deal with. The results are clear: HMOs are, in fact, more efficient. They did make savings—but the savings didn't go to the government. They went to the beneficiaries in extra benefits because of the risk adjustment issue. When setting its premium rates, Medicare didn't adjust for risk correctly, which meant that even though the government thought it was saving five percent, it was not. The government paid more than it should have. Thus the questions we should ask are these: (1) How much should the government save and how can you set rates better? (2) Would this be true if everyone were in an HMO? (Risk doesn't matter as penetration increases. If the markets have gotten more fully penetrated we should repeat some of the studies on which the estimates are based.) It will be interesting to watch that debate proceed.

More generally, analysis by Miller and Luft, using more recent evidence, shows that HMOs still seem to save money. HMOs have fewer hospital admissions and somewhat shorter length of stays. However these differences are less than what was found in comparisons between fee-for-service plans and HMOs in the past. You would expect this because the market has gotten more competitive and fee-for-service has adjusted, as well. There is also more variation across the HMO industry than was true in the past, or at least more variation in current studies of HMOs than was found previously. HMOs now use fewer really expensive services but provide more preventive services. There are issues of how to do that clinically in an effective manner, but the direction of movement is hopeful.

2. What Kinds of Managed Care Plans Generate Savings?

While this direction of movement is encouraging, it does not tell you how much savings there will be, only that there are some savings. The real question has become whether group HMOs or IPA (independent practitioner association) models produce more savings, and it is hard to reach a firm conclusion about this, yet. From current studies it is not clear that group practice capitated plans save any more than the network IPAs.

Will putting Medicaid enrollees into managed care save money? It is difficult to draw conclusions based on current data. In the available studies of Medicaid patients, few were in an HMO.[3] Most of the studies were of primary care case management models. So much is at stake in going to Medicaid managed care that a lot of research on this is now being funded. Soon we will know more. It is hard to generalize from current Medicaid managed care studies because of all the differences among providers and

How Well Does Managed Care Control Costs?

Medicaid population groups. I think we are going to learn as we go forward. I am not sure there really are short-term savings from Medicaid managed care if you do it right.

The evidence is inconclusive about whether Preferred Provider Organizations (PPOs) that offer discounted rates to large purchasers of their services save money for the system as a whole or only for their preferred customers (i.e., do they charge others more, in order to compensate for bargains struck with their large-volume users?). It also is not yet clear how much impact including more really sick people in capitated payment plans will have on their cost savings over time.

We also don't know whether the massive shift that is now occurring to managed care plans will be a one-time saving or will continue to produce savings over time. Managed care continues to evolve, which means that conclusions based on studies at an earlier point in time may not apply to what is happening now. Change is happening relatively rapidly and the data are lagging behind.

A second problem limits our ability to draw conclusions about how the form of managed care affects savings. We are dealing with small numbers. There are between 500 and 600 HMOS, but about 100 of them have most of the enroll population so their practices will produce most of the effects that we see. In addition, there is not a lot of utilization data available. If one studies changes over five years, the conditions responsible for savings may no longer apply to the managed care market. Studies are not impossible, but one would have to be really creative in one's analysis to produce conclusions that are relevant to the policy questions being asked today. Those questions may not be policy relevant when the research is over, depending on how organizational practices evolve. Researchers really need to think carefully about what the right questions are and whether their research will be very useful in the future.

3. Can Managed Care Generate "Enough" Savings?

Can managed care generate enough savings? Don't ask me what is enough. Enough is whatever who's paying is willing to pay, I think. You could say "enough" is how much it costs to give a certain minimum standard of care. You put those two definitions of "enough" together. If there's a gap, then there's a question to be answered.

Right now, however "enough" is defined, research evidence leaves the question unanswered. Different pieces of research vary in the way they classify different types of managed care plans. It is not clear that coverage is coded in the same way from study to study. Consequently, we do not know whether inconsistent results from study to study reflect differences in study design or real variations in what is happening. Thus I will continue to question any conclusions we now draw about real cost savings when we compare different forms of managed care organizations or PPOs. We do know that there are savings from managed care—at least from traditional HMOs. We probably also know that managed care is not the magic bullet that will take care of all the issues of cost. And we are not clear on exactly how much savings managed care produces. Probably the savings are more than a one-time occurrence, or at least could be. If you have a coordinated system of care it is easier for the system to respond than if it is in pieces.

Research is much better at projecting by tracking the past and extrapolating in a linear way to predict the future. For someone like me who doesn't really believe that things change that much, it is incredible that so much is genuinely in flux. I don't know how you project what additional changes will occur in health care organization, or how you project policy changes themselves into that equation. There is a lot of uncertainty. Predictions can't be as precise when you don't know the direction or rate of change. That's the problem which makes the question about amount of savings from managed care unanswerable. Managed care is increasing, competition is changing, and we don't know what is going to happen with governmental regulation. We are also getting different kinds of people enrolling in HMOs. The high dollar spending goes for care to sick people and disabled people. Policymakers are just starting to realize that in Medicaid, and people are starting to think about how you move that into your projections of cost. There is much less managed care research on sick people, on people with chronic diseases and on unemployed people than there is on the rest of the population, except for the elderly, where there has been some research. But even most of the research on the elderly deals with the *average* elderly client, not the oldest or sickest group. Consequently, research doesn't tell us the answer about opportunity costs.

Cost savings from managed care should not be confused with total savings from other changes in the implementation of health care policy. Nor should cost savings necessarily be equated with better care. A lot of physicians are being trained for whom there will be no demand, because of the kind of specialized care they offer. Keeping them as part of our system of health care providers increases total costs, independent of what managed care plans do. How equitable is that? Again, total costs will be affected by whether or not the Medicaid budget gets transferred to a block grant. Republican governors today [April 1995] were proposing that 40 percent of the block grants should not have to go to health care or to nutrition. If Medicaid spending goes into the block grants, if efforts are made to include the currently uninsured, and if risk adjustment policies affect payments to managed care plans, costs will be affected by things that are not

4. What Lessons Have We Learned?

A few things *are* clear, however.[4] What lessons have we learned?

(1) Historical research suggests that people are about equally satisfied with managed care and with not-managed care. While results of various studies differ a bit, I think it is clear that people are much more satisfied with the money and the cost of managed care plans, but more dissatisfied with the interpersonal care that is found in large, managed care plans than is found in not-managed care. Independent of the level of satisfaction, however, there are some issues that the market has affected; people are joining managed care plans in great numbers.

(2) There is equal pressure to contract and to expand the number of physicians affiliated with a managed care plan. However the plans that are expanding are also very selective.

(3) Managed care plans now emphasize selectivity of staff based on cost performance, along with quality of training. Utilization management is a growing trend.

(4) There is evidence that managed care plans are not just giving their physicians cost incentives. They are also looking for satisfaction and quality.

(5) There is more risk-sharing with specialists.

(6) There is more emphasis on quality assurance. HMOs do this more than PPOs. NCQA accreditation is clearly having an effect on managed care practice.

These are encouraging trends, which suggest that increasingly in the future approaches to cost savings will be balanced by concerns for quality of care. Because of measurement problems, however, judging how well these goals are achieved, or what balance is struck among competing goals will probably continue to be difficult.

Finally, (7) from a policy perspective there is no substitute for judgment. By that I mean that judgments will have to be made and information is going to be limited. It also means that numbers can be used to prove any point in a lot of areas, because there is so much uncertainty. (Depending on what assumptions you make, things look very different as you analyze data.) That also means, I believe, that researchers should focus more on description and analysis of the facts and not just try to look at explanations of what is causing what. Current analysis may or may not answer questions that will be important later. But if we describe current practices clearly, policy makers will be able to reassess the implications of our evidence as circumstances change.

Notes

1. Robert H. Miller and Harold S. Luft, "Managed care plan performance since 1980: A literature analysis," *JAMA* 271:1512-19, May 18, 1994.

2. Randall Brown, et al., "Do Health Maintenance Organizations Work for Medicare?" *Health Care Financing Review*, Fall 1993, 7-23.

3. Robert Hurley, Deborah Freund, and John Paul, *Managed Care in Medicaid: Lessons for Policy and Program Design*, Ann Arbor, MI: Health Administration Press, March 1993.

4. M. Gold, R. Hurley, T. Lake, et al., "A National Survey of the Arrangements Managed Care Plans Make with Physicians," *NEJM* 333:1678-83, December 1995.

40
Managed Care: Stages of Development

John E. Billi, M.D.

First, I would like to put some of Jon Gabel's figures in the context of what's happening in the state of Michigan. If we look at the state of Michigan's population of around 10 million, the *New York Times* suggests that the penetration of managed care in Michigan is now at about 19 percent and has been rising slowly but steadily over the last decade. There was actually an inflection in the curve in the early to mid '80s that has plateaued for the last few years. In contrast the HMO penetration in the Medicaid program has increased very dramatically. After looking at the national figures, the state of Michigan has elected to move the Medicaid population into managed care, as a way of controlling costs in this very difficult population. Beginning this past year and finishing in 1995, the state administration has moved the population of Medicaid into managed care programs.

If you look at the state of Michigan, the highest percent penetration of managed care is in Washtenaw, Livingston, and Muskegon counties where 30-50% of the non-government insured population is in managed care. The I-96 corridor, the population center of Michigan, has a penetration of managed care that ranges from 20 to 30 percent. The more rural areas obviously are much lower. Those of you who have been looking at managed care are familiar with a model that has been developed and used by practically every health care consulting firm which shows the four stages of market. In Stage One, there is very little managed care penetration. Health care occurs mostly through private practitioners, independent hospitals, and indemnity insurance. Stage Two is characterized by some management of

---

This presentation was made on April 1, 1995, at the University of Michigan Forum on Health Policy. It was subsequently edited in June 1997, by the author.

care, formation of PPOs, and managed care beginning to take a foothold. In Stage Three provider groups are coming together, forming larger provider groups. There is some provider network formation, some hospital affiliations, and managed care is growing. Stage Four is a so-called mature market, such as we see in Buffalo, Minneapolis, and California where managed care penetration is above 50 percent. Most of their small hospitals are gone; they have merged into larger hospital networks or closed. Physicians have merged into group practices or at least are linked by multi-hospital provider organizations. In Michigan we are experiencing all four stages simultaneously. In the Upper Peninsula and in the less industrial counties in the center of the state we have no or very low penetration of managed care, below 10 percent. As we look south towards Muskegon and down into southeast Michigan, the penetration is higher.

In Michigan the evolution of the market seems to be stuck at about Stage Two and a Half, or Stage Three, rather than moving on. With the presence of the UAW and the auto companies in this state, there is a tremendous inertia. Initially, this is on the stationary side, but once it starts moving, the inertia will be on the motion side. I expect these markets actually to evolve very quickly once the UAW and the auto companies move to a more substantial embrace of managed care. Although we have four stages of managed care market development in the state of Michigan, what we really have is akin to a supersaturated solution. All the ingredients are present and ready to crystallize into a much more aggressive and much more competitive market. We are starting to see that come about now. Every now and then a crystal gets dropped into the solution and a few new crystals form but it hasn't yet produced the dramatic flood that we expect to see. Essentially, all the ingredients are here. I think we can look forward over the next few years to a very rapid evolution into a Stage Four market.

One reason the market evolution has been delayed here has to do with the excellent insurance coverage that the bargained-for populations fought hard for and have maintained as a right of the working population of the state. This is an accomplishment of which the unions are rightfully proud. In addition, the salaried ('white collar') population in industry in Michigan often has first-dollar coverage. When excellent or first-dollar coverage is present with very little out-of-pocket premium, it is hard for an HMO to enter the market, offer more services, and voluntarily woo the population to a managed care plan. If an employee population already has excellent coverage, choice of providers, and choice of facilities, what can be offered to that population to persuade them to give up some of that and enter a plan in which they are managed? Interestingly, however, despite that lack of a carrot, a significant percentage of the population has moved into managed care. They have done so without the more draconian employer actions that have been used in some other states to precipitate that market transition.

Regarding co-pays, I want to share one of my favorite managed care anecdotes. The health minister of the Nicaraguan government under the Sandinistas, a socialist government, was visiting the University of Michigan School of Public Health after the Sandinistas were thrown out of office. In a seminar he recounted all of the fantastic accomplishments that they had made under the Sandinistas: bringing health care into the community; a great reduction in infant mortality; open access of health care to rural populations — really a number of dramatic accomplishments. Someone asked him what he would have done differently is he had to do it again. He said, "I would have had co-pays. Because we were giving the care away for free many people really thought it wasn't worth anything. If they had just paid something they probably would have had a higher sense of the worth of the care they were receiving." I find that interesting in light of what we know of the effect of co-pays in terms of decreasing utilizations, not only if the utilization is discretionary but also for utilization that is essential.

The number of HMO plans in Michigan rose for a while and then shrank a bit and plateaued out. Often in markets there is at first a proliferation of plans and then, as groups—either groups of physicians in hospitals or small investors—realize that this is going to be a very difficult market to crack, there is a coalescence of the plans with smaller plans being incorporated into larger plans or else larger national corporations deciding the location isn't as attractive as it looked initially and they pull back. There's been a number of false starts by national companies. Last year most of the big five insurers in the country did not have Michigan on their list of top states to crack. They didn't have a Michigan strategy. They were waiting to see what happened with the other political and financial factors in the state.

The top plans in the state of Michigan represent quite a spectrum of types of managed care plans. The largest plan serves almost half a million subscribers. This large group model plan owned by the Henry Ford Health System almost doubled its size by acquiring an IPA model HMO. This acquisition of an IPA model HMO by a group model HMO has transformed Health Alliance Plan from one of the classic group models with tight linkage between providers and the managed care entity into a heterogeneous plan with a wide diversity of providers. All of these acquisitions and linkages make for some very unusual arrangements, in which one provider group can have half their business tied up in one of their clinical competitor's managed care products. Here is an example of the convoluted relationships which exist throughout southeastern Michigan right now. My wife is a pediatrician who works for a group practice which was purchased by the Detroit Medical Center, which is Wayne State University's medical center. Almost half of her patient population was with Maxi Care HMO, which is now owned by the Health Alliance Plan, which is a part of the Henry Ford system, which is a competitor of DMC. Other large plans include the Blue Cross managed care plan which is over the 300,000 mark; M-Care is now up over 70,000. In addition to SelectCare's managed care product, they also have several hundred thousand more members in a PPO product.

This kind of information sends chills down the spines of hospital administrators and sends ripples of pleasure through the for-profit markets. The venture capitalists, who are now increasingly interested in for-profit managed care plans, love to see hospitalization rates that are falling in the state of Michigan but are still in some instances one and a half or two times what they are in California. They see the potential for removing large quantities of care and therefore large sums of money out of the provision of health care in the state of Michigan. Of course, whether we will ever get close to California's figures of hospitalization is really unclear to me. Michigan ranks near the top among states in such measures as chronic illness, smoking rates, and cardiovascular disease. Whether it is appropriate to compare our hospitalization rates with some of the sunbelt states, where populations may have migrated because of excellent health, is not clear. Michigan represents a great target of opportunity. I think the big five national for-profit insurance companies are going to come back here licking their chops as the market starts to move into the next phase.

I would just like to make a couple more general comments about Jon Gabel's presentation. First, in the Congressional Budget Office studies, some of the discrepancy in utilization between the IPA HMO model and the more tightly managed group model HMOs has to do with the dated nature of the information. The IPA and physician organization HMO models are evolving rapidly and starting to look more and more like the tighter managed staff and group model HMO. In the traditional IPA and physician organization models, groups of independent physicians who were spread throughout a community belonged to a managed-care plan and submitted their bills pretty much like it was Blue Cross/Blue Shield, who paid a check. The only difference was they were negotiating a rate with a managed care plan rather than with an indemnity carrier. Those have fallen by the wayside. As capitation and more centralized utilization management comes to the IPA model HMOs it is not surprising that the utilization figures are improving. I think Dr. Gabel has more recent information than CBO. In addition, though, I believe that there *is* favorable selection that has been documented in HMO enrollment. Some investigators, even in our own School of Public Health, have looked at some managed care plan tactics that have been used to discourage older or less healthy people from enrolling. These include using enrollment forms with very small print, or putting the enrollment office on the second floor so you have to climb the stairs to get there. I think those anecdotes are not representative of the industry as a whole. However, if you look at managed care advertising you rarely see advertising of extensive durable medical equipment, special seating chairs for children with chronic disabling diseases and the like. The advertising is directed to a much healthier population. As you can tell, I am quite concerned about the for-profit entry into the insurance market. I think that it is very telling that the California HMO industry uses what is called a medical loss ratio. The medical loss ratio represents the percent of health-care dollars that are spent on health care. In other words, in the investor view, the amount of money that has to be spent on health care is viewed as costs to the system. What's remaining above that can be used for administration and also for profit. I think many of us are staggered at the percent of premium that is going to profit in some of these California systems as the for-profits keep down payments to providers but keep premiums at a competitive level. Money that comes out for profit and money that goes out to administration is not available to provide health care to the patient. We've got to keep the patient's benefit in mind.

41

The Ethics of Incentives in Managed Care

E. Haavi Morreim, Ph.D.

Introduction

Ethical issues can be found in managed care on both a policy level and a clinical level. On the policy level, managed care organizations (MCOs) face questions of justice as they determine what kinds of care to provide for whom, and when. They must balance the needs of individual enrollees against those of the larger group. MCOs must set limits on facilities, for instance, from hospital beds and clinic offices to medical staff. And new technologies, such as autologous bone marrow transplant for breast cancer, offer uncertain potential to save lives at very high cost. Each individual subscriber has a legitimate claim to the care that he needs, yet MCOs must guard against excessive expenditures that could threaten their fiscal (vi)ability to serve the other subscribers with the care to which they are morally and contractually entitled.

These decisions create ethical issues on the clinical level. MCOs manage resources, not just by policies governing facilities and costly new technologies, but also by bringing cost-consciousness to the delivery of health care. Utilization review (UR) can limit physicians' clinical autonomy. If the guideline does not fit a patient's needs, the physician faces conflicts of obligation, pitting his contractual duty to honor the MCO's rules against his fiduciary obligation to serve each patient's best interests. Incentive systems, on the other hand, leave physicians considerably freer to exercise their clinical judgment, but only by creating conflicts of interest that pit their own interests against their patients'.[1]

This article argues that these ethical problems are partly the product of an economic structure that brings the economic incentives of physicians into harmony with those of the MCOs while leaving patients under a com-

---

The author has adapted this article for this publication from an article which appeared in Trends in Health Care, Law & Ethics, 10(1/2), Winter/Spring 1995, 56-62.

pletely different set of incentives, and thereby expectations. Whereas providers are rewarded for delivering a conservative level of care, patients' economic insulation encourages them to ignore costs and to demand a high level of care as their entitlement. The article then proposes that if MCOs rewarded patients for using the system conservatively, patients would have more reason to consider which care is worthwhile and physicians' incentives could be shifted toward promoting quality of care. Changing patients' economic incentives will not resolve all the moral issues of managed care, but it can considerably ease policy conflicts between patients and MCOs, and reduce physicians' clinical conflicts of interest and conflicts of obligation.

Historical Perspective

Until recently, modern health care financing was largely retrospective, fee-for-service and generous. Insurance reimbursed largely according to whatever fees providers said they customarily charged, and rarely challenged medical (i.e., spending) decisions. Insurers passed on cost increases to businesses that in turn reaped tax write-offs. Providers were economically insulated, knowing that they would be paid for virtually any service rendered (the more services the better), and most patients were likewise insulated from costs, either by first dollar coverage through the workplace or by a cost shifting in which those who could not pay were subsidized by those who could.[2]

The system was, in essence, an Artesian Well of Money. Virtually no one had much reason to worry about the cost of care. And so long as money was no object, certain values prevailed. Among them:

- potentially beneficial care should never be denied on account of mere money;
- an individual's (in)ability to pay should be irrelevant to the kind and level of care he should receive;
- physicians should never compromise their patients' care in order to save money, except perhaps where the patient is paying (thus presuming that insurance money is not ultimately patients' money);
- other things being equal, it is generally better to intervene too much than too little (high-tech is better than low-tech is better than no-tech).[3]

These "Artesian" values, alongside the inflationary reimbursement system and other factors (such as the rise of high technology and the aging of the population) sent health care costs into the upward spiral that governments and businesses are now trying so frantically to stem. Cost containment initially focused on controls, such as wage/price freezes and regulatory limits on construction and capital acquisitions.[4] However, as controls failed, it became evident that providers' Artesian incentives had to be changed.

In 1973, Congress permitted health maintenance organizations (HMOs) to reverse almost completely the providers' traditional incentives to maximize care. Under the necessity to provide all subscribers' care within a fixed annual budget, HMO physicians and hospitals questioned the necessity of many standard forms of care, including the facile use of hospitalization and aggressive technology, and focused instead on keeping patients healthy and delivering only necessary interventions in appropriate settings. HMOs were not just permitted, but expected to ensure physicians' cost-consciousness with appropriate incentives.[5]

Even the fee-for-service sector saw incentives change. In 1982, Congress established Diagnosis-Related Group (DRG) reimbursement, setting a fixed fee for each hospital admission of Medicare patients. Instead of reaping revenue by keeping patients longer and providing more services, hospitals now could only profit by limiting length of stay and intensity of care.

Significantly, DRGs directly affected only hospitals, leaving physicians under Artesian incentives. Clashes were inevitable as hospitals needing to "do less" confronted physicians accustomed to "do more," so hospitals sought to bring physicians under the new incentives. Nasty memos from annoyed administrators eventually gave way to more concrete tactics, such as publishing physicians' spending patterns at staff meetings in hopes of using peer pressure and embarrassment to change old habits.[6] More recently a far more powerful tool has emerged: economic credentialing, the denial or revocation of staff privileges for high spenders.[7]

If patients and treatments are to be effectively "managed," the principal instruments of medical practice, namely physicians, must operate under the same constraints. Hence, we are witnessing the creation and development of corporate entities and financial arrangements meant to bring physicians into concert with payors, managed care organizations and hospitals. If fully aligned, this trio of payors, providers (doctors and hospitals), and managed care organizations will be organized cooperatively and positioned to produce the change necessary to rewrite, even revolutionize, American medicine.[8]

Note in this description that patients are not listed among the financial players. They remain in the Artesian Well, excluded from the new economic incentives. In another example of alignment language, Sulmasy notes that "[w]hat is envisioned under managed competition is thus a three layered system. The government manages HMOs, HMOs manage physicians and physicians manage patients. All three would have strong incentives to spend less on health care."[9] As above, although the passage identifies four parties—government, HMOs, physicians and patients—only three are contemplated as players in managing care.

Admittedly, patients' economic insulation is beginning to erode. Few people with indemnity insurance still enjoy first-dollar coverage, while many more face increased cost-sharing. But the effect is limited. More important for this discussion, patients in MCOs remain especially insulated from the economic consequences of their health care decisions. Typically, copayments are extremely modest—a few dollars for a physician visit or prescription.

The justifications for continuing patients' economic insulation vary: it is feared that any economic incentive would create financial obstacles to needed care, or that patients might make medically foolish decisions in order to save money, or that patients are incapable of understanding economic factors enough to take reasonable account of them in making decisions (even though they are entitled through the principle of informed consent to make vastly more complicated medical decisions). The defects in these rationales are addressed elsewhere.[10] Instead, this article focuses on the ways in which this profound discrepancy between providers' and patients' incentives creates serious ethical problems and how, even within MCOs, bringing patients' incentives into alignment with providers' can ameliorate those problems significantly.

Diverging Incentives: Formula for Trouble

The consequences of these sharply divergent incentives are serious. To begin with, patients with an Artesian mentality often believe that health care is free, that they have an unlimited right to the best medical care, spare no expense.[11] If consulted about the providers or treatments their health plan should offer, they may well answer "everything."[12]

Second, and more important, because patients remain insulated and naive about the economics of care, their preferences about their health plans are largely disregarded. Patients are steadily losing control. Employers choose the plans, the plans choose the providers, and the plans with their providers choose the treatment options. The patient is largely left out, and often has just one choice: take it or leave it.

The combination is a dangerous, vicious cycle. The same economic insulation that renders patients too naive to use resources prudently—and, therefore, not fit to participate in resource decisions—gives them every Artesian reason to demand the best of everything. They pay little or nothing for their care, and have little or no reward for frugality. Accordingly, patients lose plan, provider and treatment choices while employers, plans and physicians pocket the savings.

This combination of patients' high expectations and lack of control can translate into substantial pressures on physicians. Physicians still largely control health care resources through their license to practice medicine and their power of prescription. But patients can still exert demands, sometimes by appealing to the physician's ethic of fidelity, and sometimes by threatening to use their lone remaining weapon of control: the lawsuit. [13] As a result, physicians are caught systematically, sometimes hopelessly, between the conflicting incentives of patients and health plans. Patients insist "do more," while MCOs command them "do less."

The inevitable result is adversarial. Patients may become adversaries of physicians who refuse to prescribe a requested medication or authorize a referral for consultation. They may feel that their physician is a stranger who neither knows them nor cares about them.[14] Alternatively, physicians and patients together may be adversaries of the MCO. Where a physician wants to "do more," he can adeptly game the system to extract extra resources.[15]

Attempting to minimize such controversy and gaming, many MCOs take care not to disclose their cost constraints to patients, particularly incentive arrangements. If patients do not know that physicians increase their income by decreasing patients' care, it is thought, they may be less suspicious when they do not receive the level of medical care they expected. Indeed, some MCOs actually have "gag clauses" forbidding physicians to disclose to patients any information that might reflect poorly on the MCO. One large managed care plan, said to represent about 85% of Cincinnati physicians, recently gagged its participating physicians, ruling that they "shall take no action nor make any communication which undermines or could undermine the confidence of enrollees, potential enrollees, their employees, plan sponsors, or the public in [the plan] or in the quality of care which [its] members receive."[16] Such secrecy is yet another adversarial element, as MCOs presume patients cannot be trusted with information about the health plan they have bought.

Resolution: Bringing Patients into Incentives

At the policy level, patients are excluded from important resource decisions that profoundly affect them and, at the clinical level, physicians are placed in systematic conflicts of interest that threaten traditional obligations of fidelity. If this is so, then perhaps those problems might be reduced, at the policy level, by including patients in resource decisions and, at the clinical level, by bringing them into the economic incentives that guide physicians and MCOs.

Clinical incentives could involve patients better in decisions about the more modestly priced, routine kinds of care—the minor expenses that other kinds of insurance do not cover at all. On the other hand, most of the other money spent on health care is for a relatively few patients with severe acute injuries and illnesses and costly chronic conditions. Here there is rather little room for financial incentives, since the costs run so high. Rather, plans need prudent resource policies to govern what sorts of care should be provided for whom. Here, too, patients should be involved in resource planning. It is they whose lives are most intimately affected and, ultimately, it is they who are paying the bills.

1. Policy Level

The first policy-level change should be for MCOs to inform patients about their resource policies. This information would encompass physicians' incentive systems and other utilization controls, such as therapeutic substitution requirements.[17]

Arguably, the commonplace practice of keeping such arrangements secret is ethically and legally wrong. And practically speaking it is probably not even possible much longer.

Morally and legally, physicians already have duties to disclose incentive schemes to patients. This is because physicians are fiduciaries, and fiduciaries have clear legal and ethical obligations to promote their beneficiaries' interests, even above their own. They also must disclose any conflicts of interest that might encourage them to place their own interests above their patients'. Because MCO incentive systems create conflicts of interest by paying physicians more money to deliver less care, physicians are obligated to disclose them.[18]

Arguably, if physicians must disclose these incentives, so should the MCO that created them.[19] MCOs can also be regarded as fiduciaries, both as financial insurers and as providers of care.[20] As such, they too would owe common law duties of disclosure and the utmost deference to the interests of subscribers.[21] Arguments based on contract law may also apply. If HMOs, as drafters of their contracts with subscribers, have not clearly specified limits on services, or in their advertisements have exaggerated the level of care they deliver, they may be at fault for fraud, breach of contract or other civil wrongs.[22]

Practically speaking, concealment is hardly feasible much longer. Once physicians make the necessary disclosure, the MCOs' question whether to disclose it is moot. For another thing, a rising tide of lawsuits cites MCOs' failure to disclose incentive arrangements among their allegations.[23]

Beyond disclosures, the MCO should actively involve subscribers in important policy decisions. Should patients with myocardial infarction receive costly TPA, which may or may not yield slightly improved survival, rather than much cheaper screptokinase? Should the plan pay for endless intensive care of patients in a persistent vegetative state? Should the plan cover costly but promising new treatments who medical value is not scientifically documented, such as bone marrow transplant for breast cancer?

Policies governing what levels of care MCO covers should at least be influenced, if not determined, by those who are most affected by them and who ultimately pay for them, namely patients. Federally qualified HMOs were originally required to have policy boards, with at least one-third of their members subscribers. Although that requirement has largely disappeared, most states require some subscriber participation in the health plan's policy decisions.[24] Some HMOs have long traditions of involving subscribers.[25] This element of managed care needs to be reinvigorated.

2. Clinical Level

Unfortunately, such policy participation probably will not work well until the major problem—the incentive discrepancy—is resolved. So long as patients experience virtually no economic consequences of their medical spending decisions, it remains easy to expect unlimited benefits. So policy preferences may simply amount to a demand for the best, spare no expense.[26] This may be particularly true in MCOs, where cost sharing is minimal.

At the same time, financial consequences must not represent barriers to care. After all, a centerpiece of managed care is assured access to care without financial impediment. Thus, the goal must be to reward patients for prudence without impeding needed care.

There are many ways to construct such a system, but only one will be outlined here. Analogous to the Medical Savings Account,[27] each subscriber might begin each year with a certain number of "HMO-dollars" or points. Each time the subscriber receives medical care, points could be deducted, perhaps on a standard per-service format or maybe proportionate to the intensity (cost) of the actual services delivered. To encourage preventive care, patients might earn extra points for seeking immunizations, mammograms or the like. Those with chronic illnesses might likewise be awarded points for securing important follow up care. Patients wanting interventions exceeding the MCO's guidelines, such as a CT scan for ordinary tension headaches, or a costly drug not on the formulary, might "purchase" it by spending points.

Patients would still, of course, retain complete access to care. The points serve strictly as a reward for prudence, not a barrier requiring cash in order to secure care. The incentives are also indirect in that, unlike the copays and deductibles that many people now face, points are not pitted against current expenditures—one does not weigh health care directly against food at the time one decides whether to seek care.

At the end of each year, points might be redeemed for cash, or rolled over into the next year's account, or perhaps used toward in-kind rewards, such as health club memberships or even ordinary household goods. The important feature is that conservative use of health services is directly, personally rewarded without creating financial barriers to care. All essential care is still completely covered.

Advantages of Bringing Patients into the Financial Incentives

There are many reasons why it is morally desirable to bring patients into alignment with providers' financial incentives. First, it respects patients as competent adults. Principles of autonomy and informed consent have long held that patients are entitled to determine what will happen to their own bodies. In the medical context, this means that the competent patient is entitled to accept or reject whatever interventions a physician offers, even for reasons that others might deem foolish or frivolous. It would be odd indeed to hold that, although a person is entitled to decide whether to refuse a lifesaving blood transfusion, or to undergo a risky experimental treatment, that person will not be permitted to decide how to spend his own money, on the ground that he might make a mistake, or that he might forego (what someone else has decided is) necessary care.

And it is his own money. Although the U.S. health care system has remarkably preserved the illusion that Someone Else, not the patient, pays for care, it is time to dispel the myth. Patients pay directly through out-of-pocket cost sharing; they pay as employees through foregone wages, other benefits, or even jobs; as taxpayers through higher taxes; and as consumers through higher prices.

Second, returning a measure of economic accountability to patients is probably the only way that they can regain a measure of control over their medical choices. So long as others such as employers or MCOs incur the direct costs and savings of medical resource use, they must and inevitably will control their costs—and thereby patients' care. Reciprocally, so long as patients are shielded from the economic consequences of their medical decisions, they have neither reason nor opportunity to consider which care is really worth its cost.[28] Hence, their preferences are likely to be regarded as economically and medically naive demands, and they will not be permitted to participate in important resource decisions. Their health plans, providers and treatments will be chosen by others—take it or leave it. Under an incentive system, however, the more that patients have reason to ask "Do we really need this?" and "Can we safely watch and wait?", the less will outsiders need to. Only then are patients likely to be awarded greater control.[29]

A third advantage of bringing patients into financial incentives is its potential for restoring trust within the physician-patient relationship. The current system controls costs either by dictating, from the outside, what physicians can and cannot do, or by placing physicians under incentives. Either the physician is helpless as others forbid him to do what the patient requests, or he is in a personal conflict of interest.

If patients had reason and reward for considering costs more carefully, there would be less need for outsiders to decide which care is worth its cost, and thereby less need for intrusive and costly UR, and less gaming of the system. Indeed, the very concept of "managed" care presupposes that some third party must manage the economics of health care on the assumption that physicians and patients cannot manage on their own.

Reciprocally, when the patient has a stake in the costs as well as the outcome of care, there is less need to incentivize the physician. At that point, the physician who explains that an intervention is unnecessary or unduly costly is no longer the enemy guarding a third party's resources. He is an ally helping the patient to look out for the patient's larger interests, financial as well as medical. Patients do, after all, have lives outside the medical system and can have priorities they consider more important than buying medical products and services. Such a physician will be in a powerful position to help patients once the latter are under financial incentives to avoid unwise medical decisions for the sake of short-term rewards. Probably the ideal incentive structure would reward physicians for quality of care, while rewarding patients for prudent cost-consciousness.

Finally, some other practical advantages might be anticipated. When patients have money as well as health interests at stake even in minor health care decisions, they may be more interested to hear information and make choices carefully, thereby becoming more responsible for decisions and their outcomes. Where patients are more responsible, evidence indicates that they tend to be more satisfied with their care (even with adverse outcomes) and less apt to be litigious.[30]

In the final analysis, it is difficult to justify keeping patients insulated and isolated. If they are treated more as responsible adults, accountable for their decisions with real economic consequences that nevertheless do not impede access to care, there may be considerably less adversity and mistrust in a relationship that should be, above all, a healing experience.

Notes

1. AL Hillman, "Financial incentives for physician in HMOs: Is there a conflict of interest?" *N Eng J Med* 1987, 317:1743-1748; DF Levinson, "Toward full dis-

closure of referral restrictions and financial incentives by prepaid health plans," *N Eng J Med* 1987, 317:1729-1731; RA Berenson, "In a doctor's wallet," *New Republic* 1987, 196:11-13; H Scovern, "A physician's experiences in a for-profit staff-model HMO," *N Engl J Med* 1988, 319:787-790; G Povar and J Moreno, "Hippocrates and the health maintenance organization: A discussion of ethical issues," *Ann Intern Med* 1988, 109:419-424; EH Morreim, "Fiscal scarcity and the inevitability of bedside budget balancing," *Arch Intern Med* 1989, 149(5):1012-1015; EH Morreim, "Gaming the system: Dodging the rules, ruling the dodgers,"*Arch Intern Med* 1991, 151(3):443-447; EH Morreim, "Cost containment: Challenging fidelity and justice, *Hastings C Rep* 1988, 18(6):20-25.

2. EH Morreim, *Balancing act: The new medical ethics of medicine's new economics.* Doredreche Kiuwer Academic Publishers, 1991; SM Butler, EF Haislmaier, eds. *Critical issues: A National health system for America.* Washington: The Heritage Foundation, 1989; P Starr, *The Social Transformation of American Medicine.* Basic Books, New York, 1982.

3. EH Morreim, "Redefining quality by reassigning responsibility,"*Am J Law Med* 1994,20(1-2)79-104.

4. EH Morreim, *Balancing Act*, pp. 9-21.

5. *Health Maintenance Organization Act of 1973.* (42 U.S.C. §300e).

6. EH Morreim, *Balancing Act*, p. 33.

7. JD Blum, "Economic credentialing: A new twist in hospital appraisal processes," *J Legal Med* 1991, 12:427-473; B Bjornstad and B Mohlenbrock, "Economic credentialling in the era of integrated health care," in *Integrated Health Care Delivery Systems,* A Fine, ed. New York: Thompson Publishing Group, Inc., 1993, 39-56; *Hassan v. Independent Practice Associates, P.C. 698. F. Supp 679 (E.D. Mich, 1988).*

8. LI Sederer, "Managed mental health care and professional compensation," *Behavioral Sciences and the Law* 1994, 12:367-78; at 367 (emphasis added). Other commentators use similar language. "Aligning incentives across the organization is another key to success." ; MC Rogers, R Snyderman, EL Rogers, "Cultural and organizational implications of academic managed-care networks," *N Eng J Med* 1994, 331:1374-77 at 1376; See also: K Terry, "Is this the best way to divide HMO income?" *MedEcon* 1994, 71(19):26B-26F, at 26D; RC Hall, "Social and legal implications of managed care in psychiatry," *Psychosomatics* 1994, 34:150-158 at 150.

9. DP Sulmasy, "Managed care and managed death," *Arch Intern Med* 1995, 155:133-136.

10. EH Morreim, "Of rescue and responsibility: Learning to live with limits," *J Med and Philos* 1994, 19:455-470; EH Morreim, "Redefining quality by redefining responsibility," *Am J Law and Med* 1994, 20(1-2):79-104.

11. C Havinghurst, "Prospective self-denial: Can consumers contract today to accept health care rationing tomorrow?" *U Penn L Rev* 1992, 140:1755, 1785; U Reinhardt, "American values: Are they blocking health-system reform?"*Med Econ*, 1992, 69(21),126-141; U Reinhardt, "You pay when business bankrolls health care, *Wall Street Journal*, Dec. 2, 1992 at A-14; J Weaver, "The best care other people's money can buy *Wall Street Journal*, Nov. 19, 1992, at A-14.

12. D Azavedo, "Why can't other HMOs work as well as this one?" *Med Econ* 1994,71(7):102-110.

13. Patients also use such suits against MCOs and insurers to gain access to costly care they fell they deserve, even where it may not be covered by their policy.

See WP Peters and MC Rogers, "Variation in approval by insurance companies of coverage for autologous bone marrow transplantation for breast cancer," *N Eng J Med* 1994, 330: 473-477.

14. RH Miller, HS Luft, "Managed care plan performance since 1980," *JAMA* 1994, 271:1512-1519.

15. EH Morreim, "Gaming the system: Dodging the rules, ruling the dodgers," *Arch Intern Med* 1991, 151(3):443-447.

16. The author goes on to observe that "[t]his was a bold demand for a company that a 1988 federal jury had found to have fixed prices, violated securities laws and engaged in racketeering and which had drawn fire from its doctors for reducing authorized laboratory services and instituting a 'preferred drug' list." SC Wooley, "Managed care and mental health: The silencing of a profession," *Internat J Eating Disorders* 1993, 14:387-401, at 394. See also: J Orient, *Your Doctor Is Not In: Health Skepticism about National Health Care*. New York: Crown Publishers Inc., 1994 at 159: "The details of that contract are generally kept secret from the patients and for good reason. The contract might forbid the doctor to make derogatory comments about the plan. It will set forth the financial incentives that the gatekeeper has for denying or restricting care. It will delineate the barriers that the gatekeeper will have to overcome (phone calls, forms, committee meetings, etc) in order to obtain approval for any unusual procedures he wants his patients to have."

17. GJ Glover and BN Kuhlik, "Potential liability associated with restrictive drug policies," *Seton Hall Legis J* 1990, 14:103-113.

18. *Moore v. Regents of the University of California* 793P 2d479 (Cal. 1990) (cert. denied 112 S. Ct. 2967 (1992); EH Morreim, "Economic disclosure and economic advocacy: New duties in the medical standard of care," *J Legal Med* 1991, 12(3): 275-329.

19. EH Morreim, *Balancing Act*.

20. WA Chittenden, "Malpractice liability and managed health care: History and prognosis,"*Tort and Insurance Law J* 1991, 26: 451-496, at 475; JB Stern, "Bad faith suits: are they applicable to health maintenance organizations?" *W Virginia L Rev* 1983, 85: 911-928. G Povar and J Moreno, "Hippocrates and the health maintenance organization: A discussion of ethical issues," *Ann Intern Med* 1983, 109: 419-424. HMOs may even be seen as fiduciaries with respect to the physicians or other providers they enlist. See *Sanus/New York v. Dube-Seybold -Sutherland*, 837 S.W. 2d 191 (Tex.App. Houston [lst dist.] 1992).

21. *Egan v. Mutual of Omaha Ins Co*, 598 P.2d 452 (1979); *Davis v Blue Cross of Northern California*, 600 P.2d 1060.

22. LV Tiano, "The legal implications of HMO cost containment measures," *Seton Hall Legis J* 1990, 14:79-102. WA Chittenden, "Malpractice liability and managed health care: History and prognosis. *Tort and Insurance Law J* 1991, 26:451-496. Note that such suits are limited by ERISA law: if a health plan is obtained as an employment benefit, most such common law causes of action are preempted in favor of much more limited Federal remedies.

23. M Meyer and A Murr, "Not my Health Care," *Newsweek*, January 19, 1994 at 36-38. EJ Pollock, "Jury tells HMO to pay damages in dispute over refused coverage," *Wall Street Journal*, December 28, 1993, at B-4.

24. PA Younger, C Conner, KK Cartwright, *Managed Care Law Manual*. Gaithersburg: Aspen Publishers Inc. 1994.

25. D Azavedo, "Why can't other HMOs work as well as this one?" *Med Econ* 1994; 71 (7): 102-110.

26. *Ibid*.

27. P Gramm, "Why we need medical savings accounts," *N Eng J Med* 1994; 330: 1752-53.

28. EH Morreim, "Of rescue and responsibility," *J Med and Philos* 1994, 19: 455-470; EH Morreim, "Redefining quality by reassigning responsibility," *Am J Law and Med* 1994, 20 (1-2):79-104.

29. *Ibid*.

30. B Rice, "Educate your patients without taking more time," *Med Econ* 1992, 69(19): 92-105; BR Barber, "Participatory democracy in health care: The role of the responsible citizen," *Trends in Health Care, Law and Ethics* 1992, 7(3-4): 9-13; RS Shapiro, DE Simpson, SL Lawrence, AM Talsky, KA Sobocinski, DL Schiedermayer, "A survey of sued and nonsued physicians and suing patients," *Arch Intern Med* 1989, 149:2190-2196; DA Redelmeier, P Rozin, D Kahneman, "Understanding patients' decisions: Cognitive and emotional perspectives," *JAMA* 1993, 270:72-76.

42

Managed Care and Quality Assurance

Tom Simmer, M.D.

Within the health maintenance industry variations in standard of quality, in contrast to practices regarding physician incentives and reimbursement, are not quite as extreme as some presenters have suggested. Approaches to quality management are far more consistent. Although not long ago the approach to quality management was locally defined and driven, two major changes have standardized and energized quality management programs throughout the country.

These two changes are the transformation from a quality assurance to quality improvement focus and the emergence of the NCQA — National Committee for Quality Assurance — as the recognized accrediting body for health maintenance organizations. The NCQA has itself promoted change through two mechanisms—the development of explicit standards for accreditation of HMOs and the promotion of HEDIS (Health Plan-Employer Data and Information Set) indicators of organizational performance.

Until just the past few years, quality management programs consisted mainly of individuals such as myself who would review medical records to determine if the care met the community standard of quality. Various indicators were developed which identified possible aberrant episodes of care. Such actions were undertaken with great solemnity and issues were brought before a committee of peers. All such efforts were highly confidential and constituted a sort of "due diligence" on the part of the managed care organizations which had taken on this obligation as the cost of restricting members to a defined panel of physicians. The methods of inspection had actually become quite elaborate over time. Small armies of nurse reviewers pored over records of patients who had been readmitted to hospital shortly after discharge, or had suffered unexpected complications following surgery. Efforts made to improve quality were highly variable and not at all consistent either in content or sophistication from plan

---

This paper was presented at the University of Michigan Forum on Health Policy on April 1, 1995.

to plan. Everything related to quality was highly proprietary and benchmarking performance across health plans was rare. Looking back on these days of not-so-long ago, one marvels at the widespread assumption which prevailed—that the processes of care were fine but for the occasional aberration. Actually focusing efforts on improving the care processes was beyond all but a few of the nation's managed care institutions. In fact, the concept that organizations should relinquish control over defining and recognizing quality to the "customer" of the service was not only foreign to the practice of quality assurance, it was antithetical to it. No one knew what the customer wanted because the customer was not thought to possess the competence to make such a judgment. Quality assurance, however, did not actually improve care. While such efforts remain a necessary part of all quality management programs, they no longer comprise the main thrust of such programs.

With a goal of achieving accreditation by the NCQA, organizations have been redesigning quality management programs to adhere to the many and diverse NCQA standards, which, among other things, call for demonstrated clinical improvement arising directly from quality management efforts initiated within the health plan. Such efforts should support the delivery of preventive services and, in addition, the management of specific disease entities. Full accreditation has proven to be a tall order which consumes the energy of the entire organization, particularly at the time of initial review, since so much infrastructure must be assembled to conduct successful plan-wide quality improvement.

This sudden development of accountability to an accrediting organization was accompanied by an even broader form of accountability represented by HEDIS. With public reporting of performance, accountability becomes public. What a change! It had been accepted on the basis of reason and tradition that the best care could be attained at the institutions, generally academic, which held the greatest reputation. That reputation, in turn, was the product of research and publication in the area of interest. It was not necessarily related to the satisfaction or even the medical outcomes of the persons receiving care.

Thus, in the early 1990s, very little capacity for quality measurement or improvement existed within the industry. The quality improvement model required not armies of inspectors, but fields of data covered by legions of data analysts. The evolution of quality management within most organizations went from a data panic, to data frenzy, and then to data madness. Simultaneously, and with little warning, all HMOs embraced the philosophy of clinical process improvement along the Demming line. The transformation which Demming called for was neither easy nor cheap. The forces promoting fundamental change were not to be resisted. American industry, long helpless—if not indifferent—to the soaring costs of medical ben-

Managed Care and Quality Assurance

efits, became suddenly activated. Local successes by coalitions of purchasers in the 1980s became a national effort embodied in the NCQA accrediting standards. So powerful was support given to this effort that HMOs perceived that those who failed to gain accreditation would soon find themselves locked out of their own markets. With this recognition of the NCQA as the main accrediting body for HMOs, the definition of quality—and with it the design of quality management programs—resided in a private organization largely driven by health care purchasers. Advocacy for the patient was taken from the health care professionals and deeded over to employers who possessed not only a paternalistic concern for their employees and their families, but also the commanding role of "payor."

This transfer of control over the definition of quality could not have occurred as long as quality improvement efforts maintained the shield of secrecy which the concept of "confidentiality" had afforded. The Health Plan-Employer Data and Information Set (HEDIS) called for *public* reporting of numerous indicators of performance hitherto considered privileged. Major employers had long been dissatisfied with existing information upon which to distinguish competing HMOs. Considering the magnitude of the purchasing decisions in terms of dollars, the purchasers had long passed the point of frustration in dealing with the health care industry. Many began to view HMOs as organizations which absorbed multiple millions of dollars, but whose primary function was to deny services to people. Although there were certainly differences in cost, virtually no objective information regarding the quality of care could be evaluated by the purchasers. Examples of employers withdrawing huge accounts from health care institutions which failed to meet expectations brought prompt and predictable response from managed care organizations. The message was clear: HMOs failing to report performance according to the standard HEDIS format risked the loss of business from the large, organized purchasers.

The internal workings of HMOs—the actual medical care—had in fact never been measured by the vast majority of organizations. It was certainly not the custom to report it publicly. In the process of developing the HEDIS format, the purchasers were shocked at the lack of performance measurement within the industry. Not only was there no measurement, but there was no infrastructure within most HMOs to make measurement possible. It became clear that accurate and timely measurement would require changes at numerous points throughout the continuum of care. Data measurement relies on data collection and this must be done at the point of service. There are thousands of points of service at every HMO and collecting the type of data needed to support quality measurement and improvement would represent a major change and commitment. Even those with the commitment found themselves organizationally unsuited to the task. The burden imposed by the change in paradigm cannot be understated. I have heard the opinion expressed—in all sincerity—that HEDIS is a plot by large HMOs to drive smaller ones out of business.

The employer community interprets protestations that HEDIS is burdensome and likely to drive up administrative costs as resistance on the part of the industry to change. Money spent in quality improvement is not only justified but essential. There is also the view that quality improvement reduces waste and may lead to savings which are difficult to recognize at first. The quality indicators in the HEDIS 2.0 document are rates at which the following occur among members who have been continuously enrolled in the HMO during the necessary period of service: childhood immunizations, cholesterol screening, mammography screening, cervical cancer screening, prenatal care within the first trimester, emergency room visits for asthma, and timely ambulatory care for patients hospitalized with depression. In addition to the six quality indicators, HEDIS requires reporting in several other categories of interest to employers, such as member satisfaction and utilization management. It is almost unfathomable to employers that such basic information isn't effortlessly available within managed care organizations. The truth is that such information requires enormous effort and even today can only be achieved through a process relying heavily on the cumbersome process of medical record review. It is also true that such information is worth knowing and public reporting of performance will provide strong impetus to quality improvement.

Employers hope to use this comparative reporting to rate and choose HMOs with whom to contract. Consequently, HMOs which fail to report out their HEDIS performance will find themselves severely disadvantaged in the marketplace. While there are many who will dispute the utility of HEDIS in supporting large purchasing decisions, there is recognition within the industry that these are the new rules of engagement and no single entity has the stature to resist. HEDIS is certain to evolve, and it is unlikely that it will become simpler or less burdensome in the process.

What lies ahead? A natural outgrowth of public reporting of performance is the imperative to improve that performance. The legions of data analysts will be followed by a corps of project managers whose job it will be to translate measurement into improvement. Employers and their employees and families will make choices among competing health systems based on comparative performance. Quality management in managed care will continue to move in this direction as long as the marketplace demands it.

43

Provider Perspectives in Managed Care

Macdonald Dick, M.D.
Tom Carli, M.D.
Duane Kirking, PharmD, PhD

Remarks by Macdonald Dick, M.D., Pediatric Cardiology, University of Michigan Medical School

I would like to comment on a possible impact of managed care on health care from the perspective of a physician. Although I am a specialist in pediatric cardiology, I think my remarks extend beyond this focal point. Tertiary disease states in the very young and the very old consume much of our health care resources. As we struggle to achieve an equitable balance in the distribution of these resources among the various health care needs of our citizens, a number of issues surface.

The creative tension between the service, commercial and scientific aspects of medicine has always been with us. Further, the predominance of one over the other has varied over time. From antiquity through the Middle Ages, medicine was grounded in science (such as it was) and service, although just barely at times. From the Renaissance through the 19th century, medicine as a commercial enterprise expanded, until hypothesis-driven and data-dependent (scientific) medicine emerged to compete for center stage. The Flexner report in the first decade of the 20th century subdued the boisterous, free market system which openly pitted commerce against science and education. The 20th century then witnessed parallel and complementary growth in the service, entrepreneurial and scientific impulses of medicine, to the point where medicine has, in a real sense, become a victim of its own success. We are now engaged in a great national

---

These remarks were presented as part of a panel discussion which closed the April 1995 University of Michigan Forum on Health Policy and were subsequently edited by the speakers. Susan Dorr-Goold and Rod Hayward served as moderators.

debate regarding the optimal ways to satisfy several competing interests, namely to maintain the current scientific level of medical care, to provide wider distribution of primary medical care, and, finally, to realize the promise of molecular biology. The candidate *du jour* to achieve this goal is managed care.

The first concern I have is the nature of managed care. Clearly, medicine has been a business since its inception and, equally clear, has moved from predominantly a "cottage industry" form to predominantly a "corporate" form. Managed care provides one of the mechanisms to accelerate the move to this more organized and alleged cost-reducing mode. Nonetheless, for-profit managed care systems introduce into the health care delivery system motives and behaviors (profitability, stock holders interests, stock market mergers/takeovers) that may render the purposes of health care delivery secondary to that of the market. Thus, it can be envisioned that a well-managed health care system that is "profitable" would be subject to the marketplace and could be bought and sold, and, then, altered by its new owners in a way distinctly different from its original intent. Other business mores impact the system as well. Large business organizations build a culture that is extremely hierarchical; financial rewards are distributed in a way that protects and favors this top-down administrative structure. Other "perks" such as titles, bonuses, and excessive retirement/discharge financial packages that exist within business structures have largely been developed outside the medical environment.

These administrative devices, considered a part of the standard reward system in large corporations, set up artificial differences in the collegial atmosphere that is necessary to provide seamless care to a patient or a population of patients, and they move the centers of control and power directly from those charged with delivering services to patients to those charged with increasing profitability. The business model would further turn the focus from the issues of the patient and the culture of science and service to issues of the employer and the culture of business and large organizations. The current delicate, dynamic balance between patient service and science on one hand and prestige, power, and money on the other will be tilted to the latter. The role of individual self-awareness and values that, for the most part, motivate individuals, and which arise out of each person's particular origins, education, and experience, will be devalued. In short, we will be managing patients, not caring for them.

All of the foregoing is not to say that medicine cannot benefit by a number of rigorous business practices; it simply means that these aforementioned features are neither particularly useful nor desirable. One can imagine that highly selected, rigorously trained and educated members of such an organization (namely, the physicians and health care workers) would be the least remunerated in a system that believes its greatest talent lies in its administration.

To effectively reform our health care system without unbalancing the scale of interests between medicine and business requires identification of appropriate leadership. The situation fairly demands it. To preserve the desirable aspects of this balance requires medical leadership. To depend primarily upon individuals with business and economic backgrounds, who are inclined to confuse leadership with management, to define the new relationships is to upset this balance and render reform hollow, and more importantly, unworkable. In short, the members of the medical culture comprise the more appropriate useful reservoir for leaders of the health care industry and for health care reform .

The second concern follows the first—namely, quality care. The measure of medical quality is elusive and comprises many factors. Traditionally physicians have measured quality in terms of morbidity and mortality; consumer groups tend to examine quality in a more global way, including patient satisfaction, relative cost, associated amenities, as well as a number of other indicators, that for the most part, originate from the business and advertising community and may have no relationship to scientific medicine based on human biology. Patient perceptions are deceiving and limited; it makes no sense to identify high satisfaction for a treatment that has no scientific basis. Numerous suspect treatments, fads, and even some apparent but unproved rational treatment are all behaviors that patients may perceive as desirable. Attention to outcome research, the current vogue, may shed light on these issues and certainly is a vital element that should be supported by managed care and health care reform. Physicians and their health care colleagues are deeply interested in its development and are critical members of its practice. Nonetheless, it remains to be seen if such measures will actually deliver quality care at a reduced cost.

A third concern arises out of the place of education and research in managed care systems. Professions are defined by a number of factors, not the least of which is that a profession is charged with the development and transmission of its particular body of knowledge. Managed care systems do not seem to support an educational structure that would ensure that medical practice and the biomedical science which underlies it will continue to have the support of the public and the public's dollar in the foreseeable future. Thus, the return in the short run may be offset in the long run.

It has been said that the encounter between patient and physician did not have a greater than 50% change of being beneficial to the patient until about 1913; it could equally be said that the acceptance of medicine based on science and experiment did not begin until the 20th century and it was not widespread until the 1960's, almost two decades after the dedication of the National Institutes of Health. This growth of scientific-based medicine is not coincidental to our interest in managed care at the present time. Without the scientific and technologic advances of medicine that have occurred over the last two and a half decades, all financially supported by the current health care system, including funds generated by taxation (National Institutes of Health), funds generated by medical practice, academic health centers, and philanthropy, and funds generated by the health care industry (pharmaceutical and device companies), medicine would not have progressed to a situation where it is best served by organizing corporate structures. We would all still be operating in a "cottage industry" if this increasing body of knowledge had not required specialization and coordination of medical care services. However, current models of managed care do not include the cost of research in their proposals; this is a significant flaw.

Some believe that physicians need to attend business school or obtain master's of public health to be full and equal partners in the current health care reform. I disagree with this assertion. It is not that medical students or physicians cannot learn from the business, public health, and legal communities; indeed, I submit that they can and do. Similarly, our colleagues in other endeavors can learn from medicine. I remember receiving a flyer form the business school of the university where I attended medical school asking if I thought it was necessary for medical students to have courses in medical economics and business administration during medical school. I wrote back, somewhat indignantly perhaps, that clearly the business school faculty did not understand the nature of biomedical science, its complexity, and the enormity of material to be digested in a four-year program. Furthermore, they did not seem to understand that the single unique skill a physician brings to the physician-patient encounter is based on the scientific method and the scientific body of knowledge. Law schools like to talk about teaching medical students to think like a physician. In short, to use the scientific method in the care of their patients. This objective is sufficiently challenging to take up the curriculum of most medical schools, particularly today when molecular biology holds real promise for a profound understanding of the mechanisms of disease and the development of fundamentally new treatments to address them. It would be counterproductive to have the talents of medical students who show promise in the laboratory or clinic to instead head up the corporate ladder. It seems to me it would be far more useful to have the successful physician and successful health care administrator arrive at the board room from different directions, offering different perspectives, but uniting in a common goal of developing comprehensive, up-to-date, compassionate, and cost-effective health care delivery systems. It is often said, in overly respectful and hushed tones, that the executive health administrator has a fiduciary responsibility to his/her organization; the implication is that anyone else's responsibility does not carry quite the same weight. I would submit that the physician has an equal fiduciary responsibility to his/her patient and the group of patients he/she serves. After all, fiduciary means "a special relationship of trust."

Recent issues in medical ethics have focused on patient autonomy, patient participation in medical decision making, issues of fairness and justice, and the role and regulation of medical science. The new emphasis shifts our focus to profitability, market system, constant growth, and profit and loss statements. In short, managed care threatens to transform medicine from a human service based on scientific knowledge and applied biology to a product based on profit. Although elements in this transformation are inevitable, its impact would be best served by physician leadership, not business leadership. Such physician leadership would possess, by virtue of his/her education and experience in human biology, the particular badges of the profession such as knowing and honoring medicine's origins, its strengths, its flaws, its history, its science, and its direction. Such a leader would empower his/her colleagues and would much more likely be successful in bringing both parties to pragmatic health care reform.

A fourth concern arises out of the apparent, implicit managed care notion that the application of biology to the human condition is an exercise that can be reduced to simple processes with highly predictable outcomes. Health care organizations tend to feel their job is to treat "wellness" as opposed to "sickness." In reality, many individuals (particularly in our graying population) are dealing with complex, multi-system health problems in which the outcomes are determined by a complex set of variables such as genetic factors, health risk behavior, support networks, and environmental influences. There is little recognition that many of the current disorders of modern life, in a large part, derive from the wide variety of human behavior in a free society (i.e., smoking, alcohol, illegal drugs, guns, non-use of seat belts, overeating, excessive stress, over-population, single parenting, both parents working, incomplete parenting, etc.). Public policies and reforms that do not address these social problems that emerge from this variety of life, will make little dent, certainly in the demand, if not the cost, of health care services for our citizens.

The final concern arises from the nature of tertiary disorders. They have a lower prevalence than common illnesses, and their treatment is highly time-, technology-, and labor-intensive. This is especially true for children who happen to have complex chronic medical diseases. The prevalence of complex disease in this group is so low that the affected children become medical orphans in the competition for health care dollars, and because of political reasons, namely no vote, their problems are included only as an afterthought among the more common but similarly complex disorders in the adult and elderly. The value of an individual in our society is held extraordinarily dear, especially the life of a child, until, perhaps, it is time to pay the bill. It always amazes me that the great majority of young parents, in any culture, even those cultures without a strong creed of the individual, take better care of their children than they do of themselves. There is no doubt something deeply biologic going on here. We need to think about the cost of denying available technology to that endangered child. There is a difference in rationing tertiary care between illnesses aggravated by unhealthy life choices and those illnesses visited upon children through no decision or action of their own. These are difficult and profound issues that not only impact health care systems but also illuminate the real values of our culture.

To conclude, I have perhaps overdrawn the difference between the world of medicine and the world of business, but not much. Medicine has been a business since the beginning and business enterprises can be motivated by forces other than profit. Furthermore, individuals in any human endeavor are driven by varied, complex and often competing motives. Neither profession has much of a hold, much less a monopoly, on virtue. Nonetheless, in the aggregate, the emerging pattern in health care delivery in the United States is clearly moving from the patient-physician model to the patient-provider-payor model. Efforts to retain the values and advantages of the former while developing the guidelines and provisions of the latter should be a critical part of the health care reform movement. I would suggest that a major principle of such efforts would be that physician-leaders and the profession they represent are at the center of the discussion.

It is important to say that I do not believe that most physicians are constantly preoccupied with the potential impact health care reform will have on either their private or professional life. Concerned, yes; preoccupied, no. It can be said that medicine is to biology as engineering is to physics. Both professions are dependent upon very sophisticated and complex bodies of knowledge. Medicine has been impacted by many legitimate interests and forces from society for centuries; it is a "real-world" enterprise. There's an oft-stated aphorism, paraphrased for the delicate ear, that, "physicians make poor businesspersons." An equally arguable corollary is that, "businesspersons make poor physicians." Let us not exclude each other, nor anyone else, from the table in this most important public discussion.

Remarks by Tom Carli, M.D., Psychiatry, UM Medical School

I want to focus my comments on the tremendous impact these changes are having on physicians and clinical services. It's recognized that this is happening. When I was looking for ways to describe the effect of managed

Provider Perspectives in Managed Care

care on academic medicine, I came across an old Chinese proverb that said, "When the tiger enters the temple it's best to include him in the ceremonies." There's that much of a recognition of what is happening. There is a tremendous amount of uncertainty and people do not do well with uncertainty, especially physicians.

I want to speak from the perspective of psychiatry and try to generalize from it. Psychiatry has been the canary in the coal mines in terms of managed care because we were hit with managed care a good six years before the rest of medicine was hit. We were hit for good reasons: escalating costs—far exceeding the costs of the increases in other health-care costs, flagrant abuses, tremendous variations in practice patterns. All the things that are wrong with the current system were wrong in spades with psychiatry in the '80s. So it didn't take much savvy for employers to take a look at mental health services and decide they needed to carve them out and manage them. Consequently, we have been dealing with this for a long time. We are still dealing with it. The recent American Psychiatric Association election was a bitter contest between an old guard private practitioner who was going to defend against the dragons of managed care vs. a new-age, kinder, gentler managed care psychiatrist. He lost. There are still fights, but I think the perspective of psychiatry can help us.

Jon Gabel suggests that the name of the game is controlling hospital utilization. That has been the major change in psychiatric services—developing alternatives to inpatient care and developing a well thought out continuum of care. Alternatives to hospitalization have been the key to turning psychiatric expenses around. Clearly that has to happen with the rest of medicine. Dr. Goold suggested that sociologists should study these changes in medical practice. I would also recommend this as a great study for public health grad students. There could be a combination study by professionals from the fields of sociology, public health, and organizational psychology. Here is a golden opportunity to look at how complex organizations change fundamentally. Dr. Goold also raised the issue of what is going to happen to the sick, the poor, and the old. Psychiatry has been grappling with this one, too, under managed care, because we have many, many chronic and persistent and severe illnesses. How do you deal with them when you have 20 outpatient sessions? How do you deal with them when you have utilization review? In heavily managed areas, psychiatric inpatient lengths of stay are now at five days. We've seen a falling off from 30-day inpatient stays four years ago; now we are down to 10. Still, that's high. We've got to get down to five. How do you do that with the chronically mentally ill?

The same question is going to be posed or is being posed for chronic renal failures, for chronic neurologic diseases. How are these chronic illnesses going to be managed under managed care? Dr. Morreim discussed effects of managed care on physicians. She argued that care is better and cheaper when continuity of care is available. We are finding this in mental health. The initial ideas are that physician extenders would be useful. (Physician extenders, for a psychiatrist, sounds too much like phallic narcissism. Let's call them mid-level providers.) Actually, some California highly-managed HMOs are finding it may not pay to have the less expensive person up front. When we split medications and psychotherapy, in the long run it may be more cost-effective to have the same person doing both the meds and the therapy. Continuity of care is cheaper. A lot of work needs to be done in how you organize that continuity of care.

Now let me comment on the major impact on academic medical centers Dr. Morreim brought to our attention. Physicians have always functioned as soloists, as lone rangers. Health-care systems of the future must become more like well-oiled orchestras or symphonies. In academic medical centers, say, how do you take a bunch of soloists and make them part of a team? This is probably the biggest challenge large systems of care have right now. Finally, I want emphasize the tremendous uncertainty with which we are all struggling. We heard about the lack of good research questions, about rudimentary outcome studies that are only now being done. We are not in a crisis, we are in a developmental transition. We are in a phase of many, many years of change. Unfortunately, many people don't do well with that. We are seeing a lot of demoralization. We are seeing a lot of physicians retiring early. We are seeing a lot of paranoia. We are seeing a lot of entrepreneurs jumping at new ideas. We are seeing a lot of experimentation with new clinical delivery systems. All of this is good, actually. If, at the other end of this developmental transition, we end up learning how to live with limitation, learning how to use treatments that have efficacy and effectiveness rather than what Dr. Morreim calls habit and hunch, then I think we are all going to be better off.

Remarks by Duane Kirking, PharmD, PhD, UM College of Pharmacy

I believe I am the only non-physician health professional on the panel this afternoon. Although issues addressed today relating to physicians and the health-care system in general are relevant to other professionals as well, each of us also has areas of particular interest. As a pharmacist, my primary concern is seeing that medications are used in the most appropriate manner to achieve desired health-care outcomes. Medications are a small percentage of the health-care dollar, about 10 percent in this country and perhaps a third of that is included in overall inpatient expenses and therefore often not considered. People haven't worried much about medication costs until the last few years, but when that 10 percent starts to approach

$100 billion a year, it amounts to something major. The overall price increases in pharmaceuticals in the early 1980's combined with the introduction of some very costly individual medications more recently has engendered substantial interest in doing something about what is perceived as the problem of overly high medication costs.

Managed care has positive or negative implications for medication use depending upon whether managed care organizations view medications as a means for achieving optimum health outcomes as efficiently as possible or as a commodity to be purchased as inexpensively as possible. For example, a method commonly part of managed care programs is the drug formulary. As originally conceived, a drug formulary is a means to identify and encourage use of the most appropriate medications from a therapeutic point of view with secondary consideration of product cost. An outcome of a properly designed formulary is decreased complexity of information with which physicians and others have to deal, so they don't have to contend with the information overload inherent in understanding 20,000 drugs. Unfortunately, the guiding question in determining what products are on the managed care formulary has frequently become, "what's the cheapest product?" Moreover, because of the vagaries of the pricing of pharmaceuticals, the cheapest product this week may not be the cheapest product next week. Or a product may be cheaper in one institution and more expensive in another. These complexities not only increase the difficulty for prescribers in dealing with medications, they may undermine the importance of identifying the best medication for the particular patient.

A second technique increasingly used by managed care organizations is drug utilization review, which is the process of evaluating the quality of medication use and then developing programs to correct any problems that are identified. A simplistic review program that targets physicians who prescribe greater than the average number of an expensive medication and informs them via a form letter that they should prescribe cheaper medications is not likely to have a major impact. Alternatively, a program that identifies true prescribing problems and works with patient specific information and in a supportive educational manner is more likely to increase the rate of optimum drug therapy.

There is some evidence that managed care is changing the way it looks at medications. The growing concept of disease management considers medications part of an integrated whole rather than as a commodity to be cost-minimized. While the successes of such programs remain to be carefully determined, their presence is an indication of how application of managed care principles may positively affect medication use.

Let me comment on one developing phenomenon that may not be widely known. Recent years have seen the growth of organizations that deal exclusively with the pharmacy benefit component of a health plan.

These specialized managed care groups, called pharmacy benefit managers or PBMs, are responsible for managing the drug benefit through mechanisms such as formularies, utilization review processes, provider incentive programs and manufacturer pricing incentives. These PBMs currently manage about 100 million covered lives. (We used to call them patients or customers or clients. Now it's covered lives. I guess that's better than covered bodies.) To the extent PBMs take advantage of their specialized expertise to promote appropriate medication use they have the potential to have a positive influence on health care. Through recent acquisitions the five largest pharmacy benefit management companies, which manage 60 percent of those 100 million covered lives, have come to be owned by or have other arrangements with drug manufacturers. Critics suggest that the cozy nature of the relationship between the producers and managers of medications is like having the fox guarding the hen house. At a minimum, the issue of conflict of interest must be considered as these new managed care arrangements seek to provide cost-effective drug therapy.

There are other issues related to managed care's role in proper medication use. But let me close by noting the need for research on the design of medication monitoring systems, the best ways to modify prescribing practices when necessary, the appropriate incentives — financial and otherwise to support positive change, and even research on what constitutes the optimum role of medications including the almost totally unexamined issue of *underutilization* of medications. A major deterrent to much of this work has been lack of accessible data and specifically the difficulty in integrating medication use data with disease and other patient data. Managed care organizations have the potential to support this research through the increasing presence of integrated databases necessary to do much of this research. Providing the means to capitalize on this capability be one of the best ways managed care can have a positive impact on achieving optimum medication therapy.

SECTION FIVE
The Realities of Health Care Reform: Positions, Publics, Processes and, Of Course, Power

Section Five
The Realities of Health Care Reform: Positions, Publics, Processes and, Of Course, Power

Marilynn M. Rosenthal

Introduction

The years 1992 to 1996, reaching towards the end of the century, saw new scenes in an ongoing public policy drama.

What FDR began in the 1930s when he developed the American version of the Welfare State, continues to play out in the first Clinton administration 60 years later. It was political theatre, 1990s style, but the denouement is still unclear. What America saw was an act where hard positions were taken, the public was manipulated and the political process sputtered, jammed and jolted. But the main action was played out in the American market where change continued without legislation.

One of the central issues was guaranteed universal access to health care, an old, old theme in this ongoing drama. First raised as a possibility in the early decades of the 20th century, and raised episodically since, it eludes the American public. Every other Western, capitalistic democracy has embraced universal access to health care. The Clintons tried yet again for Americans. Nor were the Clintons successful in persuading the country that we ought to have something resembling a coherent, coordinated system. Rather, the country is more comfortable approaching selected issues on a piecemeal and incremental basis. Over the decades this has included public health measures, building community hospitals, targeted insurance and services, research institutions and funding, HMOs, limited cost containment and now, selected insurance industry reform.

This is "The American Way," laid out in a constitution that eschews large scale change. No American Presidency has ever tried comprehensive health system reform until the Clinton Administration and that failed with

---

This paper was written in June 1997.

a vengeance. However, learning from the experience of the 103rd Congress, the Clintons then rewrote their part of the script to recognize that incrementalism, as unsatisfactory as it may sometimes be, is what works.

This book brings together a wide array of actors in the most recent debates: political ideologues and political compromisers, diverse economists, social scientists, interest groups, bureaucrats and policy shapers. They provide us with a detailed panorama of who tried, and how they tried, to shape the issues, public opinion, the political process, and the market to create the 1990s reality of health care policy and delivery in the USA.

The Clintons seemed determined to continue expanding the Welfare State at a time when other nations are cutting back and reshaping it for a new age of leaner central government. In hindsight, this was an anachronistic goal. We are at the threshold of another era, that of a post-industrial society where the State is shrinking in size and scope, where no new (overt) taxes are possible, where less regulation is better, local variation encouraged, individualism enlarged, and where new technologies are reshaping pieces of our society in ways we hardly understand. Other large social trends now influence what happens in our society and in our health care system.

The recent national debate on health care was edifying—it was a national educational seminar. Not only did more of the population begin to understand the complexities and intricacies of health care issues, but it has also been led to consider more closely its assumptions, positions, evidence and perceptions. We were forced to get a bit smarter at distinguishing between fact and fiction. Or at least to recognize more clearly that many people don't and won't make that distinction.

So, what is it we learned in 1992-96? What explains what happened? And what's next?

Various Ideologues and Other Frames of Reality Reference

Section One of this book introduces us to those who would create reality for the rest of us. These are the political ideologues and experts espousing a variety of points of view on health care reform in general and particular aspects of it, like cost containment. Those representing partisan views (Niskanan-Conservative Republican, Wilensky-Moderate Republican, McDermott and Nichols Left and Moderate Democrats) are ideologues along the political spectrum. They see the health care "crisis" quite differently. For Niskanan, there isn't a crisis. It's more an issue of perverse insurance incentives for which he has clear solutions. Wilensky accepts that there are serious problems and accepts the need for mild forms of government regulation but has considerable confidence in the market. McDermott is as adamant and clear as Niskanan but thinks that there is a terrible crisis, the only solution to which is a government-funded universal insurance system modeled on Canada. Nichols, representing the White House position, defends a Clinton version of managed competition. The moderates in both parties (Wilensky and Nichols) are the most willing to compromise.

A group of economists who talked about cost containment strategies, present a similar range of views. Economists have been the most prominent social scientists as advisors in the 1990s health care debate. Davis thinks we can solve the cost containment problem by expanding Medicare to all the population and using the DRG approach. Bailit is happy to let market competition do the job; Kronick agrees, but only with strong government regulation (a managed market) and Pauly thinks we're asking the wrong questions; maybe we can spend more on health care and less in some other sector. For him, the challenge is to determine what level of growth is ideal and live with it.

Whose version of "reality" is correct? Whose version of what the problem is and what we ought to be doing is "right"? We might turn to the social science researchers to see what empirical studies tell us. What are the facts? What do the data say?

The frame-of-reference of the researchers is in many ways the most interesting in the book. Their training requires that they not only discuss their methodologies, but the assumptions on which they are based and the difficulties they confront in gathering data. Their training requires them to include disclaimers, recognition of problems of validity and reliability as well as limitations on interpretation. Sheils, Swartz and Mark all describe the difficulties in collecting data, the problems of timeliness and the assumptions that lie behind methods and analyses. Sheils does a particularly good job of this, indicating how different assumptions lead to quite different policy implications. Mark seems to think that policy is driven by data but Swartz complains about the wrong interpretations and inappropriate uses to which her data were put. Nichols highlights the problems of timeliness, admitting that some insiders on the Hill knew about the figures that informed the Clinton plan: they were from 1987 and already out-of-date.

Ideological partisans of various political positions must speak with great confidence and authority. Admissions and disclaimers would undermine their ability to persuade. Those who gather the facts are duty-bound to inform their audiences of all the limitations to what they know. While our ability to describe simple trends that involve counting is relatively good, anything beyond that is rife with complexity and confusion. The health care system, and all its myriad parts is complex, confusing and, in fact, filled with contradictory trends and ambiguous situations. Further, it is continually changing in its various and multiple corners.

Research has become increasingly and remarkably sophisticated. But the challenges are great. The recognition of those challenges is important. Among other things, it forces us, as Mark points out, to distinguish between data, fact, evidence, anecdote, guess, belief and judgment. Even between fiction and fantasy.

This is something partisans rarely do. Not only do they often ignore what research can tell us, they often use those parts of research that suit their predetermined points of view. Or they simply obfuscate, perhaps deliberately. Perhaps this is too harsh a judgment. Payton, in her analysis of the 103rd Congress sees rationality overcoming political deal-making. But insiders Dingell and Hayes paint quite another picture. The role of ideology and partisanship is to produce a "vision" of what ought to or can be. But surely we are better off if that is based on some element of reality.

The partisans want to persuade the country that their version of reality is the right one. The social scientists try to do that as well. Both claim to have analyzed the situation or crisis correctly. However, the partisans go well beyond their declarations. They are active advocates and compete for our support. They are determined to shape our 'opinions' and in doing so, exploit the less rational elements of perception.

The Fine (and Refining) Art of Opinion Formation

The interest groups represented in this book are predictable in their positions on health care reform. Some are sophisticated enough to make their argument compelling, to indicate the overlap between their own interests and the nation's interests. In some cases, the overlap is significant.

The Ford Motor Company, for example, complains about unfair international competition from auto companies in other countries that don't have to include the price of health benefits in the price of their products. Small business, the locus of job creation in America today, complains about the financial burden of employee health benefits. All the interest group statements make claims, but not all claims are equal. Some don't have the weight or lobbying clout or unified constituencies of the large corporations, the small business associations and the insurance industry.

The major interest groups lobby in two ways: for the attention and votes of members of Congress and for the support of the American public. They were, and are effective in both efforts. The American public, that is a random sample of it, was surveyed episodically between the Clinton 1993 State of the Union Address and the debates on the Health Security Act in the 103rd Congress. As the polling experts (Bowman, Frankovic and Immerwahr) describe it, public opinion changed over time as the debate accelerated, more information became available and the confusion and complexity of the issues unfolded. And, we may add, as the efforts of some of the interest groups accelerated.

Noteworthy were the 'Harry and Louise' TV ads funded by the Health Insurance Association of America. They effectively conveyed all of the criti-

Section Five: The Realities of Health Care Reform

cisms mounted by those most against the Clinton plan. It was Big Government control, it was lack of choice, it was costly, it was poor quality. The accuracy of these claims is a separate issue altogether. The ads helped shape perception and opinion in many sectors of the public. The lack of validity and factual information however, was no greater than among the Single Payer advocates. They were not so widely heard or seen, but where they were, they also ignored facts, especially those about the Canadian Model they touted: its costliness, its inability to contain the rate at which costs were rising, its shortages and waiting lists. Facts were rarely important because they contradicted deeply held views.

Although a few newspapers and TV stations tried periodically to explain the complex issues and problems involved, most Americans, most interest groups and most Congressional leaders either clung to preconceived ways of thinking or were swayed by clever Madison Avenue techniques. The facts, as best we could marshal them, rarely dominated the debates and public thinking.

Like the good social scientists they are, the polling experts do not hesitate to discuss methodological problems and point out the difficulties of accurate polling. Despite this, it is possible to identify the consistent attitudes that emerged, while other attitudes and perceptions changed as the national debate and the TV infomercials flooded the country. The public repeatedly supported universal coverage, portability, tax breaks for small businesses, crackdown on Medicaid and Medicare fraud. But the public was also adamantly against anything that looked like Big Government or tax increases.

This information and accusations of big government were used to defeat the Clinton bill and strengthen Republican Congressional numbers in the midterm election. The real issues of access for millions of Americans, affordability, equitable standards, and quality assurance were ignored. The widespread public disgust with both parties after the 103rd congress lead the 104th to take a different approach.

Contention, Then Pragmatism, in Congress

Those who would shape our reality through the legislative process struggled with gridlock in the 103rd Congress and then with pragmatic, if limited, progress in the 104th. Power struggles in an increasingly fragmented Congress and weakened White House played themselves out in these two sessions with different but related scenarios. Increasingly sophisticated lobbyists (crypto-political parties as they have been described) plied the Capitol Hill offices, building on PAC contributions. In addition, they worked the grass roots back in selected home districts. Both the Democrat and Republican leadership tried in vain to impose party discipline.

The Republicans had a bit more success since the 1994 election possibilities loomed. Both parties' leadership faced increasingly independent-minded colleagues. The White House, without a strong electoral mandate and without good Hill contacts or strategy, was helpless in the face of fierce partisan fighting in the five committees crucial for the passage of the Health Security Act. The workings of those five committees are described in Section Three of this book. Dingell's committee, most reflective of the composition of the House, was unable to report anything out, despite its chair's consummate political skills. Even the worthy and respected compromisers on the Senate Finance Committee did not succeed.

Congress was the battlefield on which the ideologies clashed, skirmished and fought to legislative reality. The public committee hearings of Education, Energy, Ways and Means, Finance and Labor and their private meetings saw all the positions and concerns expressed. Committee hearings, with testimony of various interest groups and businesses underscored the immense complexity of the issues and the contradictory and cross-cutting needs of different segments of the nation. They also provided opportunity for committee members to score partisan points and appeal to their constituents. And there were the back rooms where the congressional compromisers like Mitchell and Chafee tried to negotiate, bargain and build consensus. Dingell, Feder and Kosterlitz, in this book, describe these processes as do the descriptions of the 103rd and 104th Congresses.

The 103rd was overwhelmed with acrimony and ended in gridlock and a Republican springboard for recapturing the House in the midterm elections. In the 104th, scaled-down, quiet, less public negotiations produced the Kassebaum-Kennedy bill, directed at the concerns of middle-class voters: portability, pre-existing conditions, better tax breaks for small businesses and limited, standard insurance forms. Important steps, although close examination of the details reveals that each of these succinct terms is more circumscribed and limited then their PR titles suggest.

Why the limited success in the 104th? A public displeased with the bipartisan vituperations. Clinton's determination to address health care issues. Positioning for the 1996 election. The hard lessons of defeat making it easier to accept a strategy of incrementalism. Serious attention to the persistent themes of concern in the public opinion polls. So Congress, in its 104th session, showed anew its preference for selected instrumentalism and practical, rather than ideological, legislation.

The Founding Fathers would be pleased.

The Market (Whatever That Is) Goes Its Own Way . . . Despite Evidence

The original Clinton Health Security Act was deeply committed to its own version of "Managed Competition". This concept, developed primarily (in its current form) by Alain Enthoven of the Stanford Business School, promotes a body of selected government regulation to, as Richard Kronick puts it, provide a "helping hand to the invisible hand" of the marketplace.

There have been criticisms and counter criticisms about the uses of the concepts of managed competition but the failure to pass the Clinton bill left the market to proceed albeit regulated to some extent in already established programs like Medicare. The market continues as a powerful shaper of health care reality in the USA. And its favorite shape is "Managed Care" as the model for organizing the delivery of health care.

Now an umbrella term, with multiple variations, managed care is a term used to cover a wide variety of health care plans that 1) offer a preselected network of doctors and hospitals; 2) have pre-negotiated levels of reimbursements for providers; and 3) have some controls over the services offered. The details of each of the three elements, however, vary widely.

Each member of a managed care plan chooses a primary care doctor who manages all care and provides as much of that care as possible, sending the patient to a specialist only when clear need is established. The emphasis is on prevention, outpatient services and seeking low cost at all levels. The various managed care approaches differ in contractual relationships and financial incentives to providers, range of benefits and services, and degree of choice for the consumer.

Doctors in the various plans are either on salary, on capitation, or getting a pre-negotiated set of fees. The doctors are often also on various bonus arrangements tied to performing preventive services, low referral rates to specialists, low hospital admissions rates, and short hospital stays. While there is indication of increasing numbers of doctors on salary, a doctor in private practice can be participating in a number of different managed care contracts (with different financial incentives trying to influence clinical decisions) as a way of guaranteeing patients.

From the consumer's point of view, the issues are range of choice of doctor, the amount of deductibles and co-pays and quality of care. Very few consumers understand the convoluted contractual arrangements under which their doctors may work. From the employer's point of view cost, cost control and quality of care are issues. Employers are increasingly pressuring for lower premiums (which usually means limiting benefits) or at least a slower rise in the cost of premiums.

Control is the central issue for all groups: Control over costs, control over consumer choice and control over providers' clinical decisions.

Just as we saw controversy and contradictions in the uses and misuses of data in the studies of impact of programs and in public opinion polling, data about managed care exist but are constrained in the usual ways: Definitions; assumptions; changes over time.

A July 1995 meeting of major health economists and insurers noted that premiums dropped 1% last year after 10 years of climbing up to 18% annually. Part of the drop results from the spread of managed care, especially HMOs that most closely control treatment decisions as well as pay doctors and hospitals less. Other evidence suggests that managed care may save money in its first few years but costs then start to climb again.

What does the evaluation research reveal about managed care performance? Documentation of growth would suggest some proof of 'success' in controlling costs but the studies are mixed. For example, a U.S. Government Accounting Office study, published early in 1995, found little empirical evidence that employers' overall health care costs have been significantly controlled. There may be initial slowing that then accelerates; savings may accrue in plans that serve healthier employees; ability to save depends on tightness of controls including limiting choice for consumers and for physicians' clinical decisions.

Meanwhile, in the state capitals, legislation of all sorts is pending. For example, many state medical societies are promoting the passage of "any willing provider" legislation which would prevent HMOs and other entities from selecting only the most cost-effective doctors.

States are passing or considering legislation to limit too extensive or too sparse benefit packages, and "right to know" laws permitting patients to know how their doctors are compensated. In December, 1996, the Department of Health and Human Services informed all Medicare managed care entities they could not restrict doctors' information to patients.

Managed care is growing in the programs for which federal and state governments are responsible: Medicaid, the joint state-federal insurance for the poor which covers 37 million people (one half of whom are children) and Medicare, the federal insurance for those over 65. Although the numbers in managed care for both Medicaid and Medicare are around 10%, this is expected to grow. Fifty big employers across the nation are encouraging their retirees to enter Medicare HMOs.

Both President Clinton and the Congress have submitted budget bills which will impact Medicaid and Medicare, producing a ripple effect throughout the health care system. Federal spending on health care has been doubling annually. The Clinton and Congressional proposals differ

Section Five: The Realities of Health Care Reform

in the amount of the reduction to each program and in the phase-in time. The states will now receive their portions of Medicaid in "block grants" which reduce or eliminate Federal regulations, allowing the states to design their own programs and determine eligibility and scope of benefits. All proposals emphasize the increased use of managed care.

Supporters of managed care for Medicaid and Medicare argue it will reduce unnecessary care, close inefficient hospitals, and control overpayment to doctors. Critics suggest it will increase costs of private insurance, increase the number of the uninsured, threaten the best and most needed hospitals and eliminate charity care.

Managed care settings are rife with potential ethical conflicts, particularly challenges to the traditional trust relationship between doctor and patient. The doctor now must balance responsibility to patients and responsibility to the managed care organization. The concern is whether there is an inherent conflict between reducing expenditures which limit services, and maintaining quality.

Some for-profit managed care companies report great success in controlling the rise in costs. The New York Times business section recently reported that the three biggest for-profit HMOs are "squeezing every penny possible out of doctors and hospitals . . . (and) rewarding their CEOs with sizable pay packages." Morreim's paper in this volume captures this market trend in her admonition to 'follow the money.'

The increased market penetration into health care and the growth of business thinking and business models in what has for so long been considered a service area with an altruistic underpinning, is the greatest single challenge to the American health care system. The much touted market is by no means always successful, either in producing profits, efficiency or quality. It remains to be seen what will happen in various corners of a commercialized health care system. Charles Schultze, in *Public Use of Private Interest*, wrote: "Market-like arrangements not only minimize the need for coercion . . . they also reduce the need for compassion, . . . brotherly love, [and] cultural solidarity as motivating forces behind social improvement."

Will the corporate and small business purchasers of health insurance for their employees do a better job of deciding medical need than doctors? Managed care is insisting that doctors look more carefully at outcomes for patients and push to reduce the boundaries of uncertainty in medical practice. This is promising, but only if quality supersedes cost control. In what ways will a managed care administrator be a stronger advocate for the patient then the patient's doctor? This is not to argue that the doctor has always acted with the best intentions for the patient, but that the more distant administrator hardly seems an improved substitute.

The health care business world's instruments to guarantee quality, NCQA and HEDIS, have established elementary ways to measure quality although the Joint Commission is moving towards more rigorous patient outcome measures.

We have a long road to travel before producing authentic quality measures focused primarily on results for patients. What is most hopeful is that the medical profession, beleaguered by the market changes, will move to supervise itself more rigorously and improve its own clinical standards.

The market continues to give us managed care, despite its questionable accomplishments. The most financially successful models of managed care are built on the tightest control of doctors and patients, a model that strictly limits choice for both. One of the persistent themes the public opinion pollsters find is the desire for choice. Despite this and the lack of substantial evidence that managed care manages to control health care costs, it continues to spread in the United States.

Paul Ellwood, the Father of Managed Care, is quoted in the Dec. 8, 1996 magazine section of the New York Times, saying," The trust in Managed Care is really deteriorating rapidly . . . (if this can't be reversed) . . . everything will go down the tubes."

Larger Social Trends That Shape Reality

The fate of the Clinton Health Security Act which was defeated during the 103rd U.S. Congress can, to a great extent, be explained by understanding the larger social trends that have continued to shape the society of the U.S. and those of other post-industrial countries in the last decades of the 20th century.

One of the major trends is the devolution of central government. Coupled with the inability to raise taxes, (no matter how high or low those taxes might actually now be), has been the development of philosophies of 'local control.' Critiques of the inefficiencies and ineffectiveness of big central government have also grown. These latter perceptions are widespread in the U.S., sweeping away the areas in which central government may still play important roles that only it can accomplish effectively. The Clinton-Gore "reinventing government" program leading to reduction in the federal payroll and block grants to the states are manifestations of this devolution. The Clinton Health Security Act suggested a reinvigorated role for central government in ensuring universal standards and regulation of the market. But those very characteristics buck the long term trend towards devolution.

The slowly changing nature of the American political process stymied the passage of the Clinton bill through Congress. The political strategy of the Clintons seemed to ignore weak party discipline on the Democrat side of the aisle. Not only were key committee chairs ignored and committees

Section Five: The Realities of Health Care Reform

left structured for other issues, but the Democratic leadership had a difficult time controlling increasingly independent congressmen. The proliferation of independent health care bills undercut the President's bill as did the intransigence of the Democratic Party's left, right and center.

Not only did the President come to office with a small majority, but he occupies a White House that has been progressively weakened since the Nixon administration.

And both Congress and the White House now face the increasingly powerful influence of interest groups. As manipulators of public opinion and major contributors to election campaigns, they play a larger role in the political process then the voting public.

Corporatization, as the major organizing form of the market, plays a role in a variety of ways. Health care delivery is a late-comer to the corporatization of American life. The business orientation and profit-taking of the corporate world conflict with the traditional service orientation of health care delivery in hospitals and doctors offices. The Clinton bill reflected a number of trends in the health care system already underway. It invented nothing new. But the corporatized picture of the delivery system the Health Security Act reflected so starkly was offensive to professionals and consumers alike. At the same time, it was more than familiar to the large insurance companies and the major American international corporations.

Particularly the latter understood how the Clinton bill would relieve them of some of the burden of employee health premiums and increase their competitiveness in international markets. Herein enters the dynamics of the 21st Century international market place and the role of government to expedite the success of American business enterprise.

Powerful Trends Operating at Cross-Purposes

How shall we think about individual actors and the larger social trends? The role of Hillary Clinton, Ira Magaziner, Ted Kennedy, John Dingell, John Chafee, Christie Ferguson, Newt Gingrich, Bob Dole, William Crystal, John McDermott, Michael Bromberg and other effective lobbyists . . . the list goes on and on. They act and their action is important in the myriad of waves and eddies that are generated in the larger trends. That intersection of individual and society makes things happen in months and years but the larger waves, across the decades, seem inexorable.

Short-term realities get shaped in the processes described in this book. They ultimately fall into the shape of the long-term trends or, remain as small pockets of anomaly like the Amish in post-industrial America. As we examine history, we are hard-put to find a major reversal of long term trends.

And Now, An "Agenda for Incrementalism"

The impulse for health care reform in the United States did not go away after the 103rd Congress as many predicted. Our elected officials responded to the public perception that they were do-nothing scoundrels only interested in their own re-election and incapable of responding to the needs of the American people. So, during the 104th congress and shortly before the 1996 elections, Congress passed the Kassebaum-Kennedy bill, a piece of incremental legislation that addressed a number of issues, particularly of concern to Americans who already have insurance. The two issues most touted were felicitously called "portability" and "pre-existing conditions".

Portability implies you can take your current insurance with you when you move to another job and pre-existing conditions suggests that you cannot be refused insurance because of a pre-existing condition. In the usual and increasingly annoying way politicians have of hyping what they manage to get passed in Congress, neither of these tells the whole story. These benefits are constrained in a number of ways. For one thing, you have portability for a limited time and you pay major premiums in either instance. But the bill also raises the tax breaks for small businesses offering health insurance, and mandates some simpler insurance forms as well as instituting a limited experiment with Medical Savings Accounts.

These are all useful for the middle class and it will be important to evaluate how well they work. These are important steps for people who are already insured, and will encourage additional insurance for employees of small businesses. The President also set up, in the Fall of 1996, a panel to suggest legislation to protect patient interests in HMOs. These are all certainly important.

One of the tasks central government is suited for is imposing reasonable standards across the country. With Medicaid now part of block grants, it is likely that unevenness of benefits and service will increase. However, the unresolved issues are monumental: universal access, a standard, high quality benefits package, regulation of the insurance industry, lowering administrative costs and authentic quality assurance mechanisms. Can and will these be addressed in additional incremental legislation? Or, will they be left to the mercies of the market?

We now understand in deeper ways the heterogeneity, the unevenness and complexities of policy positions, the political and market processes, public opinion and interest group behavior in the health policy arena.

We have learned anew that the power of perception is greater than facts and evidence. This continues to complicate the struggle to gather and use facts more accurately. Those with power or wanting to increase their power will continue to use or ignore research selectively, as it suits their purposes.

Section Five: The Realities of Health Care Reform

We can, however, talk about an "Agenda for Incrementalism." With only a few die-hards around still romanticizing about an entirely new system, most health policy advocates and analysts, led by President Clinton, have accepted incrementalism. What strategy can make the most of this approach, acceptable to legislative bodies and to the public?

An "Agenda for Incrementalism" should have four arenas: (1) Quality Assurance, (2) Access, (3) Financing and Cost Control and (4) Corrections in the Market.

In the *Quality Assurance* arena, outcomes research and practice benchmarks will spread, enhancing clinical effectiveness, reducing useless clinical practice and medical errors. Herein lies an authentic approach to cost savings. This has to be medically-led and medically implemented. Elwood's idea for turning the National Committee for Quality Assurance into a governmental FDA-type agency merits serious consideration.

In the *Access* arena, the next step is to cover all children who are currently closed out of the health care system. This is both morally laudable and political feasible. The next category to be covered is the increasing numbers of part-time, contract and sub-contract workers. A growing number of these are middle class who know how to make the political system move on their behalf. Then those who fall between Medicaid requirements and working poor. And finally, those with inadequate insurance.

One of the most daring ideas in terms of *Financing* is to shift funds from Defense in this post-cold war era where generals themselves call nuclear armament wasteful. A group of Democrats in Congress have already declared that they will promote this. The growing movements of self-care, prevention, health promotion (including unrelenting pressure on the tobacco and liquor industries and the continuing government attacks on Medicare and Medicaid fraud) will continue to help reduce costs along with increasingly efficacious medicine. The Point Of Service product will encourage educated cost sharing. More attention should be paid to the various segments of the medical technology manufacturers to inspire the creation of cost-saving technologies. And in this arena, a determined examination of managed care entities who claim cost savings to see whether surpluses lower premium, is in order.

As for the *Market* which is spreading cost-driven Managed Care with a vengeance, it needs correction of its excesses. Various levels of government and the courts can be seen doing exactly that in time-honored and familiar ways. Our changing health care system has entered the first stages of disclosure and rating. This is a pattern the country has seen in the securities industry where market excesses spurred government regulation. The Department of Health's new HMO disclosure regulations are a good opening shot. The creation of report cards, weak as they are, can be developed to greater rigor. The corporate leadership in rating managed care and HMOs will contribute as well.

Some important lessons have been learned or relearned. The complexities of the tasks ahead are underscored. But a bold "Agenda for Incrementalism," political will and determination can still move the country forward in small but meaningful ways.

Health Policy

Health Policy

Understanding Our Choices from National Reform to Market Forces

EDITED BY

Marilynn M. Rosenthal and Max Heirich

Westview Press
A Member of the Perseus Books Group

All rights reserved. Printed in the United States of America. No part of this publication may be reproduced or transmitted in any form or by any means, electronic or mechanical, including photocopy, recording, or any information storage and retrieval system, without permission in writing from the publisher.

Copyright © 1999 by Westview Press, A Member of the Perseus Books Group

Published in 1998 in the United States of America by Westview Press, 5500 Central Avenue, Boulder, Colorado 80301-2877, and in the United Kingdom by Westview Press, 12 Hid's Copse Road, Cumnor Hill, Oxford OX2 9JJ

A CIP catalog record for this book is available from the Library of Congress.
ISBN 0-8133-9023-0

The paper used in this publication meets the requirements of the American National Standard for Permanence of Paper for Printed Library Materials Z39.48-1984.

10   9   8   7   6   5   4   3   2

Contents

Introduction: Understanding Our Choices
Max Heirich 1

Section One:
How Can We Solve the Problem of Getting Affordable
Health Care to the Entire American Public?

Introduction
Max Heirich 13

Part One: The Alternate Positions and Their Critics

1. Next Steps Toward Health Policy Reform:
   A Conservative Approach
   William A. Niskanen 17

2. The Case for a Single-Payer Approach: A Liberal Voice
   Jim McDermott 23

3. Managed Competition as a Route to Markets That
   Serve Public Needs: A View from Near the White House
   Len M. Nichols 33

4. Health Reform: What Will It Take To Pass?
   A Moderate Conservative Stance
   Gail R. Wilensky 45

Part Two: Cost Containment: What's Working? What Isn't? Why?

5. Is Managed Care Working? The Payer Perspective
   Howard Bailit 59

6. Is the Health Care Cost Problem Solved?
    Karen Davis. 63

7. Managed Competition: Helping Hand for the Invisible
    Hand—How the Clinton Plan Would Use This Strategy
    Richard Kronick 69

8. Who's Afraid of Health Care Spending Growth?
    Mark V. Pauly 75

Part Three: Projecting Likely Economic Consequences of Planned Changes in Health Care: Strategies and Problems

9. Health Care Reform Projections and the Line
    Between Fact and Fiction
    Tami Mark 81

10. Paying for Health Care Reform: Alternative
    Financial Models Compared
    John F. Sheils 87

11. Financial Access to Health Care
    Katherine Swartz 99

Section Two:
Constraints on Choice: The Deepest Concerns of Interest Groups and the Public at Large

Introduction
Richard Lichtenstein 105

Part One: The Public and Health Reform Public Opinion Polls

12. Public Opinion on the Clinton Health Care Plan
    Karlyn H. Bowman 109

13. Health Care: The Limits of Polling
    Kathleen A. Frankovic 115

14. First Impressions and Second Thoughts: Public
    Perceptions of Health Care Reform
    John Immerwahr 121

Part Two: Interest Groups' Concerns with Health Care Reform

<u>Professions</u>

15. American Medical Association and Michigan State
    Medical Society
    Louis Zako 127

16. American Public Health Association
    Eugene Feingold 129

17. Health Care Reform: What Do We Do Now?
    Carol Franck 131

<u>Business</u>

18. Health Industry Manufacturers Association
    Position on Health Care Reform
    G. Gregory Raab 133

19. Health Care and the U.S. Auto Industry
    Charles T. Pryde 135

20. Small Business Association of Michigan
    Position on Health Care
    Gary Baker 139

<u>Health Care Systems Providers</u>

21. The Federation of Health Systems
    Michael D. Bromberg 143

22. Suggested Standards for Insurers
 Julie Goon 149

23. A Vision Renewed: Health Care Security
 Health Insurance Association of America 153

Insurers

24. Getting Inside Health Care Interest Groups
 Robert Asmussen 159

25. Blue Cross Blue Shield of Michigan Foundation
 Ira Strumwasser 161

Labor

26. Health Care in America: A Time for Change
 William Hoffman 163

Section Three:
Constraints on Choice: The Legislative Process—
Views from the Inside

Introduction
 Marilynn M. Rosenthal 169

Part One: How the Executive Branch Positions Itself for Health Care Reform

27. President Clinton's Evolving Ideas on Health Care Reform: In His Own Words
 As compiled by Anand Parekh 171

28. The Politics of Health Policy Reform: An Inside View from the Clinton Administration
 Judith Feder 183

Contents

Part Two: How Congress Works

<u>*103rd and 104th Congresses*</u>

29. Political Strategies in the Long Run: Decades of Efforts at Health Care Reform
 An Interview with John Dingell 189

30. Inside the Senate Finance Committee
 An Interview with Katherine Hayes 197

31. The Politics of Health Care Reform
 Julie Kosterlitz 205

32. The Politics of Comprehensive Health Care Reform: Watching the 103rd and 104th Congresses at Work
 Sallyanne Payton 211

**Section Four:
Change Without Legislation:
The Managed Care Revolution**

Introduction
John E. Billi 237

Part One: Managed Care: Its Permutations, Its Quality, Its Ethics, Its Costs, Its Politics

<u>*The Vision for the Future*</u>

33. Some Thoughts About Managed Care
 An Interview with Gail L. Warden 241

<u>*Issues*</u>

34. The Politics of Managed Care: The Regulatory Issues from the American Medical Association Perspective
 Thomas R. Reardon 247

35. Ford Motor Company's Perspective on Managed Care
    Charles T. Pryde 251

36. Will Managed Care End the Need for Managed Competition?
    Richard Kronick and Max Heirich 255

37. Managed Care: The Legal Viewpoint
    Sallyanne Payton 261

Research

38. Managed Care: Reform without Legislation
    Jon R. Gabel 267

39. How Well Does Managed Care Control Costs?
    Marsha Gold. 277

40. Managed Care: Stages of Development
    John E. Billi 283

How Does This Affect the Patient?

41. The Ethics of Incentives in Managed Care
    E. Haavi Morreim 289

42. Managed Care and Quality Assurance
    Tom Simmer 301

43. Provider Perspectives in Managed Care
    Macdonald Dick, Tom Carli, and Duane Kirking 305

Section Five:
The Realities of Health Care Reform:
Positions, Publics, Processes and,
Of Course, Power
Marilynn M. Rosenthal 315

About the Contributors

Robert Asmussen is executive vice president of Blue Cross Blue Shield of Michigan, Detroit, Michigan.

Howard Bailit is former senior vice president of Health Services Research, Aetna Health Plans, Hartford, Connecticut. He is a professor and head of the Health Policy and Primary Care Research Center, University of Connecticut.

Gary Baker is president of Online Technologies Corp. He was the president of the Small Business Association of Michigan, 1993-1994.

John E. Billi, M.D., is associate dean for Clinical Affairs at the University of Michigan Medical School.

Karlyn H. Bowman, is a resident fellow at the American Enterprise Institute in Washington, D.C., where she studies public opinion.

Michael D. Bromberg was the executive director of the Federation of American Health Systems in Washington, D.C. for 26 years.

Tom Carli, M.D., is a clinical assistant professor of psychiatry in the University of Michigan Medical School.

Karen Davis is president of The Commonwealth Fund.

Macdonald Dick, M.D., is the Ammon Rosenthal Collegiate Professor of Pediatric Cardiology and professor of pediatrics and communicable diseases in the University of Michigan Medical School.

John Dingell (D, Mich.) has served as a Congressman representing Michigan's 16th District since 1955. During the 103rd Congress, he was chair of the Energy and Commerce Committee, as well as chair of the Oversight and Investigation Subcommittee.

Judith Feder, Ph.D., was Principal Deputy Assistant Secretary for Planning and Education in the U.S. Department of Health and Human Services during the first Clinton Administration.

Eugene Feingold was, at the time this presentation was made (March of 1994), president of the American Public Health Association. He is professor emeritus at the University of Michigan School of Public Health.

Carol Franck is executive director of the Michigan Nurses Association.

Kathleen A. Frankovic, Ph.D., is director of surveys for CBS News.

Jon R. Gabel is director of survey research, KPMG Peat Marwick, in Arlington, Virginia.

Marsha Gold, Sc.D., is a senior fellow with Mathematica Policy Research, Inc.

Julie Goon is vice president of government affairs with the American Association of Health Plans.

Katherine Hayes is a legislative assistant to Senator John Chafee.

Max Heirich is an associate professor of sociology at the University of Michigan—Ann Arbor. In addition, he heads the Worker Health Program at the University's Institute of Labor and Industrial Relations and coordinates, with Marilynn M. Rosenthal, the University of Michigan Forum on Health Policy in Ann Arbor.

William Hoffman, Ph.D., was, at the time of this presentation, director of the Social Security Department, United Auto Workers, Detroit, Michigan. He is now president of Oster Enterprises.

John Immerwahr, Ph.D., is a Senior Research Fellow at the Public Agenda Foundation, and is also Assistant Vice President for Academic Affairs at Villanova University.

Duane Kirking, PharmD, PhD, is an associate professor of pharmacy administration in the University of Michigan College of Pharmacy.

Julie Kosterlitz is a contributing editor of *National Journal*.

Richard Kronick, Ph.D., is an associate professor, Department of Family and Preventive Medicine, University of California at San Diego. He served as a Senior Health Policy Advisor in the Clinton administration.

Richard Lichtenstein, M.P.H., Ph.D., is an associate professor of health management and policy in the University of Michigan School of Public Health.

Tami Mark, Ph.D., M.B.A., is a former Senior Analyst, Office of Technology Assessment, Washington, D.C.; she is a Senior Research Director, Project HOPE, Bethesda, Maryland.

Jim McDermott, M.D. (D. Wash.) is a member of the House of Representatives and a physician. He serves on the Committee on Ways and Means Subcommittee on Health.

E. Haavi Morreim, Ph.D., is a professor of medical ethics at the University of Tennessee's College of Medicine.

Len M. Nichols is a principal research associate with The Urban Institute in Washington, DC. He was the senior advisor for health policy at the Office of Management and Budget during 1993 and 1994.

William A. Niskanan is chairman of The Cato Institute.

Anand Parekh is an Inteflex medical student at the University of Michigan, Ann Arbor, Michigan.

Mark V. Pauly, Ph.D. is a professor in the Department of Health Care Systems at the Wharton School, University of Pennsylvania.

Sallyanne Payton, LL.B., is a professor of law at the University of Michigan Law School. She served as an advisor to the President's Task Force on National Health Care Reform in 1993 and subsequently as a Special Advisor on the White House Domestic Policy staff.

About the Contributors

Charles T. Pryde is the health policy and corporate issues manager for governmental affairs for the Ford Motor Company.

G. Gregory Raab, Ph.D., is vice president, government affairs for the Health Industry Manufacturers Assocation (HIMA).

Thomas R. Reardon, M.D., is a trustee of the American Medical Association.

Marilynn M. Rosenthal, Ph.D., is a professor of sociology in the University of Michigan—Dearborn College of Arts, Sciences and Letters. She is the director of the Program in Health Policy studies there and coordinates, with Max Heirich, the University of Michigan Forum on Health Policy in Ann Arbor.

John F. Sheils is vice-president of Lewin-VHI, Inc., Fairfax, Virginia.

Tom Simmer, M.D., is the senior associate medical director of quality management, Health Alliance Plan, Henry Ford Health System, Detroit, Michigan.

Ira Strumwasser, Ph.D., is executive director of Blue Cross Blue Shield of Michigan Foundation, Detroit, Michigan.

Katherine Swartz is associate professor in the Harvard School of Public Health's Department of Health Policy and Management.

Gail L. Warden is president and chief executive officer of Henry Ford Health System, Detroit, Michigan. In 1995, he served as the Chairman of the American Hospital Association.

Gail Wilensky is senior fellow at Project HOPE's Center for Health Affairs in Bethesda, Maryland. She served as administrator of the Health Care Financing Administration under the Bush administration and as deputy assistant to the president in the Bush White House.

Louis Zako, M.D., is past president of the Michigan State Medical Society.

Introduction
Understanding Our Choices

Max Heirich

What This Book Is About

During a critical period in health policy formation the University of Michigan Forum on Health Policy (sponsored by the Program in Society and Medicine of the University of Michigan Medical School) invited a series of key advisers, members of Congress, Congressional aides, business leaders, members of health provider interest groups, and others with a direct stake in the outcomes, as well as a few journalists and economists, to the campus to discuss what was happening. They engaged in frank discussions with one another and with the campus community about how choices for health care reform were changing through time. In addition, a student seminar traveled to Washington to observe the political process at work as various Congressional committees debated health care reform measures, and met with lobbyists, congressional staff, and others shaping the outcomes of those debates. The time period for these discussions, 1993 to 1996, included the period when the U.S. Congress was debating and rewriting the Health Security Act proposed by the task force appointed by President Bill Clinton. It extended through the congressional elections which became something of a political referendum on those proposals, and through the period following control of Congress by Conservative Republicans, when rapid changes were occurring in the organization and funding of health care, but were occurring independent of national legislation. The exchanges which took place on the University of Michigan campus between advisers to the White House and members of Congress, between economists and health policy experts of varying political outlooks, representatives of various interest groups affected by health care reform, and the academic community shed new light on the nature of the problem, the nature of the political process, and the realistic choices that now lie before us.

This book gathers together the heart of that dialogue, grouped and edited in a way to let it speak to the choices currently confronting Americans. It offers a rare glimpse into the frank exchanges that could sometimes occur between proponents of quite different solutions to the dilemma of health care reform. The book begins with papers presented shortly after the 1994 congressional elections, when it was clear that Congress would not endorse some variation of the Health Security Act proposed by the Clintons. Advisers to Newt Gingrich, conservative leader of the House, to former President Bush, and to President Clinton explained their different strategies for health care reform, discussed the heart of the differences between them, and what they saw as possible ways to proceed now. They were followed by experts who discussed different strategies for cost containment, and analysts who discussed what can and cannot be known about the most likely economic consequences of contending cost containment proposals. As had been true of the larger national debate, experts advocated three rather different roads to health care reform.

Many readers will be familiar with the broader strategies for health care reform that have been in contention during the 1990s. At one end of the spectrum have been advocates of a single-payer plan for cost control and for universal access to services. They urged Americans to imitate the Canadian model for health care, in which the government pays all health costs through a tax-based system, hospitals operate on annual budgets and serve all who come to them, and physicians' fees are set in consultation between the state or provincial government payer and medical associations.

At the other extreme have been advocates of free market solutions to health care dynamics, who argue that in the United States, government regulation of an industry, be it state or federal regulation, never works in practice. Instead, they argue, unfettered competition can bring down prices and produce innovation that will solve health care problems more creatively than monolithic national planning. Each problem in health care should be addressed individually, through a series of incremental reforms that leave the market place in tact. Make one reform at a time, they argued, and then see who is still left out. Interfere with normal market mechanisms as little as possible.

Clinton's advisers, in contrast, took a middle road between these two ideological positions, and their reform strategies borrowed evenly from each school's arsenal of proposals. Arguing that there was neither the political will nor the tax base necessary to reorganize American health care on the Canadian model, but that the market does not get services to everyone when left to its own devices, they urged the federal government to define the problems in health care that need solution and then enact laws that would create market incentives (positive and negative) for insurers and health care providers to provide services to all Americans, within a price range that could be afforded by those who pay for care. That middle position, as is well known, was attacked by advocates of each alternative.

Introduction: Understanding Our Choices

Single payer advocates found the Clinton version of managed competition unduly cumbersome and unnecessarily expensive because it continued a role for the American insurance industry, which they argued could be replaced more economically by a tax-based system. In contrast, free market advocates objected that the Clinton version of "managed competition" was more "managed" than "competition", and that government regulation lay at the heart of its reform strategies, a strategy they saw as long discredited in American political practice.

Readers who have followed the political debates about health care reform will be familiar with the arguments briefly described above. However contributors to this volume go far beyond the political arguments that surfaced in public debate. Because the discussions which took place at the University of Michigan involved key advisers in each camp who now were addressing each other and an academic audience already familiar with their general argument, advocates of each position cut to the heart of their own and opponents' assumptions, and provided both detail and analysis that often has been lacking in debates aimed at the general public. One does not have to be an expert to follow their remarks, but even those who know these arguments well will find much food for thought.

We hear, also, from experts who looked beneath the arguments and the economic projections made by proponents of each reform strategy, teasing out the current evidence about how serious the problems of access to health care actually are for various groups of Americans, and what can now be known and what remains unknowable about the most likely consequences of implementing each health care reform strategy. Then, with advisers' theoretical and technical proposals firmly in view, this book directs attention to the practical constraints that limit the freedom of the executive and legislative branches of government to choose and implement particular health care policies. Public opinion experts probe the deeper concerns of the public that limit choice, and representatives from a variety of interest groups who are active in the health care debate make clear their preferences and explain why this matters to them. Interest group representatives from associations of medical professionals, health care provider systems, insurers, business and labor explain their preferred solutions and occasionally explain why they are acting as a veto group blocking other reform proposals. Key participants in the executive wing, and in Congress, as well as keen observers from the press and academia, describe the practical political constraints that have shaped health care reform efforts in Washington. Although this helps explain how and why political gridlock stymied legislative health care reform efforts during this time period, we see these sections of the book as more than a retrospective look at what went wrong. Understanding how interest groups and congressional decision-making interact gives us a deeper understanding of the practical political realities that will affect what range of policy choices will be viable in the future.

This time period saw the failure of most legislative attempts, but the greater success of private efforts at health care reform. Within two years the health care delivery system had changed remarkably, and in some of the directions advocated by the Clinton health insurance reform task force. The majority of Americans now were enrolled in capitated payment, managed care plans, and hospital provider networks had consolidated, leaving far fewer competitors in health care delivery. This reform without legislation was accompanied by a drop in cost inflation. It was not clear, yet, whether this was true cost containment or simply a temporary drop in price increase, as had happened before during periods of high competition and rapid consolidation of the market, one that would reverse once competitors had been eliminated. The number of Americans lacking health insurance continued to climb, however, and the character of the health care system was changing fundamentally. We include papers given at a Health Forum devoted to the managed care revolution, in which advocates and critics of the changes now taking place discussed what is happening to costs, to access, and to doctor-patient relations.

The level of conversation that these Health Forums evoked between key advisers of different ideological convictions was unusually candid, and occasionally self-examining on their part. They paid their audience the compliment of assuming a fair degree of knowledge about the context of the current health care policy debate, the major positions that were in contention, and the nature of the political stalemate that now affects health care decision-making. A few of the economists assumed that their audience also understands the economic principles underlying the health insurance market. Readers who have such a background may want to go immediately on to the papers themselves, letting key players in health policy formation and analysis explain their understanding of the nature of the choices before us. Not all readers will be that familiar with the issues in question, however. For them, the rest of this chapter will provide a brief introduction to the debate by answering a series of questions.

What Is At Issue in the Debate About Health Insurance Reform?

The health safety net that Americans constructed during the first two decades following World War II has weakened. It offers no support to 40 million Americans currently, and until 1996 offered little support to another 25 million Americans whose most serious, ongoing health problems were not covered.[1] How much the 1996 legislation prohibiting exclusion of "pre-existing conditions" by health insurers will raise premium prices,

Introduction: Understanding Our Choices

and how this will affect the number of Americans without health insurance remains to be seen. How serious a problem all this creates is a matter of heated debate, but—given the cost of health care in America, lowered tax revenues and problems of state and federal deficits, as well as the problems the cost of health care now creates for the business community—there are no simple and obvious ways to mend that safety net. No wonder the debate about health care reform has drawn so much attention and concern: the stakes are high, both for the economic vitality of the nation and for the health of the population.

What is at issue in the health care policy debate, most Americans realize, is access to health care services for a constantly growing portion of the American public who can no longer afford to pay the cost of services, and for others who have had difficulty gaining access to care even when there is money to cover their costs. Equally at issue, of course, is the problem of cost containment: for over three decades, as most Americans are now aware, health care costs have risen at about twice the rate of general inflation, with only occasional and short-lived interruption to this trend. Under these circumstances answers to the questions, Who pays? How much? For what? And for whom? have major implications for all who are touched by the health care system. Those answers also affect who will have access to basic health care services and who will not. While problems of access and cost involve much more than the availability of health insurance, guaranteeing payment for services becomes critical for tackling the problems that remain.

Who Will Be Affected by the Outcome of This Debate, and Why?

The present American health care system seems to work fairly well for about three out of every four Americans. Thus the vast majority of Americans are well-served by the arrangements we have now, and most hope that others can be included without diminishing the quality or convenience of the care that they themselves now receive. For many workers, health benefits have been a hard-fought victory, an important part of their standard of living. Indeed, in recent years some of the largest labor unions have traded continued health benefits (which are not taxed) for what otherwise would have been higher wages. They are determined to make sure that health care reform does not decrease their income by lessening services they can have without increasing their wages in return. Many health care receivers, as well as providers of care and third party payers for care, look warily at proposals for reform, recognizing the need to do something but determined not to be a loser as health care reforms move forward.

Solving the twin problems of access and cost would be difficult enough, but even more is involved in this debate about health care insurance reform. The growth in health care costs has important implications for the economy as a whole. Health care employs more Americans than any other sector of the economy, and several parts of "the health care industry" have been consistent growth leaders in the economy for four decades. During the past quarter century health care has doubled its share of the gross national product.[2] Participants in the health care industry resist any changes that would weaken them financially; moreover for the sake of the economy as a whole the health care industry needs to remain strong. However, because of the formulas now used to reimburse health care expenses, other segments of American business, the federal and state governments, and private households often find themselves captive to increased price demands from health care providers. Since health care in the U.S. costs about twice as much per person as it does in most other industrialized countries, overhead costs for health benefits have affected American businesses' ability to compete in the international market (and with foreign products in the American market), contributing its part to the U.S. negative balance of trade. Increases in health care costs have also created serious problems for state and federal budgets. Solving problems of access and cost containment together, in ways that are equitable for business, government, and private households, consequently, is a high priority not only for those now left out but also for major institutional interests. The health care industry itself has too much at stake to remain passive in these discussions.

In addition to its impact on health benefits spending, businesses are affected by what the more rapid inflation in health care costs does to cost of living adjustments to wages. That also affects government obligations for social security and welfare payments. Not surprisingly, as medical costs have increased, public and private third party payers have refused to pay for some health expenses, passing those costs on to private households. Health care cost, thus, has become a two-edged sword. On the one hand, it cuts a bright swath: the increasing prosperity of American health care has helped keep the American economy vigorous in growth. But on the other hand, that growth creates serious problems for those who pay for it.

When Did the Health Care Cost Inflation Dynamic Begin, and How Does Insurance Affect It?

From 1920 to 1950 the cost of health care stayed steady relative to the growth of the economy, averaging between 3.5 and 4.5 percent of the gross national product. Then widespread introduction of health insurance began to change the cost of health care. Blue Cross Blue Shield hospitalization insurance had become available in the 1930s and some employers began to pay for it as a pre-tax "fringe benefit" during World War II. In the 1950s, labor-management contracts guaranteed this benefit for a large portion of the labor force.[3] During the 1950s health care costs increased a bit,

Introduction: Understanding Our Choices

with the cost of new hospital construction and widely available hospital insurance. By 1960, health care costs had increased to 5.5 percent of the gross national product, but few were hurting because of these higher costs.[4]

The cost of health care increased sharply after 1965, however, when Congress gave the federal and state governments responsibility for paying for the health care costs of the elderly and people on welfare, the first public health insurance legislation to survive the legislative process. The federal government provided Medicare insurance for persons over 65 who had retired, including both their hospital costs and part of their doctor fees. The federal government and the states split payment responsibility for persons on public welfare, and the states decided who among the poor could and could not be enrolled for welfare payments and consequently for Medicaid.[5]

Once public funding became available everything began to change quite rapidly. Within five years the overall cost of health care in the U.S. had doubled, and the cost of hospital care had quadrupled.[6] Hospitals, assured of a clientele that would need many services, began to expand their facilities and to invest in high tech equipment (such as intensive care units, dialysis machines, and expensive diagnostic equipment). They simply increased charges for their daily operating costs sufficiently to pay for these investments. When Congress responded by cutting off federal funds for hospital construction, the hospitals simply borrowed the money (at high interest rates) and continued their expansion plans. Indeed, hospitals that did not continue to upgrade risked losing their physicians (and the patient revenue each physician generated) to a more modern hospital. The cost of hospitalization increased still more rapidly, for now both the borrowed money and high interest costs had to be added onto the other expenses that were part of daily operating charges. Hospitals set a uniform daily rate, which meant that both private third party payers and the government were subsidizing the costs of upgrading and expansion. The pharmaceutical industry, hospital construction, hospital equipment, and hospitals themselves became growth leaders in the economy.[7] Gradually the entire area of health care delivery began to refer to itself as "the health care industry". Despite a variety of efforts to contain these costs, health care inflation has proceeded at twice the general inflation rate for most years since 1965.

Business and government, thus, became captive to cost inflation because of the obligations they had taken on and the ways that health insurance reimbursement arrangements worked. In 1960, health benefits cost business the equivalent of about 15 percent of their after-tax profits. In 1989, health benefits cost the equivalent of 98 percent of their after-tax profits.[8] (I.e., if they had not been paying for health care, business profits would have doubled.) For the federal government, health care spending commitments began to rival defense spending. The states found by the early 1990s that Medicaid's portion of the state budget had increased from about 3 percent to 15 percent, with the figure due to go higher still.[9] Health care costs were rising so sharply that few private households could pay for a major health crisis out-of-pocket. Many families without health insurance were forced into bankruptcy when a medical crisis occurred.

What Has Been Done Already to Try to Tame Health Care Cost-Inflation?

Neither the government nor business has stood by idly during the past 25 years that this accelerated cost inflation for medical care has been occurring. President Nixon tried imposing direct price controls and found they did not work: costs continued to rise because physicians and hospitals simply increased the number of services they billed at these fixed prices. Congress then passed legislation authorizing the establishment of Health Maintenance Organizations (HMOs) that would receive "capitated payments"— a fixed amount of money annually for each enrollee—in exchange for responsibility for the total care of that patient. It was hoped that HMOs would keep people out of hospitals (in order to preserve their income) and would emphasize preventive measures that would lower costs for care.[10]

Businesses responded to the cost increases by self-insuring for health benefits, and began to assume a more aggressive bargaining role for prices for services. Self-insurance began with passage of ERISA in 1974, which allowed businesses to self-fund retirement and health benefits programs. By the mid-1980s business health coalitions had formed in 93 metropolitan areas; they were monitoring health providers costs and designating some health care providers as Preferred Provider Organizations (PPOs). The larger companies bargained with their PPO for discounted rates, in return for a guaranteed volume of users. In addition, the business health coalitions often invited HMO chains to extend into their metropolitan area, as a way of increasing competition locally. After ERISA, the large health insurance companies that had developed during the 1950s and 1960s lost their large corporation accounts because these corporations self-insured. The insurance companies recouped in two ways: they got contracts to manage the health disbursements for large corporations; and they began to set up their own HMOs, so that they could compete for the business of actually providing health care to the employees of large corporations.[11]

With these changes, the corporatization of American health care began in earnest. Meanwhile government reforms of the 1980s intensified the dynamic for change that was occurring. The government still paid hospitals for each admission of Medicare patients. A new policy regrouped pay-

Introduction: Understanding Our Choices

ment into DRGs (diagnostically related groups of admissions), clustering diagnoses not by type of illness but by average cost for treating that illness. Medicare hereafter would reimburse hospitals a flat amount, depending upon the DRG category into which the initial admission diagnosis fit. Hospitals that could treat for less could keep the difference; if a patient's care cost more the hospital would have to absorb the loss.[12] Parallel Medicare funding policies for the reimbursement of physician's services (the Resource-based Relative Value Scale), introduced in 1992, provided government-set reimbursements for 85 percent of all procedures physicians use with Medicare patients.[13] In addition, government legislation encouraged the establishment of "for-profit" medical care whose income would be taxable and whose competitive business skills, it was hoped, would result in cheaper prices for care.[14]

What Interests Have Been Most Affected By Recent Health Care Reforms?

These changes in funding reimbursement have led to a fundamental restructuring of medical care and the relations between hospitals, HMOs, insurance companies, physicians, nurses, and patients. Hospital utilization has dropped sharply. HMOs now keep patients out of the hospital whenever possible and hospitals make more money if patients being paid for through DRG formulas are released quickly. More services are provided on an outpatient basis (because these were not subject to the DRG and R-BRVS payment rules). Consequently, some hospitals have closed, enough so that the community hospitals' bed count decreased by 100,000 beds between 1983 (when DRGs were introduced) and 1990.[15] Many public hospitals could not survive on their Medicaid and Medicare income and were sold to private for-profit companies. Many for-profit companies refused to accept Medicaid patients, thus aggravating the problems of getting access to care for the poor.

Hospitals themselves have regrouped, forming large hospital chains that can use economies of scale for purchasing and be in a better position to bargain for Preferred Provider status with large companies. For-profit and not-for-profit hospital chains now dominate the market. One out of every nine hospitals is now owned by a for-profit corporation.[16] HMOs use more primary care doctors and nurse practitioners, and less specialists than is true for indemnity-financed (fee for service) care, so that specialists are beginning to be in oversupply in many metropolitan areas. The relations between physicians and the business management of HMOs has varied, but the independence of physicians is very much an open question currently, affecting not only their incomes but standards of medical practice.

Have These Changes, Which Have Basically Restructured Health Care in America, Really Saved Money?

Until 1995 health care cost inflation continued at twice the rate of inflation. Capitated payment plans were about 5 percent cheaper than fee-for-service care, but their rate increases paralleled cost increases for health care in general. They were not changing the underlying dynamic but simply damping its effect a bit.[17]

In response to the health insurance reform debate of 1993 and 1994, many employers created incentives that moved their employees into capitated payment plans; by 1995 the majority of privately insured Americans were in HMOs or other programs that had a fixed cost annually. The HMOs expanded rapidly and entered a fierce competitive war. Hospitals and other health care providers consolidated into large provider networks as part of the restructuring of the health care market. For the first time in several years, health care cost increases for 1995 did not double the general inflation rate; it was not clear whether the dynamic of cost increase was changing or whether this reflected temporary price adjustments as competition led to greater consolidation of control over health care services.[18] It was clear, however, that everyone is being affected by the changes in health care delivery that the attempted insurance reforms have set in motion.

Because of the unique history of American health care, economic principles now affect much of its operation. However, the debate about health care reform cannot simply be reduced to a discussion of economics. When health problems arise, health care is not an optional commodity for private households to use or ignore, although many households now are forced to do so. Because health services often cannot be deferred, the lack of a universal insurance system to pay for health care now creates financial crisis or premature death for many Americans.

Because a wide range of earlier reform efforts failed to stop the inflation of health care costs or the erosion of access to health care services, the policy debates chronicled in this book become all the more important. How can we solve the problem of getting affordable health care to the entire American public? How do the deepest concerns of interest groups and the public at large constrain the choices that can be made? How have these affected the legislative process? In the absence of legislative overhaul of health care, how has private reform (the managed care revolution) affected access, cost, and quality of care?

Although this volume includes papers given at four different Health Forums, the argument remains remarkably coherent, as key advisers, technical experts, and decision makers discuss the choices before us and the practical constraints that affect how we proceed. We would like to have included the discussions that followed papers, as members of the audience and presenters interacted with one another. Space limitations preclude that choice. Nonetheless, the arguments presented here take account of one another, inviting the reader to probe more deeply the choices that now lie before us for health care reform.

Notes

1. Emily Friedman, "The uninsured: From dilemma to crisis." *Journal of the American Medical Association*, 265(19); 2491-2495, May 15, 1991.

2. Health Care Financing Administration, Office of the Actuary: Office of National Cost Estimates, "Trends in national health care costs, " 1991.

3. Paul Starr, *The Social Transformation of American Medicine: the Rise of a Sovereign Profession and the Making of a Vast Industry*. New York: Basic Books, Inc., 1984, 252-254, 311.

4. U.S. Government, Economic Report to the President, Annual Report of the Council of Economic Advisers, Appendix B: Statistical Tables, Table

5. Ted Marmor and Ann Marmor, *The Politics of Medicare*. Chicago: Aldine Publishing Co., 1970, 59-93, Starr, *op. cit.*, 368-370, Robert Stevens and Rosemary Stevens, *Welfare Medicine in America: A Case Study of Medicaid*. New York: Free Press, 1974.

6. Health Care Financing Administration, Office of the Actuary: Office of National Cost Estimates, "Trends in national health care costs, " 1991.

7. See, for example, *Standard and Poor's Industry Survey*, from 1959 onwards (beginning December 17, 1959, D20-22).

8. Katherine R. Levit, Mark S. Freeland, and Daniel R. Waldo, "Health spending and ability to pay: Business, individual and governments: Health care costs 1990. *Health Care Financing Review* 10, Spring, 1989, 3ff.

9. J. D. Rockefeller IV, "A call for action, " *Journal of the American Medical Association*, 265 (19) May 15, 1991, 2507-2510.

10. Joseph L. Falkson, *HMOs and the Politics of Health System Reform*. Chicago: American Hospital Association, 1986.

11. Katherine A. Lewis, *Private Sector Investment in HMOs*. Excelsior, MN: InterStudy, 1981; Leslie Scism, "Travelers Inc. and Met Life to form HMO; Met Life plans to purchase some Travelers assets to fund joint venture," *The Wall Street Journal*, June 14, 1994.

12. Commission on Professional and Hospital Activities, *Length of Stay by Diagnosis Related Groups, July 1984-July 1985, Discharges*. Ann Arbor, MI: CPHA Probe Series, 1986; Robert J. Fitzgibbon and Bernard E. Statland, *Survival Manual for the Clinical Lab*. Oradell, NJ: Medical Economics Books, 1985; Donald Lee Zimmerman, *DRGs and the Medicaid Program*. Washington, DC: Intergovernmental Health Project, George Washington University, 1984.

13. Resource-based relative value scales were discussed in detail in a series of articles appearing in the Journal of the American Medical Association (JAMA) 260, Oct. 28, 1988. See also Howard J. Anderson, "R-BRVS creates incentives for hospital-physician outpatient care," *Hospitals* 65:31, Feb. 20, 1991; Mary Jane Fisher, "New Medicare fee structure for doctors' services," *National Underwriter (Life and Health/*

Financial Service Edition) 95:3+, June 10, 1991; Joseph T. Donnelly, "R-BRVS as a financial assessment tool," *Health Care Financial Management* 47:44-46, Feb. 1993; William C. Hsiao, Daniel L. Dunn, Diane K. Verrill, "Assessing the implementation of physician-payment reform," *New England Journal of Medicine* 328:928-33, April 1993.

14. Eli Ginzberg, "For-profit medicine: A reassessment," *New England Journal of Medicine* 319: 457-61 September 22, 1988; David E. Lindorff, *Marketplace Medicine: The rise of the for-profit hospital chains*. New York: Bantam Books, 1992.

15. American Hospital Association, *Hospital Statistics:* Table 2-a, "Trends in utilization, personnel and finances in short term hospitals." Chicago: American Hospital Association, 1989-1990.

16. *Ibid*.

17. John Gable, "The changing world of group insurance," *Health Affairs* 7(2) Summer, 1988, 48-65; J. Gable, S. DiCarlo, C. Sullivan, C. and T. Rice, "Employer sponsored health insurance, 1989," *Health Affairs*, 8(2), Summer 1989, 116-128.

18. Milt Freudenheim, "Health costs for workers in U.S. rose last year, reversing 1994 drops," The New York *Times*, January 30, 1996.

SECTION ONE

How Can We Solve the Problem of Getting Affordable Health Care to the Entire American Public?

Section One
Introduction
How Can We Solve the Problem of Getting Affordable Health Care to the Entire American Public?

Max Heirich

How much reform of the health care system is necessary in order to get affordable health care to the entire American public? And what kinds of reform could make health more affordable—both to individuals who pay for it on their own, and to the public and private third party payers who now finance the bulk of health care spending? These questions underlie the arguments presented in Section One, and are supplemented by a related set of questions: What have we learned about strategies that actually work to contain cost increases? What's working? What isn't? and Why? And how reliable are the cost estimates being prepared to help us anticipate the most likely consequences of choosing one or another strategy for health care reform? These sets of inter-related questions engage the attention of the national experts whose differing views contend with one another in Section One. Most of the authorities are economists, as fits the focus on costs, possible enlargements of the market of health care consumers, and strategies for cost containment.

Part One is titled, "What is a Realistic Way to Make Health Care Reforms?" President Reagan's Council of Economic Advisers chairman, who went on to advise House Majority leader Newt Gingrich, President Bush's top health policy adviser and policy implementer, and one of President Clinton's most trusted health care economic advisers give strikingly different analyses of the problems that need to be addressed and the best route to finding affordable health care. William Niskanen, of the Cato Institute (a conservative policy institute) questions whether the "health care crisis" is of the proportions others claim, provides his own analysis of the size of various uninsured populations and the seriousness of access problems for different groups, and questions the conventional strategies for raising funds to cover their health care needs. He offers a radically different solution to the problem of access and cost containment than that of any of our other contributors to this debate. Len Nichols, of the Urban Institute (a liberal policy institute) and a major adviser to President Bill Clinton, offers an unusually frank discussion of the politics of economic planning, showing how key political decisions orient choice among economic options. He includes an equally frank discussion of the technicalities and limits of budget/spending projections, as seen from his earlier position at the Office for the Management of the Budget (OMB) and as an assessor of various projections done by health benefits management firms. Gail Wilensky, who was President Bush's top health adviser, lays out the alternate routes that can be taken in dealing with health benefits packages and their financing and the costs of doing each. She poses a trenchant challenge to the choices made by the Clinton Health Insurance Reform Task Force. To round out this discussion of routes to health care reform, we include a reprinted article by Jim McDermott, a physician and member of the U.S. House of Representatives. McDermott questions the market assumptions that underlie the debate among Presidential advisers. Instead he advocates reforming the U.S. health care system so that it more nearly resembles the Canadian health care plan, using government taxes to eliminate the need for insurance and making the government a single payer able to negotiate more reasonable rates for health care services.

In Part Two, titled, "Cost containment: What's Working? What Isn't? Why?" the debate continues, now focused more narrowly on ways to get *affordable* health care. Howard Bailit, a senior vice president for the Aetna Health Plans HMO, uses a variety of current economic data to argue that capitated payment plans with managed care have, in fact, begun to tame the cycles of constant cost inflation and may be making health care more affordable. Karen Davis, a former health policy economist in earlier Democratic administrations, and now executive vice-president of the Commonwealth Fund, musters her own economic analysis to challenge Bailit's conclusions, warning about the temporary nature of downward trends in health care spending and arguing that health care spending has *not* been brought under control. She closes with a discussion of the kind of challenge that Medicare and the growing number of elderly persons brings to cost control. Rick Kronick, of the University of California San Diego Medical School and a major policy adviser to the Clinton Task Force on Health Insurance Reform, re-examines the policy of managed competition which guided Clinton planning proposals for a Health Security Act. He explains why he believes the market needs to be "managed" if all Americans are to get access to health care, and explains the logic behind the cost containment strategies of the Health Security Act. Mark Pauly, an economist at the Wharton School, University of Pennsylvania, reexamines medical spending trends to ask "Who's afraid of health care costs?" and challenges a number of assumptions that have underlain most health policy debate. He sees quite different cost containment issues for public and private third party payers,

Section One: Introduction

insists that the problems are not being solved by managed care, and poses an ethical challenge to those who would limit discussion of health care needs to economic concerns.

In Part Three, titled "Projecting Likely Economic Consequences of Planned Changes in Health Care," three economists who are experts in health benefits analysis and cost projections sharpen our understanding of the limits of trying to forecast the costs of different health reform plans. Tami Mark, currently Senior Research Director with Project HOPE in Bethesda, Maryland, and formerly of the Office of Technology Assessment, describes the range of cost estimates that have been made, the five-step analysis OTA uses when projecting the most likely cost consequences of different health reform proposals, and concludes with observations of the relation between political will and slippage in cost outcomes. She recommends an incremental approach to health care reform, and cites the need for flexible reforms and ways to monitor their cost consequences. John Sheils, vice president of Lewin VHI, Inc., a benefits management company, explains how Lewin made cost estimates for providing universal insurance coverage for all Americans, with a uniform benefits package similar to the recommendations of the Clinton Task Force, and suggests how the additional costs would vary, depending on whether an employer mandate was used, an individual mandate, or a single payer plan. His conclusions may surprise you. Katherine Swartz of the Harvard School of Public Health discusses sources of error and slippage in making estimates of who is insured and uninsured, and of what the costs will be of implementing different proposals. Her discussion of who is uninsured, when—and what the *real* health implications of this are, clarifies a number of previously confusing arguments about health care reform. She also discusses the nature of data that are needed to let policy makers make more informed decisions, and challenges researchers to do better work in this regard. Section One of this book, in summary, lays out the economic assumptions that guide policy advisers of different ideological convictions, looks carefully at the evidence of what is happening to health care costs currently, and identifies both the potential and the limits of projecting costs for different policy choices.

In reading this section, it might be useful to consider some core questions as one ponders the strikingly different arguments being presented:

How important is it for all Americans to have guaranteed access to health care services?—a basic right for citizens in other industrialized countries, but an open question here.

How much cost would this add, to whom, and what strategies look most promising for controlling costs? What degree of risk is involved in trying them?

What limitations, if any, on current quality of services would be acceptable in order to extend coverage to all?

If there is a conflict of values between access to care for all and limits on public expenditure for budget balancing, how should they be resolved?

What do we, as Americans, take most seriously as underlying values and responsibilities to one another?